THE BROKEN PROMISES OF AMERICA AT HOME AND ABROAD, PAST AND PRESENT

AN ENCYCLOPEDIA FOR OUR TIMES

VOLUME 1

Douglas F. Dowd

Common Courage Press   Monroe, Maine

Library of Congress Cataloging-in-Publication Data is available
from the publisher on request.

ISBN 1-56751-312-3 paper
ISBN 1-56751-313-1 cloth

Common Courage Press
Box 702
Monroe, ME 04951

(207) 525-0900; fax: (207) 525-3068
orders-info@commoncouragepress.com

See our website for e-versions of this book.
www.commoncouragepress.com

First Printing

Printed in Canada

This book is dedicated to Paul M. Sweezy (1910-2004). From the 1930s to the present, his works and generosity of spirit have been indispensable to those seeking to move our world toward decency, sanity, and safety. The book is also dedicated to the young of today and tomorrow who now and in the future will carry those efforts forward.

Contents

Volume 1

Volume 2

Introduction to Doug Dowd

Douglas Dowd is not your usual economist. Although he has all the proper credentials that higher education demands, was head of the economics department at Cornell University, taught at Johns Hopkins, the University of California at Berkeley, and various universities in Italy, he is a troublemaker in the profession.

To put it simply, he is a radical economist. That suggests that he has been influenced by Marxist theory. But he has also been influenced by Thorstein Veblen (*Theory of the Leisure Class*), who had his own idiosyncratic critique of capitalism, thought Veblen died just before the great crash of 1929. Dowd, who wrote an admiring book about Veblen also had as an ideological mentor the much overlooked by prescient Robert Brady, *Business as A System of Power*.

Dowd belongs to the tradition of radical American economists like Paul Sweezy, Paul Baran, and Leo Huberman. In the pages of the periodical they founded, *Monthly Review*, they insisted on an independent socialism, refusing to be bound by Marxian orthodoxy, but adapting its insights to the particular conditions in the United States.

When I was searching, sometime in the early 1980's, for a readable survey of American economic history, I found it in Douglas Dowd's *The Twisted Dream: Capitalist Development in the United States Since 1776*. After that he wrote a number of books on the U.S. economy, as well as a book *The Waste of Nations: Dysfunction in the World Economy*, published in 1989, designed to clarify the confusion around the phenomenon known as "globalization."

There is another characteristic of Doug Dowd which is quite rare among scholars, even more rare among economists, and (I say this with some trepidation) not easy to find among radicals: a delicious sense of humor. Of course there are many people in the academic world who have a sense of humor, but do not reveal this in their writing, which remains properly sober. Not so Dowd. His writing, like his speaking, whether in formal lectures or in conversation, is infused with a sly, ironic sensibility. This is most evident in his memoir-history *Blues For America*, in which he gives us a delightful economic history starting with the year 1919, which was also the year of his birth.

There is not a trace of the ivory tower in Doug Dowd's writing. The only tower he seems to have paid attention to was the one that gave him navigational aid when he was a pilot in the Army Air Corps in the second World War.

When, after the war, he took up his various posts as a professor of economics, he did not confine his radicalism to the classroom. He became a prominent speaker for teach-ins and demonstrations, and an admirable example for students as an activist scholar and public intellectual.

In the present volume he has set for himself a formidable task: to give us, his readers, an honest, unsparing look at our nation. He aims to demolish, with careful attention to facts and to history, those myths which feed nationalist bias, which prevent us from looking with clear, critical eyes, at this country's behavior.

What you will find in these pages is an overwhelming amount of information about this country: its political system, its economic system, its culture. But what gives all this data coherence is a powerful belief in the ideal of a good society, and an unflinching look at the ways in which the United States does not measure up to this ideal. The implication is not that we must simply observe these facts cynically, but that we must enter the fray, and change those facts.

There is a prevailing myth that the United States has been a benign member of the world community, that our government seeks only to do good in the world, and that it may stray occasionally from this objective, but its intentions are honorable. Even when political leaders and mainstream journalists acknowledge, as they have been doing recently, that the United States is an "empire," they insist that it is a benevolent empire. "Imperialism light" is the phrase used by one scholar.

However this description of U.S. behavior in the world does not square with the national history. Very soon after the war for independence against England was over, the new government began its long violent march across the continent.

The attendant mayhem was concealed by euphemisms. The words "Louisiana Purchase" did not convey the consequent expulsion or annihilation of the Indian tribes that lived in that territory (something that in our time might be called "ethnic cleansing"). Military attacks on Florida, leading Spain to turn it over to the United States, became registered in schoolbooks as "Florida Purchase." They had not yet learned the term.

In 1898 the United States extended its realm overseas. A short war in Cuba (the Spanish-American War) liberated the Cubans from Spanish rule, but not from U.S. rule. A long, bloody war in the Philippines, to "civilize and Christianize" the Filipinos, as President McKinley put it, gave the U.S. a colony on the other side of the Pacific Ocean, which it occupied for half a century. Then followed numerous military expeditions into the Caribbean to create governments friendly to our economic and political interests.

After World War II, the threat of communism, genuine for the people of Eastern Europe, but wildly exaggerated with regard to the United States, became an excuse for U.S. military intervention in Iran, Guatemala, Chile, Vietnam. And even after the Soviet Union fell apart, and the fears of "world Communism" had dissipated, American intervention continued: in Panama, in Iraq, in Afghanistan, and again in Iraq. Now "terrorism" replaced Communism as the justification for imperial expansion, with as little attention to understanding the roots of terrorism as there was to understanding the reasons for revolutionary upheavals in the Third World.

Douglas Dowd examines the economic consequences of sustaining a militarized nation and a succession of wars. He dissects the grandiose claims that "the market" and "deregulation" will benefit everyone. And he is acutely aware of how these political and economic factors distort American culture.

I believe readers will find his ruminations on our society as fascinating as I have. He helps us understand the world around us with a perceptiveness we do not find in traditional education or in the media. And most important, he may provoke us to turn that understanding into the kind of civic action for peace and justice which from time to time has made us proud of the American people.

Howard Zinn

Preface

The beginning of the path that led to the making of this work was paved with the wisps of young idealism, literature, and poetry rather than the bricks and lumber of political economy and history. When I began to read in the 1930s, the books that struck me first and stayed with me were the "USA" trilogy of Dos Passos, the novels of Sinclair Lewis and of F. Scott Fitzgerald, and the poetry of Carl Sandburg and Walt Whitman.

In their different ways, they all wrote—or sang—of an "America!" whose dreams and ugly realities had always been caught up in a struggle in which the dreams almost always lost. As I read those and other books, the world was writhing in its most disastrous economic depression and seeking to recover from its worst war, while acting so as to bring on still another one whose horrors went beyond what was previously conceivable—as measured both in how many were killed and who they were, and in the consequent social breakdowns. In the midst of all that, and in part prompted by it, there was a bloody general strike in my city of San Francisco.

It was enough to make a youngster think and pay attention, as did serving for four years in a war. Thus it was that when, with the critical assistance of the GI Bill, I went to the university, it was not with the aim of getting a job, but of seeking to learn how and why all that horror had come to be "normal."

As with so many others at that time, it seemed to me not only that we must, but that we could see to it that such processes would never again occur; and that the USA, the only strong nation still standing, would take the lead in assuring that.

We were wrong. As this work seeks to show and explain, those who slowly but surely rose to power after 1945 had other goals in mind; in their ability to pursue and move toward their definition of success they have brought us now to the point where a still worse global disaster looms, this time in both the social and natural realms. No individual or book can do much to stave that off; but each of us can do our bit. This is mine.

I have written many critical books and essays, and this one is among the most critical, but its structure as a small encyclopedia is its distinguishing characteristic, not its tone. In a conventional narrative book of socio-historical analysis it is quite simply impossible to provide anything like an ample discussion of the many elements and dimensions of what's gone wrong with our fabled "America!" and its "dream"—past and present, at home and abroad. Not least is that so because the USA is unique among nations in having <u>had</u> such a dream, both for those here and elsewhere. There has been no German, Italian, English... "dream"; what came closest in history was the "<u>liberte', egalite', fraternite'</u> of France, and that was crushed almost as soon as it appeared, in the years of Robespierre and Napoleon. We have meant something to ourselves and the world which We the People have allowed to be betrayed—since our beginnings.

Thus this book. Its structure and content are meant to make it feasible for what I take to be some tens of millions of our people who are much upset by what exists and what seems to be in the offing; it has been written in the hope it can serve as a means by which people can simultaneously learn and <u>unlearn</u> what is necessary to strengthen the courage of their convictions.

I have come to that conclusion that such is needed because of the specific background for this book; namely, the combination of my teaching and political experiences over several decades. I have taught economics and economic history continuously since 1949 in the USA and, (since 1966) in Italy; along with that, since the early 1970s I have also taught and still teach free "community classes" at different locations in the San Francisco Bay Area. The classes have been a very positive but also a disquieting experience; the reasons for the latter, as well as my political experience along the way, gave the final push toward this work.

The students in those classes have ranged in age from 18 to 80, in occupation from student to professor, from hospital worker to doctor, from service station attendant to engineer, and they have been of all "races, creeds, and colors." Their political positions have run from mildly liberal to strongly radical; and although all have been reasonably well-informed and skeptical of the received wisdom, they have been "unreasonably" inadequate in the face of what one <u>needs</u> to know to function well and confidently as social critics and political activists.

Despite that those students have all been intelligent and eager to improve their understanding, most have not had the time or the opportunity to read more than a few books; understandably, for except for a fortunate few, only those whose <u>job</u> it is to read can one come even close to dealing adequately with the need for information and analysis.

Moreover, whether because of TV, our manner of education, or the frenzied nature of our times, my strong impression is that the <u>length</u> of what most read is that mostly confined to what is found in periodicals and newspapers. I think both the attitudes and the level of knowledge of those students represent a significant percentage of our society. The form of this book, about which more in a moment, is designed to suit the realistic needs and possibilities of those people in these times.

The 160 or so entries of this book cannot treat of <u>all</u> of that which is essential; that would require a much larger encyclopedia, beyond the competence of any one person. The areas I deal with here are those which are vital and that I have found it repeatedly necessary to explicate, clarify, and/or substantiate. What I have done here, it must be added, must be seen only as part of a continuing process; but even doing only that has required a large book. However, it can be read usefully in "small segments" and serve as a primer for confronting the problems of our society.

Note also that some of the matters considered in the text— Iraq, the presidency, the economy, for example—may well undergo serious changes after the book's publication. Let's hope they will be for the better, not the worse; in any case, they will have been too late for inclusion.

The entries will normally be consulted singly, but it is hoped that readers will respond to the frequent cross references found within most of them (noted in **bold**). The lengths of the matters treated vary greatly: some consist of a paragraph or two (e.g., **preemption, embedding**) others a page or two (e.g. **rich and poor**), some dozens of pages (e.g., **health care**); some are concerned with persons (e.g., **Nixon**), some with processes (e.g., **corruption**), some with major social patterns (e.g., **big business. inequality**), some with mixtures of all these (e.g., **Bush II**, which considers the man, his administration's policies, and its principal members).

It is also hoped that readers will pursue the not only such **cross-**

references but also the numerous citations of books and articles. As the latter appear, the author's name is printed in FULL CAPS. If more than one book of an author is cited, the NAME will be followed by the publication year. Periodical references will usually be parenthesized, abbreviated, dated, and italicized: (*NYT*, 2-14-02). The Foreword and Afterword seek, respectively, to provide the perspective of the book and suggestions for next steps. As the book begins there is a listing of Abbreviations (e.g., *NYT: New York Times*), at its end a substantial Bibliography. There are no footnotes.

It may be noted that among the hundreds of bibliographical references, those citing Karl Marx (1818-1883), Thorstein Veblen (1857-1929), and contemporary writers Howard Zinn and Kevin Phillips occur more frequently than others. This is not because they provide all the answers—nobody has or could—but because, from their different times, places, and perspectives, they have so insightfully raised so many fundamental questions.

It is relevant in that connection to point out that in his day Veblen was probably the most astute and admiring of U.S. readers of Marx while, at the same time, his most acute critic (see DOWD, 1964/2000); and that Zinn and Phillips would see themselves as being toward the opposite ends of the political spectrum.

In that Marx and Veblen both wrote in a world very different from today's, no matter how well their analyses fitted their own times they can only be taken as guidelines for ours; in my opinion, nonetheless, what they provided remains essential. In that they both recognized how rapid and far-reaching social and technological changes had become in the modern era, they would not have expected their analyses to have retained full validity a century or more later. But their reasoning has held up remarkably well; it is to that I often refer.

My frequent resort to the works of Zinn is quite simply because his *People's History of the United States*, "written from the bottom up" is valuably unique in its breadth and scope and tone. As a critic, Phillips may also be unique. Marx, Veblen, Zinn (and I) are deeply critical of **capitalism**; Phillips is not. The seeming aim of Phillips (as was that of KEYNES) is to keep capitalism from doing itself in. The point of departure for his many recent books has been to underscore the ubiquitous economic and political **corruption** and **inequalities** of the United States. As a bedrock conservative, his writings amount to a warning that the "America!" he supports—capitalist but truly democratic—has become a "plutocracy" and in doing so has moved toward self-destruction. To make his argument, Phillips has provided an extraordinary amount of data—invaluable for conservatives and liberal/left critics alike—all put forth within an enlightening historical setting.

The uniformly critical tone of this book may lead some readers to be outraged and to see it as a set of unfounded rants and raves. I neither seek nor expect to change such minds; my aim, rather, is to fortify the convictions of those already skeptical of what passes for "common sense" by providing plausible and documented analyses derived chiefly from the works of governmental reports, reputable writers and, in the case of articles, of mostly establishment periodicals (such as *The New York Times*, *Business Week*, and *The Wall Street Journal*).

All of those sources are in principle available to all, of course; in practice, unfortunately, the hustle and bustle and pressures dominating most people's lives prevent or deflect them from pursuing that available information; meanwhile, university students are taught almost entirely by those who accept the socioeconomic status quo and its principles as gospel. I hope some of them (and their profs) will read this book.

This "primer" is put forth as but one step toward breaking through those conventional and academic barbed wire fences. The lengthy bibliography is meant to assist readers to take the needed additional steps. Saying so, I add that many teachers must occasionally wonder if they are not being arrogant in their belief that they have "something to teach." That may be so; but the best among us do our work in a spirit of solidarity, of sharing what we know (or think we know), while knowing that we too have much to learn. Marx put it aptly (as one of the "Theses on Feuerbach") when he urged that "the educator himself needs educating."

Then there is the matter of repetition. Reference works such as this are rarely read from beginning to end; almost all readers search out what they wish to know about this and that as the occasion warrants. Even so, if one were at the same sitting to read, say, **poverty**, and **inequality**, and **education**, he/she would find some of the materials in each repeated (if also in different ways) in the others.

That is appropriate, especially in <u>this</u> work; one of its principal arguments is that a society is an <u>organic</u> phenomenon: as with the body, all "parts" live in some dynamic interaction with all else. As the old jazz/blues/scat song had it, "The toe bone's connected to the <u>foot</u> bone; the foot bone's connected to the <u>leg</u> bone; the leg bone's connected to the <u>hip</u> bone...." All those bones in their turn live within an anatomy, physiology and nervous system..., and so on. What happens to any one part of the body in small or great degree affects and is affected by what happens in all the rest. So it is with processes and relationships <u>within</u> an economy and <u>between</u> them and the other realms of the entire society. In short, the repetition you will see is purposive, not accidental.

Finally, I wish to express my gratitude to those whose advice, assistance, and support have kept me moving toward this work's completion. The students in my classes in the San Francisco Bay Area and in Italy are to be counted in that group; their spirit and their questions, their hopes and their fears, have over the years been vital to my energy and motivation.

My esteemed and talented friend Howard Zinn, although he is always pressured to do more than time permits, took a good look at an early draft and made useful suggestions; all were appreciated although not all were taken. I have been helped in many ways by Michael Slaughter, a professional musician and student for many years in my community classes. Some years ago he established a Web site for the classes (<www.dougdowd.org>) which, along with numerous other generosities with his time and skills, have been important for me and many others.

In the very week in which this work was accepted for publication by Common Courage and I was asked to edit and update as soon as possible, my wife and I found ourselves without a place to live (or work), for reasons having to do with the casual way in which agreements about time are taken in otherwise marvelous Italy (where I am half of each year). Two dear friends came through at that critical time, and I am deeply indebted to both. Enrica Casanova insisted that we stay in her very comfortable apartment, and Annamaria Oscarino went well out of her way to make it easy for me to use my computer (and practice my cello) in hers. Thus it was that more than a month of what could have been a nightmare was transformed by two generous-spirited friends into a pleasure.

The contribution of Greg Bates of Common Courage Press has been wonderful. He made what is often an annoying and frustrating process into one which at times was often almost joyous. I commend Common Courage, his press, to other writers on the verge of wondering whether the effort is worth it, after all.

Last and heartfelt are my loving thanks for the very existence and wisdom of my wife Anna Hilbe and her uniquely marvelous way of offering criticisms and assistance. I would not have begun and could not have completed this book without the loving energy and morale I receive from her; with a lift of the eyebrow, a murmur or a smile, she has done all that could be done to temper my foolish tendencies and to encourage what may be their opposite. That full success in such a Sisyphean task would always be beyond reach is not her fault.

Abbreviations

AAA: Agricultural Adjustment Administration
AFL: American Federation of Labor
AP: Associated Press
BLS: Bureau of Labor Statistics
BW: Business Week
CA: Covert Action
CCC: Civilian Conservation Corps
CIO: Congress of Industrial Organizations
D&S: Dollars & Sense
EPA: Environmental Protection Agency
ERP: Economic Report of the President
FCC: Federal Communications Commission
FDIC: Federal Deposit Insurance Corporation
FEPC: Fair Employment Practices Commission
FM: Fortune Magazine
FTC: Federal Trade Commission
GAO: Government Accounting Office
GDP: Gross Domestic Product
GE: General Electric
GM: General Motors
GATT: General Agreement on Tariffs and Trade
HC: Hartford Courant
HMOs: Health Maintenance Organizations
HUAC: House Un-American Activities Committee
IBRD: International Bank for Reconstruction and Development ("World Bank")
IHT: International Herald Tribune
im: il manifesto (Italy)
IMF: International Monetary Fund
IRS: Internal Revenue Service
ITT: International Telephone and Telegraph
LAT: Los Angeles Times
LBO: Left Business Observer
MJ: Mother Jones
MM: Multinational Monitor
MNC: Multinational corporation
MR: Monthly Review

NAFTA: North American Free Trade Agreement
NATO: North Atlantic Treaty Organization
NRA: National Recovery Act
NSA: National Security Administration
NY: *New Yorker*
NYA: National Youth Administration
NYRB: *New York Review of Books*
OPEC: Organization of Petroleum Exporting Countries
OSHA: Office of Safety and Health Administration
OSS: Office of Special Services
PBS: Public Broadcasting System
PWA: Public Works Administration
S&L: Savings & Loan Banks
SEC: Securities and Exchange Commission
SFBG: *San Francisco Bay Guardian*
SFC: *San Francisco Chronicle*
TIPS: Terrorism Information and Prevention System
TN: *The Nation*
TVA: Tennessee Valley Authority
UN: United Nations
UNICEF: United Nations Childrens Fund
UNRRA: United Nations Relief and Rehabilitation Administration
USDA: U.S. Department of Agriculture
USDE: U.S. Department of Education
USGPO: U.S. Government Printing Office
USNWRP: U.S. NEWS & WORLD REPORT
USS: United States Steel Corporation
USSIC: U.S. Senate Intelligence Committee
USSR: Union of Soviet Socialist Republics
WHO: World Health Organization
WP: *Washington Post*
WPA: Works Progress Administration
WSJ: *Wall Street Journal*
WTO: World Trade Organization
ZM: *Z Magazine*

Foreword

It is useful to begin with America—That we call ourselves, simply, "Americans" and refer to all others who live in the Americas with a qualifying adjective—Latin, South, Central or Canadian—is not a crime, but its constant usage does qualify it to be considered one of the many ways in which we display our arrogance.

We have to call ourselves something, of course; but even "the Americas" must grate on the ears of the many tribes and cultures settled here millennia before the European invasions. Its origin is usually (but not always) seen as the first name of the Italian explorer Amerigo Vespucci who, in the early 16th century drew the first map of the western hemisphere. Better Amerigo than Vespucci, probably: "Vespucci, Vespucci, from sea to shining sea...? " Better still, what the people already here had called their land? (MARTINEZ)

As was suggested in the Preface, what follows could easily be seen as the diatribe of someone who hates this country. Quite the contrary; it is a critique and a warning for those who, like myself, have had a lifelong love affair with what has always stirred us and others when we or they think of "America!" Nowadays we are increasingly joined by foreigners; the English novelist Penelope LIVELY put it succinctly in her prize-winning novel *Moon Tiger*, when she described the USA as "a marriage of all that's admirable with all that's appalling."

Love of country should never mean acceptance of <u>anything</u> we do (or don't do) at home or abroad; not when it defiles what our country is supposed to stand for: decency, freedom, opportunity for all and, among other ideals, peace. When these are betrayed, love requires determined efforts to set matters aright. The long popular USA slogan "My country, right or wrong; but my country!" has all too often been interpreted to mean "anything goes" when <u>we</u>—but not others—do it.

The USA is by no means unique in living by such double standards, nor in committing crimes against humanity, society, and the environment here or elsewhere; of course not. No society has been or is without culpability for many of the matters discussed in our "**A**" to "**Z**s" (which, when referred to in the text will be as just now printed in **bold**; and authors in FULL CAPS). Whether the reference is to "**arrogance**," or "**zoos**"; or, for example, to the mistreatment of women, the USA is far from being among the worst offenders. Rather, the charge of what follows is that we

"Americans" see our nation as unique in the number and kinds of its virtues, one that has steadily cured itself of what faults it may have once had.

The bitter truth, however, is that although we have had every opportunity to become a truly wonderful society, we have failed to shed our past faults and now evolve toward something the opposite of wonderful: The gap between our realities and our ideals, despite important changes now and again, has widened to resemble the Grand Canyon.

Not all, but a large number of the ugly realities comprised in the **A** to **Z**s may be placed into a few categories seen as having been mutually supportive: a) **Racism** and other forms of prejudice, b) violence and **militarism**, and c) a seemingly insatiable and socially sanctioned **greed** for money, for things, and for **power**. Their continuous interactions dominate our habits of thought, feeling, and behavior; they have become an important part of what it means to <u>be</u> "an American." The damage thus done to others and to ourselves is all the more potent because we are normally unconscious of our misdeeds; or, worse, often see them as positive. We often behave, feel, and think as racists not only without qualms, but unknowingly; similarly with our reflexive militarism, which we see as "defense of freedom..." or some other palatable notion. Even less do we see greed as applicable to <u>us</u>; rather, we see ourselves as "striving," as "hard-working," as "enterprising," not as a people for whom MORE! of almost everything has become an ever-present inner command.

Over our history, the ongoing mix of the foregoing have been the main shaping forces of the USA and what we are as a people, integral to the special nature and great strength of U.S. **capitalism**. They have become as normal to us as the "institutions" of marriage, of driving on the right side of the road, as the Thanksgiving dinner.

Now an anticipatory look at each of those three areas; that done, this <u>Foreword</u> will close with a comment on the socioeconomic practices of the USA that have so badly damaged the natural **environment**, and that now threaten the very survival of life on earth; a major consequence of our guiding socioeconomic system.

The USA did not of course invent itself; we grew from British roots, not out of thin air. We begin by noting Britain's defining importance in the centuries of our colonial existence; an influence never entirely supplanted by what are often seen as uniquely "American" characteristics.

<u>Like father, like son.</u>

This nation was the first to break itself loose from colonial status in the modern era; that we were able to do so against Britain could be seen as surprising given that it was soon to be the most powerful nation in the world. Vital to our victory was that Britain was thousands of miles distant from our shores at a time when transportation and communications were very slow and undependable; had we been within hundreds rather than thousands of miles, militarily there would have been no chance for us to gain independence from Britain.

At least as vital, however, was that those who led and largely fought the revolutionary struggle were themselves English by birth or origin. As such, they took for granted what was taken for granted by the English, saw themselves as having the same rights and, like them, saw themselves as a superior people.

Moreover, the colonies—more so than any other society in history— easily evolved along capitalist lines; and, like the British (and the Europeans generally), the evolving "Americans" were energetic and merciless regarding geographic conquest in both the colonial and national periods.

In being so the colonists were demonstrating what may be seen as an axiom: When a relatively great power takes over a weaker one, not its best but its worst characteristics come to dominate in the weaker society. And so it was. As will be seen, however, the colonists were less restrained by tradition than the English as they applied its worst characteristics: they lived ruthlessly, heedless in pursuit of gain, oblivious to their victims' woes; all that and more despite the inspirational words of The Declaration of Independence.

When England moved toward becoming "Great Britain" and the "United Kingdom" it did so by taking over the neighboring lands of Ireland, Scotland, and Wales, with varying degrees of ferocity—worst of all for the Irish, the first people they subjugated. (see WOODHAM-SMITH; CAHILL; MCCAFFERTY). On a much larger scale we did the same, as "westward went the course of empire."

But there was also a major difference: As Britain moved toward its global empire, its home population was almost entirely "British" (until the late 20th century). Not so for the USA. In addition to our cruel and lethal importation of millions of Africans as slaves for two centuries—more than half of whom died en route—and except for the "**Indians**" whom we disposed of ferociously, our population was <u>entirely</u> made up of peoples from elsewhere—all of whom soon learned to be treated badly by others, and to do likewise.

Racism and Prejudice

The USA is the nation to whose shores have come more peoples from more different societies than to any other. Far from seeing ourselves as extravagantly blessed by such a profusion, we have instead generated the most lengthy and complex categories of prejudice in the world. That might well be seem an exaggeration to many readers; it is not. Dozens are the categories of those who, irrespective of place of origin, ethnicity, color, or religion, have over time been openly or covertly described by epithets of everyday usage —with those demeaned also demeaning others: a perverse equality.

Forgive me as I now alphabetically list some of these dirty names. Even though I was born and grew up in one of the least bad of U.S. cities, San Francisco, these are the names I heard from childhood on: bohunk, chink, dago, gook, greaser, greaseball, gringo, honky, injun, jap, jewboy, kike, limey, mick, nigger, nip, polack, prot, redskin, slanteye, spic, squarehead, wop, yid...; the list goes on, many of them not "sounding" offensive to our ears because we have come to take them as "normal." But what's in a name?

Ask those against whom they are used. As children we learned to sing "sticks and stones may break my bones, but names will never hurt me." But those to whom such epithets are hurled—especially children—know better. When applied in the economic, political, and social realms, such names mean discrimination and prejudice affecting jobs, housing, voting, medical and legal treatment, and much more. For all too many Native, African-, Chinese-, Mexican-, and Japanese-Americans, it has meant, in addition, beatings, rape, unjust arrest and imprisonment, prejudicial and baseless executions, and lynchings. (see **crime and punishment, prison-industrial complex** and **death penalty**.)

Over time, probably most of our citizens either ignored or overlooked such crimes; but, when known about, even now, all too often they are cheered, noisily or silently.

Militarism and its Violence

Virtually all societies have been militaristic from time to time, some more than others; the USA ranks near or at the top among those "others." That should be surprising, given that until the mid-20th century the vast oceans surrounding us made us virtually impregnable, and that our unparalleled natural resource base made us the least needy of all nations. From our colonial period on, however, we have turned to violent ways and means to construct our present boundaries; that achieved, toward the end of the nineteenth century we began our continuing <u>global</u> expansion.

For a majority of the people of the USA the foregoing words would seem utterly implausible. That connects all too well with the substance of this book, one of whose several elements has to do with the continuous aggressive behavior of the USA, from its first days to the present.

To illustrate that behavior and, at the same time, to suggest the tone of the book, herewith a preliminary set of historical facts on how easily and frequently we have resorted to military ways and means:

<u>To the shores of Tripoli</u>. Ask the citizenry of the USA to characterize our behavior as a nation when faced with controversies with other societies: Are we prone to use persuasion, or do we employ force and violence? A strong majority would in effect respond, "We are a peace-loving nation, always seeking what is demonstrably in the best interests of all, except when provoked."

Such attitudes can stem from **arrogance**; usually they are a result of arrogance combined with ignorance. As a people, we pay dangerously little attention to history; "We cancel our experience. It is an American habit," as Clifford Odets put it in the 1930s.

Our ignorance is a natural outgrowth of an easy insolence that has socialized us to see our nation as superior to all others, not just in its sheer economic and military strength, but in its morality, its ideals, its sense of justice; indeed, to see our great strength as a <u>consequence</u> of the application of those virtues.

But the USA has been neither the most virtuous of societies nor among the most peaceable. Here a brief outline of a small portion of our very warlike history.

William A. WILLIAMS, in his <u>Empire as a Way of Life</u> provided an annotated list of U.S. "interventionist activities" between 1798 and 1941. The listing is only of <u>undeclared</u> wars, of which he found <u>154</u> in those years (including the Cuban and Philippine wars 1898-1909). Here a representative <u>sample</u> of the 154 instances, in chronological order: (see BLUM/2000, 2004/ for those after 1945)

1798-1800: Naval war with France, including land actions in the Dominican Republic.

1815: The second Barbary war (Tripoli, Algiers, Tunis), involving a fleet attack on Algiers. (There were also the first and third Barbary wars).

1822-25: Four landings on Cuba, in pursuit of pirates.

1827: Greece. Landing parties hunting pirates (again).

1838-39: Sumatra. Two landings, to punish natives for depredations on American shipping.

1843: Africa. Four U.S. vessels landed 200 marines to discourage piracy and to punish attacks on U.S. ships.

1856: China. Attacks for the protection of U.S. interests. By 1895 there had been seven such attacks on China.

1858: Uruguay. Two landings to protect U.S. property during a revolution in Montevideo.

1860: Angola, Portuguese West Africa, "to protect American lives and property when the natives became troublesome."

1863: Japan. Between 1853 (when Admiral Perry "opened" Japan) and 1868 there were six U.S. interventions to advance and protect U.S. interests.

1872: Korea. Two landings, to punish natives for "depredations" on Americans. Repeated in 1888.

1899-1901: Philippine Islands. To protect American interests following the war with Spain, and to conquer the islands by defeating the Filipinos in their war for independence.

1903-14: Panama. U.S. Marines to protect U.S. interests during canal construction.

1906-09: Cuba. The Cubans won their independence from Spain in 1898. In 1903, the U.S. Navy took Guantánamo (southern Cuba) as a naval base; 1906-09 the U.S.A. "intervened" militarily "to restore order, protect foreigners, and establish a stable government."

1911-27: China. As nationalist revolution and connected conflicts began, the U.S.A. intermittently landed and functioned to protect U.S. interests with, by 1927, 5,670 U.S. troops ashore and 44 U.S. naval vessels.

1918-20: Soviet Russia. In June and July, 1918 Marines were landed near Vladivostok to protect U.S. interests; in August an additional 7,000 were landed, and stayed until 1920. At Archangel, 5,000 U.S. troops joined other "Allied forces," suffered 500 casualties, from Sept. 1918 until June, 1919; all this and other interventions to support the Tzarist and Kerensky forces. (No war was declared.)

1920: Guatemala. Landings to protect U.S. interests.

Such a listing in the years after 1945 would be as long or longer (again excluding <u>declared</u> wars). Many of those "interventions," will be discussed in the pages to follow, including Angola, Cambodia, Chile, the Congo, El Salvador, Honduras, Nicaragua, Laos, and Panama.

It is difficult to find many years in our entire history when we were not openly or covertly engaged with others militarily in North, Central, or South America, in the Caribbean, the islands of the Pacific, in Asia, Africa, the Middle East, or Europe. Only one of those hundreds of wars, World War II, may be seen as defensive— unless, and very much to the point, one sees the **Cold War** as defensive; about all of which, more later.

Institutionalized greed

It is generally agreed that the USA is the most capitalistic of all societies. That is to say something else: Ours is the society in which there have been fewer obstacles to and more encouragements for the accumulation of private wealth than any other, come what may.

Just as there is much to be criticized in other modern societies, there was much to be criticized in the traditions that characterized and constrained ancient, medieval, and early modern societies; of course. But there was also much of value, not least the implicit recognition that "we are all in the same boat," and the related understanding that "economic" activities must be balanced <u>within</u> a set of primary institutions and social values, rather than, as in the "ideal" capitalist society, allowed to dominate the larger social process. As TAWNEY put it:

> To found a science of society upon the assumption that the appetite for economic gain is a constant and measurable force, to be accepted, like other natural forces, as an inevitable and self-evident datum would have appeared to the medieval thinker as hardly less irrational or less immoral than to make the premise of social philosophy the unrestrained operation of such necessary human attributes as pugnacity or the sexual instinct. (1926)

But that is precisely what has become very much the "primal force" in the USA, with only occasional interruptions such as those of the New Deal of the 1930s and its 1950s-60s offspring. Writing in mid-19th century Britain, MARX observed that "Accumulate! Accumulate!" was the "Moses and the Prophets" of capital, that is, of the <u>business</u> class. Today, that persists, but to capital accumulation must be added the voracious seeking after power for business (among others) and, with the deepening of **consumerism**, the accumulation of consumer goods and services—now the passion of almost all in the USA, as well as, increasingly, in the "americanizing" world. The harmful consequences of the obsession with MORE! MORE! have been many, in the economic, political and social realms. Ultimately, the most devastating of all will be found in the always spreading and deepening destruction of the **environment**.

You can't fool Mother Nature

Blessed as the USA has been in both the quantitative and qualitative dimensions of its natural resources, it is perhaps understandable that we would have been more careless than others in their use. But carelessness had moved to recklessness already as the 19th century closed; by the end of the 20th century, we were verging on eco-suicide. Nor, as our treatment of **buffaloes** shows, was our spoliation of natural resources separate from our strong tendencies toward violence and our racism (in this case, toward "**Indians**"), destroying the peoples and their social structures. Without a second thought.

The first indications of just how destructive our use of resources could be was by **farmers**, as the westward movement went on and on and the Plains were settled and farmed. Those lands might well have served sensibly for grazing; they certainly were not suited for the staple crops wheat and corn for which they were and are used. There were many indications already by the late 19th century that things were going to come unstuck; that became glaringly obvious with the devastating **dust bowl** of the 1930s, whose many ominous signs in the past had been ignored.

But what was to be true for the wrong-headed use of the Plains states was also true for what became the heavy use of pesticides; for the misuse of water supplies; for the death of forests, the over-mining of minerals; the overuse of oil and coal; for the drying-up of streams, lakes, bays and rivers and serious damage, even, to the surrounding oceans, to the ozone layer—part of a long list of environmental wrongs combining stupidity with

greed, and **waste** with destruction.

To all that one must add in the deadly pollution of the air and the water, the death of both flora and fauna, and the steady movement toward gridlock as well as asphyxiation in our cities and suburbs. And, as is daily more obvious, global warming.

But there is something else. Not all, but all too much of what has gone wrong has been due to the great successes of the auto industry in making **cars** our Number One passion—treated at length in its place.

In sum

Taken together the contents of this book stand as a condemnation of our society as it has been and as it is. Many decades ago, William Carlos Williams, among the most noted U.S. poets, observed of our past that "History begins for us with murder and enslavement, not with discovery." W.H. AUDEN was speaking to the British long ago in "Get There If You Can and See the Land You Once Were Proud to Own"; its closing words speak to us, today:

> If we really want to live, we'd better start at once to try;
> If we don't, it doesn't matter, but we'd better start to die.

advertising/public relations

There was a time when to advertise meant to inform the public where to buy something at what price. That was long, long ago, when almost all people were having a hard time finding the money to stay alive, before mass consumption, let alone **consumerism**, had set in.

The first whispers of what modern advertising should mean were noted by DICKENS in his *Hard Times* (1854)—along with his devastating descriptions of education and exploitation. As that century neared its end, VEBLEN (1899) heard them as already loud voices creating the first steps toward "conspicuous consumption, conspicuous display, and conspicuous waste."

Not until the early 20th century would there be a sufficient percentage of the population with incomes above sheer subsistence to provide the mass markets for durable consumer goods that are critical for the profitability for 20th century industrial **capitalism**, they in turn critically dependent upon always more deft advertising techniques.

As modern advertising began, so did **public relations**—the one to sell products, the other to sell ideas; soon, they had morphed to become indistinguishable in ends and means and, by now, in their personnel. The journalist Joe McGinnis captured the formation of that family in his book *The Selling of the President*, on whose cover was a cigarette package with **Nixon**'s head sticking out. (McGinnis had accompanied the entire 1968 campaign of Nixon.)

Modern advertising is not meant to inform; its role is to <u>mis</u>inform, <u>dis</u>inform, tantalize, and to nourish and to stimulate our irrational fears, hopes, and inclinations. In doing so, it simultaneously 1) leads us back to or freezes us in an adolescent state; 2) isolates and feeds what might otherwise be minor feelings of greed and envy while supplanting natural feelings of compassion and generosity, bringing out the worst and helping to stifle the best in us; and 3) makes social and self-harming fools of us, leading us (as Paul Baran once put it) "to want what we don't need, and not to want what we do." (BARAN, 1969; ENSENZBERGER, EWEN, SCHILLER)

Implicit in the foregoing is that despite and because of our many strengths, in comparison with other species we are fragile and vulnerable. But where other species are vulnerable to <u>other</u> species

that are their natural enemies, we have become our own worst enemies.

We have the capacities to be and to create what no other
species can, and we have done so: Beethoven and Hitler, the piano
and the atomic bomb, hospitals and death camps. What or which we
do as a species depends upon the social processes within which we
live; the social processes **capitalism** depend in critical part for their
"healthy" functioning upon stimulating our greed, our envy, our
cunning, our selfishness, our ability to hate and harm, our fears.

In this matter, as in so many others discussed in this book, our
times and the USA are far from being unique, nor is advertising the
only means by which such tragedies are produced: we need only call
to mind Nero's Rome and its cruel irrationalities. But, in the matter
of modern advertising in the USA, we are dealing with what we
choose to see as the most desirable of all societies. In that **arrogance**
we have not been alone, either; our historical competitors include
all the great and some of the not so great societies: Rome, Britain,
France, Germany, China, Japan....

Advertising/public relations have done much to feed that
pride—and to undercut its realities. Advertising techniques have
become essential for the selling of things, ideas, and politicians; as
such, aided and abetted greatly by **spin**, they have also shaped the
social process; or, more accurately, misshaped it by exploiting our
many vulnerabilities.

It seems clear that all mammals have a need for dignity, taken
away from many mammals by us in **zoos**, lost by all of us in diverse
ways, whether at work or play, lost much more for those discrimi-
nated against because of gender, "race, creed, or color" in all realms.

Whatever the locus or rationale, dignity for the human animal
translates easily into a need for self-esteem. That need can be satisfied in many positive ways; all too often it is taken care of in ways
harmful to self and others.

Interestingly, Alexander de Tocqueville saw this early on in our
history, in his *Democracy in America* (1845). While praising the
USA to the skies as the most democratic of societies, he also saw us
as plagued by **conformity**, wracked by our fear of being different. He
took this to be the Achilles heel of our democracy—this before
there was anything like what we call advertising. About half a cen-

tury later, Thorstein VEBLEN commented on the same matter, in his own way:

> The usual basis of self-respect is the respect accorded by one's neighbors. Only individuals with an aberrant tempera-ment can in the long run retain their self-esteem in the face of the disesteem of their fellows. (VEBLEN, 1899)

It is but short a step from that to "keeping up with the Joneses," who in turn are "keeping up" with their " Joneses, those they see as better fixed than themselves—represented most fully in the popular response to the advertising for **cars**, from the 1920s on. When that began, the slogan became "You are what you drive"; now its not entirely unconscious motto seems to be "You drive what you want people to think you are." ("Vehicle Viagra....," *NYT*, 7-13-03)

Veblen categorized such behavior as "emulation," and saw it as a major means by which the powerful retain their power. Making us uneasy in these ways has risen to a fine art in the worlds of advertis-ing and public relations. In that respect, already in the 1940s the main academic demand for psychologists was in the realm of social psychology, and the demanders were large corporations and adver-tising agencies.

These are the days of "More!" and "Shop 'til you drop" and (although not put this way) "borrow 'til you're bankrupt," Those siren songs are what we hear and see from **TV**, in the print media's ads (and articles), in films, our clothing logos; it has become the social air we breathe, beginning with when we are children: "In the U.S., kids see 40,000 commercials a year on **TV** alone." ("Is tide starting to turn on advertising in school?" IHT, 2-18-03)

So thorough is that contamination that we have become unconscious of it, as we have with the polluted air; we neither can nor do seek to distinguish between ads and non-ads—whether as regards goods and services or politicians and policies. Indeed, it has been found through polling that a rising percentage of TV watchers have come to prefer the commercials (and "infomercials) to the pro-grams they accompany. (BARBER)

In the USA alone, spending on ads went from $222 billion in 1999, to $244 billion in 2000, to over $250 billion in 200—with an additional $231 billion spent outside the USA. "A billion here and a billion there," wisecracked Senator Dirksen (R., Ill.) a generation ago, "and pretty soon we'll be talking big money!"

Which is worse, having our minds managed to lead us to buy stuff we don't need and can't afford, or to getting us to vote for politicians who have been bought and paid for by those who have given them the money to buy enough TV time to get elected? Don't ask, they are one and the same thing; the money to pay for the ads for goods and services comes from very much the same group of rich and powerful individuals and companies who buy the politicians. <u>Item</u>: in **Bush II**'s record-breaking campaign finance efforts in 2003—expected to raise $200 million—it was reported that the **CEO**'s of major contributors (those raising over $200,000 <u>from their employees</u>) were among the highest contributors.

As the 19th century ended, its **corruption** of politics led to the common view that U.S. democracy had been replaced by a U.S. plutocracy. (JOSEPHSON) That tendency continued through the 1920s, but was then halted; for a while: in the 1930s and its severe depression, the populace moved itself to form **unions** and to participate in politics enough to carry us toward democracy. That set of processes endured up through the 1960s but began a reversal as the 1970s ended, taking us to where we are now: a bought and paid for plutocracy, differing from its predecessors in many ways, but mostly in its greater intensities, dangers, and social destructiveness. <u>Caveat emptor</u>, the Romans said. They had it right. (PHILLIPS, 2002)

Does it not matter that advertising has now become common in **education**, from K-12 through the university? Or this? In the article "Heartfelt Advice, Hefty Fees" (*NYT*, 8-11-02), we learn that in addition to the long-standing practice in films of having all actors smoking with labeled drinks, we now are shocked—shocked!—to discover that,

> In a rare interview, Lauren Bacall appeared on the NBC "Today" program (3-22-02), telling the host about a good friend who had gone blind from an eye disease and urging the audience to see their doctors to be tested for it.... And then she mentioned a drug called Visudyne, a new treatment for the disease of macular degeneration. Neither NBC nor Bacall revealed that she was paid for it.

The story goes on to note others who have done the same (Larry King, Rob Lowe, et al.) It is clearly possible that none of what

Bacall said was true, of course; and why need it have been? But tough talking, heart of gold Lauren Bacall, my and millions of others' favorite? Give us a break, Lauren! (I'm still sucker enough to think Bogie would have vetoed that sleazy act; although, on second thought, Bogie was one of the non-stop smokers in films, even though it was killing him.)

As a result of the publicity concerning this and many other such incidents, in late August CNN issued "a new policy and will tell its viewers about the stars' financial ties to corporations." (*NYT*, 8-23-02). It will be interesting to see how such statements are phrased: "Our lovely guest this evening, having been paid $10,000 to say so, will tell us how Zowie Cream has changed her life." Or what?

Meanwhile, in a world agonized by malnutrition and starvation, mal- or no education and dreadful or no housing, something just under $500 billion is being spent globally on ads every year. That's not just obscene, it's insane.

And it's dangerous. Quite apart from the fact that a very high percentage of the commercial advertising is for products—most especially **cars**—which we must buy and use less, not more, an always rising percentage is devoted to politics and politicians, and the advertising and public relations worlds become one.

Public relations expenditures divide into two prinicpal functions, 1) "institutional advertising," meant to give a "good name" to companies/industries seeking, for example, to avoid environmental or anti-**tobacco** regulations; or **HMOs** arguing against national health insurance; or a giant agribusiness company (in acting as "sponsors on presumably non-commercial public TV), such as **Archer Daniels Midland**, that seeks to deflect attention from its criminal price-fixing behavior in global markets, and the like; and 2) the function of favoring particular politicians or policies in an upcoming electoral contest.

But there is a third element, vital in itself; namely, the ways and means of public relations used to create or maintain a favorable "image," as for a **Bush II** and his policies. You may have noted how frequently in recent decades the principal advisor of the President of the United States has been an advertising man: a **Haldeman** for **Nixon**, a Mary Matalin for **Bush I** (and **II**), a James Carville for

Clinton, a Karl **Rove** and **Andrew Card Jr.** for **Bush II**. (That **Bush II**, he gets a <u>lot</u> of help; and he needs it.)

An interesting sidelight is that not long after both Matalin and Carville and their adversarial bosses had left the White House, they (M&C, not their presidents) were married. Both remain active, Carville with a TV show, Matalin helping Bush II. Wouldn't it be loverly to eavesdrop on some of their conversations? And what does that tell us, if anything, about the depth of their political persuasions? Does it matter?

affirmative action

The first "affirmative actions" in the USA were undertaken as the Civil War ended, providing a

> brief period in which southern Negroes voted, elected blacks to state legislatures and to Congress, /and had/ free and racially mixed public education in the South. (ZINN, 2002)

In those years (1865-1875), three constitutional amendments had been enacted: The XIIIth outlawed slavery; the XIVth proclaimed that "all persons born or naturalized in the United States" were citizens; and the XVth that citizens' right to vote "shall not be denied... on account of race, color, or previous condition of servitude."

It all worked, for a while; but only so long as northern (black and white) troops were there to see to it. However, in those same years strong economic and political forces were also at work seeking to undo whatever progress had been made.

> The southern white oligarchy used its economic power to organize the Ku Klux Klan and other terrorist groups. Northern politicians began to weigh the advantage of the political support of impoverished blacks—maintained in voting and office only by force—against the more stable situation of a South returned to white supremacy, accepting Republican /that is, northern/ dominance and business legislation. (ibid.)

The economic situation in the 1870s was a very heavy straw that broke the very weak back of progress toward social decency: 1) What became the longest depression in U.S. history—1873-1895—produced social unrest in the North while, at the same time, 2) the muscles of U.S. industrial capitalism were flexing, hungry for access to always more resources, the building of always more railroads, always more production and profits. The undeveloped South was prime territory for the resolution of both matters.

The North's ticket for easy entry to that beckoning feast was **"The compromise of 1877."** The hanky-panky in Florida that gave **Bush II** the presidency had its precedent set in the election of 1876—just as what PARRINGTON called "the great barbecue" was roasting the meat. The server on that occasion was a Congress so corrupt as to make ours today seem only mildly so, with its own version scurvy deals; the protaganists were the South and the North. The South's white supremacists got what they wanted, as did the capitalists of the North. In doing so, they brought into existence the conditions which in the late 20th century would require the nation once more to seek "affirmative actions" if it was to have even the appearance of a free society:

> The Compromise of 1877 did not restore the old order in the South. It did assure the dominant /southern/ whites political autonomy and non-intervention in matters of race policy and promised /them/ more than a share of the blessings of the new economic order. In return, the South became, in effect, /an economic/ satellite of the /North/. (WOODWARD) (my emphasis)

That devlopment and its consequences are pursued further under both **racism** and **slavery**; suffice it to note here that it was not until the 1960s that any positive steps were taken to move the USA toward realization of the XIVth and XVth Articles of the Constitution—with, all along the way, "strong forces" doing what they could to halt and reverse that realization.

What may be seen as preliminary steps toward what is now called affirmative action were taken during World War II. With the largest part of production devoted to the war and paid for by federal contracts, it was relatively easy for the government to legislate the "Fair Employment Practices Act." (FEPC)

FEPC required that all companies receiving government contracts hire without discrimination. With war's end, however, so ended FEPC. Efforts to continue it occurred here and there; but the hill leading to social equality was both steep and slippery, more than symbolized when, in California in 1946, a referendum was put to the voters to have a California FEPC.

During the war, California had undergone a large influx of both blacks and whites from the South (still reeling from the **Dust Bowl**); it was they who built the thousands of ships and planes (etc.), and received good wages in the process.

Hard to believe though it may be now, the general expectation right <u>after</u> the war was that the bad times of the 1930s would return. That fear and an ever more intense racism interacted with a full-scale business-financed media and extraordinary billboard campaign of blatant racism meant to scare the hell out of the voters. Duly scared, they voted FEPC down, two to one. That was in California, not Mississippi.

The term affirmative action itself was introduced for the first time in 1961, when **JFK** created the Equal Opportunity Employment Commission; its provisions lacked the teeth of enforcement; however, some teeth were provided in the **LBJ** civil rights legislation that outlawed discrimination in federal jobs.

Since the 1970s "affirmative action" has served as a battle cry for those who strongly support <u>and</u> those who strongly oppose measures to counter discrimination—most generally in jobs and education. That sharp-edged conflict is unlikely to diminish and, if ever "settled," seems likely to be won by its opponents: Those who support "affirmative action" do so from different bases, and are often at odds with each other, with "moderation" the majority view among them; those who oppose, although also diverse in their opinions, are not as riven by differences as the supporters, and also have easier access to those with economic and political power.

Given the many dimensions and deep roots of **racism**, what was legislated in the 1960s was comparable to using a stick to beat a tiger—a stick that had the perverse effect of waking up a snoozing tiger. Worse, its claws came to be sharpened first in the economically stagnant years of the 1970s, then most cleverly by **Reagan** in the 1980s. The result was that an ofen <u>unconscious</u> racism for most of our people became <u>conscious</u> for all too many.

Except for an isolated few <u>none</u> of our political or educational leaders have <u>ever</u> engaged in an attempt to teach the people of the USA about and against prejudice and discrimination and racism. World War II's FEPC, for example, was shoved down the throats of business; or, more accurately, oiled with profits so it would slide down smoothly.

JFK's executive order for "affirmative action" was for <u>federal</u> employees as was the employer provision of LBJ's Civil Rights Act. Just how insubstantial federal efforts in this realm were was revealed over and over again during the civil rights struggles in the South. Only by extraordinary—and usually failed—efforts by those in the civil rights movements were they able to gain protection from violent racists—the history-distorting, **FBI**-lauding film "Mississippi Burning" to the contrary notwithstanding.

Here a personal recollection: One of the most thoughtful <u>and</u> when utilized attempts to undo a sordid past was LBJ's "Head Start" program. On its surface a program to provide education to under-privileged (itself a euphemism) pre-schoolers, Head Start provided funds to provide not just education, but food and medical care and counseling to small children. The scope of the program was a recognition that hungry and demoralized kids are not likely to be able learn well. I was in the South for the summer from 1964 through 1966. In addition to trying to enable blacks simply to <u>register</u> to vote (effectively illegal then), some of our group also participated in the local Head Start program. (This was in southern Tennessee, on the Mississippi border.) Not only were we harassed, jailed, and even beaten for seeking to register black citizens, but the Head Start sessions had to be held secretly, in barns or houses—taking the chance of being beaten by outraged white locals. When I went to report this to the local (Memphis) **FBI** office (on whose bulletin board was nailed a photo of Supreme Court Justice Earl Warren stating "Impeach Warren!") I was rebuffed as though I were—to use today's words—a terrorist.

A key provision of Head Start was that it be both funded by and administered through the federal government. The reason for that was that the southern states could not be trusted to utilize the funds in its spirit, and that <u>none</u> of them could be trusted to <u>not</u> spend them for other purposes in times of fiscal crisis. Now, with all 50 states in such a crisis, the Bush administration has proposed to provide the funds to the states and leave it to them to do as they will. Only those who care strongly will even notice.

All of this is understandable, given that our political leaders have grown up in the same society as the rest of us, a society where the majority attitudes toward "people of color" and toward "women," are seldom if ever treated critically in our education. We are a people almost entirely <u>un</u>educated concerning our own history in any serious respect, let alone the ways in which we have mistreated, abused, even exterminated "people who are different." Different from what, or whom? To ask the question is to point to the combination of cruelty and absurdity of our patterns of discrimination: We are <u>all</u> among the "different" in terms of color, ethnicity, religion, national background; and half of us are female.

The 2003 ruling by the Supreme Court on affirmative action is but one more flaccid step toward continuing confusion and conflict which, over time, is likely to mean <u>more</u> discrimination in education and jobs rather than less.

Some day, somehow, the people of this country must find ways to see our diversity as a blessing, not as a threat; to see fairness and justice to all as a standard higher than **competition**; to recognize that those who are rich and powerful were, <u>most</u> of them (see **inequality**), "born on third base, and think they've hit a triple"; and that <u>most</u> of those of us who are well-fixed in our work and comfortable in our lives, <u>most</u> of us, had a "head start," had good luck, because of our gender, color, parents, where and when we were born—something in addition to or other than our hard work and brains. Those fine religious words "Do unto others as you would have them do unto you" may be too dreamy for the likes of our citizenry today; OK, back to realities. They reveal the hypocrisy of those who criticize today's affirmative action efforts.

The 2003 Supreme Court decision in the Michigan Case allows "race" to be taken into account, but disallows quotas. In doing so, they managed not to notice the elephant in the living room:

> No one raises concerns that preference in admissions given to athletes, cheerleaders and children of wealthy alumni causes self-doubt or stigma /as argued by Justice Clarence Thomas/. The fact that this concern only rises to prominence when it comes to considering race as one of many factors in admissions illustrates how difficult it will be to overcome the lingering discrimination in American Society. (Alan B. Krueger, "Economic Scene: The Supreme Court finds the 'mushball middle' on affirmative action." NYT, 7-24-03)

One of that living room elephant's prime beneficiaries was **Bush II**: Into prestigious Andover (after being turned down by a Texas prep school), then Yale, then Harvard's business school. He got into Andover because, get this, they "wanted Texans to diversify their student body;" into Yale because his grandpa was on the Yale Board (+ Texas again), and into Harvard..., just because. (<u>NYT</u>, Nicholas D. Kristof, "A Boy and His Benefits," 1-2-03) And that's why we have a such well-informed President.

Africa

As with our other geographic groupings (**Asia, Europe,** etc.), the intent here is merely to highlight the most egregious instances of U.S. interventions; often, the countries discussed are also part of other essays (e.g., **Cold War, imperialism,** etc.).

The critical and horrendous damages done to the peoples of Africa began well before there <u>was</u> a USA, and continued and deepened in the imperialism that took hold in the 19th century. In the earlier period, the major damage wrought to Africans was through an earlier slave trade; it was greatly multiplied from the 16th century on. (DAVIS, D.B., NORDHOLDT)

As one European nation after another began its exploitation of the human and natural resources of that bountiful continent, they moved from working with pre-existing African slave traders to transforming every dimension of African life—not least and, in the long run, most devastatingly, by creating artificial boundaries—"nations"—which separated whole ethnic groups to squeeze the resulting portions into imperial borders. Within those borders they were simultaneously deprived of the right to be themselves and required to live under the rule of Europeans who neither knew nor cared about them as human beings.

Today's terrible warfare and its genocides (as in the Congo) are a direct consequence of that European voraciousness and arrogance. The USA thrust itself into Africa in the 20th century, as we became <u>the</u> global power—doing so to profit from Africa's immense resources and as part of the **Cold War.** As the suffering of Africans continues and worsens, their oppressors' motives cannot be of much interest to them; they should be to us, however.

As will be seen, damaging though our direct and recent intrusions in Africa have been—and except for our earlier major role in the slave trade—they have been of a smaller magnitude than in the other regions discussed later; not because we have held back for reasons of decency but because in all the countries discussed below, the Europeans were there in force as well—and/or because there was less at stake for us.

It all began in Angola, and then shifted over to the Congo; we look only at them, and that all too briefly.

Angola

It was one of the first of the areas to be "discovered" by the Europeans—in 1482, by the Portuguese navigator Diego Cao, soon after he had "discovered" the Congo (on Angola's northern border). To its enduring misfortune, and like the Congo, Angola was and is rich in human and, even more, natural resources. The slave trade was the main attraction from the 17th into the 19th centuries, with Central Africa its doomed source: Ten to fifteen million men, women, and children died on the "western vogage," in order that 4-6 million who survived might be enslaved in the USA alone. (see **slavery,** and NORDHOLDT, and D.B. DAVIS)

The slave trade was ruinous to the African people and their economies, all too similar to what occurred to the native tribes of Latin and North America. (WRIGHT) That trade, like most colonizing activities, was a <u>coastal</u> operation; but when industrial **capitalism** and its **imperialism** took hold in the 19th century, the European penetration not only went beyond the coasts geographically, but into the social anatomy, physiology, and psychology of all the peoples of Africa, as it rendered them powerless and destroyed their cultures. (DOBB)

The colonialism imposed upon the peoples of Angola began in the 17th century and lasted until after World War II. Then virtually all colonized/imperialized societies were able to declare their political independence and have their own flags— but not their own economies nor their own "politics."

The U.S. presence in Angola was prompted by two matters: 1) its rich mineral resources; 2) its attempts to be truly independent, and the ways in which that brought it into the **Cold War.**

The movement toward independence in Angola was simultaneous with that of the Congo, and despite many differences, was destructively similar. From the beginning there were two opposing forces, 1) Jonas Savimbi's UNITA, initially supported—and partially created—by the USA and the Union of South Africa and 2) IMPLA, led by Augustin Nero, seemingly indigenous, ultimately militarily supported by the **USSR** and **Cuba.**

Although by 1975 IMPLA had won, and created the Republic of Angola, UNITA's forces continued their war until 1988, by which time at least half a million Angolese had died, the nation's infrastructure had been destroyed, and the economy was in a slough of despair. A truce was established, leading to the departure of Cuban troops; nonetheless, UNITA resumed fighting, financed still by the USA (with CIA assistance). (POWERS, 2002).

The effort to disarm Savimbi's zealous fighters continues at this writing (summer, 2003). There is no doubt that without U.S. and South African intervention, the IMPL forces would have won through democratic processes; the intervention of the USSR and of Cuba <u>followed</u> U.S. intervention—neither for the first nor the last time.

The Congo

The disasters imposed upon Angola from outside were multiplied for the Congo, beginning in the 17th century and worsening up to this moment. The Congo had the misfortune not only to be more populous and richer in natural resources than Angola, but also to have been invaded and ruled over by a Belgian, rather than by the Portuguese.

Note "a Belgian," rather than "the Belgians." The Congo was unique in that respect; the Belgian was Leopold II, King of the Belgians, a megalomaniac who, although subject to the Belgian government at home was free to do what he wished in his activities of what became <u>his</u> Congo. (See HOCHSCHILD; quotes to follow are from his <u>King Leopold's Ghost</u>.)

The Congo is an area at least equal in size <u>and</u> resources to the USA east of the Mississippi. Leopold took it over with the clear intent to make it his own, for reasons both financial and egoistic. His ego was satisfied by powers virtually unique to the modern world (until Hitler), and his finances grew in proportion to the trade in slaves, ivory, and rubber. It is estimated that he alone was responsible for the death of 10 million people.

After much in the way of massive lying and deceit, the Belgian government (at the instance, mostly, of Belgian businesses that wanted some of that Congo for themselves), literally "bought" the Congo from Leopold, for what today would amount to billions of dollars—an outrage in itself, but a hill of beans compared with what Leopold had done to the Congolese people. That can never be undone, even as its reverberations continue. A reading of CONRAD's Heart of Darkness, along with HOCHSCHILD, tells most of what needs telling of that history; it could cause you to gag at the depths to which some of our species can sink.

After World War II, independence movements took hold in the Congo, as in most other long-colonized societies. In the Congo's capital of Leopoldsville they came to an explosive head in 1959, when continuing demonstrations were bloodily suppressed by Belgium's Force Publique. By 1960, Belgium saw the light and grudgingly "allowed" independence; and then, with help of the **CIA**, succeeded in poisoning its independence to death.

In the Congo's first election ever, the charismatic Patrice Lumumba was appointed Prime Minister by a governmental coalition. From the beginning he argued that political independence in itself was insufficient for true independence, that the Congo could not go it alone economically. So he called for all of Africa to free itself from outside political control and economic dependence and to work together as a regional economy: Only then could the Congo use its vast resources of cobalt, copper, diamonds, gold, manganese, tin, and zinc for its own rather than foreigners' well-being. HOCHSCHILD tells what came next:

> Anathema to American and European capital, he became a leader whose days were numbered. Less than two months after being named the Congo's first democratically chosen prime minister, a U.S. National Security Council subcommittee on covert operations, which included CIA chief Allen Dulles, authorized his assassination. Richard Bissell, CIA Operations Chief... later said, "The President /Eisenhower/ would have vastly preferred to have him taken care of some way other than assassination, but he regarded Lumumba as I did and a lot of other people did: as a mad dog... and he wanted the problem dealt with.

(The easily accessible DVD film "Lumumba" provides a vivid and heart breaking account of that continuing tragedy.)

The problem was "dealt with" in early 1961. After being kidnapped and badly beaten and tortured, Lumumba was "secretly shot.... A CIA agent ended up driving around the city with Lumumba's body in his car's trunk, trying to find a place to dispose of it."

The man who then became the Congo's bloody dictator for over 35 years, Joseph D. Mobutu, "had been spotted as someone who would look out for /outside/ interests. He had received cash payments from the local CIA man... while Lumumba's murder was being planned."

Enough. Mobutu carried out Leopold's tradition, exploiting and murdering his own people. When **Bush I** (former head of the CIA) was U.S. President, Mobutu was greeted by him as "one of our most valued friends." Earlier he had been welcomed by President **Reagan** as "a voice of good sense and good will."

When Mobutu died in 1997 (at one of his numerous villas on the Riviera), his personal fortune was estimated at $4 billion.

alienation (see dehumanization)

anti-colonial imperialism

The concept is that of the U.S. historian William Appleman WILLIAMS (1969); it is worth a brief look for the insight it gives for the hypocritical stance typical of our nation and ourselves as a people regarding our long and continuing imperialist history.

Our anti-colonial history neither began nor ended with Britain; what became the USA had the "footprints" of the Spanish, French, Dutch, Russians, and Mexicans upon it, up to the mid-19th century; then, and especially after the Civil War, the USA was moving toward becoming the great economic power it was by the 20th century.

From our colonial beginnings until the USA extended to both oceans from east to west, and from the Gulf of Mexico to Canada from north to south, we had expanded with rarely an interruption; but we never saw ourselves as what we were becoming: the richest and most compact empire ever.

In that all we were doing was to expand within the space that became continental USA, the word "empire" might seem forced; it would not have seemed so to those who were forcibly brushed aside or slaughtered, beginning with the many millions of "**Indians**."

Then, from the 1890s on, we began our expansion overseas. The lead was taken by farmers seeking markets for their surplus crops (already then!). With the Monroe Doctrine (see **Latin America**) as our rationale, we began by seeking to oust Spain from the Caribbean; thence to the Philippines; thence to China, with now and then a poke in the Mediterranean (see Foreword), the rationale swelling to include our right to gain equal access to all markets in the world on the basis of free competition.

The rest is history, but a history in which "free" competition was more notable for its absence than its presence. Given the rising technological superiority of the USA in both agriculture and industry as the 20th century approached and ensued, that permitted a growing economic empire for the USA, without the traditional political institutions of "imperialism." And so it has gone ever since: Thus, "anti-colonial imperialism."

Except, that is, for the areas where "traditional" political and improvised imperialist political institutions had to be installed— including warfare, as in Central America both before and after World War II and the Philippines. (Those and many other developments are treated under the geographic headings of **Latin America and Asia**.)

Be all that as it may, almost all people in the USA would be self-righteously upset to hear us called "imperialists." Or, even, "anti-colonial imperialists." Why, we're just folks.

Archer Daniels Midland (ADM)

Those who watch the PBS McNeill-Lehrer news program have the opportunity five times a week to become acquainted with ADM—"Supermarket to the World." The message is always partially true and partially false. The true portion is that there are a lot of people in the world today, that more than a billion don't have enough to eat, and that there will be lots more people in the foreseeable future. The false part is that ADM tells us they are seeing to it that they <u>will</u> have enough to eat. They ask us to visualize the world as "one big farm"; a farm which, because of their techniques will be able to feed all. As noted under **environment** (and elswhere), the world has <u>always</u> been and still is able to feed all without ADM's chemicals and associated "green revolutions"; the problem lies elsewhere (see **farmers**). Instead, ADM is part of the problem and—in "cooperation" with other giants such as Cargill (largest of all)—has been for some time, while making lots of money in the process. Some numbers and related facts:

ADM is one of the top 100 largest companies in the USA; its revenues in 2003 were over $30 <u>billion</u>; its profits, $451 <u>million</u>, up 33 percent from 2001; (<u>FM</u>, 4-5-04)

The founder of ADM was Dwayne Andreas, now CEO Emeritus; other Andreases are Michael, Senior V.P., who did some time in jail (see below), Allen, now Chairman and CEO, and Martin, Senior V.P and Assistant CEO; in short, almost a one-family show. We begin with Dwayne.

In 1995 he said "There isn't one grain of anything in the world that is sold in a free market. Not one! The only place you see a free market is in the speeches of politicians." He ought to know. A 1995 study for the Cato Institute, a conservative think tank, states that at least 43 percent of ADM's annual profits are from products heavily subsidized or protected by the U.S. government." (BOVARD)

The core areas in which ADM has been helped along by U.S. government programs are three: maize (corn) subsidies, the sugar program (via government limits on output, and thus high prices), and the ethanol subsidy (corn again). ADM is a major contributor to both Democrats and the GOP from the Farm Belt. Which helps to explain why Senator Daschle (Dem., S.D.) helped to write the bill requiring gasoline refiners to almost triple the use of ethanol by 2012, even though it increases gas prices and does little or nothing for the environment. ADM's PBS <u>non</u>-advertisement is often livened up by corn leaves waving in the wind. (MALKIN)

So much good luck! Or perhaps it's more than luck. ADM is a major contributor to those who make and sign the relevant legislation: 1992-1994, $3-4 million known; and sums like that in subsequent years. So what's wrong with that? Everyone does it, no? (BOVARD)

Maybe so; maybe not. But not everyone has the opportunity or power to engage in ADM's most spectacular activity: price fixing of agricultural commodities. And not everyone who does gets caught, as ADM has been (for at least some of it). They began to be caught and tried and found guilty in 1996, twice for conspiring to fix an elevated price on lysine and citric acid (a food additive harmful for you and me <u>and</u> the **environment**) and, a bit later, for a related major loss for its stockholders; total fines, $190 million. Then, in 2004, another settlement for elevating the price of fructose corn syrup; fine: $400 million. (<u>NYT</u>, "Archer Daniels...," 6-18-04).

Cheap at twice the price, for are not those fines, like their PBS "non-ads," tax-deductible for ADM? Bargain basement crime.

But wotthehell, it's only making food cost more in that "hungry world" they talk about on PBS. And nobody's perfect.

arrogance

"Would the Gods the giftie give us, to see ourselves as others see us," observed Sir Walter Scott long ago. Unfortunately, among the several dangerous qualities of arrogant persons and nations is that it is precisely their arrogance that does not allow them to see themselves as... arrogant.

Arrogance and its close companion self-righteousness have been common in many nations, especially those with great power; it began to splotch our attitudes and behavior over a century ago; now it is one of our defining characteristics: We're Number One.

Accompanying our arrogance has been a **double standard**—the condemnation of others when they behave in a manner that is seen as acceptable when <u>we</u> do it. Confining attention here only to the contemporary scene, ask yourself how the USA would react if <u>any</u> nation, friend or foe, were to establish a naval or air base on an island close to our shores—as, for example, the U.S. base at Guantánamo, **Cuba**—a military base which is not on an island "close to Cuba's shore," but is <u>on</u> Cuba itself—where our base has been for about a century. The most recent insult has been to locate "Camp X-ray" there, for interrogating presumed **"terrorists"** (and often doing so against international laws).

We could go on with relatively small instances such as that—

e.g., our reaction if Chinese planes had been doing observation work off the shores of San Francisco, as compared with our indignation with their response to our doing just that off their shores.

Here a brief listing of recent U.S. arrogance, two under Clinton, the rest under **Bush II**: (NYT, 7-16-01, "U.S. snubs accord on germ warfare.")

1997: The US. refuses to sign the Ottawa Treaty eliminating anti-personnel land mines.

1999. The U.S. Senate rejects the Comprehensive Test Ban Treaty.

2001. Bush says the U.S. won't OK the 1997 Kyoto pact on global warming, signed by 178 other nations.

2001. President Bush says he wants to go "beyond the constraints" of the 1972 Anti-Missile Treaty

2001. The United States rejects an international accord aimed at enforcing a 1972 UN treaty prohibiting the development, production, or possession of biological weapons.

If that were not enough, in 2002 the arrogance continued when "U.S. Links Peacekeeping to Immunity from New /International Criminal/ Court" NYT, 6-19-02) and went on to "unsign" what Clinton had signed; after which still another headline: "U.S. Fails in Effort to Block Vote on U.N. Convention on Torture" (NYT, 7-24-02).

In sum, the USA is of more than one mind when it comes to germ warfare, global warming, ABM's, nukes, land mines, torture, and war crimes: We want y'all to stop doing all those dangerous things, but don't tread on us!

What lies behind all those disgraceful decisions was all too well revealed in 1984, after the explosion in Bhopal, India. As you read this, ask yourself what the USA position would have been if positions were reversed; reversed, that is, between India and the United States. The U.S. company Union Carbide (now owned by Dow Chemical) had a pesticide producing plant in Bhopal; its gas tank in effect exploded, spewing 40,000 tons of lethal gas. Bhopal had 900,000 residents. Immediately after the explosion 8,000 died; soon after the number of dead rose to 20,000 and more than half of the other residents of Bhopal were seriously poisoned.

It was subsequently admitted by the company that the cause

was the failure to check that the overfull tank and that the company had not followed required inspection routines. That's a lot more dead and injured than 9/11 in the USA, but how many in the USA paid any attention to that tragedy? Maybe it was OK because it wasn't political, but just to keep costs down?

Be that as it may, Union Carbide has never denied its culpability; it has rewarded the paltry, indeed insulting, sum of $300-580 to the victims of the catastrophe ($480 million cost to the company which, however, may be compared with the $26.5 <u>billions</u> paid by EXXON to Alaska (our 50th state) for its oil spill—where nobody died.

That's bad enough. But not bad enough for its owner Dow Chemical (which gave us Agent Orange during the Vietnam war): 1) the then CEO of Union Carbide has managed to avoid extradition and trial in India; 2) and now Dow Chemical is <u>suing survivors</u> of the Bhopal tragedy for their recent demonstration against the company in Bhopal. Why? Because of "the loss of labor time" it caused.

Now <u>that</u>'s arrogance. But it must be said that Dow and other U.S. companies have been substantially encouraged to behave this way by their government:

> The disaster in India led the U.S. Congress to pass a law requiring companies to disclose chemical emissions. But even though Bhopal was an overseas disaster, the law it inspired applies only in the United States. Dangerous pollutants are just one aspect of corporate behavior that can be hidden abroad. (NYT Editorial, "A global right to know," (1-24-03)

Try to imagine what the folks in the USA would be saying and doing if an Indian company with a factory here had allowed such a tragedy. Why, we'd send in the Marines to grab the CEO and whisk him off to Guantanamo for a secret trial. Justice never sleeps. (im, 1-4-03)

Perhaps things are changing a bit; and perhaps not. In the article "Field hands battle multinationals" (<u>NYT</u>, 1-20-03), we find that

> ... a federal judge in New Orleans has opened the way for a lawsuit brought by 3,000 Central American banana workers seeking millions of dollars in damages, the first time one of these cases would be tried in the United States. (my emphasis)

The cause of the lawsuit is a pesticide which, when proven to cause sterility in 1977, was banned for use in the USA; but it continued to be used in "the sprawling banana plantations that supply American supermarkets." There are seven companies involved; among them Shell Oil and Dow Chemical.

Over the objections of the Bush II Administration... Nicaraguan courts have found the companies guilty, but the companies say they will not pay... the $493 million fine to affected workers. Shell issued a statement arguing that Nicaragua's courts have no jurisdiction over Shell Oil, because its headquarters are in the United States....

Let's see now: If some thousands of U.S. workers were made sterile while working at a Japanese plant in Tennessee (which exists), and they sued, and the Japanese said their HQ was in Osaka, so.... What then would **Bush II** say? Zap 'em?

One gets a clue from another telling instance of U.S. arrogance as practiced by **Bush II;** his explicit position on **preemptive** action. In a speech to 2,000 "cheering troops" at Fort Drum (7-19-02), roaring approval to "Let's get Saddam!", and after reiterating the U.S, position on the International Court by saying "The United States cooperates with many nations to keep the peace, but we will not submit American troops to prosecutors and judges whose jurisdiction we do not accept," Bush went to "make it clear that he envisioned several types of preemptive action, from boosting foreign aid, to acting covertly against potential enemies, to sending in troops...into any country that poses an imminent threat to the United States." NYT 7-20-2). The behavior of the USA in recent years would have brought a quiet smile to face of the Roman historian Tacitus. Writing toward the end of the 1st century A.D., as the plutocratic/militaristic/deeply-corrupted empire was simultaneously growing in cockiness, he observed:

> It is no use trying to escape their arrogance by submission or good behavior. They have pillaged the world. When the land has nothing left for men who ravage everything, they scour the sea. If an enemy is rich, they are greedy; if he is poor, they crave glory. Neither East nor West can sate their appetite. They are the only people on earth to covet wealth and poverty with equal craving. They plunder, they butcher, they ravish, and call it by the lying name of "empire." They make a desert and call it "peace." (TACITUS)

Roman arrogance, following the bloody path laid out before them by the Phoenicians and Greeks, was headed toward their fate, only on a broader canvas. Empires are all spawned from arrogance, whatever their other faults: It happened to Spain and Great Britain and France and Japan and..., and now <u>we</u> are in the Catbird Seat. The Gods must be weeping with laughter.

Asia

The eastern shores of Asia are about 7,000 miles from the western shores of the USA; the technology of the seas thus set certain limits to whatever designs we might have had there in the 19th century. But not for long.

In 1853, Admiral Perry sailed four ships into Yedo (now Tokyo) Harbor—"belching black smoke"—and, the next year, seven more, well-armed and demanding that Japan <u>must</u> open its economy to ours. Thus the USA ended Japan's three centuries of self-imposed isolation (the sole exception being minimal Dutch trading rights in the 17th century).

Thus, also, was Japan propelled into the tightly coordinated economic and military programs which, by the early 20th century brought it into the top ranks with the USA, Britain, and Germany. Consider the devasting uses to which Japan put its militarized economy from the late 19th century up through World War II—in Korea, China, Okinawa, Formosa (now Taiwan), and Southeast Asia—and the price its own people paid for it from beginning to end; considering all that, and comparing it with its <u>relatively</u> innocuous existence before, it seems that for all concerned, it might well have been best for the USA and the Admiral to have "let sleeping dogs lie."

As the 19th century was ending, The USA undertook many other forays into Asia; they will be treated below, beginning with those of recent years into Central Asia.

Afghanistan

Poor Afghanistan! It is a classic instance of a society having been destroyed as it became a pawn in an international struggle: its people and its land bombed and battered and planted with hundreds of thousands of land mines, insane fighting year after year by one brute force after another—in our time, the USSR, the Taliban, the

USA. Each had its cause—the **Cold War** and/or **oil** and/or religious fundamentalism—each feeding on the others, all at great cost to the diverse peoples of Afghanistan, but also those of the USSR/Russia and, now, the USA.

Here it is neither desirable nor possible to discuss Afghanistan's long and troubled history <u>before</u> the USA became involved. What is important is to see just how and when and why—covertly—we did become involved. That was not after 9/11, it was in July of 1979.

That was when Zbigniew Brzezinski, National Security Advisor to then President Carter, persuaded him to sign the first of several directives allowing the **CIA** to provide weaponry to what became the Taliban. How do we know? "Zbig" (as he liked to be known) told us, through a boastful interview given to *Le Nouvel Observateur* (1-15-98): <u>realpolitik</u>'s finest hour.

The stated intention in July, he said, was "To draw the Russians into the Afghan trap.... We didn't push the Russians to intervene, but we knowingly increased the probability that they would." Three months later, on the day the Soviet army entered Afghanistan, he wrote to Carter "Now, we can give the USSR its Vietnam War."

In doing that we also birthed the Taliban, the main force resisting the USSR. When the interviewer asked Zbig if he regretted "having supported Islamic fundamentalism..., and given arms and advice to future terrorists," the reply was "What is most important to the history of the world? The Taliban or the collapse of the Soviet empire? Some stirred-up Muslims or the liberation of Central Europe and the end of the cold war?" (Interview in "The Making of Afghanistan," by Pankaj Mishra, *NYRB*, 1-15-01). On a day later that year in Manhattan there was an event called "9/11" at a spot now memorialized as Ground Zero.

Afghanistan, a country poor in natural resources, is rich in location: it straddles the area through which the vast and as yet little-exploited oil deposits of Central Asia can be transported at least cost—to the U.S. oil giant Unocal, if it has anything to say about it; and it probably will have (if China lets it/us). Unocal has been nosing around that area for at least 20 years, hoping to have first grabs on the oil pipeline.

Oil may be irrelevant to the U.S. involvement there; and it may not be; just as it may or may not have been irrelevant for the

U.S.-**Iraq** war. The truth will have to be dug out of the always more tragic ruins of Afghanistan—where, as this is being written in the winter of 2004, a cruel but predictable (and predicted) process is underway; namely, the re-emergence of rule by the so-called Northern Alliance, along with almost perpetual warfare and the re-emergence of—guess who?—the Taliban. Congrats, Zbig.

Cambodia (and see Kissinger)

Cambodia was never a rich country, except in its culture and its natural beauty; both have suffered greatly since the USA forced them into the Vietnam conflict. Their always small population (about 7 million before **Vietnam**), has been reduced by more than 15 percent by slaughter. (JACKSON)

Like Laos and Vietnam, Cambodia was forced into becoming a French "protectorate" (1863), and then made a part of French Indochina in 1887. In 1954, as France was being defeated by the Vietnamese at Dienbienphu, Cambodia wriggled loose and became a constitutional monarchy, presided over by Prince Norodom Sihanouk.

Not all "royalty" is beloved by those over whom they rule, but Sihanouk was; he was extraordinarily popular with them, and for good reason: As the French left Indochina and the USA at first crept in and then came to dominate the peninsula both covertly and openly, Sihanouk's obsession came to be to keep Cambodia out of that war. We wouldn't let him.

The USA bombed North Vietnam relentlessly and endlessly, and left it—and Laos—looking like the cratered surface of the moon; but the ground fighting took place almost entirely in South Vietnam. The whole of Cambodia is less than 200 square miles in size. At its northeastern corner is a little protuberance called "the parrot's beak" where the USA—as with Iraq's "WMD"—claimed, and claimed, and claimed again, that we would find COSVN ("Central Office for South Vietnam"). COSVN, the almost-always-mistaken CIA, claimed was the location of North Vietnam's materiel and weapons depot for the war in the South.

There was no such depot we now know; materiel and weapons were carried from north to south on innumerable paths and tunnels. No problem: We'll bomb the hell out of Cambodia anyway, on all those paths and tunnels. Except that the bombing—the **carpet bombing**—was not confined to the northeastern corner of Cambodia.

It all began almost immediately after **Nixon** had begun to find his way around the Oval Office, in early 1969. Standing close by was his National Security Advisor, Henry **Kissinger**.

Their murderous plans for the bombing of Cambodia had the official name of "Menu," with the progression of targets adolescently and sickeningly dubbed "Breakfast," "Lunch," "Snack," "Dinner," "Dessert," and "Supper." (SHAWCROSS) Makes one proud to be an "American."

The bombing of Cambodia began on March 18, 1969; by the time it ended 14 months later 3,630 air raids had been carried out by flights of 50 or so eight-engined B-52s flying from either Okinawa or Guam, each carrying dozens of 750 lb. bombs. And dropping them from 30,000 feet, from which nobody can distinguish a hill from a valley, a person from a tree. Lots of **collateral damage**, you can be sure; and that was the intent.

All of this was illegal (see **Kissinger**), so it had to be done within a pattern of secrecy from relevant congressional committees and cabinet members and, as well, from the air crews and their superior officers. (They were given a "legal" target in Vietnam and then, at the last moment, by radio, told to switch the coordinates.) (SHAWCROSS) Everything we did in or at Cambodia broke long-standing international law; pshaw! Old-fashioned rules? Ishkabibble; we're the USA.

So the USA set out to defy and depose Sihanouk and to control Cambodia by secretly bombing and enlisting the assistance of a right-wing general named Lon Nol. At a moment when Sihanouk was out of the country (in Paris), Lon Nol (assisted by the USA) pulled off a coup; "Cry Havoc! and let slip the dogs of war."

Lon Nol was unpopular, the very popular Sihanouk was unable to return, and various existing but small groups—among them the left-wing Khmer Rouge—were struggling for control. As the USA continued its heavy bombing in the spring of 1970, the Khmer Rouge, entirely a product of the breakdown of traditional Cambodian society, moved in and took over. It then proceeded to transform a very bad situation into something incredibly worse: they deliberately killed at least a million of their own people, literally destroyed Phnom Penh, and created the a nightmare that continues to this day.

Commentators in those years and since have rarely if ever placed the blame on the USA and its passion for defeating the North Vietnamese at whatever costs. The costs were high for the USA, but very small indeed in comparison with what happened to the people of Indochina. The following long quote from Sihanouk (from an interview in New York in 1979) is worthy of attention:

> What separated me from Lon Nol in 1970 was that he wanted to make war against the Communists and invite the United States into Cambodia. I knew that if we did so we would be completely involved in the Vietnamese war, we would lose our peace, and everything in Cambodia would be destroyed. If the United States had refused to help Lon Nol after the coup, he would have collapsed. I would have returned and stopped the war. It didn't happen because Nixon and Kissinger didn't want Sihanouk back.... There are only two men responsible for the tragedy in Cambodia today, Mr. Nixon and Dr. Kissinger. Lon Nol was nothing without them and the Khmer Rouge were nothing without Lon Nol. /But/ the results were the opposite of what they wanted. They demoralized America, they lost all of Indochina to the Communists, and they created the Khmer Rouge. (Quoted in SHAWCROSS)

The U.S. invasions of **Cambodia**, **Laos**, and **Vietnam** were rationalized by the "domino theory": "Unless we stop them (= USSR and/or China) there, the whole row of dominoes from Vietnam to Laos and Cambodia, to Thailand and Burma, to Pakistan and India..., the whole row would be knocked down.. all the way to the Mediterranean."

That theory didn't work out well: We did lose, all three countries were badly damaged, millions were killed, and "all the way to the Mediterranean" is dominated by neither the USSR nor China.

So there we were, continuing and deepening our long tradition of destroying native peoples in the name of something or other. Just for the hell of it? No, man, just for the **preemption** of it; our right and duty.

China

The USA first began to intrude on China late in the game, preceded much earlier by, among others, Britain. We stuck our nose into their affairs first in 1899, with our "Open Door Policy." It may be seen as a preview of today's **globalization** and **free trade/free markets** efforts or, as some see it, as an extension of the Monroe Doctrine from the western to the eastern hemisphere, as an application of the **anti-colonial imperialism**, concurrent with conquests in the **Philippines**.

Our Open Door policy took the form of identical notes from our Secretary of State (John Hay) to England, France, Germany, Russia, Italy and Japan, stating that "all countries should enjoy perfect equality of treatment for their commerce and navigation." It is revealing that the note was <u>not</u> sent to the Chinese government. Nor was it answered by its recipients.

It <u>was</u> responded to, however; a year later China answered with what came to be called "the Boxer rebellion." It was an effort of a group of Chinese (then called "fanatics") fighting against all non-Chinese present. But only for a while. Shortly thereafter, both the USA and all other parties except the Japanese found themselves fully occupied in battles elsewhere; the USA in the Philippines, the Europeans in Africa, subsequently all of us, in World War I.

We had taken our first steps in Asia in 1853, when U.S. ships broached **Japan**'s isolation, followed by our several years' fighting in the Philippines. After the 1899 attempt, we left China alone until World War II.

During that war, the Chinese were our allies against the Japanese. But already, and for many years previously, there had been emerging two Chinas: Nationalist (Kuomintang) and Communist, led, respectively, by Chiang Kai-shek and Mao Tse-tung.

The civil war between them had taken hold already in the 1920s (MALRAUX, SNOW); during World War II both sides fought (separately) in cooperation with the USA in the fight against Japan throughout China—the Nationalists from their HQ in Chungking, the Communists throughout the interior.

After the war, the civil war resumed in earnest, coming to a head in 1948-49. The Nationalist forces were routed, Mao declared the People's Republic of China, and Chiang Kai-shek, with the substantial assistance of the U.S. Navy, took his team and as many supporters as he could to Taiwan (previously Formosa); there, having proclaimed it to be China's he established a dictatorship—which, as in South Korea, lasted for a quarter of a century or more.

From that beginning until today Taiwan has been seen as under the protection of the USA. Our naval and air forces have never left the area, which they patrol 24 hours a day. There have been moments of respite, as in the early 70s, when **Nixon** and **Kissinger** were seeking a rapprochement with China as a lever against the USSR; in exchange for Nixon to be welcomed to China for talks with Mao, he agreed we would see Taiwan as part of "One China." And that we have done, "sort of," as they say in New Jersey. (HERSH)

The unrelenting hostility of the USA to "Red China" has of course had many negative consequences for both countries and, as well, for **Korea** and **Vietnam**. As noted with respect to the latter two, just as it is impossible to know what their fates might have been had they not become pawns in the **Cold War**, the same is so for China. Revolution against the merciless authoritarianism of Chiang Kai-shek, like that of the Russian revolution against the Czar was fully justified. (GURLEY)

There was reason to believe that the Chinese Revolution (as also that of Russia and Vietnam) would lead to a better life for their people—economically and politically. They were never given a chance; in all cases, if their revolutions were not to be overturned by one or more western powers, they had to militarize. Because also, in all cases, they were economically weak, the pressure on their resources and production required constraints which were entirely unlikely to be accomplished democratically.

Now we shall never know; were such possibilities ever to occur again for them or for other societies swept up in the tidal waves of the Cold War and/or now, **globalization**. we'll put stop to them, sure as shootin'.

Indonesia

The Portuguese were the first to intrude into "Southeast Asia." When they did so in the 16th century they were the tail end of a pre-capitalist tradition; the Dutch were on the cutting edge of just emerging capitalism. So it was that in 1602 there came to be a large basket of very rich islands called the Dutch East Indies in.

The Dutch, with a population under 2 million, were nonetheless the economic leader of Europe at that time. It was they who provided the strongest momentum for the emergence of **capitalism** in that era; they who, in the 18th century were vital in financing what became British <u>industrial</u> capitalism.

All that, both despite and because their natural resources were minimal. They were dominated by the sea, but learned to use it: they became the best shipmakers (in a preview of mass production techniques), and they constructed all those dikes, not only or even mostly to keep the sea away, but to give them more land on which to cultivate crops. They sold many ships to others and used at least as many for what was the first global trading network, stretching from Norway around to North America, from Holland around Africa to Japan.

They became the leading commercial and trading power in the 17th century and its leading financial power in the 18th: they were what the UK would be in the 19th century, as the UK was what we became in the 20th—with quantum leaps of power from one stage to the next. In their plantations and their tight rule, the Dutch were also the first to give a glimpse of how **colonialism** would become **imperialism**, going beyond coastal trading into internal production and by creating a government in their own name.

Its agricultural resources were just right for "trading capitalism": relatively bulky products traded within the East, lightweight "spices" easy and safe to transport all the way to Europe. They became the leaders, indeed the founders, of the "spice trade." That conjures up visions of pepper and ginger and such; and indeed they were part of it. But the spice trade consisted of at least 350 different commodities, some for eating, but at least as many for medicinal and "cosmetic" purposes. (BOXER)

That was long ago. By the end of World War II, the Dutch, along with <u>all</u> other Europeans (except the Swiss and the Swedes) had been flattened or worse by war. That is, <u>all</u> the imperialist powers were weak and needy while, at the same time, the USA was at its most powerful, and awash in abundance.

As the war ended, the imperial<u>ized</u> countries almost without exception had strengthened their efforts to throw off those who had taken over their countries; including the people of the Dutch East Indies. The Indonesian independence movement was led by Sukarno (or Soekarno). In 1948, the USA had placed pressure on the Dutch to relent; in 1949, independence was declared, and Sukarno headed up the new Indonesia.

It would be pleasing to think that U.S. pressure on the Dutch had been because of a regard for the freedom and independence of the many peoples of its 14,000 islands. Perhaps that <u>was</u> a factor; what is certain is that the area is not only of great strategic importance, but that it is rich in mineral resources, not least **oil**.

More's the worse, Indonesia, like so many other newly-independent countries, had the misfortune to achieve its freedom in the early stages of the **Cold War** <u>and</u> to be rich in resources <u>and</u> to be located near to both China and Indochina; as both, already in 1949, became a focus of hostile U.S. attention.

In 1955, Sukarno organized a conference of non-aligned countries—calling themselves "Third World" (the first usage of that term). From then on, Sukarno—much like Lumumba in the **Congo**—was a thorn in the side of the USA. His government was overthrown by Suharto in 1965, and at least 1,000,000 were killed, a large percentage of them from the large Chinese population of the area. There ensued a rightwing dictatorship distinctly friendly to the USA in terms of investment and trade (and votes in the UN).

As with so many newly-independent countries where the USA intervened for its own purposes, after 1965 Indonesia became the center of spreading oppression and terror in its own and adjacent territories—not least in East Timor, brutally taken over and suppressed and struggling to this day to find its own way. To this date, however, there has been no admission of the responsibility of the USA for the frightful costs paid in those countries—in the Congo, Chile, Central America, the Philippines, Southeast Asia, Greece.... (BLUM, 2004)

Japan

As the 20th century began, it was becoming clear that there were two major powers fronting the Pacific Ocean, the USA and Japan. Both were industrializing rapidly, the resources of one the most abundant in the world, the other's among the most meager.

Both were also aggressively expanding their sway over contiguous (and not so contiguous) lands: the USA in Central America (Nicaragua and USA-created Panama), the Caribbean, the Hawaiian Islands and the Phillipines; Japan, most importantly in Korea and Formosa before 1900, and in China by the 1930s.

Had there been no Hitler, no Mussolini, no European War II, it is within the realm of probability that at some time in the 20th century Japan and the USA would in any case been having it out militarily. Nor is it irrelevant to recall that when the USA <u>did</u> enter World War II, it was in response to Pearl Harbor, not to stem European **fascism**; and even then, having declared war against Japan after the attack, we did <u>not</u> enter the European war until after Germany declared war against us.

That being so, it is also relevant to recall that although the weight of 1930s public opinion in the USA was against involvement in <u>any</u> war, that was not so for **FDR**; if for mixed reasons, he spoke and acted as though he understood that more was at stake in that war than the mere wellbeing of Germany's neighbors.

The eminent U.S. historian Charles BEARD was convinced that FDR's desire for U.S. involvement was such that he contrived to provoke the Japanese, going so far (as Beard saw it) as to allow (even to provoke) the attack on Pearl Harbor, even though we had evidence it was going to occur; given the widespread opposition to war in the USA, only an attack would change public opinion. As indeed it did.

Be that as it may, it is necessary to keep <u>pre</u>war history in mind when considering <u>post</u>war U.S. behavior in the Pacific region—in occupied Japan itself, but also as regards the other "hot spots" of East Asia discussed above: China, Indochina, and Indonesia. We intervened in all of them; we regarded the Pacific Rim as "our backyard"—if also somewhat more distant than Central America, for which that phrase was used in the years of our involvement in the upheavals in **Guatemala, Nicaragua**, and **El Salvador**.

U.S. policy toward war-flattened Japan was decided in Washington, but administered by the authoritarian General Douglas **MacArthur**. Both because of and despite MacArthur's doings, the policies suiting U.S. needs and possibilities in eastern Asia were put in place: economically and politically, Japan would adjust its institutions to harmonize with emerging U.S. **monopoly capitalism** and our global stretch; militarily it would serve as an extension of our strengths.

Our Japanese policy was closely-linked to our overall Far Eastern policies: We must dominate as much of the region as possible, both to provide markets and resources for Japan with, at the same time, Japan serving as a key location for our wars in Korea and Indochina; Japan (and its colony **Okinawa**) taken together served as our "aircraft carrier," and our supply and "recreation" bases for soldiers, sailors, and aircrews. If Japan and Okinawa lost a certain freedom and dignity in the process, they—at least the best off of them— gained economically. (C. JOHNSON)

Also to be kept in mind is that the atomic bombs dropped on **Hiroshima** and Nagasaki may—or must—be seen as "the first shot of the **Cold War**," with defeated Japan serving both as a test for the new weapons <u>and</u> as a warning to the USSR. (ALPEROVITZ, WITTNER) Here, as in the discussion of the Cold War, I think it useful to incorporate information from my own wartime experience.

> I was in charge of air-sea rescue for my bomb group; we had very little to rescue off the shores of Japan in the last six months of the war: Japan had always depended on imported oil; by the spring of 1945, air and sea attacks had effectively blockaded Japan, leaving its supplies depleted. Their entire military machine was grinding to a halt: all air, land, and sea transport, factory production, aircraft fuel, anti-aircraft functioning, everything had been weakened them to the point of non- or dysfunction. In my rescue function I was also on Staff in the bomb group; because our group was scheduled to be the first posted in Japan, we had to be informed of the forthcoming invasion of Japan, already in its advanced planning stage in June. At the same time we were discussing that, we now know, Japan was communicating through the USSR concerning a peace agreement. President Truman claimed to be balking on one matter only: He insisted that the Emperor step down. Hiroshima of course ended the war. For reasons never stated, Truman's insistence that Hirohito step down was forgotten. The Emperor still sits. It is hard to resist the conclusion that the USA wanted to drop those bombs. Come hell or high water. (HERSEY)

And the world will never be the same.

Korea

On the awful list of the all too many peoples who have been devastated by invaders over the centuries, Korea stands tragically near the top. Since their beginnings, the Koreans have had the misfortune to be bounded by Imperial China on the mainland and to be a stone's throw from Imperial Japan on the sea; both have seen Korea's people and resources as exploitable objects.

In the discussions of the **Cold War**, it was argued that the deaths of upwards of four million Koreans (plus almost 60,000 U.S. soldiers and innumerable Chinese) were the product of a senseless power struggle between the USSR and the USA and, subsequently, the Chinese. The entire history of that conflict may be found in MATRAY; those wishing to find the irrefutable basis for the position taken here may find it in the two scholarly volumes of CUMINGS, and its more popular version (with CAVANAGH).

For further discussion of the Korean War, see **Cold War**; in what follows the current situation will be the focus, with a brief introductory background note.

The cold war struggles of the USSR, USA, and China that impinged upon countries left most of them with dictatorial regimes comporting with the wishes of the cold war "victor": see **Africa, Asia, Europe, Latin America**, and the **Middle East** for elaboration. Among them, Korea.

As noted in the Cold War discussion, Korea was made into a North and a South Korea by the USSR and the USA just as the war ended; an instance of mutual paranoia whose tragic consequences and whose conclusion is not yet in sight.

After the Korean war's cease-fire, the governments of both nations were ruled over by dictators, a Communist dictator in the North, supported by the USSR, a fascist dictator in the South, supported by USA. (CUMINGS)

To repeat what is argued concerning China, Russia, and Vietnam, it seems beyond sensible doubt that the Koreans, left to themselves after 1945, and although there would have been a struggle over who would rule the nondivided country, would all have been better off today than they are, as would be the world, as would be, of course, the several millions dead and their families.

By the 1980s, after much struggling by its ordinary citizens, and with no visible help from the USA, South Korea began to emerge from the fascism we had encouraged to be brought into being. That path has yet to have been trod to completion, nor is it made smoother by the ambiguous presence of 37,000 U.S. troops, the connected if unadmitted domination by the USA over South Korea's foreign policy or, following the economic collapse of 1987, by the **IMF** and U.S. companies in its economy.

Meanwhile, North Korea, devastated in every human and social dimension by the USA's pitiless bombing and shelling from air and sea, emerged with what may be the tightest and most dangerously armed dictatorship in the world—at least among the smaller countries.

As this is being written (2004), not a few are trembling as North Korea intermittently shakes its nuclear fist at the USA. Perhaps it does so as a bargaining chip for improving its condition; perhaps not. It would be reassuring to be able to believe that the USA will handle the ongoing nuclear crisis with good sense; experience suggests the opposite.

To those, and they are many in the USA, who laud our "victory in the Cold War" as they create or acquiesce in our own fist-shaking against the "axis of evil," here a request: Spare us your victories.

Laos

As the USA saw things, the defeat of the French at Dien Bien Phu in 1954 left a dangerous power vacuum in Southeast Asia; the war that had defeated France had been fought out almost entirely in Vietnam, and had been won almost entirely by the Viet Minh. Thus, when the USA called the Geneva Convention and dominated its agreements—most importantly that Vietnam would be split in two at the 17th parallel—there was nothing comparable affecting either Cambodia or Laos; until later, that is.

Anti-French movements had been stirring in both of those countries before 1954; by 1958, in both of those small countries (6-7 million in Cambodia, 2-3 million in Laos) elections were held for their own national governments. The ongoing political chaos involving center, left, and right factions prompted the USA once more to call a Geneva Convention (1961-62).

The principal factions in Laos by that time were the Pathet Lao (the rough but independent equivalent of the Viet Minh), and the right-centrist Kong Le/Prince Souvanna Phouma faction. The USA supported Souvanna Phouma, Kong Le (a mercenary soldier) departed for Paris and never returned, and the Prince became the de jure ruler of Laos; the de facto ruler was the USA.

As in Cambodia, the USA had for some years deployed thousands of armed and non-armed covert agents in Laos under various names; by 1962 they had been reorganized under one heading, USAID (U.S. Agency for International Development); its mission was to suppress the Pathet Lao.

It was a mission with many dimensions, the most destructive of which was the continuous and heavy bombing of real or suspected Pathet Lao hideouts. What were called "hideouts" were peasant villages and fields; thus ordinary Laotians—like ordinary Vietnamese and Cambodians—became targets for U.S. bombers, at ground level or from above 30,000 feet.

The main "city" of Laos is Vientiane. When I had the occasion to be there in 1970, the war still on, I was able to visit and speak with hundreds of bombed-out Laotian refugees (with a translator, of course). They had been placed in open sheds with thatched roofs, where 100 or so people—men, women, children—occupied a space fit for, perhaps, 20—"fit" in the sense of their being space to lie down comfortably as though in a ship's bunk; nothing more than that. (BRANFMAN)

USAID had been functioning there for many years, as had the **CIA**. The CIA had its own airport, which it used to furnish the military and subsistence needs of its own and those of subsidized Laotian army led by General Vang Tao. USAID was a major presence in Vientiane, and the main information source for journalists; it also built the modern palace of Prime Minister Souvanna Phouma.

I had occasion to interview the Prince in his palace (see DOWD in N.S.MCCOY). As we sat in his elegant and air-conditioned villa, I asked the Prime Minister how he, working with the still covert U.S. forces, could permit his people and his country to be destroyed. He blithely answered that "it is for their own good."

What was good for them was this: from the air, all that the eye could see on the Plain of Jars (the center of the Laotian country) and the surrounding hills were bomb craters, numberless thousands of bomb craters. The interview ended abruptly; the Prince wanted to take his daily swim in his USAID-built pool. I wanted to vomit.

The French had been there for almost a century; the US for more than a decade. The progress their combined efforts provided for the Lao were: no railways, two doctors (one for each million + inhabitants), three engineers, and 700 telephones, little education, none of it in the Lao's language. There was, however, a certain income from the lively heroin trade of the "golden triangle," a product of the CIA, which is given the principal credit for the massive drug addiction of U.S. GIs in the war. (MCCOY, CHOMSKY, BRANFMAN)

Like the rest of Indochina, one could see that, once upon a time, Laos had been a marvelously beautiful country of gentle and hard-working people. Nevermore.

Okinawa

Strictly speaking, Okinawa is a "prefecture" of Japan, whose possession it became in the 17th century; factually speaking, it is a colony of the USA. It is a small island about the size of Los Angeles County, and one of the most densely-populated areas in the world, their lives made more difficult because about one-fifth of their prime agricultural land is occupied by the 39 U.S. military bases.

Neither Japanese nor Okinawan courts have any jurisdiction over these U.S.-occupied lands. Whatever the onus of U.S. occupation is for the Okinawans—and it becomes always greater—it has been a boon for the U.S. military: "in 1965, Admiral U. S. Grant Sharp, Commander in Chief of American forces in the Pacific, stated that the United States could not fight the Vietnam war without its Okinawan bases." (C. JOHNSON)

The behavior of the military and its personnel on Okinawa from 1945 to this day, had it been that of, say, Soviet troops in occupied Czechoslovakia, would receive the most scathing condemnation from us. Setting aside the demeaning effects for the Okinawans of <u>being</u> occupied and surrounded by jostling GIs always and everywhere, there are these non-trivial matters: The Okinawan air is poisoned by the innumerable military land vehicles, and by the "noise pollution" of never-ending artillery practice and military planes; their agriculture has been sharply curtailed by having their lands taken from them (beginning in 1945, and continuing); there has been serious soil and coral reef erosion from daily artillery and bombing practice, and land poisoning from runoff jet fuel and other toxic substances; in 1995 and 1996, 1,520 "depleted" uranium shells were fired into a nearby Okinawan island. They had been used first in the first Gulf War, where they produced the uranium oxide gases seen as the cause of "Gulf War syndrome."

If all that were not enough, there has been the aggressive sexual behavior of U.S. troops, most publicized after the rape of a 12-year old girl by two marines and a sailor in 1995. One of the rapists—6 feet tall and 270 lbs.—stated that the three had embarked on the rape "just for fun," had picked the girl at random as she was leaving a stationery store. They rented a car, bound and gagged her, raped and beat her. (Nor has such behavior ended: in July of 2003, another U.S. soldier was convicted of the rape of a young Okinawan girl.)

The Commander of all U.S. forces in the Pacific, Admiral Richard C. Macke, subsequently remarked to the press (C.JOHNSON) "I think the rape was absolutely stupid. For the price they paid to rent the car, they could have had a girl." Oh.

But perhaps our military personnel have such harsh lives that they can be forgiven for such behavior? Not quite. They spend a lot of time on Okinawa's beautiful beaches, for one thing. For another, taxpayers will not be amused to learn that the fun-loving rapists and all active-duty military personnel on Okinawa (and, one assumes, on our other foreign bases) receive either rent- and utility cost-free housing on base or housing allowances ranging from $500 to $2,000 a month, depending on rank and family size. These benefits are supplemented by generous cost of living allowances. (C. JOHNSON) Imperialism is hell.

Philippine Islands

It used to be said that the British amassed their vast empire in "a fit of absent-mindedness"; some have asserted the same as regards the Spanish when they took over the Philippines, about 500 years ago. If they did have something on their mind it was location, for the early colonial contest between Spain and the Portuguese—already established in India and on mainland China.

This is to say that when the Spanish <u>did</u> take over the grand archipelago of the Philippine Islands (named after Phillip II), its gold had yet to be discovered, so there was little to exploit except the fish in the sea and food from the land—of little meaning for distant Spain. Thus, although the Spanish imposed their rule and their religion on the native peoples, there was little ferocity entailed over the centuries—by comparison with either their activities in the Americas or, more to the point, with what transpired when the USA moved in. Just <u>how</u> we moved in, as narrated by then President William McKinley, presaged both the mentality and the rhetoric of **Bush II**.

> When I received the cable from Admiral Dewey of the taking of the Philippines, I looked up their location on the globe. I could not have told where those darned islands were within 2,000 miles!/And later, in speaking to a group of ministers about his decision to "take" the islands: /The truth is I didn't want the Philippines, and when they came to us as a gift from the gods, I didn't know what to do with them.... I thought first we would only take Manila; then Luzon, then other islands, perhaps, also. I walked the floor of the White House night after night until midnight, and I am not ashamed to tell you, gentlemen, that I went down on my knees and prayed Almighty God for light and guidance more than one night. And then one night it came to me this way...: 1) We could not give them back to Spain—that would be cowardly and dishonorable. 2) We could not turn them over to France or Germany, our commercial rivals in the Orient—that would be bad business and discreditable. 3) We could not leave them to themselves—they were unfit for self-government—and they would soon have anarchy and misrule over there worse than Spain's was. So 4) there was nothing left for us to do but to take them all and to educate the Filipinos, and uplift and civilize and Christianize them.... And then I went to bed and went to sleep and slept soundly. (quoted in ZINN, 2000)

It took us four years and the killing of over 300,000 Filipinos to quell the opposition led by Emilio Aguinaldo. In 1934, some decades later, Congress legislated that the islands should have their independence within 10 years; it was granted after World War II.

Just as that war ended, the Philippine Constabulary—which had worked <u>with</u> the Japanese during the war—was newly armed by the USA. It set out for four years to eliminate the "Hukbalahap"— the group that had worked <u>with</u> us (including my bomb group's rescue operations) and <u>against</u> the Japanese during the war. (see **Cold War**.)

All things considered, after independence the Philippines might well have gone their own way. The main movement to kill off the "Huks" and, as well, the islands' economy and foreign policy were directed by the USA and the long-standing local elite (called "caciques"). All too soon, our work came to be done by the Philippines' first dictator, Frederic Marcos.

Ultimately, as democratic movements once more began, Marcos fled with his accumulated millions (or billions), to the Hawaiian Islands. The deaths, corruption and other socioeconomic damage done to the their society over the past century may, one day, be undone; as with Korea, Laos, Cambodia, Vietnam in the East, and so many others on other continents, to achieve that will require more than hard work.

Taiwan (see China)

Vietnam

Introduction Even to approximate adequate comprehension of the decades—not just years—of disaster we produced in Vietnam, this will have to be an extended discussion.

Ask most people in the USA when the war in Vietnam began and the reply would be "early 1965, after Congress passed the Tonkin Gulf Resolution." But, as noted under **Cold War**, I observed the beginning of U.S. involvement in Vietnam in December, 1945, at least 20 years earlier, when U.S. Merchant Marine ships in Manila harbor were being loaded with British and Dutch soldiers to be sent off to Haiphong. Why? To "hold the fort" until the French could arrive.

I saw that while waiting to return to the States after the war. What I did not know was that in those same days, twelve more such U.S. ships in Europe had been diverted from their task of taking U.S. soldiers home in order that, instead, they could "transport 13,000 French soldiers halfway around the world to Saigon." (YOUNG)

First, a note on my principal sources and of my competence in this area. Partly because of the experiences just noted, and partly because of the 18 months or so I had spent in the Philippines (after more than a year in New Guinea), when I re-entered the University of California (Berkeley) to study after the war, one of my fields became Southeast Asia.

When I joined the faculty there as a Lecturer in 1950, one of my three courses was "Economic Development in Southeast Asia." Later, when I taught at Cornell in the 1950s and 1960s, I was part of an interdisciplinary program where one of my colleagues was George M. Kahin, head of its Southeast Asian Studies Program, and author of a comprehensive historical study of Vietnam: *The United States in Vietnam*. (1968) Consequently, from the 1950s on I was a reasonably well-informed and much-concerned observer as the war in Indochina expanded in scope and violence because of U.S. intervention.

Over time, I have depended greatly upon the work of Kahin and, more recently, upon that of Marilyn Blatt Young and Daniel Ellsberg. The source of the above quotation about French troops and of much more that follows is the comprehensive scholarship of YOUNG, *The Vietnam Wars: 1945-1995*. I shall depend on her detailed and thoroughly documented analyses and, as well, upon Ellsberg's unique *Secrets: A Memoir of Vietnam and the Pentagon Papers*. (2002)

Ellsberg, in addition to having been a Marine Captain in Vietnam, was a top official in the National Security Council in the mid-60s and spent over a year in Vietnam in 1965-66 as the USA officially entered and escalated the war. Although initially in favor of the war (hoping there would be limited bombing and civilian casualties), Ellsberg became increasingly upset at what he observed in Vietnam and, later, in Washington; for example, the nature and effects of air strikes on villages:

> The lead plane fired rockets with white phosphorous warheads at the village, perhaps to mark the target for the others, which dropped bombs and napalm. White phosphorous explodes like a blossom. It spreads out brilliant white petals... with crimson tips. It's a gorgeous site. When /it/ touches human flesh, however, it burns down to the bone. In Vietnamese civilian hospitals... I'd seen children who had been burned by it and others who had been burned by napalm, which leaves a different kind of scar. You can't put napalm out with water either. I'd seen both of these in the Marines... and I know they are very effective weapons. We think of them as saving the lives of our troops, especially when we're the only side using them, as in Vietnam, but when I was a marine, I didn't want to be saved by

them, any more than I wanted to be saved by nuclear weapons. (ELLSBERG, 2002)

It was his dismay with such cruel slaughter, and with his participation in what he came to see in the White House as a combination of deep corruption and horrendous tragedy that led Ellsberg (helped by his two children) in 1971 to mimeograph the 7,000-page "Pentagon Papers" and, at risk of imprisonment, to give them to the *New York Times* (and Senator Fulbright). In doing so, he made it possible for others to plumb the bottomlessly ugly truths of life at the White House.

In her Preface, YOUNG summarizes the customary explanations for the USA's role in Vietnam: 1) to bribe the French (as noted under **Cold War**), 2) "... to provide Japan with Southeast Asian substitutes for the China trade the United States had embargoed..., /and/ 3) because Vietnam was a crucial part of the U.S. enterprise of reorganizing the post-World War II world, according to the principles of liberal capitalism."

As time went on, the <u>official</u> reason was to secure the freedom of the Vietnamese from an assumed Communist, USSR-controlled totalitarianism; but as the successive regimes in South Vietnam became always more totalitarian and oppressive to their own people, reaching their depths with General Nguyen Cao Ky (an open admirer of Hitler) it became less embarrassing for the official reason to become saving Vietnam from being handed over to the <u>Chinese</u> Communists—with whom the North Vietnamese were mistakenly seen as being allied; "mistakenly," because China had invaded the north repeatedly for at least a thousand years, and mutual enmity was strong.

Or, we may summarize U.S. goals in the words of a 1965 Defense Department document, as revealed in the *Pentagon Papers* (published by the *NYT* in 1971), I quote:

> US aims: 70%—To avoid humiliating US defeat (to our reputation as guarantor). 20%—To keep SVN "—South Vietnam—" (and then adjacent) territory from Chinese hands. 10%—To permit the people of SVN to enjoy a better, freer way of life.

All the above-noted arguments were made in public statements and repeated in the media, although with the "percentiles" very much <u>reversed</u> in favor of "freedom." The government was invited to make its position clear in the numerous "teach-ins" that began in 1964 and that became widespread by 1965. They were organized by a few dozen university professors knowledgeable about Southeast Asia. Typically a teach-in involved two speakers, one representing the CIA, the State Department, or the Pentagon, against a professor opposed to the war. At first, the audiences were small and inclined to accept the governmental positions; by mid-1965, the student audiences became huge—doubtless influenced by the threat of being drafted—and the governmental speakers came to be boo-ed.

An experience with one of the boo-ers when I was present is worth citing: In a 1965 teach-in at a university in Muncie, Indiana, after I had argued that our aims in Vietnam had very little to do with freedom, my opponent—the U.S. Consul in Saigon—in exasperation said, in effect, OK already, what we <u>are</u> there for is to prevent China from taking over all of Asia.

As the meeting ended, a U.S. Marine in uniform approached me and said, "Goddamn you, Dowd! I've done two tours in Nam and am on way back for a third, and <u>now</u> I learn I'm being fucked over!" "Don't blame me...," I started to say, but he was already gone.

By early 1966, we could find <u>no</u> governmental speakers; after a few arguments against an empty chair, the teach-ins were replaced with mass demonstrations, organized by the Mobilization Against the War in Vietnam ("the Mobe").

The teach-ins were intended to show the many dimensions in which the government's arguments for the war were fallacious, whether as regards what might be seen as best for the Vietnamese, the people of the USA, or for world peace and wellbeing. It is fair to say that "the broken promises of "America!" were represented in microcosm by the Vietnam war: 1) our racism, 2) our militarism and penchant for indifferent violence, 3) our greed for power, 4) our steady descent into the corruption, dishonesty, and hypocrisy required if that war was to be supported and to be conducted in its ferocious manner, 5) our utter disregard of the human, social, and environmental disaster we were creating, and finally, 6) our arrogance in assuming that we had the <u>right</u> to decide what was best for the Vietnamese, no matter what—epitomized by the army colonel who said "We had to destroy the village /of Ben Suc/ in order to save it."

All the foregoing elements interacted each step along the way, as will be seen in what follows.

From Dienbienphu (1954) to Tonkin Gulf (1965).

When the Japanese were defeated in 1945, they had occupied Vietnam for five years. In those years, the Japanese "had devasted the economy, creating a famine in the North that killed between 1.5 and 2 million people," as the continuing French administrators looked on (until the last weeks of the war). (YOUNG)

This only strengthened the determination and energies of the Vietnamese to have their freedom. Initially, those efforts were made in the North where, led by Ho Chi Minh, resistance had grown for decades. As noted under **Cold War**, while **FDR** was still alive, through the USA's OSS agents in the North, he had promised the Viet Minh that Indochina would move toward independence after the war.

Unfortunately for the Vietnamese, Cambodians, Laotians and U.S. GIs killed or wrecked by the war, FDR died before the end of the Pacific war; when he died, so did his aims for an independent Indochina.

In the presidential election campaign of 1944, it was well-known that FDR was fatally ill, so the choice or Vice President was more than usually important. FDR's V.P. since 1932, Henry Wallace, was very much in accord with the domestic and foreign policies of the "liberal" FDR; precisely for that reason, the conservative wing of the Democratic Party, dominated by "the Solid—that is, racist—South" dumped Wallace and made Harry S. **Truman** the candidate; within less than two months after the inauguration, Truman was inaugurated as President.

Truman had a small haberdashery shop when he was plucked for political service by the notorious Big Jim Pendergrast's machine (Kansas City, MO); he was "placed" in the U.S. Senate. Whatever else may be said of Truman, good or bad, all agree that his war experience had led him to admire, even to cherish, the military. He went along with **Hiroshima** without blinking an eye, and was an early enthusiast for the **Cold War**—and for **McCarthyism**, even though it later backfired on him. (See **Truman**)

Accordingly, Truman had neither the understanding nor the

inclination to resist his foreign policy advisors as the USA shoe-
horned the French back into Indochina, nor as the French presence
and ferocity produced an always rising Vietnamese resistance and
then a full-fledged war, Truman went along with financing and arm-
ing the French: Into the quagmire, without looking back.

As 1946 became 1950 and then 1952, the USA had also
become embroiled in the war in **Korea**, which it could not and did
not win. The new president, Eisenhower, who had argued for us to
get out of Korea and (partly for that reason) was elected president in
1952, nevertheless continued our policy of increasing assistance to
the French, even as—in part because—their casualties continued to
mount.

Instead of taking the position he had urged for Korea, Ike
became, instead, a leading spokesman for the "domino theory," arguing that the French must hold out in Indochina, then the principal
"domino": The loss of Indochina, Eisenhower told a press conference... would bring in its train the loss of Burma, Thailand,
Indonesia, Malaya; threaten Japan, Formosa, the Philippines,
Australia, and New Zealand. In economic terms it would deprive
"the world" of Southeast Asian tin, tungsten, and rubber. Finally,
Japan "must have /that region/ as a trading partner or Japan, in turn,
will have only one place in the world to go—that is, toward the
Communist areas in order to live." The French were assured that
every resource, save only American combat troops and nuclear
weapons, would be at their disposal. Before the war ended /20 years
later/, some American officials were ready to offer both. (YOUNG)

As will be seen, that was especially so as our own involvement
wore on, up to and after the shock of the Viet Minh's Tet Offensive
of 1968. The Geneva accords of 1954 had provided for reunification
elections to take place throughout Vietnam. In Saigon, President
Ngo Dinh Diem had taken control with the assistance of the USA;
he quite sensibly refused to have reunification elections; "sensibly"
because it was evident that such an election would result in a reunit-
ed Vietnam presided over by a democratically-elected Ho Chi Minh.

Diem's always more repressive regime gave rise to the National
Liberation Front (NLF) in the South. Although fighting the same
fight as the Viet Minh, initially they had no ties with them; the NLF
was forced to function underground, and soon became an effective

guerrilla force (derisively called the Viet Cong)—and the main target of what would become a decade or more of U.S. efforts to root them out and destroy them.

As will be noted below, the means used were unspeakable, constant heavy bombing of South Vietnam—considerably more than upon the North—and the use of weaponry all of which, aimed at civilians as they were, should be considered under the heading of war crimes. (see YOUNG, and **collateral damage**)

As that was evolving, the U.S. presence in all of Indochina was rising, much of it <u>overtly</u> in South Vietnam, all of it <u>covertly</u> in the North and in Laos and Cambodia—whether in the form of Green Berets, CIA agents and <u>their</u> agents (and their "Golden Triangle" heroin trade /MCCOY/), or in the U.S. Military Assistance Advisory Group (MAAG), whose operations had begun as early as 1950.

By 1960, <u>admitted</u> U.S. military personnel in Vietnam stood at just under 1,000; when JFK was assassinated in 1963, there were more than 16,000. By that time MAAG had been "upgraded" to become MACV, the U.S. Military Assistance Command—which was more than a mere shift of terminology. (YOUNG)

In tandem with this increase in U.S. military activity, Vietnam began to serve as a laboratory for counter-insurgency techniques and weapons. In the spring of 1961, a joint U.S.-Vietnamese testing center was established whose first project was an evaluation of herbicidal warfare: the use of chemicals to poison food crops and strip the foliage in areas in which guerrillas were known to operate.

Chief among those chemicals were Agents Orange, Green, White, and Blue. Orange and Green contained <u>dioxin</u>, now admitted by the government to be a cancer-causing agent; what today is called a "weapon of mass destruction." Its widespread and increasing use in Vietnam began in 1961—four years before we "entered the conflict"—and continued for an entire decade, until 1971. Some of the details are horrifying:

> ... planes sprayed the herbicides directly over at least 3,181 villages. At least 2.1 million inhabitants—and perhaps as many as 4.8 million—would have been in the villages during the spraying operations... in South Vietnam, whose total population at the time was less than 17 million... Almost 80 disorders have been associated with exposure, including cancers of the lung

and prostate and more than a dozen other malignancies.... (SFC, "Seeing red over Agent Orange: U.S. understated use of dioxin during Vietnam..." /4-21-03/) (my emphasis)

There was rightly much hullabaloo about the many thousands of U.S. GIs made seriously or fatally ill from this weapon; but about the enormously higher numbers of Vietnamese whose lives were shortened and ruined, along with their lands? You have to search to find a word. Nor have we done well by the GIs who had their lives ruined, shortened, or ended because of Agent Orange (and its fellow dioxins). Analyze this:

> Nearly 400 Americans who died as a result of the Vietnam war... are not eligible to have their names inscribed on the Vietnam Veterans Memorial... /including those/ who died of the effects of Agent Orange exposure. ("Ceremony Honors Veterans Not on Memorial," *NYT*, 4-22-03)

Already as such operations began in 1961, it had become the "mode" for the USA to give **spin** names to our military activities, even to the point of being repulsively cute about them. This one was called Operation RANCH HAND, its motto "Only We Can Prevent Forests." In the first eight years of that operation <u>one hundred million pounds</u> of herbicides were dropped on over <u>four million acres</u> of South Vietnam, its <u>intent</u> stated as the intimidation of peasants—men, women, children—from cooperating with the Viet Cong. (YOUNG, my emphasis, and note, that was just <u>South</u> Vietnam.)

The foregoing was occurring five years <u>before</u> the USA had an official <u>military</u> presence in Indochina. From then on, it expanded both qualitatively and quantitatively, with the years before and after our official entry overlapping.

A major element of that overlapping was the general "pacification" program. The "strategic hamlets" were among its main elements. The practice was to bulldoze innumerable villages suspected to be guerrilla strongholds, and to herd all their former inhabitants into a spot where new "houses" surrounded by barbed wire and guard towers were constructed—most of this to be paid for by the villagers themselves. (YOUNG)

That strategy was meant to intimidate the villagers and to get rid of the NLF—who, however, IF they had been there simply exited into nearby territory, to return when they wished: Not the best way to "to win the hearts and minds of the people." (YOUNG) If MACV had seen the Vietnamese people as human beings, rather than as "gooks," they might have understood that such steps would only increase Vietnamese opposition both to the puppet South Vietnamese government and to its master; as indeed it did.

Diem, as head of government in those years, did not of course wish to be seen as a "puppet." His main means of proving that, he thought, was to disallow the official use of U.S. troops to subdue the NLF—while nonetheless allowing the other official activities just noted. Meanwhile, the U.S. paid for and U.S.-trained Army of the Republic of Vietnam (ARVN) was of low morale and associated low competence, plus having unknown numbers of NLF sympathizers in its ranks.

By early 1962, the growing weakness of ARVN relative to the NLF had led the U.S. to consider organizing a coup to overthrow Diem; two weeks before JFK was assassinated, Diem _was_ overthrown, and he and his brother killed. (YOUNG) It is believed that JFK was in on it; whether or not _he_ was we may be certain that _we_ were; we wanted Diem out, and he was overthrown.

Subsequently, one corrupted government after another was created, reaching its low point with General Nguyen Ky, an avowed admirer of Hitler (and now living it up in Los Angeles). ARVN wobbled its way along the paths cut out for it by the USA, always costing more lives for both themselves and NLF soldiers _and_ countless heedlessly killed villagers, while ruining the economy, the land, and the people—and, to some degree, the USA.

In the years following JFK's death, his close advisors revealed that he very much wanted out of Vietnam in 1962 and 1963, but feared that if he pulled the USA out, he would be accused of being "weak on communism," and lose the 1964 elections. In one variation or another, the same came to be true of **LBJ** who, in his memoirs, said "Losing the Great Society was a terrible thought, but not so terrible as the thought of being responsible for America's losing a war to the Communists. Nothing was worse than that." (KAHIN, 1986).

And so **Nixon** moved into the White House. He tried to squirm his way out of Vietnam and failed, for his "peace efforts" involved leaving it divided, with the South independent of the North and dependent upon the USA. When finally we <u>did</u> get out, it was only because of the chaos following Watergate.

Thanks goodness for Watergate. ELLSBERG (who had top clearance in the National Security Council) shows that had the choice came down to losing the war or using nukes, Nixon's NSC had made up its mind: nuke! The irony there is strong: fate and arrogance in 1972 led Nixon to be caught in the crude illegalities that led to Watergate—one of which was his hiring of thugs to steal Ellsberg's files from his psychiatrist's office. Tricky Dick done did himself in. Fortunately.

But in 1963, the story had only begun to be told. What followed after our official entry in the war in 1965 made the previous decade seem almost easy. After Diem, one South Vietnamese government after another came into being and either fell or was pushed out. Thus, in 1964, it was a General Khanh who, after he had engineered a coup, took over. His inadequacies were so substantial that then U.S. Ambassador Lodge took it upon himself "to coach the General in the art of the fireside chat, boasting that he had done the same for General Eisenhower." (YOUNG)

Meanwhile, newly-installed President LBJ in 1964 authorized "OPlan 34-A." It was the more ferocious next stage of the "pacification" program. It entailed an increase in the pace of covert actions against Hanoi and an increase in the overt actions in the South: stepped-up air and naval surveillance, commando raids against bridges, railways, and coastal fortifications, and increased bombing and strafing (by U.S. pilots) of positions held by the Pathet Lao and of North Vietmanese villages on the Lao border, in order to discourage support for North Vietnam.

Reminder: we were not at war; formally, that is, although (as noted above) in November, 1963 there were already 16,000 (admitted) U.S. military personnel in Indochina. When, after 1965, we <u>were</u> at war, as will be seen below, all the foregoing was intensified throughout Indochina. (YOUNG)

In January of 1964. General Nguyen Khan overthrew the Minh government; his own government was soon seen by his U.S. advisers as "sliding into terminal demoralization," and deemed to need a big victory to boost morale. In 1967, the Pentagon historians summarized the logic of the moment for McNamara:

> Khanh would not be able to feel that assurance of victory until the U.S. committed itself to full participation in the struggle, even to the extent of co-belligerency.... The problem for U.S. policy-makers, therefore, was to find some means of breakthrough into an irreversible commitment of the U.S.

But, President Johnson was advised, "'co-belligerency' must await some overt act of war on the part of Hanoi, and none seemed to be forthcoming." (YOUNG) Shucks.

Then, as if by magic, the 1964-65 Gulf of Tonkin scenario began its run. Belatedly, those deeds having been done, we discovered (ELLSBERG) that the script had been touched up in all of its critical scenes. Lights! Music! Roll!:

Act I. August 2 and 4: U.S. destroyers *Maddox* and *Turner Joy* report attack by North Vietnamese patrol boats. August 3: Hanoi endorses Soviet call for reconvening the Geneva Conference.

Act II. August 5-7: Congress discusses and passes the Gulf of Tonkin Resolution, authorizing the U.S. to go to war against North Vietnam.

Act III: December, et seq: Overt bombing of the Ho Chi Minh trail and North Korea, intensified bombing, etc., continues in the South.

Number of admitted U.S. troops: 23,000. (YOUNG)

The Tonkin Resolution was described by Under Secretary of State Katzenbach as "the functional equivalent of a declaration of war"—finally! Not only had we helped arrange and paid for the French Indochinese war since 1945 (see **Cold War**), we had taken it over surreptitiously after 1954. Although it seems certain the USA would have continued and increased its participation without the disgracefully casual approval of Congress—Senate: 88-2, House 416-0—the Resolution gave a certain legitimacy for what would become always more devastating and costly to one and all: The U.S. troop figure of 23,000 just noted rose to an average of over 500,000 for most of the next five years, almost 60,000 of whom were killed; but the numbers of Vietnamese, Laotian, and Cambodian dead went added up to more than three million dead (to say nothing of many more than that wounded, displaced, their lives ruined).

It is important, therefore, to show at least some of the dishonesty and doubletalk that underlay the Tonkin Gulf Resolution. (The details and documentation of the foregoing and what follows are found in YOUNG and ELLSBERG).

The presumed Tonkin Gulf incidents and congressional action all took place in August, 1964, before which, as has been discussed above, the USA had been aggressively, even ferociously involved.

Be that as it may:

Item: On July 30, South Vietnamese commandos, accompanied by American "advisers," used U.S.-financed gunboats to conduct heavy raids against two islands in the Gulf of Tonkin (offshore from the northern parts of North Vietnam). The next day, the U.S. destroyer Maddox itself arrived there and exchanged gunfire greetings with the South Koean gunboats as they were returning to Danang.

Item: On August 2, the destroyer again cruised close to the offshore islands, which were again under attack by the South Vietnamese commandos. That time, the Maddox was pursued into the middle of the Gulf by three North Vietnamese patrol boats. They veered toward the destroyer, and did not fire; but the Maddox did, with its very large 5-inch guns. The North Vietnamese held course, still without firing. Captain Ogier of Maddox subsequently reported that he was pleased. Why?

> Of course, you know, if they had just turned and run away after we'd started firing at them, we could have been in real trouble, because they could have said "Here we are in international waters and you went and fired at us." But they came on and fired torpedoes at us, which was good.

Quite apart from the fact that the U.S. ship had fired at them, there is another problem: it just didn't happen that way. John B. STOCKDALE, a Navy pilot overflying the entire action later said that "with the best seat in the house from which to detect boats," he failed to see anything at all. "No boats, no boat wakes, no richochets off boats, no boat impacts, no torpedo wakes—nothing but the black sea and American firepower." Plus, Commodore Herrick, on board the Maddox, reported to his superior that "Review of the action makes many reported contacts and torpedoes fired appear very doubtful..." (YOUNG)

Nonetheless, the next morning, August 5 (the day the Resolution came to Congress), Stockdale and his fellow pilots were ordered to "retaliate" against targets in North Vietnam. Saying to himself "Retaliate for what?" Stockdale nevertheless "led this big horde of airplanes over there and we blew the oil tanks off the map." (ibid.)

Two days later, the Resolution was passed.

Not quite Pearl Harbor, but "... policy makers had found a means to break through into an irreversible commitment of the U.S." (ibid.)

Keep in mind the actions of the USA from 1945 up through 1964 as you now read the opening words of the Congressional Tonkin Gulf Resolution:

Whereas naval units of the Communist regime in Vietnam, in vio-
lation of the principles of the Charter of the United Nations, and international law, have deliberately and repeatedly attacked United States naval vessels lawfully present in international waters... /and/

Whereas the United States is assisting the peoples of /Southeast Asia to protect freedom and has no territorial, military or political ambitions in the area, but desires only that these people should be left in peace to work out their own destinies in their own way....

Except for the two senators who voted against, my mother would have made all of them wash their mouths out with soap, and spanked them. They deserved much worse.

From 1965's escalation toward the light at the end of the tunnel, 1968.

The light at the end of the tunnel, as someone has said, was the headlight of an oncoming train: the Tet offensive of 1968, which began at the siege of Khe San and ended at Hue. The North Vietnamese lost great numbers of men and women in that battle and would lose still more in years to come, but it was there and then that they also won the war.

After Hue, the USA mumbled and stumbled, arranging more than one peace conference, withdrawing our ground forces

("Vietnamization"), and continuing "only" with safe and easy **carpet bombing**—of Laos and Cambodia, as well as Vietnam: Over 3,000 high-level carpet bombing missions in Cambodia alone, in 1969. (SHAWCROFT)

"Nothing lost save honour," when you drop 'em from B-52's at 32,000 feet: a mix of insanity and obscenity.

Those were the years of always more numerous and larger demonstrations against the war in the cities of the USA and, perhaps even more pointedly, the years when returned war vets organized themselves into the understandably very effective Vietnam Veterans Against the War (VVAW) and, more pointedly than that, when the "grunts" still in "Nam began to rebel in one form or another: by "soldiering" (GI talk for goofing off) and by "fragging" (shooting and/or blowing up) their officers.

In the States, one fall day in 1969, the "Moratorium" and the "Mobe" combined forces to produce a national demonstration in which at least 20 <u>million</u> people stood somewhere to demand an end to the war.

The people of Indochina and of the USA had to wait until 1975 for peace to break out (and not even then, in

Cambodia), had to wait until the monstrous morons on top did themselves in. They had brought enormous human, economic, and social cost and waste to the Indochinese and their own peoples, but little or no damage to themselves. And their successors are at it still. YOUNG quotes the French journalist Bernard FALL—with many years of experience in Indochina behind him—as having said, in December, 1965. "The incredible thing about Vietnam is that the worst is yet to come." And he was right:

> Between 1965 and 1973, the USA dropped on Indochina more than four times the bomb tonnage it dropped on all of Europe and Asia in World War II. And among those bombs were the infamous "daisy-cutters," used against peasants in rice paddies (along with white phosphorous and **napalm**), and the deadly **cluster bombs**, with which a pilot could "lawnmower" anyone on a path several hundred feet wide and many yards long. (SLATER)

The terminology used to categorize our military actions in Vietnam is more revealing than it was meant to be: "search and destroy"; "pacification"; "clearing operations"; "uprooting";

"Operation Masher"—which, as Westmoreland belatedly realized, made for <u>very</u> poor **public relations** with the people of Indochina.

The basic problem for the USA was in not being able to distinguish friend from foe. It wasn't so much that to the Yanks all the Indochinese looked alike, but that there was reason to believe that virtually all of the Laotians, Cambodians, Vietnamese, even in the South, seemed quietly or dangerously hostile to our presence.

And why not? For both military and non-military U.S. personnel to see the NLF and Viet Minh forces as "gooks" was bad enough; but few Vietnamese in ARVN or in bars or in "cathouses"—whoever, wherever—would believe that the rough and aggressive Yanks ever saw even their Indochinese allies as human—exemplified by the mass murders at My Lai 4 in 1968. (HERSH, 1970)

That My Lai was unexceptional was revealed in a <u>NYT</u> report by John Kifner decades many decades after the fact, "Ex-G.I.s tell of Vietnam Brutality." (12-19-03)

The information to follow came from some of those who committed the acts.

Item: "For seven months, U.S. 'Tiger Force' soldiers moved across the Central Highlands, killing scores of unarmed civilians— in some cases torturing and mutilating them...."

Item: "Tiger Force was not a 'rogue' unit; its members had done only what they were told to do and their superiors knew what they were doing."

Item: From a sergeant who was a section leader in one such unit: "It was always about the body count...; the colonels were saying, "You guys have the green light to do what's right... It was out of hand very early. There were hundreds of My Lais. You got your card punched by the numbers of bodies you counted."

Anything goes, for freedom and democracy.

Throughout the war, both before and after Tonkin Gulf, there was a distinct lack of enthusiasm on the part of most of the ARVN to exert themselves militarily, let alone to take great risks—whether because they distrusted their own government or ours; or, for who knows how many, because they had always been, or soon became, silently on the side of the NLF or the Viet Minh.

In short, in pushing its way into Vietnam the USA had

embarked on a path strewn with land mines of its own making—literally and figuratively. By November, 1965, there were already
220,000 U.S. troops in Vietnam, with another 110,000 on their way,
with many more to come in ensuing years: over 5 <u>million</u> before
1975.

Without knowing it, the USA was repeating the experience of
the French that led to Dienbienphu, albeit on a much grander and
more destructive scale for all concerned. What was central to the
failures of both the French and the USA was their inability to comprehend that as they stepped up their attacks, their opposition was
growing even more in consequence—not only in numbers, but in its
ability to second-guess and outwit us.

The U.S. military was then and even more so is today, techno-
logically-oriented from beginning to end; it was never able to grasp
even how the NVA (North Vietmanese Army) and the NLF supplied themselves, let alone how they so often managed to inflict
more casualties on our troops than vice versa, despite our overwhelming ground and air fire power; or, where we <u>were</u> able to inflict
more than we suffered—"killing at a distance" (SLATER)—how
they would not only rebound, but do so in greater numbers.

At the root of such incomprehension lay another vital difference: The Vietnamese fighting against us knew very well what they
were fighting for and against; the Vietnamese "on our side" and the
U.S. GIs may be forgiven for being confused; so were their "leaders."

Enough about the ugly details of the war. If "Vietnam" had any
virtue to it all, it could be found in what it <u>could have</u> taught us
about the dangerous idiocies of U.S. foreign policies, still today making their way with only slight modifications of rhetoric, but with
much the same, possibly even more horrific consequences. A final
note: Robert MCNAMARA, Defense Secretary for JFK and LBJ,
put his memoirs together in 1995. In them he reflects on both **Cuba**
and Vietnam—and indicates how dangerously wrong-headed he and
the USA were in those heady days.

More recently (February, 2004) he appeared before a U.C.
Berkeley audience. A fair summary of what he said is 1) the war in
Vietnam was wrong from the beginning, and became always more so,
and we knew it; 2) that he had serious misgivings about what is now
going on in Iraq, and, <u>but</u> 3) "drew the line at directly criticizing his

counterparts still serving in the government..."

(<u>NYT</u>, 2-6-04, "McNamara flashes Berkeley the peace sign." Birds of a feather stick together no matter what, it seems. Or should that be "turkeys of a feather...."?

assassination

This discussion could just as aptly occur under **arrogance** or, even better, **double standard**. The USA has always prided itself on being a "frontier society," where that is meant to point to a fierce spirit of justice and the intense pursuit of it, <u>by</u> one and all, <u>for</u> one and all. If anything, the frontier was characterized by brutality and brawling, institutionalized thievery and murder (neither least nor only against the "**Indians**") and justice wasn't even a dream, let alone a reality.

Assassinations, if not by that name, were common, and "taking the law into your own hands" something of a euphemism for them. It is surely relevant to our larger and subsequent history that almost all of us were brought up on stories, films, and games making heroes of the "cowboys": Bang! Bang! You're dead!

So it is not surprising that the practice of lynching at home has infiltrated our treatment of those we despise or fear abroad. Worse, it should be said, is that when we have done so, it has been self-righteously accepted; when others do the same, however, we pounce upon them in indignation.

What does it mean, "when we have done so"? We have <u>never</u> done so, almost all of us would say. The vast majority thinking that does so for two related reasons: 1) Our leaders seldom tell the truth about such matters; 2) if and when we do find out about it, our position is to the effect "Well, it was OK, because...," whereas we would never find that "because" if—for example—the Soviet Union or China or Cuba assassinated a leader of some other country. Still, "when did <u>we</u> ever do so"? How about these (only these recent) "incidents"?

Item: See **Latin America... Cuba**, for Castro.
Item: See **Asia.... Vietnam** for Diem.
Item: Democratically-elected Salvador Allende of Chile died in a coup d'etat (9-11-73) financed and supported by the U.S. government. (see *Kissinger*)

Item: In April of 1986, President Reagan authorized an air raid on
   the home of Col. Muammar el-Qaddafi of Libya; it missed
   him but killed his daughter. The Reagan administration
   never acknowledged that Colonel Qaddafi was the target,
   nor did it publicly speculate two years later that Libya's
   bombing of an American jetliner over Lockerbie, Scotland,
   killing 270 people, was Colonel Qaddafi's revenge for the
   death of his daughter.
Items 1,2,3: In the middle of the last century, at the height of the
   Cold War, the United States often wished, sometimes
   planned and occasionally took concrete steps to kill foreign
   leaders. In addition to those noted above were Patrice
   Lumumba of the *Congo*, Rafael Trujillo of the Dominican
   Republic and Abdeul Karim Kassem of Iraq. These plots were
   wrapped in the deepest secrecy and vigorously denied until
   the facts were finally exhumed by Senator Frank Church in
   1976. ("When Frontier Justice Becomes Foreign Policy," by
   Thomas Powers, *NYT* "Week in Review," 7-13-03) (my
   emphasis)

Powers wrote that in response to the current publicity concerning the prolonged hoopla for taking out Oh sure, there was that
presidential order of **Reagan**—having washed his hands after
Qaddafi—stating that "no person employed by or acting on behalf of
the U.S. government shall engage in, or conspire to engage in, assassination." (ibid.) That settled that.

Or did it? It didn't prevent **Bush I** from going ahead secretly to
take out Hussein; nor did it prevent **Bush II** from doing so publicly—with, natcherly, a Texas-like $25 million reward for the killer.

It's a fair guess that such goings-on go down pretty well with
most of the people in the USA. Is that because Saddam is uniquely
horrible? Or because we can get away with it—as we did, for example, against Qaddafi (except for the 270 dead on that plane).

big business

When Adam Smith laid out the analytical basis for free market
("laissez-faire") capitalism, it wasn't because he trusted either the
means or the ends of businessmen, "...an order of men," he observed,
"whose interest is never exactly the same with that of the public,

who have generally an interest to deceive and even to oppress the public, and who accordingly have, upon many occasions, both deceived and oppressed it." (SMITH)

His *Wealth of Nations* (1776) was an appeal for a fully competitive economy which, if it functioned properly, would frustrate business attempts to achieve the unlimited profits and power they pursue. His central aim was that the market protections and restrictions of his time be done away with; that done, he hoped and expected that the economy would become one in which all firms would be small—very small; that is, the percentage of a given industry's output produced by any one or even several firms would be so insignificant a percentage of the industry's entire output that none could have control over supply; all would have to respond to an entirely-uncontrolled market—which is what he meant by free—whose "invisible hand" of competition would transform individual self-seeking into the wellbeing of society.

A pleasant dream with, however, two stubborn realities that subsequently shattered it: 1) Even when the **competition** he depended upon prevailed—as it did in the USA in staple agriculture, coal mining, and cotton textiles—it was devastating for **farmers**, for coal miners and for coal companies, in one way and another; consequently, all those just mentioned sought to find ways to interfere with, that is, to control the markets:

Farmers: After decades of finding themselves ruined by the excess supplies and low prices of the free market, they began in the 1920s to seek and to gain governmental control over their output and pricing; free competition in coal mining produced ruined lives for the miners (who thus fought for unions, and bankruptcies for their small owners (who were replaced by giant companies); and cotton textiles, that once "perfectly competitive" industry could not survive even with its brutal worker exploitation; it too became another segment of big business.

It needs adding that Smith took as given that for **profits** to be made, workers must be exploited: because they were propertyless, they could survive only by working on the terms of those who owned and controlled the means of production—that is, the means of life. Nonetheless, Smith believed that with widening and deepening industrialization that in the long run that system would be "the best of all <u>possible</u> worlds." Secondly, just as Smith believed that internal "economic freedom" was essential for industrialization in Britain, David Ricardo, his most important follower (in his *Principles of Political Economy and Taxation* /1817/) argued similarly as regards <u>global</u> trade barriers. Neither foresaw that the very success of the sought-for industrialization, when achieved within the capitalist framework, would create a world rendering vain the benign elements of their hopes.

Why vain? Because it was and is in the very nature of the industrialization process to obliterate the tiny firms constituting the "invisible hand": Half a century or so after the first factory (1815), the galloping technological advances unleashed by industrialization and mass production had begun to make it both possible and <u>necessary</u> for firms to enlarge and become gigantic. This they did in order to defend themselves from otherwise "destructive competition" and/or simultaneously to increase their profits by their ability to control their markets. The best defense is a strong offence.

The USA, given its rich resources and vast spaces, its large population and broad markets, took the lead in that race (closely followed by Germany). In the decades after 1860, when the mergers of formerly competing companies sped up—in railroads, then iron and steel, then oil, then....—the resulting process was called "the combination movement." By the first years of the 20th century, the "invisible hand" had become a well-concealed fist.

Thus, what had been 5,300 industrial firms in 1897 had become 318 corporations by 1905. Most spectacular were the mergers in iron and steel which in 1901 created U.S. Steel—the first billion dollar company in the world—one company composed of what once had been 750 different companies. But all that was just a beginning. (JOSEPHSON, DU BOFF)

Before World War I, a "merger" was many companies ending up as one, all in the same industry. The interacting economic demands and possibilities just before, during and after World War I—substantial technological progress, the emerging importance of physics and chemistry and electrification and motor vehicles and radio and strong and subsidized markets—created a set of enormous stimuli for mergers.

But these were not only <u>within</u> an industry—"horizontal" (e.g., among many steel companies)—but also <u>between</u> industries—"vertical" (steel companies buying up bridge building companies and coal mines)—and <u>among and between</u> industries and even sectors—"conglomerate" mergers.

All records were broken throughout the 1920s, in terms both of numbers and the value of mergers; it was then that today's processes first took hold: big companies buying up big companies. By 1929, the assets of the largest 200 non-banking corporations had doubled, rising at an annual rate of over 5 percent, while those of all other corporations rose by only 2 percent (BERLE & MEANS).

By 1955, all this had already gone far enough to prompt *Fortune* (FM) to begin its annual "Fortune 500 Largest Industrials." Over time, FM added special issues for the "50 Largest Financial, Utility, etceteras" and then, in the 1990s, the 500 Largest <u>Global</u> Firms, with many other listings.

In 1995, in its 40th anniversary issue of the "500" they noted that the revenues of that year's 500 largest U.S. <u>companies</u> were equal to 63 percent of the GDP (gross domestic product) of the USA, and far exceeded those of Japan and Germany; and so it goes year after year, with small variations—upward.

That ever tighter concentration of economic power, nationally and globally, is a consequence of the explosion of the older combination movement into what are now called **mergers and acquisitions** (M&As) whose present rat-a-tats began soon after World War II;

> Commencing in the early 1950s, merger activity registered progressive increases and reached a frenzied pace in 1967-1970, when more than one of every five manufacturing and mining corporations with assets exceeding $10 million was acquired. (ADAMS & BROCK)

But the best—or worst—was yet to come. As capitalism has developed over time, it has produced—has <u>had to</u> produce—more and more changes in more and more areas of existence, and to do so at an always accelerating rate. In those same processes more social harm is done, more private gain is had; and socio-economic processes become always more frenzied, always more speculative and more fragile, at home and abroad.

In our day, the framework within which the stepped up M&As

occur is called **globalization** (or "New World Order," or "neoliberalism"). Call if what you will, it is both cause and effect of several decades of "disequilibria" (the term economists give to periods of crisis, chaos, or imbalance).

The 1970s were years of a unique economic crisis called "stagflation"; almost a decade of simultaneous and prolonged rising inflation <u>and</u> rising unemployment. In complicated ways those years gave rise to a set of connected developments which, among other results, sped up and transformed M&As, leading to one record-breaking year after another, continuing and accelerating as this is written. (RAVENSCRAFT & SCHERER, DU BOFF):

1. Both the defensive and offensive motives for M&As increased, along with an effectively novel set of behavior patterns called "hostile take-overs" and "leveraged buyouts"; its main actors were called "corporate raiders."

Notable among the latter were Carl Icahn, T. Boone Pickens, Michael Milken (the inventor of the "junk bond," who picked up $500 million in one year, and a jail sentence in another), and Ivan Boesky. Boesky is my favorite. He gave a (much applauded) commencement speech at the UCLA Business School entitled "Greed is Good"—just before he too got caught and was whisked away to do (very short) time. The stage had been set for the emergence of the buccaneering **CEOs** now so common.

2. That had been preceded in the 1960s by the emergence of the **MNCs**—"multinational corporations." Further acceleration and internationalization in the 1970s created the need for a name change: **TNCs**—"transnational corporations." One thing leads to another, so from the 1980s on the latest modification of **imperialism** called globalization was born.

3. Among the many changes taking hold in that emerging set of processes, those creating the most harm and instability were **downsizing and outsourcing** and **financialization**—further stimulating another and global outburst of **M&As**, especially in **oil, cars,** and telecommunications.

Here some examples of the U.S. merged companies and their values from that period:

Telecommunications: 1998 and after, AT&T merges with
    Telecommunications Inc., then with MediaOne ($133 bil-

lion); Bell Atlantic with GTE ($71 billion); Vodaphone and
Mannesman ($151 billion); Owest Comm. with US West
($49 billion); Viacom with CBS ($37 billion);
Oil: EXXON and Mobil ($68 billion); BP and ARCO ($34 bil-
lion);
Autos: DaimlerChrysler ($40 billion).

In 1998 alone, there were 12,500 M&As, with a total value of
$1.6 trillion. (*FM*, 4—15-99)

The value of the M&As for the 18 leaders between 1998 and
2002 (14 of which were U.S.) was more than $321 billion; the total
announced value global M&As between 1995 and 2002 was over $7
trillion; and the total number of deals for those same years was in
excess of 65,000. (*IHT*, "Here they go again," 1-25-03)

In 2001, the Top Ten U.S. companies (those in **bold** to be discussed separately) in order of revenues, were `Wal-Mart,
ExxonMobil, **GM**, Ford, Enron, **GE**, Citigroup, ChevronTexaco,
IBM, and Philip Morris. (*FM*, 4-15-02) By 2002, the Big Ten said
bye-bye to naughty Enron, brought American International Group
(whoever that is) and Verizon up, as Altria Group (a pleasant name
for ex-Philip Morris) went down to No. 11. (*FM*, 4-14-03)

> The combined 2002 revenues of that Top Ten were over
> $1.3 trillion. GDP is not an equivalent measure for firms' rev-
> enues, but it serves as an "order of magnitude": the combined
> revenues of those companies were just about equal to the GDP
> of either Italy or Great Britain. (*FM*, 7-21-03)

Mergers have an exciting and a brutal quality to them; so does
a prizefight. But in the latter case only the fighters are harmed;
today's rampant M&As also harm the "spectators." Their always
more concentrated power, in being also always more heedless, helps
to explain the behavior of many of the their **CEOs**, who in turn
have been big players in the **financialization** of the U.S. and the
global economy; their related political influence through their **lobbyists** and their domination of **campaign finance** assure that more of
the same is on the way.

Those damages are all the greater when we understand that the
high concentration and the uses of that power in the **media**—where
industrial giants such as **GE** (which owns NBC) are also able to
mold not only our desires for their products, but our political think-

ing and our cultural existence. (BARBER)

Despite all, the giant companies and their bought and paid for media and politicians continue to profess the existence of and their faith in "the free market," aided and abetted by an accompanying supporting chorus of shameless mainstream economists; their "trained incapacity" (VEBLEN) allows them to be self-satisfied in their ignorance.

Postscript:

If all that was not enough to raise your ire, try this: In 2003, it was reported that "Feds classify giant firms as small businesses." (*AP/SFC*, 7-11-03)

> Among the companies designated as small businesses are.... Verizon, the largest phone company in the nation and Verizon Wireless, the company's joint venture that is the largest U.S. wireless provider. Also, Barnes & Noble, the top U.S. bookseller, AT&T Wireless, and /big surprise:/ KBR, a Halliburton subsidiary, one of the world's largest providers of oil field services /not least in Iraq/ and part of the company Vice President Dick Cheney ran before taking office in 2001.... (ibid.)

Suffice it to point out that l'il ole Verizon had revenues in 2002 of over $66 <u>billion</u> and profits of $4 <u>billion</u>. FM, ibid.); if Halliburton/KBR is "small" where does it get the $180,000 it pays our **Cheney** for the rest of his life?

Moreover, this chocolate cake has two layers: once a company <u>is</u> classified as "small" it is eligible for federal government contracts for which otherwise it would <u>not</u> be eligible; and "once a company's status <u>is</u> mischaracterized, it stays that way through the life of a con-tract—which can be 20 years." (ibid. Revenue data for Verizon, <u>NYT</u> 7-30-03, "Verizon and Unions Meet with Mediator.")

So how did such a set of mistakes occur? Well, after all, how could anyone in the Bush administration know that Verizon is a sort of big? Or know that KBR/Halliburton has picked up a few $billions in Iraq? Never heard of 'em. We're in good hands.

boys and girls/men and women

The injustice and abuse with which women are treated in the USA has much in common with the atrocities of U.S. **racism** and

slavery; but along with the similarities there are many differences:

1) They are similar in that neither is confined to the USA; different in that the oppression of racism/ slavery has been more severe than that of women's oppression in the USA, harsh though both have been.

2. They are similar in that however serious the socio-economic *inequality* of the USA, it is more so for the victims of racist and gender oppression—to say nothing of their combination for women of color—than for the racists and the sexists; although, as will be seen later, all workers have lost and their employers gained from the breach of worker solidarity in both respects.

3. In addition and even more damaging, though impossible to measure, all concerned suffer from the attendant diminution of their humanity. In Germany, the slogan for the "place" of women that fits almost all societies was "<u>kuchen, kirche, kinder</u>"—that, or something worse. The damage done to women by that categorization in Germany (and something similar or worse elsewhere) is beyond measure in all of social existence; but men have paid little or no attention to how they have diminished in their own lives in forcing their mothers, lovers, daughters, and sisters into that mold.

4. A basic similarity for both forms of oppression is that an unknown but probably high majority of people act and feel toward these "others" in prejudicial ways—but <u>unconsciously</u>, so deeply ingrained are the attitudes of disdain, fear, scorn, hate, and **arrogance** resulting from our socialization. These attitudes have been "taught" to all of us—racism for centuries in the USA, and very probably from our species' beginnings for the oppression of women.

5. The differences between "centuries" and forever gives added importance to women's oppression. Not only is it more widespread and deeper than racism in our "social genes," but something more: that experience has "taught" almost all of us to see half of all human beings as being inferior to the other <u>half</u> in one way and another; in consequence, all men (and many girls/women), in becoming habituated to thinking prejudicially, have become unthinkingly open to accepting other prejudicial views as well.

6. The consequences of women's enduring mistreatment neither begins nor ends there; it has found its way into every nook and cranny of our lives, allowing men's predilections to shape and set the standards for almost all of our social institutions: We live in "a man's world." It has been a nasty world for most, most of the time—harmful to all, as is argued in many of the essays of this book, such as education and waste. <u>What man hath wrought</u>. Among the many appalling effects of that history has been the systematic and lifelong disadvantaging of girls/women. It begins in the life at home as children and continues as adults, works its way through **educational** levels from K-12 to the Ph.D., and manifests itself in all other walks of life: on the job (and which jobs are granted), in **entertainment**, in... everything; generation after generation.

The resulting abnegation and distortion of both human and social needs and possibilities is mind-boggling. That is especially so if we concentrate on what has thus been lost to all, what life <u>could</u> have been and could be, as contrasted with what it has been and is. How explain this set of crimes and tragedies?

The "predilections" or solidly-rooted tendencies of men can be seen as resulting from the combination of our genetic makeup (which makes the male generally stronger) and, finally more important, with the prehistoric social processes of survival in our original natural environment. The 150,000 years of that prehistoric environment make "historic time" seem like an hour compared with a month.

The basic instinct for <u>all</u> species is of course that of survival. It has two elements: <u>reproduction</u>, and the adaptation to the natural/social environment by <u>production</u>, in order to eat sufficiently and to be protected against the weather and surrounding enemies.

Men and women participate in both of those, but in different ways. In comparison with women, men's involvement in "reproduction" diminishes sharply soon after children are born; were women to have behaved similarly, our species would not have survived. Whether or not we term "maternal" behavior as "instinctive," it is clear that there is nothing comparable for men, despite that some men show substantial affection and other positive attitudes and behavior and, of course, through their "production" do much to support children's lives.

In the tens of thousands of prehistoric years, men's "production" was that of hunters and warriors, providing production, protection, and aggression. Women, in that pre-agricultural epoch, searched for and gathered food. Moreover, and importantly, once a settled agriculture had become possible, it was women who became the farmers. The nature and meaning of what Veblen called "the maternal bent" does not usually end with the activities of mothers and their children; it extends also to the general tendency of women to be "motherly" whether or not they themselves have children. It isn't that men never behave in similar ways (as distinct from being "buddies"), but that those who do are exceptions.

Implicit in the foregoing is that men's main functions in the deep past entailed prowess in the realms of violence, in contrast with the relatively peaceful realms of home and field. By the time that technology and production had improved sufficiently to allow "civilization" (that is, cities) to develop, those who ruled over them and, subsequently, over nations and empires were those who had mastered the arts of violence. (CHILDE, VEBLEN /1899/)

That desperately limited sketch of millennia of change perforce neglects exceptions here and there; but the basic processes are generally agreed upon, Thus, here and there a Cleopatra ruled, but the list of rulers is denominated by a Julius, a Henry, a Louis, until modern times. Then, when ancient and medieval developments were shoved aside by the emergence of nation-states and industrial **capitalism**, men continued to rule in suits instead of robes, not just in business but almost everything else except kindergartens and nursing, ruled over almost always by male bureaucrats and doctors.

That has begun to change in some few countries, including the USA, as women have increasingly (in a small minority) come to take up "man's work" as doctors, lawyers, professors, politicians..., or U.S. Marines. But in doing so, indeed often in order to do so, women frequently do—often must—"act like men." That may or may not mean dressing like men; it almost always means to be aggressive, ruthless, heartless, tough.

Almost, but not always: In keeping with recent legislation, women are increasingly able to fulfill themselves as human beings more than in the past—in realms ranging from medicine to universities to politics to sports, where a noticeable percentage in fact do behave differently than men, to their pleasure and our benefit. However.

The desirable changes achieved amount to no more than a beginning of what is necessary. And even for those very limited changes to occur, a substantial women's movement was essential. Its beginnings go back a century and more, years in which those who constituted that movement—as with their counterparts in anti-racist movements—were treated with scorn, contempt, and even punishment.

Nor should it be forgotten that even now the lives of <u>most</u> girls and women in the USA—and even more so for most of the rest of the world—remain more like those of the deep past than the emerging present—at home, at work, in school, on dates..., wherever.

Moreover, as also with anti-racist reforms, it is doubtful if a majority of men have welcomed or acquiesced in the beneficial changes that have occurred; for most men, the progress has been accompanied by sighs of disbelief, resignation, scorn; even rage.

On top of which, the movements toward women's equality with men and those for the equality of people of color appear now to be stalled, as with so much else in the socioeconomic sphere. That takes us to another consideration; the ways in which racial and gender oppression meld with linked conservative to reactionary trends now dominant in the larger political realm.

There cannot be genuine democracy in a society rife with racism and sexism; but to make progress on either of those fronts requires doing so on both at the same time and, as well on other fronts—most obviously to improve incomes and conditions of work. Success in all those struggles would require the reorganization of the existing structures of socioeconomic power that created, depend upon, and that profit from socioeconomic inequality; the structures, that is, of **capitalist** society.

The struggles for democracy have been many since capitalism's birth; until recently their most frequent focus and successes were those against workers' **exploitation**.

"Recently" refers to the past century or so, and particularly to the years after World War II. The vital center of those struggles was for independent and strong **unions**. In the USA they began both to encounter great resistance and to make progress in the 1930s, and considerably more so by the 1950s. Also after World Wawr II, and building on prior efforts, two other movements against injustice and inequality began to take hold: the civil rights and womens' movements.

What never did occur, except rarely, was for those three sets of struggles to join together to become a <u>movement</u>, a movement, that is, for justice and equality and a decent livelihood for all.

To repeat, of course progress had been made; in comparison with the conditions of workers, people of color and women a century ago with those of today, there have been significant changes for the better: improved real wages and working conditions, reduced socioeconomic and political discrimination against people of color and women, and the subtler but important changes in what may be called the "culture of opinion."

Both despite and because of those successes, since the 1970s there has been a noticeable reversal in all those areas in an always worsening trend. In past decades some important battles were won, but not the war: **unions** are much weaker today than 30 years ago; worker **exploitation** is rising (see **big business** and **waste**); **education** and **housing** are deteriorating for most; **racism**, while lessened for many, is widening to include new **immigrants** and presumed **terrorists**. Nor is it irrelevant to point to steeply rising **health care** and **pharmaceutical** costs at the very time in which coverage is falling as patients' costs rise. These are not the signs of successful struggles, but of failure.

There are many reasons why the USA has been lurching backwards in these respects. One, the absence of an overall movement was just noted. Another, which sits at the base of that "absence", is that our unique history (in comparison with all other capitalist nations) has induced our workers to be less class conscious than any other. (see **capitalism**)

Important though that has been, however, we have also been unique in the ways in which capitalist power has been able to exploit mostly male workers' **racism** and, in recent decades, their sexism: the Achilles heel of movements for socioeconomic improvement has been that all too many of us have been prone to be distracted from our own exploitation and mistreatment because of our failure to see that those who work for wages are in the same boat with all people of color, and irrespective of gender—to the great profit of those who rule. (ROEDIGER)

The foregoing has been heavy with sweeping generalizations; the specifics to follow seek to fill in some of the blanks; and, insofar as all of us have had experience with most of what follows, and some of us with even more, your memories will also provide some verification.

<u>As the twig is bent...</u> I begin with boys and girls at home, in school, at play, in dress and in speech, attitudes and behavior taught to us in our formative years, and thus very difficult to "unlearn": accepted ways of being—but invidiously different for boys and girls, to the harm of both, if also more so to the girls.

In all that is said here, to repeat, it is true that things have changed markedly in the past several decades; <u>markedly</u>, especially for those who would be reading a book such as this, and for their children. But the focus here is upon <u>all</u> the people of the USA.

Just as the USA is neither the worst nor the best place in the world for girls/women, there are also better and worse parts of the USA for this and other socioeconomic matters: Manhattan—i.e., parts of it—is less oppressive to girls/women than most of, say, Little Rock, Ark.; parts of San Francisco are better than most of Los Angeles (and parts of L.A. better than most of S.F); the North less bad than the South, etc.

But a fair estimate would be that desirable changes in the upbringing of children regarding gender differences have made little progress from where they were 50 or more years ago for <u>most</u> of the people in the USA, where "most" means a thumping majority of us; the snapshots to follow are more likely than not to be accurate for almost <u>all</u> children, still today. Would that it were not so.

So: A baby girl is born; a few years later, her little brother: Sally and Billy. The conditioning processes begin soon after birth, with Sally usually wearing something pink, Billy something blue. Cute, to be sure, but they would both look cute in pink, or blue, or orange or purple; pink and blue have taken on connotations, whether or not ever made explicit.

In most families, the <u>babies</u> Sally and Billy will be treated with equal affection; but as soon as they are able to walk and talk, that usually changes—whatever the family's "race, creed, or color."

Usually without parental deliberation, Sally will be treated as a girl en route to becoming a young woman, and then a mother; Billy as a boy on his way to manhood, to become "the man of the house." The lessons will be provided by their parents (who learned them from their parents), by their teachers, their peers, from books and film and now, not least, by **TV**.

When they enter grammar school, they will already be self-segregating with whom they chat, with whom they play and which games they play, and thus with whom they become friends. All this is arranged in a set of processes as natural as breathing in and breathing out, usually unspoken, unconscious, and unexamined, and which soon comes to define "normality."

But don't some boys and girls become friends despite all? Indeed they do; but when they do, it is not in the same way as girls/girls, boys/boys. One reason is that as time goes on they have learned to have fewer and fewer things in common; girls have learned to be together with other girls both so they can "be themselves" and for relaxation; and were two children of the opposite sex to become friends in the same way as with their own sex they would be made fun of, even tormented: Not normal.

And then there is the different clothing, the different ways of communicating, the differences in learned aggressiveness or gentleness, the differences in the kinds of things joked about or taken seriously, who learns to cook and who learns to fight..., all getting a firm grip on us already as children.

To be sure, much of that has changed and may (or may not) change even more, most visibly in the sports girls/women are now learning/being allowed to play in grade school and high school and college; and in that sports have a meaning going well beyond what is done and seen, that can become significant in and of itself—another similarity with **racism**; except that even those whites who see Willie Mays or Tiger Woods as heroic continue to see blacks as a "group" in unchanged ways.

Add to all that what boys and girls "learn" from TV—which, studies show, children watch for an average of 4-6 hours a day. (POSTMAN) Even if they watched only children's programs it would be bad enough, for most TV shows work within the same stereotypes. Worse, and as with adults, what children see on TV and film screens is a dreadful combination of violence, sexism, aggressivity, and the other values of Macho USA—"virtual realities" skillfully done, not only teaching different lessons for boys and girls, but also allowing them to become accustomed to violence in such a way as to lose any sense of what such behavior might mean in <u>real</u> reality. It is hard not to believe that increasing violence among children is thus stimulated.

Meanwhile, little girls learn that to be beautiful is not just OK, it's absolutely essential; that beautiful means being very thin with big breasts, always smiling or laughing; that the proper center of their lives is to make themselves desirable to men and, ultimately, to serve them, as "girlfriend," wife, and mother.

So, by the time they are in high school, girls have learned that to be popular with their male counterparts is to be "good sports" about sex—from which, if there is an unwanted pregnancy, for example, it is theirs to resolve. Meanwhile, the boys are learning that a real guy is one with physical prowess, at sports and with women.

As young women, if and when they get to college and are in sororities, they are not by then surprised to find that the regular weekend frat-sorority dances are normally marked by drunkenness and the expectation of pairing off for sex, up to, and even beyond "consenting" rape—not only at the worst, but at the best colleges and universities.

In short, girls and young women learn to take for granted, to admire, and to seek to become like the very stereotypes the women's movement has sought for so long to banish, while boys learn to be fools, brutes, and sexual cowboys; and those boys who manage <u>not</u> to learn all that are seen as goofballs and, often, ostracized. All this has taken hold already in early adolescence and is well-entrenched by the late teens. Thus, by the time the boys and girls are becoming young men and women they have become habituated to accepting certain roles for each other while, at the same time, a high wall has been constructed that keeps them from developing other possibilities for living and working together as equals: to their mutual benefit.

<u>So the tree will grow</u>. As is discussed elsewhere in these pages

(e.g., **jobs** and **education** and **inequality**), if a living wage is defined as provided by a job paying $14 an hour for 40 hours a week—which only 40 percent of U.S. workers receive—then 80 percent have <u>less</u> than a living wage. Seldom indeed will those who are struggling with less than that have a job doing something that is useful and interesting: collecting garbage and waiting on table, e.g., are both useful, but in addition to being badly-paid are rarely interesting, combine boredom with disgust, and are <u>never</u> fulfilling. Note that we are referring to more than half the working population with such jobs— in factories or offices, gas stations or clerking here or there etc. (Ehrenreich)

With such jobs, most husbands and wives get home from work both tired and bored—the wife somewhat more so, for she had probably taken care of the kids and breakfast and even some cleaning up before leaving for the "real" job. (As is discussed below, <u>two-thirds</u> of married women with children also work outside the home.) Neither husband or wife is in the mood to have to put up with the kids; it's usually Mom's job to do so, and she <u>does</u> so, before, during, and after the dinner she has cooked—while Dad is having a beer or a shot or two, in front of the boob tube. Even if he's a "good Dad."

And then to bed. The first few years of even what will become a bad marriage are usually sexually lively and pleasant. But after the marriage settles, the jobs go on, and as the kids and the bills and the mountains of **debt** demand attention and worry, sex too can become a routine—something the husband feels is his due even though the wife feels only exhausted.

Not that there aren't wives who are just as sexually lively as men (or more); it's just that after a couple of kids, not enough money, a bored and perhaps boring husband, and all that, at the end of the day she's more likely to want to rest than to have a workout. If she does, fine. If she doesn't, hubby will all too regularly see it as his right; i.e., her duty. And you can fill in the blanks.

There is much more that is unpleasant to dwell upon; suffice it to say that in a non-sexist world, the normal passions of males and females could, if left to themselves, produce both a considerably better physical and non-physical life for men and women—and, as well for men and men, and women and women—than do the distortions now marking the lives of almost all. So much has been lost, and nothing gained—not even for "the masters of all they survey."

On the job. Most jobs, over half of them, are neither clearly useful nor interesting for men or women; for women, they are often another area of oppression and injustice, and of human and social waste. In the poorer countries, conditions are considerably worse than in the rich countries, of course; worse not just in terms of how very wearying and life-shortening their work is, but how little control women have over their lives, including their education, and their related sex lives and health—which includes both the high birthrates and the cruelly disproportionate levels of HIV infection of women (58 percent, in Africa) compared with men), especially cruel considering that it so often incurred through coercion. (NYT, 12-29-02, "In Africa, AIDS Has a Woman's Face.")

A main element of job inadequacies for women is the formal or informal distortion of education as between them and males, and thus which "tracks" they are placed on—or kept from. Such treatment is also meted out to males, where the "push" is determined by class and "race," not sex; for young women, it is all of the above: Heaven help the young woman who is also black. You are pushed on your way to a Wal-Mart aisle or hospital hallway or, if a bit luckier, to a GM office, to becoming a nurse rather than a doctor, and so on. (And when you become a nurse, even though you are often more valuable to the hospitalized patient than the doctor, you will work many more hours, be paid much less, and be treated as a servant. (see **health care, HMOs**)

Countless women with talents at least equal to men have been tracked into stupid and low-paying jobs, women who, without oppression, with equal education and opportunity, could have made a considerably greater contribution to their own lives and to society. The same has been and, largely remains so, in **education** for men and women; but whatever the ill treatment is given men in this connection, it is doubled for women.

For, given the job, there is then what happens on an identical job to a woman. Often as not, she works more hours, is paid less, is treated shabbily to the point of mistreatment (including sexual abuse), and is less likely to have a **union** to assist her toward better conditions, pay, and benefits: in short, abused and exploited.

But surely that affects only a small minority of married women with children? Wrong. The socioeconomic changes that began to emerge in the 1970s and that went through the roof from the 1980s on, gave the United States the world's highest ratio of two-income households, with its hidden, de facto tax on time and families. Whereas back in 1960 only 19 percent of married women with children under six had worked, by 1995 fully 64 percent did, exceeding the other industrial nations. By 1999... the Bureau of Labor Statistics reported that the typical American worked 350 hours more per year than the typical European, the equivalent of nine work weeks. (PHILLIPS, 2002)

Given all the woes concerning women and children and jobs earlier, it is revealing to compare what happens in other rich countries. In Italy, for example (and Germany, and Austria, and...) when a married working woman has a child, she is entitled by law to one year off with pay; in the period before the child enters kindergarten, it may attend pre-school (an "asilo" or nest), where he or she is given careful and friendly attention, while the mother works. And, not unimportantly, if the new mother is not married, far from being scorned, she has the higher priority for such childcare. In the USA we don't have any such arrangements even for middle-income families, let alone those who are poor and thus need it most.

The inadequacies to cruelties referred to above are for the USA, not Indonesia, China, Nigeria, Afghanistan, where economic and cultural conditions might conceivably furnish some kind of admissible basis for an excuse; but in the richest and self-styled "most democratic" nation in the world?

To repeat what is noted under **racism,** what girls and women have lost through all this here and everywhere has in different degree and with partial responsibility also been lost to men; men who have never been able to have a full life because they have participated in denying a full live to all the women they have known, mothers and wives included.

In sum. So allright already, most would say; the USA is still the best place in the world. Sure, we're stupid in things like spiked heels and lousy jobs and distorted education and...; but hey! That's nothing like as bad as bound feet, having to wear a burkha, being burned to death on a ceremonial fire because your husband has died, not being able even to go to school if you're a girl...; at least here things are nowhere near as bad as that. Right?

Right. We're not that bad, but nor as regards the treatment of women are we—or the other rich countries, any country—anywhere close to being as good as we like to think we are; nowhere near as good as we would be if we saw men and women—all men and all women—as having equal rights, equal needs, equal abilities and possibilities, an equal craving for the dignity that is denied them.

But at least we are closer to that today than we were a century ago? Somewhat; "Close, but no cigar," as they say in target shooting. We are still so far away from decency, fulfilled needs and possibilities, that few if any men would trade places with women; as far away from that goal as we are from what where we could and should be for ending **poverty** and **racism** and **militarism**. Imagine, fellas, just try to imagine this: Not your wife, but you have to go through the pain of childbirth; you have to be the 24-hour guardian of the baby's/child's/adolescent's wants and needs/; you have to do most of the worrying and fretting; you have to do the cooking, the cleaning, the shopping, endure the boredom; you are also likely to have another, usually a lousy, job; you have to put up with a tired and frustrated mate coming home hungry and thirsty and..., so on. Want to trade places?

What fools we mortals be!

buffalo (Technically: bison.)

"Oh give me a home / where the buffalo roam, / and the deer and the antelope play / where seldom is heard a discouraging word / and the sky is not cloudy all day." Deer and antelope are alert and quick enough to have survived reasonably well, but the buffalo is cow-like, stands and stares—until it's too late. As "westward the course of empire" unfolded they were always too late, taking them within a hair's breadth of extinction.

About 100 years ago, the U.S. Department of Agriculture estimated there were some 1,500 buffalo in the United States, but that a century earlier there had been some 60,000,000 (that's right, million). Even assuming there were three times as many in 1900 and only one-third as many in 1800, those figures beg for an explanation. It is all too simple; and horrifying.

In an early version of a Disneyland feature, the buffalo were mostly massacred by "sportsmen" as the transcontinental railroads were built and used. Train cars were outfitted with long benches facing outward on both sides; as they passed through buffalo herds, the sportsmen would shoot them. Some corpses were left to rot where they fell, others were later assembled into lumber-like piles. Another legend for the fabled West. (BRANCH)

A very cruel sport but, some would say, wotthehell. What difference did it make? For the **"Indians"** of the Plains, it meant the white man had added to his other ways of destroying their traditional and sensible life on lands they saw as sacred; we had found another way to weaken and demoralize them.

For numberless centuries, the buffalo had been a central element of their economy, providing food, clothing, tools (from bones), and shelter; moreover, the virtual extermination of the buffalo on the Great Plains was accompanied the loss of the land itself while, at the same time, their numbers were continually added to by the **Indian removal** from the eastern states to the west. (CALLENBACH)

That devastating process, it must be said, was all too similar to the deportation of Jews from Hungary, France, Italy, Poland and Germany by the Nazis. And just as millions died during and after those "deportations," so it was for the "Indians": It has been estimated that from the first moment of European arrival on "our shores," until 1900, 6-to-9 million "Indians" in North America died from imported diseases, "removal," and fighting.

Indian removal was a popular institution. It was directed early on by General Andrew Jackson; it is agreed that his fame as a "remover" was a major reason for his becoming president. (ZINN, 2000)

That's the bad news about the buffalo. But now some good news: In recent years the number of buffalo has been rising; but the reasons are pretty awful: Now there are about 200,000 buffalo; some are raised to become "buffalo burgers," others are used as an obscene throwback to the past: About a decade ago at Yellowstone National Park, for $250 one could shoot a buffalo and—get this!—have one's photo taken with the carcass at no extra charge. (Bring your own gun; line forms to the right.)

Bush I

George Herbert Walker Bush came into power in very much the same way as his son **Bush II** would—except for the rigged election. He was the son of the rich and powerful Senator Prescott Bush. Sam Bush, Prescott's dad, was in steel and armaments, and a mucky-muck in D.C. during World War I. Prescott went on from there into international oil, and G.H.W. Bush carried on that tradition and gave it a little zip by getting involved with Enron back in the 1980s. (Phillips, 2004)

Although Prescott was a Connecticut Yankee kind of guy (and a Senator), his oil connections introduced him to the ole buys of Texas, and that's how that began.

Even though G.H.W. Bush spent some time in the squats of Texas, he, like his father and son were all Yalies. Being a Yalie then and now meant 1) you had done well in high school, and/or 2) you were a good athlete, and/or 3) you were from a Yale family, and/or 4) you were rich. Prescott got in on 1+4; Bushes I and II by 3+4: upper class variations on **affirmative action**. Yale is pretty tough, yes? Not if your folks are rich and were there before you: the insured "Gentleman's C" is ubiquitous in the Ivy League.

As with many Yalies, George I joined the **CIA** family and, as is the wont of the Bushes, started at the top as Director. After he'd been in the public eye for a while, the joke about him was that "George was born on third base, and thinks he hit a triple." (Dubya stands at home plate and thinks he homered.)

It was the habit of the CIA from the time of its birth in 1947 to seek out graduates of the top universities to join them—Ivy League+MIT+Hopkins in the East, Berkeley+Stanford in the West.

Item: The CIA made one of their early mistakes at Berkeley in 1948, when they asked me to join them—the very years when the **FBI** was busily filling up 2,500 pages against very dangerous me: Even then the CIA and the FBI failed to communicate with each other.

After emerging from the womb of Big Oil to become Director of the CIA, Bush I was a natural to be chosen to Veep for Reagan, thence—and why not?—to succeed him as President; all of that, in the hallowed Bush tradition, without breaking a sweat.

Bush I's presidential campaign against Massachusetts Governor

Dukakis became infamous—and successful—for its strategic use of the "Willie Horton" threat: An expertly constructed TV ad showing a revolving prison gate while, in the background, a scary and inaccurate story of Horton (a black man) droned on. Along the way it was made clear that Horton was imprisoned in—guess where?—Massachusetts.

The story and the visuals clearly meant to suggest that if Dukakis were to be elected President, the prisons would soon empty themselves of countless black killers. It became the main focus of the campaign and, given the polluted social air of the 1980s, it worked.

During that same campaign another and true story began to circulate, but after a flurry as brief as snowfall in April, it was quashed: Bush I, while a pilot in the Pacific war, had bailed out when his plane caught fire. Nothing necessarily wrong with that—unless, that is, you are leaving your crew behind. Bush I did just that. All pilots (and I was one) learn that the "captain of the ship" is <u>never</u> the first to bail out. Bush I broke that rule, and his crew went to a flaming death.

How do we know? Because other aircrews on his wing that day provided the story to the press. Confirmed though the story was and damaging though it should have been to one who had gained repute for heroism, the news dwindled away and was not heard from again.

Like father, like son: except that Bush I did fly in combat, and may well have kept his nerve on all other occasions (it's not easy to do). But, as will be noted below, **Bush II** was also a pilot but managed to avoid <u>any</u> occasions on which he might have been in danger.

Bush II

Himself

Quite simply because he <u>is</u> President of the USA and, as such, the most powerful person in the world, it is worrisomely difficult for most of us to see him for what else he <u>is</u>: a rich, ignorant, and feckless boy who got through private K-12 prep schools and Yale University and Harvard Business School because of wealth and family status; a dolt who has never done an honest day's work; who was <u>handed</u> a governorship and then the Oval Office with no meaningful political experience or knowledge. All he needed to become governor Texas was the Bush name, the gift of a large pile of oil stock and the ownership of a Texas baseball team (bought with easily borrowed funds from an oil company), its stadium paid for by $150 million of taxpayers' money. A newspaper summary of his rise to riches and power: (from *SFC*, 7-5-02.)

1. Breezed and drank his way through prep school at Yale and an MBA at Harvard.
2. Made head of Arbusto Energy (Tex.), funded by family friends, who lost $5 million.
3. After changing its name to Bush Exploration in 1982 (Dad then in White House as V.P.) and continuing to lose money, it was bought out in 1984 by Spectrum 7 Energy (Tex.), owned by two men who were major backers of Bush I's 1988 presidential campaign. Bush II was CEO of Spectrum 7, which had steady losses until bought out by Harken Energy (still Tex.) in 1986, when Bush II was made a Harken director, which paid him $250,000 in consulting fees and stock options.
4. Bush II spent much of the next two years working for Dad's political campaigns. After Dad won, Harken was awarded a big contract by Bahrain for offshore drilling—for which it had no prior experience.
5. In 1989, with Bush II a director and "consultant," the S.E.C. ruled that Harken had hidden $10 million in losses through the sale of a subsidiary to company insiders who had borrowed the money from Harken to make the deal.
6. Soon after, in 1990, Bush II (who sat on the board's audit committee) sold $848,000 of his Harken stock—8 days before the price fell by more than half, when the public was informed that Harken had recently lost $23 million. (*SFC*)

And oh yes, Bush II waited 8 months to file the document insiders are required to submit when they sell. (*NYT* 7-4-02)

When the latter information hit the news in July of 2002 **Ari Fleischer** had the unenviable job of reconciling at least two contradictory versions of Bush's asserted innocence reported earlier. In its story on this matter—"The Know Nothing Defense..."—the *SFC* quoted Acting Dean Hermalin of UC Berkeley's School of Business: "The know-nothing defense is a public statement of incompetence."

Bush II says it must all be OK, because the SEC looked into it
and "vetted" him. Paul Krugman had this to say about that:

> In fact, the agency's investigation was peculiarly perfunc-
> tory. It somehow decided that Mr. Bush's peculiarly timed stock
> sale did not reflect inside information without interviewing him
> or any other members of Harken's board. Maybe top officials at
> S.E.C. felt they already knew enough about Mr. Bush: his father,
> the president, had appointed a good friend as S.E.C. chairman.
> And the general counsel, who normally would make decisions
> about legal action, had previously been George W. Bush's per-
> sonal lawyer—he negotiated the purchase of the Texas Rangers.
> I am not making this up." (*NYT*, op-ed, 7-12-02)

Bush II, like his Dad, is a pilot; unlike him, he's never heard a
shot fired in anger: Other than landing on the deck of that carrier in
2003 (after a 30-mile flight) he confined his derring-do to whizzing
over Texas for its National Guard, thus exempting him from having
to display his heroism in Vietnam. And even then, he managed to
take a never-explained leave of an entire year. As the 2004 election
approached and this became a public matter, a process of intricate
razor-thin qualifications and denials filled the news. However one
managed or did not manage to cut through all that fog, however,
what remained is that a) he got into the Texas National Guard
through being a Bush, b) that he didn't serve all his time, and c) that
he got an honorable discharge under dubious conditions.
(IVINS/DUBOSE)

There you have him: one who has lived the almost stereotypi-
cal life of the loutish, classic hard-drinking fraternity boy, ignorant
as a turtle, doing his cheap imitations of James Dean, marked by fal-
sity in his walk, his talk, his smile, his frown.

And his speeches! Presidents in the modern era have had all or
most of their speeches written for them, although some could have
written their own.

Not so for either Bush, nor for the one and only **Reagan**. But
like his Dad, Bush II was born with two objects in his mouth: a silver spoon, and a foot; both larger than the father's. One can only
imagine the panic in his inner circle when President has to speak
from his own head. Some examples:

> In a conversation with the President of Brazil, he asked
> "Do you have blacks in Brazil?" Condoleezza Rice quickly inter-

jected "Mr. President, Brazil has more blacks than the USA." In fact it has more blacks than any place on earth except Africa. (Germany's *Der Spiegel* /5-19-02/)

And here some quotes from *SFC*, (9-20-01):

"Reading is the basics for all learning."
"More and more, our imports come from overseas."
"You teach a child to read and he or her will be able to pass a literacy test."
"...Teaching children to read and having an education system that's responsive to the child and to the parents, as opposed to mired in a system that refuses to change, will make America what we want it to be—a literate country and hopefuller country."
"My pro-life position is I believe there's life. It's not necessarily based in religion. I think there's life there, therefore the notion of life, liberty and pursuit of happiness."

Or, when interviewed in Genoa, as the turmoil of July, 2001 was going on in the streets: "That's what I believe and I believe that what I believe is right." (*NYT*, 7-25-01) I'm convinced.

Much will be said under **Iraq** about its phony rationale(s), etc.; here Bush II's response to Tim Russert on "Meet the Press" (2-10-04) to that disgraceful muddle:

> In my judgment, when the United States says there will be serious consequences, and there isn't serious consequences, it creates adverse consequences. /Whose side is he on?/

Finally, as the CEO corruption scandals were alarming the nation in the summer of 2002, Bush II issued what may be seen as The XIth Commandment: "In order to be a responsible American, you must behave responsibly." Is that leadership, or what?

Mark Crispin summed it up well when, in reviewing M.C. MILLER's *The Bush Dyslexicon* (*New Yorker* (7-23-01), he remarked, "In W's world, political messages resignate, racial quotas vulcanize society, outstretched hands are shaked, and Bush himself is consistently misunder-estimated."

One may be sure that Bush II's team is acutely aware of their leader's weaknesses, and aware, too, of the need to front for him. They have their work cut out for them, work whose needs and limitations they don't always recognize. For example:

> On Air Force One on Friday /June 14, 2002/, **Ari Fleischer**... brought forward John Bridgeland, director of U.S.A. Freedom Corps /to brief the press/ on the commencement speech Bush was to make at Ohio State... "He's building on...the thinking of ancient Greeks and Romans and on the principles of the founding fathers..../the president/ derived his ideas from the teachings of Tocqueville, Adam Smith, the world's major religions, Aristotle, George Eliot, Emily Dickinson, William Wordsworth, Pope John Paul II, Cicero, Abraham Lincoln and the founding fathers...." /and added/ "We've actually discussed Nicomachean ethics together." (*NYT*, 6-19-02, op-ed, M. Dowd /no relation/)

Wow. Wouldn't it be <u>won</u>derful to be able to give the President a multiple-choice exam on those ethics?

Neither intellectuality nor a fine command of language is a must for being president; but the problems exhibited above and elsewhere are not those of language but of dishonesty—a dishonesty required to protect the noodleheaded Commander-in-Chief of the most powerful—and now **preemptive**—nation. Are there any at all who will believe it when, as this or that crisis emerges, we are told "President Bush is still <u>thinking</u> that through, and will announce <u>his</u> decision soon"?

If there is an exception, Bush II <u>does</u> seem to have a mind of his own when it comes to one matter, the worst one: Even without a teleprompter, he speaks clearly, forcefully and enthusiastically about warfare. That fits in with an observation by Molly Ivins who, crazy though it sounds, writes,

> I have known George W. Bush slightly since we were both in high school, and I studied him closely as governor. He is neither mean nor stupid. What we have here is a man shaped by three intervening strands of Texas culture, combined with huge blinkers of class. The three Texas themes are religiosity, anti-intellectualism, and machismo. ("The Uncompassionate Conservative," *Mother Jones*, November/December, 2003)

U.S. politics has long been polluted by **spin** and outright lies; as with so much else, these techniques are constantly refined, not least in Bush II's public appearances. Behind him at every speech are those signs telling us what he is talking about: "Recovery," "Small

Investors' Retirement Security," you name it. Reminds one of second grade in grammar school, when the teacher puts such things on the chalkboard so the kids will know what she's talking about.

That the lines between advertising, propaganda, and public relations are increasingly difficult to find was sickeningly revealed in the week before the first "anniversary" of 9/11. In "Bush Aides Set Strategy to Sell Policy on Iraq," the *NYT* (9-7-02), we read that

> White House officials said today that the administration was following a meticulous strategy to persuade the public, Congress and the allies of the need to confront the threat from Saddam Hussein.... The White House decided that even with the appearance of disarray it was still more advantageous to wait until after Labor Day to launch their plan. "From a marketing point of view," said Andrew H. **Card** Jr., the White House chief of staff who is coordinating the effort, "You don't introduce new products in August." A centerpiece of this strategy, White House officials said, is to use Mr. Bush's speech on Sept. 11 /2002/ to help move Americans toward support of action against Iraq.... Toward that end, in June the White House picked Ellis Island in New York Harbor, not Governor's Island, as the place where President Bush is to deliver his Sept. 11 address to the nation. Both spots were considered /they said/, but the television camera angles were more spectacular from Ellis Island, where the Statue of Liberty will be seen behind Mr. Bush.... /His/ remarks, about 10 minutes in length, are to serve as the emotional precursor for a tougher speech about Iraq that the president is to deliver to the UN General Assembly the following day..., written by a team that included Mr. Bush's principal speech writer (Michael Gerson), Condoleezza Rice, Donald Rumsfeld, and Colin Powell.

In the same mode (as Bush I liked to put things) was that photo op at Mount Rushmore in August 2002, with Bush II looking stern and stony against the background of some rather different presidents. Why not move the White House to Madison Ave.? Save time and reduce the **deficit**. What happens when Bush cannot escape speaking for himself? Sheer terror for his "team," you can bet. How do you spin "Bring 'em on!"—Bush's response to reporters about the ongoing, even rising turmoil and GI deaths in July, 2003; how do you explain to the GIs on the spot, already pissed off by the unexpected length and dangers of being "there"? Especially when the man taunting the Iraqis has himself never heard a shot fired in anger at <u>anyone</u>, let alone himself. And who among his spinners didn't tremble when Bush, speaking without notes after meeting with former KGP chief Putin, said "I looked him in the eye, and I trusted him." Why not? After all, Putin, like Bush I, was our Head Spy.

Enough with the fun and games. The USA has never been as powerful as it is today—economically, politically, culturally, militarily; the quality of its leader and those surrounding (grooming?) him could well have been the voices T.S. ELIOT had in mind when, in 1925, he wrote:

We are the hollow men
We are the stuffed men
Leaning together
Headpiece filled with straw. Alas!
Our dried voices, when
We whisper together
Are quiet and meaningless
As wind in dry grass
Or rats' feet over broken glass
In our dry cellar
Shape without form, shade without colour,
Paralyzed force, gesture without motion....

Except that rats only eat each other, and do minor damage to others; the Bushies wreak havoc in all quarters of society, in all quarters of the world.

Had enough? Sorry, there's more, and it is perhaps the most troubling of all Bush II's characteristics. Earlier the view Molly Ivins of Bush as driven by the Texan trio of religiosity, anti-intellectualism, and militarism. In her probing essay "Mr. Bush and the Divine" (*NYRB*, 11-6-03), Joan Didion makes it clear that his religiosity dominates and guides the other two—whether as regards policy for Israel/Palestine (see **Middle East....**), **Iraq**, or the economy (especially, **deficits and surpluses**), or civil liberties (see **Ashcroft, terrorism**)—to the degree that even some of his most conservative supporters are beginning to wonder what genie they have brought to power:

> We have now reached a point when even the White House may be forced to sort out how a president who was elected to execute a straightforward business agenda managed to

sandbag himself with the coinciding fantasies of the ideologues in the Christian fundamentalist ministries and those in his own administration.

Now a characterization of the policies already enacted or being pushed by Bush and his advisors. Their "hollowness" exists in sinister combination with Bush's and his crew's arrogance, willfulness, fanaticism, and as yet unchallenged use of power.

His Administration's Policies

Bush II, it surely would be agreed, is not his own man—except when the occasion arises to be warlike. He speaks for those in his administration who have continued and sped up the shift to the Right engineered in the Reagan years—with the help of continuous pressures from industry and finance, from the military, and militant Christians.

What will be discussed now is treated in 20 or so of the separate entries preceding and following **Bush II**. After that an introductory sketch I shall list the many entries that treat of both the nature of the problem and the ways in which this administration is making a bad situation worse, both at home and abroad,

Taken together, the ongoing policies of this administration are at once awesome, disgusting, and frightening. What has already been achieved and what is being sought constitute an attempt not only to follow through on the aims and "accomplishments" of the decades since Reagan, but to do so in ways that conjure up a return to the political economy of Harding and Coolidge, the politics of McCarthyism and the Cold War, and an unrestrained militarism.

More's the worse, there is a set of differences that threaten something more dangerous than the earlier periods, destructive and terrifying though they were.

It is important to understand those differences if we are to understand just how perilously situated we are now: Most relevant and important among them are:

1. The concentration of economic power in the decades up through the 1970s was all too substantial; now it is drastically more so. (see **big business**)
2. Throughout the 1920s, there was a growing anti-militarist public opinion in the USA, a product of disillusionment with

World War I; but the triumphs of World War II and the socialization provided by the Cold War reversed those attitudes—until Vietnam. But since the Gulf War and, especially after 9/11, the general public became more pliant than ever as regards foreign military interventions by the USA: so long as the U.S. casualties are very minimal, and no matter their **collateral damage** to others. Our ongoing wars in **Afghanistan** and **Iraq** are deeply worrisome, with others <u>very</u> possibly on the way.

3. The arts of **public relations** and "mind management" have been honed to a fine point since World War II, whether as regards the sale of commodities or of socio/economic/military policies. That is so even without any deliberate attempts to interfere with dissent; but, such attempts are now well under way, with more anticipated (**Ashcroft; terrorism**).

In short, there is considerable evidence bespeaking a McCarthyism II—if also more subtle, more extensive, and more potent. The times that lie ahead will indeed "try our souls." Now some simple listings of the areas under siege from this administration, by category.

<u>The Economy</u>: See **taxes/tax expenditures, deficits and surpluses, deregulation, privatization, income distribution, poverty, free markets/free trade, unions, fiscal and monetary policies, financialization, globalization, IMF, et al., CEOs, military expenditures..., cars, oil, environment, waste, farmers**. All of those, in one degree or another of intensity, are casualties of Bush II, and all interact—as the foregoing also interacts with what follows.

<u>Socioeconomic policy</u>. The main elements of that policy realm are **health care, HMOs, pharmaceuticals, education, homelessness/housing, hunger**, and **social security**.

<u>Foreign policy</u>. Since World War II, U.S. foreign policy has been dominated by the **Cold War**; that has been replaced by **terrorism**, with its corollary of **preemption** and the attempts to develop non-U.S. threatening, therefore "usable" **nukes**, facilitated by improvements in the art of **spin** that permit lies and deception to reach new heights/depths, as for **Iraq**

<u>Civil rights and liberties</u>. As discussed at length under **racism** and **slavery, McCarthyism**, and **House Un-American Activities**

Committee, civil rights and liberties in the USA, though enshrined and taken for granted throughout our history, have all too often required difficult struggles, whether to be obtained or maintained; under Attorney-General **Ashcroft**, threats are rising once more, in the name of 9/11 and **terrorism**.

His Team

Abrams, Eliot, et al.

(That is, those involved in Central America with him.) He was Assistant Secretary of State under Reagan. Now Senior Director for Near East and North African Affairs in the National Security Council, Abrams was Assistant Secretary of State under Reagan. He was charged with and finally pleaded guilty to having withheld information from Congress in its investigation of that administration's efforts to arm and supply Nicaraguan contras, despite a congressional ban. He misled Congress about human rights in El Salvador, and dismissed reports of the (confirmed) El Mozote massacre as left-wing propaganda. (DANNER) He was sentenced to two years' probation and 100 hours of community service, but was pardoned by Bush I, in 1992. So he <u>must</u> be OK.

Abrams's job at the NSC is Director of its "Office for Democracy, Human Rights and International Operations." (*NYT*, 6-30-01) He is not entirely inexperienced in that his work in Central America had to do with <u>preventing</u> democracy and <u>crushing</u> human rights; everyone has to start somewhere.

Abrams is joined by other veterans of the illegal and murderous Central American activities of the Reagan years: 1) John M. **Poindexter** began his illustrious career on high when he was **Reagan**'s National Security Adviser. Under Bush II he became Director of Information Awareness Office in the Pentagon. His main program was first called "<u>Total</u> Information Awareness"; it was changed to "Terrorism Information Awareness" when the White House spinners were informed that "total" was just a wee bit too straightforward.

Of the five felony counts of which Poindexter was convicted, one concerned the clandestine financing of the Nicaraguan contras and illegal sales of arms to Iran—concerning which Reagan remarked (and, of course, got away with it): "I told the American people I did not trade arms for hostages. My heart and my best intention still tell me that is true, but the facts and the evidence tell me it is not." Facts, schmacts. (WILLS, 1988) Poindexter's convictions were later overturned "on a technicality."

The principal program of the "information" office—of which more in a moment—is unsettling to say the least, and quite a more so with the ex-admiral at the helm:

> Several members of Congress have said that the admiral is an unwelcome <u>symbol</u> because he had been convicted of lying to Congress about weapons sales to Iran and illegal aid to Nicaraguan rebels, an issue with constitutional ramifications, the Iran-contra affair. The fact that his conviction was later reversed on the grounds that he had been given immunity for the testimony in which he lied did not mitigate congressional opinion, they said. ("Congress restricts surveillance plan," *NYT*, 2-12-03). (my emphasis)

The hell with him as "symbol"; the problem is the program of his office, which is: "... monitoring Internet e-mail and commercial databases for health, financial and travel information...." on you and me. (ibid.) That would be terrifying if Patrick Henry were in charge: and Poindexter is no Patrick Henry.

He cut his own throat when, in July of 2003, his office announced <u>another</u> program, the "Terror Futures Market." Born one day, it died the next. The idea was to create "an online futures trading market where speculators could bet on the probabilities of terrorist attacks, **assassinations**, and coups." (*NYT*, Editorial, "Poindexter's Follies," 7-30-03) The wave of outrage led the Pentagon to cancel the program the next day. The *Times* concluded its editorial with "The next logical step is to fire Poindexter." Two days later Poindexter "resigned." A good first step, but no more than that: Senator Leahy got it right when he said, "The problem is that these projects were just fine with the administration until the public found out about them." (*NYT*, "Poindexter will be quitting...," 8-1-03)

To that sordid picture, we add other old pals of Central American yore: 2. John D. **Negroponte**, our new Ambassador to the UN—just in time!—appointed by Bush II, without a look back. <u>Had</u> he looked back, he would have learned that Negroponte's previous experience as an ambassador—to Honduras—was as point man for the provision of illegal arms for our illegal allies in El Salvador and Nicaragua. (DRAPER)

Numbers 3, 4, and 5: Otto **Reich** and Roger **Noriega**, both with sleazy curriculum vitae in Central America, and our new Assistant Secretary of Defense, Rogelio **Pardo-Maurer**, who not only worked with and for the contras but was himself a contra leader. (*NYT*, 8-1-01; 12-7-02) Wouldn't it be loverly to overhear a luncheon conversation between those five ex-gunsels of Reagan?

Ashcroft, John

His function as Attorney General of the USA and the most powerful lawyer in the nation is the closest thing you can find to arbiter of civil and human rights in the USA. Given that he is a pro-guns, anti-abortion, militant religious rightist and effectively against dissent (except from dissenters against gun laws, etc.) that bodes ill for how he views his duties.

Those who are old enough to have watched/listened to Walter Cronkite over past decades, will remember him as a genial and moderate commentator on just about everything; moderate almost to a fault, indeed. So his characterization of Ashcroft is worth quoting at length:

> In his 2 1/2 years in office, Attorney General John Ashcroft has earned himself a remarkable distinction as the Torquemada of American law. Torquemada was the 15th century Dominican friar who became the grand inquisitor of the Spanish Inquisition. He was largely responsible for its methods, including torture and the burning of heretics—Muslims in particular. Now, of course, I am not accusing the attorney general of pulling out anyone's fingernails or burning people at the stake (at least I don't know of any such cases). But one does get the sense these days that the old Spaniard's spirit is comfortably at home in Ashcroft's Department of Justice. ("The New Inquisition," *Denver Post*, 9-21-03)

Also: Given that he makes no bones about wishing to be President one day and that Bush II will seek re-election in 2004, the possibility that he will not have Cheney as his running mate (because of the latter's heart condition), and that Karl Rove has seen him as top choice for Bush's V.P.—well, it looks as though we have to root for Cheney (!!!) to stay well? (NY, "Ashcroft and the presidency.... 4-15-02)

Ashcroft's fervent belief in God was doubtless strengthened by 9/11. It served as a virtual <u>carte blanche</u> for him deftly to translate most of his policy wishes into a fight against **terrorism**. If he continues to do so there is much woe and harm awaiting the needy, women seeking abortions, free speech, prisoners, foreigners, union membership..., almost anyone who holds what were once upon a time becoming the accepted views as to civil and human rights.

If by his works ye shall know him, consider first what Ashcroft sought to accomplish in his six years in the Senate: He "sponsored seven constitutional amendments, which would ban abortions, prohibit flag burning, permit a line-item veto, require a balanced budget, necessitate a super-majority for tax increases, establish term limits for federal officeholders—and, finally, make it easier to amend the Constitution." (ibid.)

That was in the Senate; what has he done since he's been Attorney General? Here only some examples.

The "USA Patriot Act" steam-rolled through Congress in 10/26/01: House, 356-66; Senate 98-1. Very much like The Tonkin Gulf Resolution (see **Vietnam**).

It took courage—not our most important product—to vote against something whose full title was "An Act for Uniting and Strengthening America by Providing the Appropriate Tools Required to Intercept and Obstruct Terrorism."

That act led to the subsequently created Homeland Security Department and much else, with and without titles. Almost immediately, one of the titled organs that came into existence to insure our security was the Terrorism Information and Preventive System: TIPS.

Cute, but not funny. One of five components of what Ashcroft hoped would be a "Citizens Corps," TIPS called upon cabbies, truck and bus drivers, utility readers <u>and</u> your neighborhood mailman to "keep an eye out" for characters undertaking unusual or suspicious acts; to report by telephone, Internet, letter, whatever.

It seemed to be up and running, but it was just a little <u>too</u> crude, or too soon: The U.S. Postal Service said it wouldn't play. Terrorists, every one of 'em.

Congress finally decided not to support TIPS; at least not right away. So we're OK? Not quite.

> The first effects of the /Patriot/ Act were soon felt when the government secretly arrested and jailed more than 1,200 people in connection with its investigation of the events of 9/11. Despite demands from members of Congress, numerous civil liberties and human rights organizations, and the media, the Government refused to make public the number of people arrested, their names, their lawyers, the reasons for their arrest, and other information related to their whereabouts or circumstances.... Most arrested and jailed were Arabs or Muslims..., cab drivers, construction workers, and other laborers, with no more than ordinary visa violations, routine traffic stops /etc./. Some were incarcerated for seven months without being charged or permitted to see their families. ("The USA Patriot Act: An Assault on Civil Liberties," Jim Cornehls, Z *Magazine*, 7/8-03)

The American Civil Liberties Union filed a suit in federal court (July 30, 2003) seeking to have the sweeping antiterrorism laws declared unconstitutional, because (as stated by the group's lawyer)

> There are basically no limits to the amount of information the FBI can get now—library book records, medical records, hotel records, charitable contributions—the list goes on and on, and it's the secrecy of the whole operation that is troublesome.

Good luck, not least with the "No Fly Lists": The "List" is meant to prevent terrorists from boarding a plane. The problem, as always with such devices, is who decides and on what grounds; and whether egregious violations of civil liberties are accidents or done by design—with a later Oops! to excuse it. There have already been lots of "later Oopses," detaining, among others, known to be "strongly liberals"; peace activists; people of suspicious color, et al.

Not only at airports; anyone who as just walked around New York City or San Francisco, or D.C. has been able to see more security guards, more surveillance cameras, bomb sniffing dogs even in museums; or, if you've been to noted landmarks, or have been a librarian or university officer you will know that the government not only has used, but has gone beyond the Patriot Act. For Ashcroft, however, too much is never enough: "Patriot Act too limited, Ashcroft says: Attorney general calls for expanded powers to fight terror." (*NYT*: 6-6-03)

Understandably, but nonetheless frighteningly, large and rising numbers of ordinary people in charge of this or that have responded by going too far rather than taking the chance of reprimand for not going far enough. Take the Library of the University of California, Berkeley (UCB): UCB has not had a sterling record for the defense of civil rights/academic freedom: In 1950 it was the first university to demand a "loyalty oath" from those on its payroll (profs, secretaries, janitors....). When the State Supreme Court declared that to be unconstitutional, there was a referendum to change the constitution; it passed two to one, this time applying to <u>all</u> state employees.

Fifty-three years later, McCarthy dead and gone, UCB did it again: This time it was about Emma Goldman. You probably haven't heard of her; she died just 61 years before 9/11. She had emigrated from Russia before the revolution, became a worker and then an organizer and anarchist, then, in 1916, a great protestor against U.S. participation in the <u>first</u> World War. For which she was deported back to Mother Russia.

She was a prolific, eloquent, and much-admired writer; her substantial papers were collected and held in the Library of UCB. A private scholarly group planned to publish her papers; in order to do so, they began a fund-raising campaign to pay for it. The *NYT* reported on what happened next: "Old Words on War Stirring a New Dispute at Berkeley" (1-14-03)

> The university officials have refused to allow a /private/ fund-raising appeal for the Emma Goldman Papers Project to be mailed because it quoted Goldman on the subject of suppression of free speech and her opposition to war. The University deemed the topics too political as the country prepares for possible military actions against Iraq.

You might wonder what Emma Goldman had written to cause such fear and trembling. She called upon people, not yet overcome by war madness, to raise their voices of protest, to call the attention of the people to the crime and outrage which are about to be perpetrated on them. /And free speech/ advocates shall soon be obliged to meet in cellars, or in darkened rooms with closed doors, and speak in whispers.... (ibid. And see ZINN 1986/2002)

As this is written, despite all, Ashcroft has only gotten stronger, more effective in getting what he seeks; perhaps because he seems so unassumingly "disinterested," seems truly to believe that what he wants, he wants because it is God's will, not his. In May of 2003, he and the Administration submitted Patriot Act II to Congress. If passed, it would permit the government to engage in unchecked surveillance, secretly access credit reports, and catalogue generic information about innocent Americans. (<www.aclucalifornia.org>)

Hold on to your hats and buckle your set belts, it's going to be a rough ride, greased on its way by our next Bushie (among others).

Card, Andrew, Jr.

He is Chief of Staff in the administration, but the title is misleading. Karl Rove along with Dick Cheney and Condoleezza Rice are its "brains" for basic domestic and foreign policy, Rove for the strategy of "selling the president for re-election." "Chief" Card's main function is to work alongside Ari Fleischer/Scott McClellan to publicize the proper image.

As noted elsewhere, but worth noting at least twice, Card made further comment necessary on his duties when, in the summer of 2002, as all hell was breaking loose with the revelation that we were planning to invade Iraq—and when the UN was supposed to receive the justification from Bush—Card announced that Bush would delay his speech until "after August, which is a bad time to market a new product."

Diligent mind-shaper that he is, Card was also the guiding hand behind the (elsewhere noted) "breathtaking images appearing to demonstrate the absolute superiority of U.S. military power.../with/ the destruction of Saddam Hussein's statue..., the dramatic 'rescue' of Jessica Lynch, a panoramic vista of the bombing of Baghdad and...Bush's staged landing on an aircraft carrier" at the war's 'end.'" (RAMPTON/STAUBER) 'Nuf said?

Cheney, Dick.

Probably the most scary of the top members of the Bush Team, Cheney, Secretary of Defense under Bush I, and in tight with the **military-industrial complex**, is also in tighter with the oil industry (for which intimacies there is no little competition in Bush's cabinet).

Cheney functioned for six years as a **CEO** in the oil industry—

enough to give him plenty of documents to hide—and concerning
which he has "stonewalled," with the cooperation of the **SEC** whose
investigation of Halliburton has yet to query Cheney, despite these
well-known and relevant facts: Income from Halliburton, 2000: $36
million. Increase in government contracts while CEO: 91 percent
(= $2.3 billion). Pages of Energy Plan he has refused to provide con-
gressional investigators: 13,500. There was a brief flurry of hope in
2002, when a result of a congressional resolution the GAO sued
Cheney to obtain the names of the energy industry execs who
"might have helped the White House draft its energy policy. That's
when the Democrats were in charge of the Senate and its committees. However: On February 9, 2003, with the GOP in charge of the
Senate, the GAO announced it had withdrawn its suit.
("Investigator drops bid for Cheney panel data." NYT, 2-9-03)

Cheney was CEO of Halliburton 1995-2000. Halliburton is a
giant: #1 for oil-field services, 5th largest military contractor, and
the biggest non-union employer in the USA. Cheney's years were
those in which Halliburton got some plush Middle East construction
contracts thanks to CEO Cheney (Sec. of Defense under **Bush I**—
when, not so incidentally, he told the oil industry he was against
toppling Hussein). Beginning in 1998, using two of Halliburton sub-
sidiaries (Dresser-Rand and Ingersoll-Dresser /Dresser was Gramp
Prescott's company) the company got more than $23 million for
rebuilding Saddam's oilfields. (IVINS)

Since then, there has been an ongoing federal inquiry concerning Halliburton's accounting practices—including the reporting of
$100 million in revenue (thus boosting its profits by that amount)
by counting unpaid cost-overruns as revenue. With the help of its
auditor—also a trusted auditor for two other rogue companies,
WorldCom and Enron—they got away with it. Molly Ivins concludes her report thus:

> No one is ever going to argue that Saddam Hussein is a
> good guy, but Dick Cheney is not the right man to make a case
> against him. I have never understood why the Washington press
> corps cannot remember anything longer than 10 minutes, but
> hearing Cheney denounce Saddam is truly "Give us a break
> time." (ibid.)

In mid-July 2002, the *Wall Street Journal* quotes from a video it obtained showing Cheney and six other execs of Halliburton applauding the pliant accounting firm. Here's Cheney: "One of the things I like that they do for us is that, in effect, I get good advice, if you will, from their people based upon how we're doing business and how we're operating, over and above the just sort of the normal by-the-books audit arrangement."

Or, as Bush II said when questioned about his illegal behavior with his Harken stock, "Auditing isn't always just black and white." Food for thought.

Despite that he was CEO, and presumably in charge when this all happened, "Cheney's aides won't say what he knew at Halliburton," was the headline of an AP story (7-2-02). Can't blame him. And then, a week or so later, a public interest group ("Judicial Watch," best-known for its suit against Bill Clinton) filed a lawsuit against Cheney and Halliburton, charging accounting fraud in order to enhance share prices. **Ari Fleischer** shrugged it off as "without merit." That takes care of that.

And since he has been V.P.? Well, in December, 2001, KBR, a corporate unit of Halliburton, although already the target of a criminal investigation, was granted a large "sweetheart" (i.e., cost-plus) contract by the Army (**Thomas White**, ex-Enron V.P., its Secretary) for "cleanup" work in Afghanistan. (Op-ed, NYT, 7-20-2) After the war "officially ended" in 2003, the announcements of contracts awarded began to flow: Halliburton and its largest subsidiary KBR, plus Bechtel, have been the main recipients of the largesse from the war. So that's (and this) is what friends are for: "U.S. Gives Bechtel A Major Contract in Rebuilding Iraq: Worth up to $680 million." (NYT, 4-18-03)

George Schultz, a main advisor of Bechtel's, was Reagan's Secretary of State, and Cheney Bush I's Secretary of Defense. We may be sure that our V.P. is in no way influenced by the $180,000 a year he receives from Halliburton 'til death does them part, and had nothing to with the Halliburton/KBR's getting a cost-plus contract amounting to $7 billion over two years (assured profits of almost $500 million) for Iraq. (D&S, "The Real Winners," by Tod Tavares, 7/8-03) Just one of those things.

But, anyway, think of all the taxes they had to pay for their good work; why, lots. According to their PR rep, they paid $15 million in 2002. Say, that's a lot; or is it? It's like you paying one percent. ("Guess how much Halliburton paid in taxes," *NYT*, 1-3-04)

The popular phrase used to characterize V.P.'s is "Just a heartbeat away from being President of the USA."

Cheney is a bit closer than that. In the *NYT* (2-1-03) ("Quiet Cheney accrues power and influence"), after remarking that Cheney had recently been pretty much invisible, the article goes on to say that

> He is hardly invisible to the president...; Bush has accepted almost all of Cheney's ideas: aggressive support for an attack on Iraq..., hard line against North Korea...., aggressive criticism of Yasser Arafat..., denunciation of the University of Michigan's race-conscious admissions policies..., almost everything but his call for every American to be vaccinated for smallpox.

See? Our President does have a mind of his own.
Or maybe he's just scared of having shots?

Fleishcher, Ari

Poor Ari! He's out to pasture (and money) now; he earned it. To have to confront the cameras almost every day to explain what his Boss has been doing; oomph! There is such a thing as body language; and Ari's puts one in mind of a faithful parent trying to explain to the teacher that his son shouldn't be punished for his poor work, "Because, you know, our little doggie ate his homework." Now that he's left that job, he can relax and pile up lots money with memoirs, as whatsisname (Scott McLellan?) takes his place and continues to try to persuade the press corps that 2+2 = 5. Oh, no! That was yesterday. Today 2+2 = 9.

O'Neill, Paul/Snow, John.

Very much the self-made businessman, and Secretary of the Treasury for less than two years until eased out, O'Neill earlier was **CEO** of Alcoa, the largest aluminum company in the world. He speaks the language of rugged individualistic capitalism as though there were no other language, and to say that he is a firm believer in "the magic of the market" and an enemy of governmental intervention would be a gross understatement.

How he saw his role in the government was aptly displayed

when, after a prolonged downswing in the stock market, and "with the stock market plunging and surveys depicting Americans as increasingly worried about the way the Bush administration is dealing with the economy and corporate fraud, Treasury Secretary O'Neill, the administration's main voice on economic issues, was in Kyrgystan. 'I'm constantly amazed that anybody cares what I do' /he stated from there, July 18, 2002/." (*NYT*, "Wall St. and Washington," 7-21-2)

Well, someone up there did care, if for the wrong reasons: just six months later, his resignation was asked for by the administration; O'Neill was not only uttering bloopers brushing away fears about nuclear energy (see **environment**) but bothering Wall Street with his insouciance concerning "the dollar." Not his problem; after all, it isn't as though he were Secretary of the Treasury.

And now that he isn't, unlike most of those who have sashayed in the Oval Office and left, Mr. O'Neill has found his way toward speaking plainly about everything from deficits to Iraq.

O'Neill's replacement was announced as John Snow, CEO of the giant rail transportation firm CSX. When his appointment was announced, an official is quoted as saying, "I thought Paul O'Neill wasn't suited to being Treasury secretary; he'd have been better off running a railroad. Now they've picked a man who ran a railroad." ("A Creditability Problem," by Paul Krugman, *NYT*, 1-28-03)

But Snow has been praised by <u>almost</u> one and all. The non-praises worry about his all-too-typical record as a CEO. Two small not so irregular "irregularities have thus far been noted: 1) A loan to him for CSX of $24.5 million to purchase CSX stock valued at $32 million, a loan that was forgiven (along with those of other execs) after the stock declined; and 2) he sold 120,000 shares of the company stock for $3.8 million just a few weeks before <u>his</u> company announced a weakening of its business outlook.

The response of the White House to these disclosures was, shall we say, not unforgiving: Re: (1) and (2) Ari Fleischer ("Bush Chooses Banker for Securities Agency, <u>IHT</u>, 10-2-02) said they were "legal, appropriate and fully disclosed," and "a common practice in business. Check.

However, it's just possible that Mr. Snow is beginning to worry a bit about what will happen to <u>him</u> if the financial system goes down the tubes on his watch. In the summer of 2003, when it began to appear that corporate pension plans were already on their descent to disaster, the good news is that Mr. Snow was realistic about it; the bad news is

> that the same ailment that felled the savings and loan institutions in 1989 /see **financialization**/ is now eating away at pension funds: a mismatching of assets and liabilities. And he noted that, like the savings and loan institutions, /private/ pensions are covered by a federal insurance agency. The presence of a federal insurer in such cases is sometimes said to promote riskier behavior. (*NYT*, "New Rules Urged to Avert Looming Pension Crisis," 7-28-03) (see **Social Security**)

A "mismatching of assets and liabilities" is a polite way of noting that corporate pension fund directors are treating those funds as though they were in Las Vegas.

Powell, Colin

In a world in which the USA is serving the role of global policeman, General Powell is the "good cop," working side by side with "bad cops" Cheney, Rumsfeld, Rice, and Rove, and their assistants, Abrams, Poindexter, and Reich. As Secretary of State, Powell serves as the voice of reason and decency for the USA in global conflicts; but, reminding of a somewhat earlier process, "the voice is the voice of Jacob, but the hand is the hand of Esau": Powell then goes along with what his unreasonable and indecent associates find necessary: not least or only for **Israel/Palestine** and **Iraq** now, but for **Vietnam** when he served there.

Nice guy he may be, but when it comes to messy controversies he seems to need someone to tell him "Don't just do something, stand there!" In his memoir, he states that when he went to fight in Vietnam in 1962 (first of two tours of duty), he was "standing on principle and conviction...and watched the foundations eroded by euphemisms, lies and self-deception." (POWELL) That memoir was written well <u>after</u> many of the top people in the administrations of Kennedy, Johnson, and Nixon administrations had acknowledged that those "euphemisms" were also conscious lies, as they prosecuted the war. (For details, see ELLSBERG, HALDEMAN) But Powell stayed with it to the last, evidently understanding neither then nor since that the euphemisms, circumlocutions, blatant lies and so on were <u>essential</u> to the beginning and the continuation of our invasion of Vietnam: There were <u>no</u> acceptable foundations or principles for that war.

Nor have there been for our cooperation with **Israel** in its ruthlessness in Palestine. But Powell has explicitly stated his support for Bush's "road map," a speech which, all sides agree, Sharon could have written. Under **Iraq** (which see), once more he served as the gentle good cop who, finally, looks the other way when the time comes.

Add to those non-Powell-like policies others of their ilk he has gone along with; namely, our withdrawal from the International Court, our refusal to make our expected $34 million contribution to the UN Population Fund's international family planning (presumably because of Chinese behavior; in fact in order to solidify the anti-abortion vote), and refusal to sign the Kyoto Treaty—after all that (with more doubtless not yet come to light), one is led to wonder if our good General Powell, for the first time in his years at the top will just <u>once</u> meaningfully object?

Powell made his stragegic position clear during the Gulf War: Don't go in unless there is no alternative;and then, only if you're doing so with massive and unbeatable force. Well, perhaps we can get out of Iraq in one stinking piece; the probabilities seem ominously high that Bush and his advisors, recognizing the combined domestic and global advantages of war, will not stop there. What then, hawk in dove's clothing?

Rice, Condoleezza

Probably the most intelligent of the Bush team—and that is not meant as a sly insult—Rice is probably also the best-informed, and, up to now, the only one to have an oil tanker named after. (In the 1980s, when she was an up-and-coming young prof at Stanford, I was asked to debate her on Reagan foreign policy. I did. She takes no prisoners; she won.)

It has been remarked that Rice has **Cold War** genes. Put her brains and those "genes" together in the Office of National Security Advisor in this administration, and then try to relax regarding the evolution of our foreign policy. One of her office's main creations was the policy of **preemption**. And let the devil take the hindmost. He's waiting with open arms.

It seems clear that Bush II sees as his most trusted advisors the highly visible Rice and the almost invisible Karl Robe. It was mentioned earlier that if Cheney can't re-run for medical reasons, Ashcroft would get the nod for Veep. Maybe not; the selection of Condi at the last minute would probably be literally breath-taking— and a way of picking up a helluva lot more votes than it would lose.

Rove, Karl

First, some ABCs about the White House, for any administration. There are always speech writers, and then there is always the right-hand man or woman, who helps out on how to <u>think</u>, how to <u>decide</u>, how to <u>look</u>, and <u>when</u>, and <u>where</u> on <u>what</u> and <u>why</u>: the political strategist. Wilson had his Colonel House, **FDR** his Harry Hopkins, **Nixon** his **Haldeman**.

Bush II started out with two: softie Karen Hughes and hard-nosed Karl Rove. Hughes left the Oval Office after less than two years, seemingly shell-shocked, saying she wanted more time with her family; my guess was she wanted less time with Rove and his "anything goes" strategy: especially wars.

<u>Anything</u> that will help Bush to maintain/increase his popularity and thus be re-elected is, per se, on target; well, <u>almost</u> anything: Rove clearly believes that the next election cannot be won by moderate domestic <u>or</u> moderate foreign policies. It's OK, indeed just fine, to use words like "compassionate," so long as they're not backed up by policies. Rove is evidently confident that the hardcore religious, economic, and militaristic right are also Bush's hardcore for victory.

In an era in which cynicism is rampant, Rove seems to wish to be its king. Though born in Colorado, after becoming a college student in Texas he became—like Connecticut-born Dubya—a Texan, with a very strong political bent that began with "College Republicans." His model and idol was Lee Atwater, a ruthless and sharp advisor to, among others, **Nixon**.

Rove's and Bush II's partnership began with the gubernatorial election in Texas; having been instrumental in Bush's victory, it was easy going for him to become central to the presidential campaign; now he's top gun in the White House. His tactics remind one of

Vince Lombardi's all-American wisecrack: "Winning isn't everything, it's the <u>only</u> thing."

Or maybe it wasn't a wisecrack. As though to confirm that view, during the midterm election campaign of 2002, one element had to do with demeaning Senator Max Cleland of Georgia. Cleland, you may remember, had lost both legs and one arm in Vietnam. In addition to branding Cleland as "unpatriotic," Rove used "a television ad showing Cleland along with pictures of Osama bin Laden and Saddam Hussein; a tactic used the preceding year against Sen. Tom Daschle, when, two months after 9/11 they showed a picture of him also next to Osama bin Laden. ("Elizabeth Drew, "The Enforcer," *NYRB*, 5-1-83.)

In a rarely granted interview reported in the *NYT* ("A portrait of Bush as 'little guy's' friend," 1-24-03), Rove had this (among other things) to say: "The elimination of taxes on stock dividends is aimed at the little guy." "Give /Bush/ a choice between Wall Street and Main Street, and he'll choose Main Street every time." And after describing Bush II as a "populist," he said, "I would suspect that Theodore Roosevelt would be standing up and applauding the president's initiative on, say, healthy forests."

In the entry on **environment**, it is shown that Bush's policy is to allow the logging companies to cut what they damn well please, in the name of preventing forest fires. That ranks right up there with **Reagan**'s wisecrack when he was Governor of California and there was a campaign to save the redwoods: "See one redwood," he said, "and you've seen 'em all." Life is just a cabaret.

Rove's single-minded ruthlessness would be dangerous enough advising a president with a mind of his own, some of which we have had for better and for worse: But this pudd'nhead? He responds to every business pressure and <u>loves</u> all militaristic pressure; is then presented with well-honed words for their delivery, and, having translated them into his version of cowboy, comes to see them as his own and comes on strong: Rove and Card, Rummy and Rice, Wolfowitz and Cheney sitting by, holding their breath and counting their chips, Powell saying his beads.

More to the point, as Drew concludes, "is that the brilliant visionary who, with manic energy, remade the politics of the state of Texas—recruiting candidates, throwing opponents on the defensive, raising vast amounts of money—is now trying to do the same thing to the nation." (ibid). And, so far, succeeding.

Rumsfeld, Donald

Like almost all of the Bushies, Rumsfeld is very rich. Neither for him nor the others did the riches arise from nowhere; beginning his career in the happy days of the **Reagan** administration, he also began his political and wealth careers through understanding and sympathizing with the needs of the top companies in finance, **oil**, and/or the **military-industrial complex**; almost always, that entail conflicts of interest in policy-making.

One of the rules of the game is that problematic assets must be sold or placed in a "blind trust" to avoid such conflicts. Setting aside the unlikelihood that the mere selling or "blinding" of such assets would totally—if at all—remove conflicts of interest, it is worth noting a) that when Rumsfeld announced he had sold $20.5 to $91 million in assets, b) he also complained that filling out the "exessively complex" forms cost him $60,000 in accounting fees. (*NYT*, 6-19-02) Aw.

In addition to passing the hat for him, allow me to express my solidarity with Rummy's great pain, by reminding him that at least those fees are tax-deductible? And, as a vet of World War II, may I add my rebuke to those of many others concerning your heartfelt comment about "draftees not having been of much value"? Like his P. and his V.P. and Rice, Rumsfeld has never been anywhere <u>near</u> a live bullet. How would <u>he</u> know? Or maybe he means the <u>dead</u> guys aren't of much value? That must be it.

But Rummy's hijinks with money and lowjinks with words are of minor interest; he is after all Secretary of War ('scuse me, I mean Defense), head of the Pentagon, in a moment when the USA is setting new records for belligerence and arrogance in the world. And at that very moment, this Secretary of Defense, it is generally recognized, has as his main counsel Richard Perle.

Perle, was Head of the Defense Policy Board until the revelations that he was taking in big money from big companies he was advising. The Board had been set up and financed by the Pentagon. Just as the National Security Council was set up as an early offspring of the **Cold War**, so was this private but influential Board; and in the very hawkish Bush administration, Perle is—still—seen as Chief Hawk. ("The Neocons in Power," Elizabeth Drew, <u>NYRB</u>, 6-12-03)

Even if Rumsfeld were being counseled by Jimmy Carter, it would be worrisome: but Perle? For him, it has become clear, we are not unilateral enough; not belligerent enough; not ambitious enough for whom we'll invade. For Perle and nukes, it's "use 'em or lose 'em." Dr. Strangelove lives.

White, Thomas

One of many corporate execs now sitting in seats of power in D.C., White may be able to take first prize for conflicts-of-interest, although it would be a close race. He is now Secretary of the Army. Before that he was a senior exec at—guess?—right you are, Enron. Although (as is true for any top job) when White signed on as Army Secretary he also pledged to divest his stake in Enron but— he just plain forgot: He retained stock options for 665,000 (that's right, 665 thousand) shares of Enron until early 2001, selling $12 <u>million</u> worth just before Enron went down the tubes. He claims that despite 70 telephone calls he had with his former colleagues, there was no inside info. Hard not to wonder what all that outside info might have been.

No problem for Bush II and Ari: In early March, Ari said that "President George W. Bush has confidence that Secretary White will comply with the ethics requirements of Armed Services Committee, and that he has complied with all executive branch ethics requirements as regards conflicts of interest." (<u>IHT</u>, 3-9-02, <u>NYT</u>, 4-2-2, op-ed, Paul Krugman) Say again?

All things considered, complying with executive branch ethics requirements is not a time-consuming task.

Wolfowitz, Paul

As it happens, I knew Wolfowitz when he was a little boy; his father was on the math faculty at Cornell when I was teaching econ there. Econ was then beginning its dreamy move toward mathematization, so math profs were often at lunch with us. His father was somewhere right of center and, in my oft-expressed judgment at those lunches, a fool.

But not a dangerous one. Little Paulie (as he was called) is.

Long a buddy of Richard Perle (noted above) he is <u>very</u> dangerous, the more so in an administration dominated by his ilk.

As Deputy Secretary of Defense in an already hawkish White House, Wolfowitz <u>almost</u> makes even Cheney, Rummy, Rice, and Perle seem just a bit dovish at times. Along with Perle, Paulie became close with Albert Wohlstetter at the U. of Chicago (then also Milton **Friedman**'s hangout), and did his Ph.D. under him. The relevance of that is that Wohlstetter was in effect the dean of the school that argues "that nuclear deterrence /isn't' sufficient—the US had to actually plan to fight a nuclear war in order to deter it." (Drew, ibid.)

And Paulie learned his lessons well. With his generous help, the Bush administration is pushing hard for developing teensy nukes—teensy enough to be used without anyone knowing or caring? Or doing likewise? (see **nuclear weapons**)

campaign financing (see lobbyists)

Camp X-Ray (see Latin America....Cuba)

capitalism

<u>Introduction</u> It would not be stretching things to say that almost all of this book is about the interacting dimensions of U.S. capitalism on the whole of our social existence, past and present; for, as will be expanded upon shortly, capitalism is neither merely nor even mostly an <u>economic</u> system; its needs to become a fully <u>social</u> system have accompanied capitalist development in all of its stages: it not only rules over what happens in a factory, but, consciously or not, its main movers do and must seek to rule over the entire social process <u>if</u> it is to have its way economically.

That has been so since capitalism's beginnings, and always more so up to the present. Capitalism could not have come into being as cause or consequence of economic activities alone; from its birth pangs centuries ago to now, capitalism has both utilized and transformed its surrounding world, <u>all</u> of our existence: geographic, cultural, political, social, **military**, <u>and</u> economic.

Constant revolutionizing of production, uninterrupted

disturbance of all social conditions, ever-lasting uncertainty and agitation distinguish the bourgeois epoch from all earlier ones. All fixed, fast-frozen relations, with their train of ancient and venerable prejudices and opinions, are swept away, all new-formed ones become antiquated before they can ossify. All that is solid melts into air, all that is holy is profaned, and man is at last compelled to face with sober senses his real conditions of life and his relations with his kind. ("Communist Manifesto," MARX/ENGELS, 1967)

The medieval era of trade may be seen as capitalism's womb, and the early modern period as its childhood. (TAWNEY, 1926, 1929); in 18th century Britain it moved toward the critical and shaping decades of "industrial revolution" (MANTOUX), and was thrust into today's "McWorld" (BARBER) by two sets of mutually transforming dynamics: the insatiable appetites of capital and the endlessly accelerating technological and related scientific developments.

In consequence, capitalism and capitalist nations gained always greater strengths; by now those strengths have come to entwine both suffocatingly and irreversibly in the realms noted above: geographic, cultural, political, military, and, of course, economic. Taken together, these always more potent strengths have brought all societies, all peoples, to the world's most fragile condition ever—taken there by an uncontrolled and uncontrollable interacting set of economic, political, and military honchos hell-bent on accumulating always more power and profits. In 1951, C. Wright MILLS used the term "power elite" to understand that process; but he was concerned only with the USA; since then, all analyses, like the capitalist system itself, must be "**globalized**."

In the pre-capitalist epochs of the early Mediterranean empires, there was never a "system"—Persian, Roman, Greek, or Holy Roman—that did not become imperial in its reach and, finally, destructive to others and of itself. But no earlier social system has been either as constructive or as destructive as that of contemporary capitalism; its ability to be both or, importantly, its inability not to be both, is the focus of what follows.

All of my previous writings have had understanding capitalism as their aim; for this discussion, it would be false modesty were I not to draw upon my most relevant work, Capitalism and Its Economics.

Other than saying that, I shall make no further specific references to that book in what follows.

The wheel of fortune spins... Capitalism has undeniably brought improvements in most realms of human existence in terms of comfort, education, health, productivity, and real income levels: "In most realms," but not for most people; from the beginning there has been quite another side. The components of that other and negative side have been ignored or brushed aside by mainstream opinion makers, assisted along the way by mainstream **economists**. They like to say that "a rising tide lifts all boats"—overlooking the fact that what "boats" have existed are usually tiny and swept under by the "tide," and, more importantly, most have never had boats. But "in the long run..." the economists murmur; in the "long run we're dead," history shouts.

As noted under **environment**, two centuries ago there were fewer than one billion people in the world, most of them with Hobbesian lives: "nasty, brutish and short." Now there are over six billion. One billion lives somewhere between comfort and luxury; four to five billion live those Hobbesian lives.

Still, has it not gotten better? No. About 50 years ago I wrote an article entitled "Two-thirds of the world," where the percentage referred the poor; since then, the world's population has more than doubled and the poor now amount to four-fifths of the world.

In this what the poet MERWIN has called a "culture up to its neck in shame," it seldom occurs to the fortunate one billion that it is the relationships between the **rich and the poor** that have been vital in creating and maintaining both in that condition: The "two tribes," (to adopt Disraeli's words during the late Industrial Revolution), one relatively small and very rich, the other enormous and very poor have come to be despite and because of "progress." In those centuries, the gap between them, far from narrowing, has increasingly widened to produce today's obscenities. (see **globalization**)

"Culture of shame?" Yes, if one recognizes that with all of our much-vaunted progress over the past two centuries, and assuming the majority of people in the earlier period were materially badly-off, there are now five times as many people badly off than in that earlier "underdeveloped" world. Moreover, the badly-off majority of the deep past—whatever the dangers and hardships of their existence—were, before the onset of industrial capitalism, very probably <u>better</u> fed, clothed, and housed than the billions of disinherited and desperate people today. (CHILDE)

Moreover, the poor are not only "poor" in their material existence; in order for the rich to become so materially—and whether deliberately or carelessly is here not at issue—it was essential to pulverize the long-standing mortar of social traditions that protected human beings from the worst within and between us.

Doubtless some of what was lost is better so; but much of what was also lost was—and would today be—of great value, not least when set against the culture of commercialism essential to capitalism. (MANDER, 1992) That "culture" has naturally taken on always more stridency as capitalism marches toward always greater dominance within and between countries. (BARBER)

As if that were not harm enough, capitalism's pressures for unremitting and heedless **economic growth** hold Mother Nature as permanent hostage—the flora and fauna, the air, the soil, and the water of the planet—doomed to a slow death by capital's voraciousness and the **"free market's"** heedlessness.

Grant for a moment that the foregoing arguments are reasonably valid; how is it then that capitalism as such is less resisted and more popular now than ever? The answer lies in the sources and uses of capitalist **power**. That power is manifested in many ways; here the focus will be on three main dimensions: the economic, the political, and the cultural. All these are strengthened over time by advances in **technology** which, in the realm of communications, shape thought and feeling (among other consequences). In doing so they have facilitated the processes by which our "cultural space" has become totally dominated by commercialism, and our politics by money. (ENSENZBERGER, HERMAN/MCCHESNEY, EWEN, SCHILLER /1976/)

In what follows, it is well to remember that the three dimensions of economic, political, and cultural examined are always interacting in processes of constant and mutual transformation.

<u>The political economy if capitalism.</u> When Adam SMITH wrote what later became the "Bible" of capitalism, in 1776, he was not an "economist," but a <u>political</u> economist—as were other

thinkers (notably David
Ricardo, John Stuart Mill and Karl Marx) for many decades.

Smith well understood and emphasized the crucial nature of the relationships between "economic" and "non-economic" affairs; indeed his focus was upon doing away with the political obstacles to economic development. It is said that Smith was the "father of economics"; not quite: he was the "father of political economy"; a father abandoned by sons who created the absurd to dangerous abstractions of "neoclassical" **economics**.

Smith would have seen as absurd their theorizing about economic life without explicit concern for the **power** relationships within which economies function, upon which they are dependent, and which they constantly seek to change in their favor. Smith himself emphasized those relationships, and sought to transform them. Thus he sought to get rid of the timeworn interventions of the State and of private powers in the functioning of the economy; interventions which he saw as effectively holding back the already apparent possibilities of an industrial technology in his time—constrained by State activities such as subsidies and protective tariffs, and the power of merchant and craft guilds. It was Smith who gave credence to arguments for **free markets,** or "laissez-faire," as it was termed in his day. However, though he sought the removal of traditional controls, he trusted neither the means nor the ends of businessmen, an order of men whose interest is never exactly the same with that of the public, who have generally an interest to deceive and even to oppress the public, and who accordingly have, upon many occasions, both deceived and oppressed it. (SMITH)

In one of history's ironic twists, it was the very success of Smith's arguments that undid the kind of competitive economy he proposed, for it soon meant that the rise of private business powers much exceeding those of the 18th century Crown of England. That power arose from the giant scales of production enabled by the unleashed technology, and which substituted business rivalry (see **big business**) for Smithian competition.

Nor is it unimportant that even when Smith's "invisible hand" has existed, where markets have not been controlled by either business or government, much economic, political, and cultural harm has been and is being done—to workers, to the environment, to the sociopolitical process. (see **competition, commodification, farmers**)

Smith wrote 1776 so he may be forgiven for not knowing the dire effects of his proposals; today's economists they merely have to pay attention, but don't. Instead, they are cheerleaders, concocting fancy abstractions concerning diverse "equilibria" while ignoring the ugly realities of a system that encourages and rewards the ruthless and ignores the consequences of heedless transactions—to whose dynamics we now turn.

The heart of the matter. The extraordinary momentum of capitalism has been and is driven by three systemic imperatives: expansion, exploitation, and oligarchic rule. Capitalism could only meet those imperatives in conjunction with the overlapping and mutually stimulating "geographic" processes of **colonialism, imperialism,** and today's **globalization,** for national economic expansion requires an always broadening and deepening geographic expansion.

Throughout its history, capitalist profitability has required, and capitalist rule has provided, ever-changing means and realms of exploitation at home and abroad. The central relationship making that possible is the ownership and control of productive property— that is, of the means of life. Because it is a small group that owns and a vast majority that does not, the resulting powerlessness of that majority requires them to work for wages under conditions set by the owner in order to survive. The social relations between those two classes have from the beginning been crucial to capitalism.

Given those relations, the strengths of each capitalist enterprise and nation and of global capitalism vary in accordance with the volume, the scope, and the rate of capital accumulation: that is, the expansion of the capitalist's capital. This refers to the driving force of capitalist development, its "ploughing back" of profits, the conversion of those profits into additional capital. Capitalists as such are not driven by the desire for higher consumption (although their consumption always has been much higher than others'), but by the passion for wealth per se. Marx put it succinctly in this famous passage:

> /The capitalist/ shares with the miser the passion for wealth as wealth. But that which in the miser is a mere idiosyncrasy, is, in the capitalist, the effect of the social mechanism of which he is but one of the wheels. Moreover, the development of capitalist production makes it constantly necessary to keep

increasing the amount of the capital in a given undertaking, and competition makes the immanent laws of capitalist production to be felt by each individual capitalist as external coercive laws. It compels him to keep constantly extending his capital, in order to preserve it, but extend it he cannot, except by means of progressive accumulation. /And later Marx adds:/ Accumulate! Accumulate! That is Moses and the Prophets. (MARX, 1867/1967a)

"Capital accumulation" may seen as the basis for <u>economic</u> expansion (or growth) which, as suggested above, has always been tightly interwoven with and dependent upon <u>geographic</u> expansion —most broadly and intensively in its current expression as "globalization," the current successor to **colonialism** and **imperialism**. The national and global forms of <u>expansion</u> taken together may be seen as capitalism's "heartbeat." They in turn depend upon capital's ability to <u>exploit</u> labor, the "muscles" of the capitalist process. Capital's "brain" resides in its ability to control of the uses of state power; here called oligarchic <u>rule</u>—the third "imperative."

But how can capitalism have its way in all that? Has it not been true that, with some time lag, political <u>democracy</u> comes into existence <u>with</u> capitalist development? Yes, but. "Democracy" has many shades of being, and what most of us would like to mean by democracy—the dispersal of power equally throughout societyóhas <u>never</u> been even approximated in the capitalist (or any other) era.

To the degree that the USA even moved <u>toward</u> such a goal, it was in the post-Civil War decades. In those years, say from 1865 to the outbreak of war in 1914, and setting aside the disenfranchisement of all women and of millions of black people in the South—<u>if</u> we set all that aside, how close then did the USA come to the goal of a genuine democracy?

Close enough to have generated what was called the "Populist Movement" in the last years of the century—a movement of farmers and workers protesting the iron hand of capital over their farms, their jobs, their country. Here and there a victory—for example, pressing successfully (finally) to have those in the **U.S. Senate** chosen by voters rather than by the placidly corrupt state legislatures. If it is democracy that is our focus, the Populist movement—itself racist—was self-debilitating in ignoring or, worse, supporting the <u>deepening</u> of **racism** and its excrescences in those very years

(WOODWARD, 1956, 1963, 1966) while, at the same time, almost all males (and some females) were distinctly hostile to women's struggles to get the vote.

That is, the Populists, principal fighters for democracy in the U.S. up to World War I, did not themselves believe in it; what they did believe in was the material improvement of their own lives within the ongoing domination of society by capital—with modest reforms.

In the 80s and 90s, the very years in which their struggle was strongest and was lost, government's role in the economy was increasing, very much as a by-product of industrialization. As that was happening, President Woodrow Wilson, seen as a relatively liberal president (and a onetime political science professor), observed in 1912 that "when the government becomes important, it becomes important to take control the government." (FAULKNER)

As though Wilson had spoken directly to them (or vice versa) capital's hold over local, state, and national governments increased apace in the early 20th century: and Washington, D.C., was transformed from a small corrupt town into a large corrupt city. It was the period dubbed by Mark Twain in the 1870s) as the Gilded Age; the historian Vernon Parrington, less gentle than Twain, called those years "the great barbecue."

The barbecue was presided over by what Matthew JOSEPHSON called "the robber barons." Their baronies were those of the railroads, the mines and forests, the copper and steel mills, the machine and machine tool industries, the emerging **oil** industry, and, of course, the financiers.

They robbed nature of resources, the farmers and workers of their proper rewards, and the society of its infant democracy; they bought mayors, governors, the Congress, the White House, whole political parties: Sound familiar? (see PHILLIPS, 1994, 2002).

And now? Now the **corruption** is deeper, and the resistance less; moreover, the means of gathering the spoils today are both more numerous and more penetrating, at home and abroad. They have been so sufficient as to be able very easily to reverse the steps toward democracy beginning in the 1930s and expanding through the 1960s. It was easy for them and costly to the society in the 19th century; it is easier and more dangerous today.

Again the question, how can it be? Because, to repeat, capitalism is a <u>social</u> system, its powers ubiquitous. To even begin to understand that requires a longer look the <u>intrinsic</u> political limitations of capitalist democracy, and its third imperative.

<u>Oligarchic rule</u>. In owning the means of life—land and its resources, machinery and tools, etc.—both in principle and in fact, capital thus controls what allows us to survive. With few exceptions, we either work for the owners or not at all. But not only is capital able to force people to produce more than they receive (about which more, under **exploitation** and **profits**)—but capitalists as a **class** also <u>rule</u>. Understanding that already in the mid-19th century, Marx and Engels put it this way (in <u>The German Ideology</u>):

> The ideas of the ruling class are in every epoch the ruling ideas; i.e., the class which is the ruling material force is at the same time its ruling intellectual force. (quoted in TUCKER; emphasis in original)

Years later, as he was preparing to write <u>Capital</u>, in the Preface to <u>A Contribution to the Critique of Political Economy</u> Marx added this:

> The mode of production in material life determines the social, political and intellectual processes in general. It is not the consciousness of men that determines their social being, but, on the contrary, their social being that determines their consciousness. (MARX/ENGELS, 1967)

Both of those observations were made in an era in which political democracy did not exist even formally in Britain, the then leading capitalist society; women did not have the right to vote, not more than 10 percent of men (those who owned property) could vote; and not much more than that percentage was literate. In those times the "material force of society" sufficed to the end of firm <u>rule</u> by a very small minority—as had always been so.

But by the time Marx died in 1883 (and Engels in the mid-1890s), all that had begun to change; in the ensuing century the pace of sped up and its constituent elements spread like wildfire into the sociopolitical process, dramatically in the recent past in the realms of industry, communications, and transportation and, as well in higher real per capita incomes.

Already in the early 1970s, Herbert SCHILLER, in his *The*

Mind Managers, and Hans ENSENZGERGER in his *The Consciousness Industry* were describing and analyzing unsettling developments that would soon become <u>fait accompli</u>. Because of the "mind management" these and related developments allowed to those in power, the damages done to political democracy have since gotten much worse; but, from the standpoint of those in power, much, much better. (**media, TV,** and see BARBER; MCCHESNEY)

The higher real capita incomes noted just above were part and parcel of two major developments led by U.S. capitalism from the late 1940s on: **consumerism** and the **Cold War**. The latter was critical for the sustained economic growth of two decades after the war; and the former was essential if there was to be an ever-expanding market for consumer—especially durable—goods; and the two developments were mutually reinforcing.

That "reinforcement constituted a "double-whammy" for capitalism: the air filled with ideas which, in attacking communism soon managed to tar with the same brush even New Deal-ish policies while creating tantalizing ads "to make people want what they don't need, and not to want what they do." (BARAN, 1969)

"Not to want what we need" is <u>not</u> to want national health insurance, not to want improved education and housing, not to want genuine security for the aged and disabled, "and to want what we don't need" points to consumer frenzy over new model cars, new model computers, new model clothes, new model watches...: always a <u>new</u> this or that, paid for with always more **debt** (which, for the average family now greatly exceeds average household income)—and Mom and Pop both work to pay it off.

All of that taken together has added up to a considerably more effective means of maintaining a docile labor force than guns and sticks ever did or could; more effective <u>and</u> more profitable. In the USA, it has meant the diminution of class consciousness from its always low levels, and the strengthening of an always growing tendency to the right.

Similarly, in what after the war had become the European social democracies, it has meant the withering away of previously vigorous left of center politics; so that, in Italy, for example, the Democratic Left (inheritors of the previous Communist Party of Italy) is now virtually indistinguishable from the Democratic Party of Clinton—itself now resembling the GOP of the 1970s. From capital's point of view, <u>that's</u> progress. MCCHESNEY (1999) summed it up in a nutshell:

> Capitalism benefits from having a formally democratic system, but capitalism works best when elites make most fundamental decisions and the bulk of the population is depoliticized.

With well under half of the eligible electorate now voting and, when those who do vote are voting for effectively bought and paid for candidates at all levels (**lobbyists/campaign finance**), "depoliticization" has become the reality, as relatively progressive groups—e.g., **unions**—have been enfeebled both quantitatively and qualitatively to the point of impotence.

It is difficult to disagree with the contention of PHILLIPS (2002) that the USA is now a "plutocratic" society—that is, one ruled by the moneyed class. Contemporary USA stands in sharp contrast with the quasi-plutocracies of the past, up to and including the 1920s, and in many ways and degrees. That is so even when we compare what is ruled over in 2003 with the same elements as of 1950:

1. The economy's productivity has risen explosively, and its production of goods and services has more than tripled.
2. Population has risen from about 150 million to almost 300 million.
3. The economic, military, cultural, and political power of the USA in the world has gone from substantial to omnipotent.
4. Communications and finance have gone from being important to dominant.
5. The giant national industrial corporations of 1950 have become, through <u>mergers and acquisitions</u>, combinations that cross sectors (industry, finance, communications, entertainment—see, e.g., GE) and national borders.
6. The two major political parties, distinguishable in many ways in the past, have never been anti-capitalist but have from time to time given some representation to the non-business sector; not only has that representation moved to the vanishing point, but the capitalist viewpoint has come to be the triad of **oil**, **finance**, and **milex**.

The data and analyses of **big business** support the following conclusion: Although U.S. democracy has always been crippled by racism and the overweening power of capital, its present concentrations of socioeconomic power are qualitatively greater than any previous era. Preposterous on the face of it though it may seem, it is not an exaggeration to contend that the vital decisions affecting and directing the life of the USA in its cultural, economic, military, and political realms are made by a maximum of 10-20,000 people; and that their composition is more from business than from any other sector, followed closely by entrenched political individuals and groups (themselves usually harmonious in ideas with the business world), the military, and social groups (most clearly, now, the Christian Right).

If the 10-20,000 number seems extreme, double it to 20-40,000, or triple it. Still a plutocracy, one that controls the social process in the USA—and, to a large extent, elsewhere. Although it is impossible to prove such numbers, a serious look at the realities of **power** in the USA makes it hard to posit anything more plausible. Just what the doctor ordered for capitalism. And why not? Capitalism is its own doctor.

carpet bombing (see collateral damage)

cars

What are cars for? Certainly not safe, fast, cheap and comfortable transportation. If that's what we want, we can have all of that, within and between cities and surrounding urban areas and nearby states, with an old-fashioned invention: surface and underground rail systems—plus some buses for short trips within and airplanes for long trips between cities and countries.

What we have instead is an insane plethora of cars, while much of our air travel would be better done with trains. There are more than two hundred million private automobiles in the country; a majority of families have two and many have three. In an article entitled "One Vehicle on the Road, Two Others in the Garage," (*NYT*, 8-30-2003) we learn that:

There are now more cars in American households than drivers; the average household has 1.75 but 1.90 "personal vehicles"—and 0.86 adult-sized bikes. Only 8 percent of households are without a car.

The main use of cars is not long trips, but short ones; 91 percent use cars to get to work; 5 percent used public transit; the rest walk (or somethin').

The cars have cost a fortune in dollars to buy and insure and maintain and replace and repay with interest, drive us half-mad with the slow and dangerous driving to our jobs, our shops, and our entertainment as, meanwhile, we poison the air we breathe and warm the atmosphere toward—perhaps already beyond—the point of danger. (Flash: In January, 2003 it was reported that the centuries' long attempt to sail all the way through the fabled Northwest Passage has been done, and will soon be practical—thanks to global warming and the ozone hole.)

Why are we so nuts about cars? Mort Sahl gave one answer, back in the Sixties: "How else can ya get sexual satisfaction?" He may have had something there; a fuller answer requires looking into the socioeconomy that brought us to this baleful condition; in doing so, it will also touch on Sahl's not so funny jest.

Automobiles were produced and popular already by the end of the 19th century, both in Europe and the USA: Rolls Royces, Stutz Bearcats..., to be driven by Prince William, Gatsby, young Rockefeller, and their friends.

As the 20th century began, believe it or not, there were thousands of auto producing companies, each producing those handcrafted cars by the hundreds, and costing in the thousands. They were rich men's toys, when a horse might be bought for $100, and a loaf of bread or a trolley across town cost 5 cents. (FAULKNER)

Along came Henry Ford, his Model-T, and mass production, in 1908. But his cars were built and designed to be used for farmers to bring their goods to market, at a time of dirt roads with lots of bumps and holes. So the cars had high axles and were identical: Henry liked to say "You can have any model you want as long as it's a T, and any color you want, as long as it's black." (SWARD) (After he got rich and powerful, a lot else that he did wasn't quite as amusing, like going to Germany and embracing Hitler.)

Mass production not only made it possible for humble farmers

to buy a car; it soon became clear that it could be a consumer product. But mass production meant, at the most, a dozen companies,
not thousands. Their numbers began to slim down to the hundreds
before World War I; by 1930, there were fewer than 40 in the USA;
and then there were three—with one now half-owned by the
Germans.

It wasn't just the numbers that were changing; it was the nature
of the industry. In turn that was a consequence of what "cars" had
come to stand for. The biggest qualitative jump was taken by **GM**, in
1923. It became the giant corporation it is now by buying up and
merging Chevrolet, Buick, Pontiac, and Cadillac; as was became
true of Chrysler (Plymouth, Chrysler, Dodge) and Ford (Lincoln and
Ford).

GM's mergers were not the first; its distinction was that it was
the first to innovate in several ways at once: the annual model
change, intensive advertising, and consumer credit (with the
General Motors Acceptance Corp.) For GM, you <u>could</u> have any
color you wanted and any <u>model</u> you wanted: already by the 60s,
there would be 65 or so different "models" of Chevys alone.

But no matter the color or the model, all the cars had one characteristic in common: they were all <u>planned</u> to wear out within three
years—what the industry came to call "planned (or deliberate) obsolescence," a strategy subsequently adopted by other durable consumer goods producers, most recently, computers.

And why not? 1) For the middle and higher incomes, to have a
new car every year or two was/is a matter of "class"/and or "status:"
2) those whose incomes require them to wait more than three years
are punished by having to make substantial repairs, a main source of
profits for the auto companies.

> Item: My wife is Italian; her brothers own an Italian parts
> manufacturing company that sells globally. When I asked why
> they sell everywhere but the USA, I was informed that "We
> guarantee our parts for ten years; the vehicle companies in the
> USA don't want them."

The transformation of the car industry in the early 'Twenties
coincided with the beginnings of **consumerism**, facilitated by commercial radio (the **TV** of its time), the modern film industry, and
modern advertising—a set of processes at whose <u>producing</u> center

stood cigarettes, ("Reach for Lucky instead of a sweet"), cars, and facial soap—and, on radio, the "soap opera."

Those and closely-related developments in the consumer goods industries and the techniques of public relations may be seen as the roots of the contemporary economy, its culture, and its politics—all of them, in their particular variations, utilizing one form or another of deception and "spin," what ENSENZBERGER called "the industrialization of consciousness."

In all the relevant areas—not least, tobacco, consumerism, and bought-and-paid for politics—grave harm has been done. Among the many harms done, and whose damages are on their way to becoming catastrophic, are the social and environmental damages consequent upon—one may say, <u>required by</u>—the "successful" functioning of the automobile industry and its deadly partner, the **oil** industry.

The degree of social insanity exemplified by the numbers and uses of cars is underscored when we note that already several decades ago it had been recognized that, especially in the richer countries, cars were doing us in; that if their numbers continued to increase at the industry's expressed need—three percent annually—we would move from serious trouble to the ineffable.

Have I mentioned SUVs? Now that the well-orchestrated craze of the 90s is on its feet and running, if you are a real "Amurrican"— or, indeed, Italian, German, Briton, or Japanese—you probably have one by now.

Plagued by the global excess capacity in the industry of the 80s (which persists) the carmakers discovered that the size, the presumed greater safety (of which more below), the machismo—the pizzazz!—of the SUV was THE way to increase sales and, even more, **profits**.

So—and what good business wouldn't?—they began to concentrate their advertising and their production on the "spurious virility vehicle" (Ex<u>cuse</u> me!, sports utility vehicle). Then, not to be outdone by their recent past, the industry now curses us and the environment with something that makes the SUVs seem like those small Japanese cars of the 1960s: the <u>Hummer</u>. As most will know— and some will cherish—it is a civilian copycat of the military Humvee.

And Hey! It must be good—at least for the car companies—cuz it costs a big bundle: $50,000 for the H2, which gets 10 mpg. But you can get something more intimidating in the H1, for only twice as much: $100,000 (whose mph is a secret). That'll show those tree hugging wimps what's what.

But that's not all that's wrong or, for the companies, right about them:

1) The SUVs are far bigger than the smaller cars; their already great and rising sales have reversed the hard-won trend toward smaller cars (now of yore);
2) Their gas mileage is half or less than what was recently typical;
3) They greatly increase air pollution;
4) They take up lots more space (especially when they are a second family car), and are harder to park and to see around;
5) The death rate in their more numerous accidents is higher, its victims mostly in smaller cars:

> Item: New data from the National Traffic Safety Administration /show that/ for every 100,000 crashes involving SUVs there are 205 deaths in the other vehicle...; there are 107 deaths between a minivan and another vehicle, and 77 for a mid-sized car.... The highly profitable SUVs continue to gain market share from passenger cars and minivans, despite increasingly vocal criticism of them on safety and fuel-consumption grounds. (NYT, 1-30-03, "U.S. weighs tightening safety rules on SUVs.")

The "U.S." might well tighten them more than they were planning, in light of this subsequent report from the same Safety Administration:

Regulators said last week /4/19/-03/ that 42,850 died in traffic-related deaths in 2002, the highest number since 1990..., the population of a small city like Chapel Hill. "If /there were/ a chemical attack that wiped out an entire city, think of the public outcry and outrage...," the Safety Chief said. Rollovers of SUVs and pickup trucks accounted for more than half of the 734-death increase from 2001 to 2002; rollovers account for a staggering 32 percent of automobile fatalities, more than 10,000 annually. ("SUVs Take a Hit, as Traffic Deaths Rise." NYT, 4-27-03)

Plus, 6) SUVs cost about twice as much and, oh yes, as noted earlier, they are "highly profitable," which, for the car companies is what's right about them: SUVs produce <u>three to four times</u> more unit profit: Ford's small car, the Escort, sold in 1998 for $13,100 and yielded a profit of $2,100; its Explorer SUV sold for $27,200 with a profit of $8,600. (*NYT*, 9-24-97, 4-16-98 2-4-99) Happily for the auto giants, SUVs now account for more than half of new private motor vehicles in the USA (and are coming into their own elsewhere, as well). You may have noted that the TV ads for these cars almost always showing them whizzing over rough country and around mountainous roads—even though the industry's own market research shows that only 13 percent of their use is outside cities.

As for their higher death rates, when asked about them, GM's Director of Advanced Technology responded by saying something which was, at least for me, as endearing as it was persuasive: "Even if you're driving a tank down the road, you could always be hit by a locomotive." (ibid.) Hey, Ma! Is there a locomotive store near us? There better be; by the summer of 2003, the next leap toward hell had become a tendency: "Pickups, Bigger and With Fancy Amenities, are Displacing Cars." (*NYT*, 7-31-03). Pickup trucks have long been fashionable for non-work purposes; the reference here is the LARGE pickup:

> An S.U.V. with an open back.... /that/ weighs three tons, empty, and has enough room in the cab for /driver/, wife, two children in car seats /with space left over/.... Sales of the largest pickups have been soaring for several years...; /now/ even Japanese automakers are rushing into the market...., which now accounts to 13.2 percent—one in eight—of all vehicles sold.

They cost $40,000 and up; their fatality rates are almost 50 percent higher than the <u>large</u> SUVs; their gas mileage is of course significantly lower and, like the SUVs, they cause more pollution than all other private vehicles. (ibid.) Is that crazy, or what?

Arnold Schwarzenegger, now Governor of California one day, pointedly drove a Humvee around the streets of L.A. in March, 2003, with no laws, just traffic jams, to slow him down. There's a man who has his finger on the pulse of the public.

So whaddya think President Bush might do about all the ways in which cars are adding to our woes? Right you are: In 2003, as global warming and air pollution and car accidents were all setting new records,

The Bush administration's economic plan would increase by 50 percent or more the deductions that small-business car owners can take immediately on their purchases of the biggest sports-utility vehicles and pickup trucks. The plan would mean that small businesses could immediately deduct the entire price of SUVs such as the Hummer H2 /modeled on the military Humvee/, the Lincoln Navigator /!/ and the Toyota Land Cruiser, even if the vehicles are loaded with every available option. (*NYT* 1-22—03, "Bush tax plan would foster big SUV sales.")

Honk if you need a gas mask.

Caspian Basin (see Asia...Afghanistan, oil)

CEOs

The corporate chief executive officers of our time are the latest mutation of what began with the hardy entrepreneurs of the industrial revolution. The first industrialists built a small cotton factory or iron mill up from scratch, using their own and one or more partner's funds. Almost without exception, they worked hard at a business whose ABC's they invented along the way, as they exploited workers to the utmost and worked hard themselves at capital accumulation. Marx called them "the Messrs. Moneybags."

The modern corporate form was not even born until the 1850s, independently and simultaneously in the UK and the USA, an outcome of the need for large-scale capital if there was to be large-scale production. In his *Absentee Ownership* (1923), Veblen described them as "Captains of Industry," to be superseded as the 20th century began with "Captains of Finance."

The latter were the "rugged individualists"—otherwise known as "robber barons" (JOSEPHSON), such as Carnegie (steel) and Rockefeller (oil). They were business buccaneers who became the chiefs of the new giant corporations (see **big business**) which they ran 'til death did them part.

Whatever in the way of criticism may and has been said of Carnegie, Rockefeller, Ford, Sloan, Pullman, Vanderbilt, Duke, Swift, Swope, and other "chiefs" from the late 19th through the early 20th centuries—all as aggressive and ruthless as the occasion allowed or demanded—they were at least part and parcel of the history and the functioning of their enterprises.

If there were exceptions to that rule in the past, in today's world the exceptions are the relatively few CEOs who have been rooted in the history and functioning of the empire over which they rule.

Most of today's CEOs may—or, more usually, may not—have any knowledge of the businesses over which they preside; experience in "their" industry is not a requirement. What is required are the ethics, the quickness, and the brutality of the tiger; it doesn't hurt to have a degree in Bus. Ad., for the schools of business today do more to teach the several scams of the **M&A** and stock options world than the art of "business administration."

There are of course CEOs (and Bus. Ad. schools) that do not fall under the foregoing or subsequent generalizations; or so they say. Just as they say there are both ethical and unethical lawyers, professors and doctors who are more or less devoted to learning and healing than to wheeling and dealing. However.

However, in the past decade or so, the always rising number of CEOs whose nefarious activities now daily come to light allows one to assume that here, as in other realms of crime—legalized or not—where there's smoke there's fire; or, to change the metaphor, for every one caught in the spotlight, countless others are running loose, howling in the night.

Of the criminals, more later. But the larger scandals of the CEOs are not only those of what are seen as crimes; they are matters whose ends and means and their effects should be seen that way.

Consider first the "effects" consisting of how much CEOs receive, and for what—keeping in mind the same questions for those who are actually producing useful goods and services. The following quote covers some of that ground. In 1960, U.S. CEOs averaged $190,000 a year, 40 times that of the average factory worker. Now?

> CEO pay now stands at 531 times the pay of the average blue collar worker, according to "Executive Excess 2001," the eighth annual CEO compensation survey issued by the Institute for Policy Studies and United for a Fair Economy. CEO salaries jumped an average 571 percent between 1900 and 2000 /years of low inflation/... /and/ the pay hikes continued to rise in 2000 even while the S&P 500 dropped 10 percent.... CEOs of firms that laid off 1,000 or more workers in 2000 earned about 80 percent more, on average, than executives at 365 other top firms.

The job-cutting corporate leaders earned an average $23.7 million in total compensation in 2000, compared to an average $13.1 million earned by executives as a whole. (MM, 10/01)

Those are the figures for the <u>average</u> CEO; the figures for those CEOs of companies presently under investigation for "cooking the books" "earned 70 percent <u>more</u> from 1999 to 2001 than the <u>average</u> CEO at large companies," according to a separate report released by the Institute for Policy Studies and United for a Fair Economy. ("Cooked Books earned CEOs big dough," WP, 8-28-02)

And, mind you, the foregoing incomes, whether for the honest or the dishonest, do not include the numerous and costly free "perks" of the officers and directors of <u>most</u> of the big companies: the best health and life insurance, free air and auto travel (often in their own but company-paid-for planes and limos), country club, luxurious vacations for self and family—all of which would add a mill or so on their incomes, but not taxable.

Among the most egregious of such <u>known</u> goings-on were those of Dennis Kozlowski and Chief Financial Officer Mark Swartz, the top guys at Tyco. While busily looting the company (and its stockholders and workers) of $130 million, they received apartments as perks from the company. Dennis had one on 5th Avenue, Mark one on E. 85th Street, with two whole floors. On his expense account, Dennis listed a $6,000 shower curtain and a $15,000 umbrella stand; Tyco listed Mark's place at $15.9 million, but could only get $9.25 mill when they sold it to the CEO of Sony Music in November. (NYT, 11-30-02, "Judge Approves Tyco Apartment Sale.")

Shocking! But no surprise there. Also shocking, but not surprising: "Rightly or wrongly, the cutting of staff has tended to give a boost to a company's stock..., It's one of the ways that Wall Street evaluates top executive's performance." Thus spake Charles Peck, compensation specialist at the Conference Board, a business research and networking organization. (SFC, 9-2-01, "Staff Cuts Help Stock Prices.")

From the beginning of their reign, the early 1980s, today's CEOs have received gargantuan salaries and other forms of compensation—most famously, stock options. In that the CEO not only dominates the company, but also its Board of Directors (which oversees compensation), it is not strange that as the CEO phenomenon has spread, their incomes have multiplied. Thus, in 1981, the top ten among them were paid an average of $3.5 million a year. That's high; but they went up six-fold by 1988, to $19.3 million. Stunning! Except that by 2000 their average annual pay had skyrocketed to— get this!—$154 million. (PHILLIPS, 2002) Does that mean that they had all increased their efforts and their companies' results by over 4,000 percent? Or what?

The answer to that would have many parts to it—eager or reluctant cooperation from Directors, manipulation of stock option grants, inside info, you name it—but sitting at the heart of any set of explanations would have to be what has happened to corporate USA, what it sees as its "business" and how and for what it is run— and by and for whom.

There are no soothing answers to that set of questions. Nor are the answers to be found solely within the business world; one must examine what has been done in (at least) the past 20 years or so to **deregulate** the various sectors of the economy, whether in energy, or finance, in air transport, whatever. That shifts a good part of the responsibility over into the political world; in turn, that takes us to the realms of **campaign finance** and **lobbyists,** of which (as will be seen), there are presently 90,000 or more lobbyists functioning in D.C. alone, with each state and city also swimming in that dirty pool. And then there are the bought and paid for **media** (themselves part of big business), with their own bigtime CEOs, and their part in bewitching, bewildering but not much bothering the public. (PHILLIPS, 1994)

Much of the nervousness now besetting the financial sector (and those whose fates depend upon it, wholly or in part) has do with a second large and growing scandal intimately linked to the CEO phenomenon, that concerning stock options—their importance, how they are "handled," and their increasingly harmful consequences. Some ABCs: In addition to their usually 7-figure salaries, CEOs are given stocks with the option of holding on to them until the moment they deem most profitable to themselves. This presumably gives the CEO an added incentive to act in such a manner as to enhance the price of the company's stock, an impolite person might be led to think.

Recent history has also shown that "the manner" in which all too many CEOs have acted combines illegality and immorality with deception and swindle, by finding illicit and misleading ways of stating profits. So common is this that market "analysts" have found commonly used euphemisms to describe it: "backing in," and "tweaking numbers." Sounds harmless. But what it refers to is what companies and market analysts do after making the almost required optimistic quarterly forecasts of profits (in order to raise or maintain stock prices) is this: what they do is "... they work backwards, starting with the profit **"investors"** are expecting and manipulating sales and expenses in order to make sure the numbers come." This "tweaking of numbers" is not only common, "one hedge fund manager recently compiled a list of 20 tactics that can be used to make sales or profits better than they are." (*NYT*, 6-29-02)

Such techniques, which my mother taught me to call "lying," are much enhanced by bringing distinguished accounting firms (such as Arthur Andersen, LLP) into the act, firms whose duty is presumed to be to serve the wellbeing of the shareholders, the company, and the public—not a CEO.

Alas! Too often, we now know, the accounting companies are "in the act" as really expert "tweakers," and become mutual gainers from deception. So profits are deceptively stated, stock prices rise as the "investing public" (i.e., speculators) jump aboard, and at some point when the truth is soon to come out, the CEOs sells their stock (as do the accountants), and down the tubes it all goes. Enron is only the best known and most spectacular of these criminal activities. Just think how guilty they must feel, especially Ken de Lay, Bush I's best pal (now of yore).

Since the energy chaos produced by them, we have learned a great deal about the gambling casino the relevant CEOs made of the energy crisis, with the public the losers. There is much yet to learn, but one of its cases settled in July of 2003 reveals who some of the "respectables" were in that disaster: "A Warning Shot to Banks on Role in Others' Fraud; Two Big Banks to Pay $300 million to Settle Enron Case"; "Banking Giants Further Tangle the Enron Cases." (*NYT*, 7-29, 7-30-03)

The "two big banks" are very big, indeed they are the biggest: J.P. Morgan Chase and Citigroup. All they did was "help Enron to defraud investors," helping Enron to manipulate its financial statements and mislead investors. The $300 million will be doled out by the SEC as a partial recompense to the defrauded investors. That still leaves an ongoing mess, with still further cases involving Enron and the banks, likely to go on for many more years.

In making the settlement with the SEC, the banks did not admit guilt; what they did do, however, was pretty smart: "This money is going to do double duty," said a Columbia University law professor, "it settles all charges and is going to go as a credit against the private class action." (ibid., 7-29) Smart.

But just as the Enron fiasco would have been impossible without the **deregulation** that went from fire to flood from the Reagan years onward, so it is that in the financial sector that some deregulation has made it not only easier but downright simple for swindle to become the name of the game.

Meanwhile, another game in the corporate town: In days now long gone, the fate of a corporate boss was expected to rise and fall with the doings of his company. Silly stuff, as today's CEOs and their presumed bosses—"directors"—are concerned. For some time now a trend has been underway whose name seems to be "It depends"— depends, that is, upon CEOs' skills at persuading a Board to look the other way when "their" company goes into the red.

About half of them have succeeded in doing just that. In a feature article entitled "Did Pay Incentives Cut Both Ways?" (*NYT*, 4-7-02), David Leonhardt writes "...as profits fell for the typical company /in 2001/ by 35 percent..., pay for the typical CEO continued to climb: the median compensation rose 7 percent... to $9.1 million... in a pay survey of 200 large companies." (my emphasis)

On the same page, in a related article—"Tell the Good News. Then Cash in."— we are told that "The profits were an illusion. The multi-million dollar rewards for executives were real. Over the last few years, executives at some companies released inaccurate earnings statements and, before correcting them, sold large amounts of stock at inflated prices... It happened at major technology companies like Oracle..., Sun Microsystems..., Guess..., Xerox..., Dollar General..., Enron... and Global Crossing."

Your stomach is probably as weak as mine, so let's call a halt to these proceedings—but not without this note, having to do, as it does, with the man who one day could be sitting behind that desk in the Oval Office:

> During Vice President Dick **Cheney's** tenure as its CEO, the Halliburton /oil industry/ Corporation altered its accounting policies so it could report as revenue more than $100 million in disputed costs on big construction projects, public filings by the company show. Halliburton did not disclose the change to investors for over a year. At the time of the change—which was approved by Arthur Andersen LLP—Halliburton was suffering big losses on some of its long-term contracts.... Two former executives of Dresser Industries /once owned by Bush II's grandpa/, which merged with Halliburton in 1998, said that they concluded after the merger that Halliburton had instituted aggressive accounting practices to obscure its losses. (*NYT*, 5-22-02)

Lies, all lies.

As the Enron, Global Crossing, WorldCom, Tyco, et al., scandals went on, and despite the administration's insistence that no new laws are needed to reform U.S. corporations, Congress overwhelmingly passed new laws, asserting that all those evil corporate doings are things of the past. The laws were signed by Bush, but before the ink had dried, as Paul Krugman put it,

> The administration began issuing 'guidance' to federal prosecutors that will undermine the law's intent on whistleblower protection, document shredding and more.... Now the administration is sounding the all clear—we've passed a bill, we've arrested five people, it's all over." (*NYT*, 8-13-02)

With such enemies, the shady CEOs don't need any friends.

Postscript #1. "DaimlerChrysler doubles pay for 13 board members" (*IHT*, 2-27-03):

> Compensation for the 13 top executives totaled $54.7 million in 2002, up from $22 million in 2001... Such a steep increase could further infuriate shareholders /and the thousands of laid-off workers?/ who have been displeased with the sharp loss in the value of their shares over the last couple of years.

The board members so enriched—$4 million a year per capita—were of course themselves part of the decision-making apparatus. But let's not be too hasty; for one thing, they have to meet once a month (which couldn't help their golf game) and without their sagacity, the shareholders and workers might have been even worse off than they were. Who are we to judge? Postscript #2. This one has to do with American Airlines. As it was facing bankruptcy in early

2003, it asked its unions to vote for a voluntary cut in wages and benefits totaling $1.62 <u>billion</u>. After much turmoil, in early April they voted and agreed to the cuts. That was Act I. Act II occurred

> when workers learned that Mr. Carty /CEO/ had hid from union leaders <u>new</u> executive benefits while he was negotiating for /the workers/ deep concessions. The benefits—so-called retention benefits paid to seven executives <u>and</u> a $41 million pretax payment to a protected executive pension trust fund— had been approved... last year but not disclosed until the company made a securities filing late on April 15, just <u>after</u> the unions... had voted. ("A Taut, Last-Minute Stretch to Save an Airline." *NYT*, 4-27-02) (emphasis added)

As an economist, I provide what I think must have been the reasoning of the Board of Directors: "Look here, sure these execs allowed American to plunge toward bankruptcy. Solution? Looks like we haven't been paying them enough: Hand-em $5-6 million more apiece and better pensions, and just you watch their performance improve!" And it was a done deal. Next question?

Chicago, 1968

All hell broke loose in Chicago in the week of August 25, 1968, while the Democratic Party was holding its convention to select its candidate to replace **Lyndon Johnson**. It was a moment when not one, but several festering sores broke open; in doing so, they caused still more infections.

Nowadays, and setting **Vietnam** aside, reminiscences of the Sixties refer most always and lovingly to the Beatles and Woodstock, to the inspirational Martin Luther King and the Selma March—if also, almost as second thoughts, to the killing field of Kent State, the beatings in Chicago in '68, the mass jailings of "the Battle of the Pentagon" in '69, the assassinations of King and of both JFK and Bobby Kennedy, and, with the election of **Nixon**, the beginnings of a long swing to the Right.

The good side of all that was its combination of a growing liveliness and attentiveness with a sense of solidarity, a noticeable break from the stuffiness of the Fifties. In turn, the Sixties came to produce not just the good times and the flower children, but struggles: against **racism**, against **poverty**, and against the war in **Vietnam**. A nation cannot—or should not—be as prosperous and self-satisfied as the USA was as that decade began and continue to hide its tens of millions of poor from itself, or its riches from those who are poor; nor can it plausibly claim to be fighting for freedom 10,000 miles away while millions of its own people are oppressed at home, largely unable to vote, and subject still—if only rarely by then—to being lynched.

It seems relevant (and, I hope, not merely vain) to quote a paragraph from a Sixties article of mine, written while teaching in Italy and frustrated by my distance from the tumult and shouting at home: Now I can see it as my first stirrings toward this book. It was entitled "An End to Alibis: America Fouls Its Dream," and it concluded by commenting on what was coming to be called the government's "credibility gap":

> A credibility gap there is, between the Administration's words and the facts. The more important gap, however, is between the image that Americans like to have of their society, and what Americans work for and do, what their society is. This is not to say that, in terms of what is done, America is worse than other societies, Americans worse than other peoples; our evil consists of believing that we are better than others—and it consists as well of our being able to be so much better than we are, of our being able in fact to take our image towards reality. The gap between what Americans are in practice, and what with our ideals and our resources we should be, is as a Grand Canyon that separates actuality from possibility. President Johnson indeed represents us; like us, he cannot face—perhaps cannot comprehend—the truth. But Johnson's Gap is a line scratched in the sand; we the people have allowed the earth to open. It is this gap, this chasm between reality and ideal, that defines the American crisis. It is this gap into which "America!" slides. (DOWD, 1967)

"Chicago, 1968" lasted a whole week; as one of the organizers of the main demonstration, I was there for all of it. It had its wonderful moments even as the horror descended—as when thousands gathered here and there in parks to sing and talk and plan; as when, on "Black Wednesday," Allen Ginsberg sat on the edge of the stage in the park where and while those same thousands were being beaten by hundreds of cops; sat there, calmly, almost serenely, chanting "Om, Om, Om." It helped; a little.

But most of its moments combined horror with terror with disgust: <u>Item</u>: Presidential hopeful Eugene McCarthy being manhandled in the convention hall. <u>Item</u>: Tear gas and batons and tear-gas, again and again—men, women, and children, at least one grandmother, beaten and piled into police trucks. <u>Item</u>: Once on that Wednesday night, as the carnage went on and on, I took a few minutes to go around the block to catch my breath. As I turned back toward the chaos once more, several police wagons drew up. Out of each of them piled 50 or so Chicago cops. After arranging themselves into platoon formation, they began to march in place and then to jog toward the immense crowd, chanting in unison: Kill! Kill! Kill! Chicago's finest; "the Blue Meanies" of whom the Beatles sang.

In retrospect it seems that Chicago broke the back of the resistance, or, if not its back, its morale. That kind of violence from the authorities—and <u>the</u> authority in Chicago was "liberal" Mayor Daley—was a shock whose waves did not cease for years to come. One of those waves gave momentum to what came to be the strong rightward movement now in power in the USA. Another wave was that of a few young people who, giving up on peaceful protest, turned to even more hopeless and ultimately self-destructive means.

Still another consequence was the recognition by some that the hill we were seeking to climb was steeper and more treacherous than we had thought; all the more important, then, to grit our teeth and continue—lest the nightmare of "Chicago, 1968" completely displace the dream of "America!". The hill is steeper even now; time for us to get more serious, more involved.

CIA

Like the **FBI**, the CIA had a reasonably worthy beginning; and both went awry. The FBI's original mission was to keep interstate crime and espionage down. As noted under **Cold War** and **Vietnam,** the CIA began during World War II as the OSS (Office of Strategic Services); its mission included working behind Japanese lines in **Vietnam** (in part for air-sea rescue, in which I was involved), and its strategic bombing analyses in Europe. The latter, it is worth reminding, showed that the massive fire-bombing that burned Dresden to the ground, far from "intimidating" the enemy," strengthened

Germans' resolve—as the German "Battle of Britain" did for the British; and as our even more massive bombing of the Vietnamese would for the Vietnamese, years later. Had we asked ourselves what our reaction would be to savage bombing, might we not have guessed as much?

The FBI began to betray its legislated mission early, when it came under the direction of **J. Edgar Hoover** in the early 1920s. As noted in the discussion of his career, he ruled over the agency for half a century, until 1972; in the process he made it into an enemy of the freedoms presumably cherished in the USA. He was aided and abetted by a Congress whose members he regularly blackmailed in order to gain their permanent support. (Which leaves one to wonder what they were so anxious to hide.)

As the **Cold War** gained speed in 1947, the OSS had its mission as well as its name changed; in effect, it became Hoover's FBI abroad. But more than that. All that Hoover ever did was to use his powers to intimidate individuals and, when he chose to, to destroy their careers—in the process doing much harm to contaminate entertainment, education, politics, and weaken unions.

The CIA went—and goes—beyond that, with those actions which had dire effects abroad, as well at home.

Here, only some highlights will be noted. Skeptical and interested readers who wish to pursue further (or find substantiation for what follows) may consult one or more of the many works listed in the Bibliography, under BLUM, CAUTE, FREELAND, HALPERIN, KOFSKY, LEFFLER, SHULTZ, and WITTNER; and a compact summary of the consequences of the dirty doings of both FBI and CIA in LEBOW and STEIN's *We All Lost the Cold War*. Such books make one's head spin, and one's stomach to churn.

The CIA's publicly defined responsibilities were to gather information relevant to the national security of the USA. In the 20th century, that may be seen as a necessary evil for nations; so be it. It is what the CIA has done (and doubtless continues to do) that is neither publicly acknowledged nor acceptable that is the concern here and of the books just noted.

In our "**A to Zs,**" there are four groups of geographic regions— **Africa, Asia, Europe,** and the **Middle East**; each examines a number of countries. To one degree or another, the CIA has operated in all those countries, and has done so covertly in ways ranging from illegitimate to criminal; often as not they have bumbled and gotten things wrong, perhaps fortunately so. (BLUM)

What "things"? Item: The Cuban "Bay of Pigs" invasion by the U.S. in 1961. Getting their information entirely from anti-Castro Cubans, the CIA assured Eisenhower that an invasion of U.S. Cubans (trained by us in **Guatemala**) Cubans would trigger a counter-revolution that would overthrow Castro. JFK inherited the plan and reluctantly went ahead with it. Its results? Many of "our Cubans" were killed, many more jailed and, if anything, anti-Americanism was fueled.

Item: Using the same kind of reasoning (and allies) in **Vietnam**, the CIA repeatedly provided information indicating that the people of Vietnam, if armed sufficiently and given the opportunity, would fight on until the Viet Minh were defeated. Instead, the Viet Minh (in the North) became ever more potent militarily and kept us on the defensive while, at the same time, U.S. control over the Saigon government and its unrelenting and murderous raids against the civilian population ultimately generated the independent and separate "National Liberation Front" (derisively called "Viet Cong"). (KAHIN; YOUNG)

Item: In **Chile**, the CIA, working with the **Nixon** and **Kissinger** White House (see HERSH; BLUM), made the 1973 coup d'etat of Pinochet possible, through its provision of financial and military aid and a disinformational propaganda campaign—entailing the murder of at least 40,000 Chileans.

Item: On another level, it was the CIA during the Cold War which continually provided "intelligence" indicating that the **USSR** was either stronger or weaker than it actually was. A way of understanding its systematic incapacity is provided by the fact that the CIA was even more surprised by the fall of the USSR than the general public: They had disinformed themselves.

The complaint of all the foregoing is not merely that the CIA failed, nor that its admitted annual $30 billion budget wasted our taxes. It is rather that the USA has seen fit to have such an agency; that the CIA has been paid to develop programs under a flag that says "The End Just Justifies the Means." They do not, not in the "America!" we have been taught to admire: The use of murderous means (including torture and murder) transforms the nation using them, leaving no distinctions between ourselves and our enemies. (POWERS)

class

Walk down any crowded street in the USA and ask 100 adults at random, "What's your class?" and the answers—if any—would fall into something like the following groups:

1. Middle class: 90 percent.
2. Rich: 1 percent.
3. Working class: 5 percent (maybe).
4. "Beat it!": the rest.

Whereas, narrowly-defined,

> Sixty-two percent of the labor force in the United States are working-class people... who do not have much control or authority over the pace or the content of the work and they're not a supervisor and they're not the boss...: white-collar workers, like bank clerks or cashiers...; blue-collar workers and construction and manufacturing. (ZWEIG)

In terms of "not having much control or authority over the pace or content of their work," if we add in most teachers, nurses, bookkeepers, airline attendants, bus drivers, and many others who are in some unpleasant degree under someone's **power** who makes **profits** from others' work, and the percentage would probably be closer to 80 percent. (TERKEL, 1974; MILLS, 1956; SCHOR, 1991; EHRENREICH /2001/)

All the percentages noted above are arguable; what is not is that under **capitalism**, almost all people are working directly or indirectly for those who own and control the means of production, that is, the means of life: in this socioeconomic system there is no other way to survive.

But few who "work for a living" in the USA see themselves as members of a working "class," as has been shown in many studies. Among the most recent are those noted in the *NYT*, 1-20-03: "An elusive social class system in a less prosperous America":

Item: "... many people believe they have the chance to occupy the rich end of the income scale—despite the ever-widening income gap."

Item: "The new reality is a society in which one-fifth of Americans are privileged, with job security, high wages, and strong skills. The other 80 percent belong to a 'new working class.../which/ lacks the same security and high wages."

The USA is close to unique in its virtual absence of class-consciousness—at the bottom, that is; as will be noted later, those on top are <u>very</u> class-conscious. Those who work for wages here are that way, as with so much else, as a product of our unique history. Although we inherited the constituent social elements of a two-class system from England, our subsequent history, with its unparalleled natural resources and never-ending waves of pliant immigrants, enabled our capitalist class to function with economic ease and relatively little worker resistance. (LAPHAM) A brief survey of those processes follows.

The relevant basis for capitalist development was first solidly established in England by the end of the 18th century; it consisted of the hundreds of thousands of families which, in the past, had made their <u>living</u> off the land: the much-lauded "proud yeomanry" of England, freed over the preceding centuries from the serfdom of the medieval era.

The process that forced them off the land was called "the enclosure movement." Its guiding rationale was enhanced efficiency in agriculture. As that movement was reaching its peak in the late 18th century, the poet Oliver GOLDSMITH, in his celebrated epic poem "The Deserted Village," saw clearly what was on its way:

Ill fares the land, to hastening ills a prey,
Where wealth accumulates, and men decay:
Princes and lords may flourish, or may fade;
A breath can make them, as a breath has made;
But a bold peasantry, their country's pride,
When once destroyed, can never be supplied.

Nor has it been again "supplied." Instead, in one variation or another, that process has been repeated over and over again in the poorer countries—in the 19th century, in the 20th century and, more ferociously than ever, in today's processes of **globalization**.

Thus was created the modern working class, a class which,

because propertyless, was economically and politically powerless, easy to **exploit**. They came to be called the <u>proletariat</u>. (HOBS-BAWM, 1964, 1984)

In the early 19th century, with the beginnings of the factory system and the great expansion of coal mining (to fuel the vital steam engines in factories, trains, and ships), that new working class provided a class of wage slaves; composed men, women and children.

They worked not only in the mills for at least 12 hours a day (with no more one 30-minute break, for "lunch"); also and even more dreadfully for women children, they worked in the mines. Why in the mines? Because they are smaller than men, so the expensive mining tunnels could be smaller in diameter. Governmental reports of the period are filled with discussions of women and children on their knees, pulling the rough equivalent of today's toy wagons, of girls and women mistreated and assaulted; and of many women and children who, once at work in the mines, never again ascended from them to the light. One measure of the human costs of these process-es was its impact on health and life as the new working class was uti-lized:

> The life-span of the average working person between 1821 and 1851 <u>fell</u>: In 1821, 37 percent died by age 19, and 70 per-cent by age 44; bad enough already. But thirty years later, 1851, 46 percent died by age 19, and 78 percent by age 44. (HOBS-BAWM, 1968)

In the USA, and here setting aside the meanings of **slavery** for health and life, the working class in capitalism's shaping years—that is, roughly, 1815-1915—increased greatly through immigration over that entire period, and was very cheap indeed: a) by far the largest percentage of immigrants were 15 or over; that is, their socially cost-ly and relatively "non-productive years" were "paid for" in their home country; b) simply to <u>be</u> an immigrant meant some combina-tion of eagerness, pliability and optimism, resulting in a hard-work-ing and not only largely non-militant working class, but one that was also and everywhere weakened by **racism**. (HANDLIN)

For those and other reasons (see **capitalism**), the U.S. working class was and is, among all capitalist nations, one in which "class-consciousness" is weakest. That was so throughout the 19th century, with some moments of real or seeming exception: "real" as regards the International Workers of the World (the IWW), "seeming" as regards the Populist and trade union movements; the latter were both were seeking reforms <u>within</u> the capitalist system, rather than to bring about a truly democratic society.

A seeming exception was the period from the 1930s through the 1960s. But that again was constituted by a series of relatively successful reforms which, however, have been weakened or reversed—even though the reforms had allowed the system to work more smoothly.

Given the economic platform of the **Cold War**, that "smoothness" emerged because the earlier reforms increased the purchasing power of a substantial majority of the working class, directly and indirectly. That in turn meant **consumerism**, now the main basis for contemporary economic growth—which, however, also served to reduce the already low levels of class-consciousness.

In so doing, it also facilitated the aims of what DU BOFF aptly called "the corporate counter-attack" that took hold in the late 1970s and which has flourished ever since. Its successes may be measured in the significant weakening of the membership and the political clout of **unions**, and in the synchronous reduction of the "social wage" (health care, pensions, housing, education). That deterioration was given its greatest boost in the **Reagan** years when **downsizing and outsourcing** became common; since then, not only the Republicans but the Democrats are either against or weak-kneed supporters of the several components of the "social wage."

It needs adding that the social wage is not merely a matter of everybody being able to have a decent chance of meeting their basic needs in the realms of education, housing, and health care; also vital is the loss of dignity when those needs are <u>not</u> met—discussed at some length by SENNETT/COBB in their excellent study, *The Hidden Injuries of Class*.

Such matters have seldom been taken seriously in the USA. The steps made in that direction have always been hesitant; now they are more so. Nowadays, the **Bush II** administration finds it easy to cut back on governmentally organized policies to provide social needs and, adding social insult to social injury, is at the same acting so as to increase **inequality** and **unemployment**, while cutting the **taxes** of the very rich. If there is anything positive about those vicious processes—and there isn't—it has at least brought back into usage the term "class"—if mostly, at the moment, largely by those who support and push literally reactionary policies: those who dare to oppose them are "accused" of indulging in "class warfare."

Thus it is, that now as almost always in U.S. history, as between the capitalist and working class, those who recognize their existence as a class are the members of the ruling class. Never had it so good.

Cold War.

Introduction. Two questions: 1) When did the Cold War begin and 2) when did it end? More importantly why did it begin and, in its underlying nature and endless mutations, will it ever end? There are analyses that answer (1) by placing its beginning with the Russian Revolution of 1917; I am persuaded. (LAFEBER, OGLES-BY, WITTNER)

Soon after World War I, British and U.S. troops (among others) were sent into the territory of the new Soviet Union (the U.S. troops at Vladivostok, on the Pacific) and, at least as important, were supplying the White Army and Cossacks with materiel in their struggles against the Red Army. Attempts to undo the revolution that began in 1918 continued through the 1920s and throughout the 1930s, in forms varying from de facto economic blockades muffled support of the USSR's external enemies—including Nazi Germany. (see BOWDEN, et. al.; BRADY /1937, 1943/; OGLESBY)

Setting aside such historical analyses, what about the received view that the Cold War was "born" in March, 1946, when Truman and Churchill stood side-by-side in Independence, Missouri, and Churchill proclaimed that

> ... America stands at the pinnacle of world power.... Opportunity is here and now...; America should not ignore it or fritter it away..., for it faces a peril to Christian civilization...; an iron curtain has descended across the /European/ continent... from the Baltic to the Adriatic. (quoted in WITTNER)

Within a year the process of institutionalizing those words took hold, resulting in:

1) The National Security Act, which in turn created
2) The National Military Establishment; in its turn the

"Establishment" (its real name)

3) Consolidated the pre-existing Departments of the Navy and the Army (which had included the Air Force) into the War Department while also changing its name to the Department of Defense—just one year before Orwell wrote 1984.

4) Then the **CIA** was created, along with the unprecedented and the always more powerful

5) National Security Council (NSC). Its Director and all of its members are appointed by the President, without further confirmation, and accountable only to him. (One such Director was **Henry Kissinger**; today's is **Condoleezza Rice**.)

The conventional view also has it that the first strategic initiative of the Cold War was the "Truman (Greece-Turkey) Doctrine." As will be noted shortly, such views have been promulgated by the NSC, the White House, and decades of rarely-questioned **media** presentations. (LEFFLER)

But the realities of the Cold War's beginnings were critically different, as has been its "end"—recalling Mark Twain's remark when informed of an obituary lamenting his death": "The report of my death has been greatly exaggerated."

The Cold War's form has indeed changed since 1989, when the **USSR's** disintegration began; but its content goes marching on—not least in the new **preemption** doctrine, orchestrated as the USA prepared to invade **Iraq** in 2003.

Herewith some of the justification for seeing both the "beginning" and the "end" in ways departing from the conventional wisdom.

The beginning. I start with two events typical of the Cold War. They occurred well before Truman/Churchill and the codifications of 1947; I was witness to both of them, in the fall of 1945, the war in the Pacific having just ended.

I had been with the Air Force in New Guinea and the Philippines for almost three years. In August, 1945 "The Bomb" was dropped (twice) and, two weeks later, the war was over. Along with thousands of others, I was sitting around with nothing to do awaiting transportation back to the States (until December).

The first event was at Clark Field, the main U.S. airbase in the Pacific. The two principal participants in the event were the national Philippine Constabulary and their target—presumed members of the "Hukbalahap." All through and up to the very end of the war the Constabulary had worked <u>with</u> the Japanese and <u>against</u> the USA; the Hukbalahap had worked <u>for</u> us (including myself) behind Japanese lines in air-sea rescue work (then my main duty).

Thus it was that In the middle of night in September, 1945 I was more than casually interested in what happened: I was awakened by considerable gunfire close by at Clark Field; it was the Constabulary hunting down and killing what they took to be Hukbalahap, newly-baptized by the USA as "Communists." They were not.

The Hukbalahap were against the colonial status of their country and, as well, against the <u>caciques</u> (the large landholders and merchants) who had worked with and benefited from U.S.—and then Japanese—rule. The Huks saw themselves as "agrarian reformers"; for which they were mocked by standards which, had they been applied in our own struggle for independence, would have made "Communists" of Patrick Henry, Tom Paine, and George Washington.

Beginning that night and for years to follow, under the supervision of Air Force General Lansdale (later to play a key role in Vietnam) (ELLSBERG, 2002; YOUNG), the Huks were killed, imprisoned, or forced into hiding where, indeed, some of them <u>did</u> become Communists—a non-existent force in the Philippines until then.

The other incident was in December, just before I finally embarked for home. With nothing to do but wait all those months, I wandered around. One day, strolling around the docks of Manila, I saw some U.S. cargo ships loading soldiers and equipment. They were newly-uniformed and armed (by us) British and Dutch soldiers, recently freed from Japanese prison camps in the Malay Peninsula and what was still the Dutch East Indies.

Their destination, I discovered, was North Vietnam, their mission "to hold the fort" at Haiphong and Hanoi until the French could arrive, already en route from France on 13 U.S. merchant ships, everything organized and paid for by the USA. Ultimately it was revealed as part of an emerging set of deals meant to bribe a reluctant France, "which held the American plan for European secu-

rity and recovery hostage to its /France's/ colonial war in Indochina."
(YOUNG).

Among the many revolting elements of that U.S.-organized
event and its sequels were 1) that during the war, while Roosevelt
was still alive, an understanding had been reached with the Viet
Minh that after the war the French would have to back off from
what they had called their mission civilisatrice in Indochina
(Vietnam, Laos, and Cambodia). Those peoples could then move
toward independence, with U.S. guarantees. 2) The Viet Minh, led
by Ho Chi Minh, were Communists, but their communism arose
from their nationalism, the deep desire first, to throw off more than
a century of devastating French rule, then to begin at least a partial
reconstruction of their admirable society preceding 1830. 3) The
understanding was worked out in Vietnam during the war between
the OSS, representing the USA, and representatives of the Viet
Minh. Earlier, the OSS (Office of Strategic Services), honorable
predecessor of the considerably less honorable **CIA**, had been working with the Viet Minh: "They relied on Viet Minh networks for
intelligence information and help in rescuing downed American
airmen /an effort in which I was intermittently involved for my
bomb group/;... and the OSS gave /Ho Chi Minh/ six revolvers and
an official appointment as OSS Agent 19." (YOUNG)

Soon after the war, the Viet Minh, in anticipation of their freedom, wrote a Constitution. It was modeled upon our own, beginning
with its Declaration of Independence. And when those U.S.-paid for
ships and British and Dutch soldiers arrived and debarked in
Vietnam, it should give pause to the people of the USA that what
they saw painted on the walls as they marched through the streets of
Haiphong was "WELCOME ABE LINCOLN!" (See YOUNG and
KAHIN, 1968 for both the history of the next 50 years and its background.)

As if that were not enough, when I finally disembarked at Long
Beach, CA in December we were met by Red Cross women who
gave us coffee, doughnuts and that day's edition of the Los Angeles
Examiner—on whose front page was blazoned an editorial headlined: THE TIME TO STRIKE SOVIET RUSSIA IS NOW! So
much for the (second) war to end all wars.

That was how and when the Cold War began in the Pacific

(with other beginnings in **China**), except, of course, that it is diffi-
cult to believe that the reason was other than to intimidate the
Soviet Union and China when the atomic bombs were dropped on
Hiroshima and Nagasaki in July; they were "the first shots of the
Cold War." (ALPEROVITZ, SHERWIN)

And in **Europe**? The Cold War began in Europe when the
USSR was going to do or did... what?

First two notes: 1. Before noting the terrible weakness of the
USSR in 1946, when Churchill and Truman saw it as a "peril to
Christianity" that had dropped an "iron curtain" between itself and
the West, a question: What role had the USSR played in the
European war just ended?

Most in the USA would answer 1) that there were two fronts,
east and west, and that the USSR was just defending itself after
being invaded by Germany; and was able to do so largely through
the substantial assistance of the USA. And some would add 2) that
anyway, they were on the wrong side at the war's beginning, when
Molotov and Ribbentrop signed their non-aggression agreement.
Some truth in both; however:

The attack against the USSR began in the summer of 1941; the
USA did begin to supply the USSR with materiel in 1942 and it was
critically important; and the USSR did sign that pact with Hitler;
but why? Why would Stalin sign such an agreement with his most
hated—and hating—enemy?

A full answer cannot be given to that question here; it will
have to suffice to point out that in the early and late 30s—while the
Japanese were invading China, **fascism** was established in Italy, a
civil war was raging between fascists and "republicans" in **Spain**, and
the Nazis were spreading beyond Germany into Czechoslovakia and
Austria; with all that going on, the UK, France, and the USA, three
long-standing and vigorously anti-Soviet countries, were either
indifferent to or cooperating with Japan (selling it metals and oil),
the Italian and Spanish fascists (selling them ditto), and (in 1938)
U.S. Steel (the largest steel company in the world) signing a pact
with Germany for an international steel cartel (i.e. joint monopoly).
(Believe it or not, I was then working in the "Strategic Research
Department" in U.S. Steel's San Francisco office.)

Put all that together, and it can be seen that it was reasonable for the USSR to buy time and focus on building up its own. (see BREITMAN; BRENAN; BRADY /1937/; ORWELL /1962/; SALVEMINI; WITTNER)

2. And then there is this: In justifying our present "imperial role" in the world, it is quite generally believed that we have had to do so more than once before—in World War I and, most importantly in World War II, when the USA stood "between Nazi Germany and a takeover of all of Europe." In disagreeing with that, William Pfaff (*IHT*, op-ed, 1-2-03) states that

"Britain, not the United States stood between the Nazis and the takeover of Europe." He is more than half-wrong, despite being one of better-informed journalists. Why?

Because All the top U.S. military after that war agreed that, given the unrelenting resistance of Britain, it was, finally, the USSR that beat Hitler. Hitler had quite stupidly gone against his own military chiefs to decide that 1942 was the time to topple the Soviet Union; the western front, as he saw it, was secure, north to south; for years a critical portion of German forces were deployed to the 1,900 mile Eastern Front of 1,900 miles. Recent documents show that conflict to have been "the largest and possibly the most ferocious ever fought..., which claimed 80 percent of all German casualties in the war /and/ perhaps two and a half times the original estimate...." (Benjamin Schwarz, "A Job for Rewrite: Stalin's War," NYT, 2-21-04) The battle for Stalingrad alone claimed over 1,000,000 Soviet soldiers and civilians, and over 200,000 German soldier.

I have taken the space to note this not to jump on the journalist Pfaff, whom I admire, but because if even such an excellent reporter as Pfaff can hold such an opinion, that tells us how deeply warped our views of the Soviet Union have become; more to the point, have been made to become.

Of course, the USSR was a totalitarian state; of course its crimes against its own people were horrific. But, remembering that U.S. forces were not meaningfully participant in the European war until late 1942, one must ponder what our forces and the much-weakened British would have been facing in the West had the Nazis not been fatally wounded in the East. Which that takes us to the rationale for the Cold War.

What then was the nature and the strength of the Soviet

"threat to Christianity"? As noted elsewhere, of all the damage done during World War II—whether as counted in deaths and casualties and/or in destruction of economies, it was the USSR and its people who paid the highest price: A UN study reports that of the 60,000,000 European dead, a minimum of 28,000,000 were of the Soviet Union. (FRUMKIN) And proportionate damage was done to their entire economy—agriculture, factories, infrastructure.

More than Germany? More than Britain, Italy, Greece, Holland, Belgium? Yes. But let's assume that the damage done to the Soviet Union was <u>not</u> greater than that done to the other European countries. The sum and substance is that a) Britain had to hold on, b) the Soviet Union and the USA, respectively, had to break Germany's back and wipe them out.

For those as thoroughly indoctrinated as we have been for over half a century that "sum and..." is just wrong. Setting aside the Truman-Churchill speech, the starting-point for the Cold War is often seen as the famous 1946 cable of George F. Kennan (then the State Department's person in Moscow). Kennan saw the USSR as a threat, but as a <u>political</u>, not a military threat; as indeed, in a real sense it was: Those who had presided over the pre-war status quo in Europe had either been fascists (as in Italy, Germany, Spain and the Vichy government in France, along with smaller countries in Eastern Europe), or they had been tightly conservative. In being so, they had tainted themselves all too much to find popular support after 1945.

Throughout Europe, before war broke out and for many decades earlier, there had been significant to strong anti-capitalist movements. Many thousands of their supporters were imprisoned or killed as the fascists rose to power; of those who remained free, a large number became <u>partigiani</u> or <u>maquis</u> in Italy and Germany, or their counterparts in Germany; it was they who led the underground and military resistance to the fascists.

Unsurprisingly, after the war the political scene was marked by widespread disgust with prewar leaders, matched by substantial popularity for those who had fought against them before and during the war: In most European countries, they were and are seen as heroes.

That set of conditions, taken together with the various forms of desperation afflicting most of the people in Europe, <u>did</u> constitute a

threat; a threat to the maintenance of traditional capitalist governments and, as well, to the maintenance of **imperialism** and its bounty over the globe.

As the war ended, the popularity of <u>both</u> the Soviet Union and
the United States was high. The military strength of the USA was
the highest of any nation in history, both relatively and absolutely;
the USSR's was at its nadir. In its occupation of eastern and central
Europe, the force it applied was in effect that of <u>police</u> forces. The
USA had an incomparable air force and navy, an army of millions of
still healthy GIs (we had suffered "only" 450,000 military deaths)—
<u>and</u> nuclear weapons.

Those who knew that best in the USA were the military chiefs
of staff and the State Department. The USA set about to deal with
the crisis openly, peaceably, sensibly, and (if also, naturally) to its
own advantage with, for example, the **Marshall Plan** while, at the
same time, dealing with it covertly, aggressively and, when deemed
useful and secure, with force and guile (see KOFSKY, WITTNER,
EISENBERG, and **Italy, Korea, Vietnam, Cuba, Chile, China...,
McCarthyism, milex, FBI, CIA...**)

The "anti-communist" activities within and by the USA (all
discussed more fully in the just-noted **bold** notations), were aptly
categorized as they applied not only to the Europeans but to the rest
of the world, by Herbert SCHILLER (1989):

> /A/fter the late '40s and early '50s "McCarthyism," the
> anti-communist fever, broke out in response to what was identi-
> fied as an <u>external</u> crisis. Not at all as evident as it is today, the
> external threat then—if that term is justified at all—was (is) the
> possibility that significant chunks of the ex-colonial world
> might break away from the world business system, adopting
> some form of socialist economy. This possibility was transmuted
> by the governing class and its enthusiastic accomplices, the
> media, into the "Soviet threat." (His emphasis.)

However, that threat was continually put forth as a <u>military</u> not
a political threat; in the language in which the threat was repeatedly carried the emphasis was mostly on the military, whereas if, to
repeat, whatever threat there might have been existed was as much
despite as because of the USSR.

The cultivated prospect of the Soviet military rampaging
through Europe was intense from the late 1940s and especially in the

years of **JFK**; it was given a strong boost by **Reagan** in the 1980s. His ability to charm thought away was perhaps most notable in his successes—despite scientific scoffing from first to last—in gaining finance for the "Star Wars" program. Item: The program has been revived by **Bush II**.

Baseless and dangerous though the resulting arms race for half a century was, it was a grand success for the USA: The economic side of the Cold War was manna from heaven for the U.S. economy and its lively bedmate **consumerism**; just the opposite for the Soviet Union. The arms race caused it to distort its economy toward military expenditures at the expense of the nation's wellbeing, thereby also strengthening totalitarianism. After the fall of the USSR, the CIA bragged that this had been its intention all along. The whole sordid tale is told in, most readably by Frances FITZGERALD and Tom GERVASI.

At home and abroad the stage was continually set and changed to accord with or to strengthen the Cold War. The "cold" part of that war referred only to major power conflicts; for the once colonized world, it was one hot and disastrous war after another, only the best-known of which were those of Korea and Indochina.

The middle years. Both Korea and Indochina (Cambodia, Laos and Vietnam) are dealt with in some detail under their own headings; here the discussion is confined to their role in the Cold War. Those two wars rank among the great tragedies of modern history, and not only because their war deaths add up to upwards of 4 million in Korea (35,000 of them U.S. soldiers) and at least 3 million in Vietnam (plus 58,000 GIs)—over 7 million. Adding in the more than one million dead in **Laos** and **Cambodia**—direct consequences of the Vietnam war—gives a total close to those killed in World War I: but for countries with relatively very small populations compared with those of that war.

1. Korea. The U.S. rationale for the war was in terms of the threatened domination of the Korean peninsula by China and/or the USSR (which were then, but not for much longer, "allies"). The people of Korea were indeed in trouble; its prime source, however, was neither the USSR nor China. (see **Asia....Korea**; CUMINGS; STONE) Korea had long been a brutally-treated colony of the Japanese when the Pacific war ended in 1945; almost immediately,

the looming tension between the USA and the USSR forced a division of Korea into North and South in 1945, at the 38th Parallel.

> Japanese armies, according to the Soviet-American agreement, were disarmed north of the 38th parallel by Russia and south of the line by the United States. Lengthy conferences failed to unify the nation, for neither the Soviet nor the Americans wanted to chance the possibility that a unified Korea would move into the opposing camp. (LAFEBER)

As would be so later in Vietnam with the 17th parallel, the dividing line cut across and separated natural areas of geographic, culture, and climate. The foreseeable result was considerable confusion and conflict and, by the late 40s, military incursions by Koreans conflicting groups from both sides, building to civil war. Each side repeatedly crossed the border to the other, militarily: U.S. intervention was justified by the stated need to respond to an invasion from the north; the facts for preceding months had provided equal such justification for <u>both</u> sides. (For that point, and the entire history, see the definitive work of CUMINGS.)

The essential <u>raison d'etre</u> for the Korean war was not any concern by either the USSR or the USA for the freedom and wellbeing of Koreans; neither party could use that justification. In a recent book, Chalmers Johnson, long one of our leading authorities on Asia, undertook a re-examination of our policies there. His remarks on the background of the Korean War deserve a long quote:

> The end of World War II had proved no more a "liberation day" in Korea than for Czechoslovakia or other nations of Eastern Europe. The Japanese had occupied, colonized, and exploited Korea since 1905, just as the Nazis, following the 1938 Munich Agreement, had divided, occupied, and ravished Czechoslovakia. Both countries now underwent transformations into colonies of the victors of World War II. At about the same time in 1948 when the Communist Party of Czechoslovakia was carrying out a coup d'etat in Prague, right-wing forces in the southern half of divided Korea, then under the control of the United States, were slaughtering at least thirty thousand dissident peasants on the island of Cheju..., part of a process by which /Syngman Rhee's/ puppet regime in South Korea, a government every bit as unpopular as Gotwald's Stalinist government in Czechoslovakia, consolidated /its/ power.... Gotwald /and Rhee/ were prototypes of the faceless bureaucrats the Soviets and the Americans would use for the next forty years to

govern their "captive nations," (a term the Eisenhower administration applied to the Soviet Union's satellites). (C. JOHNSON)

A de facto civil war had begun by 1948-49. Had that civil war been fought out by the Koreans without foreign intervention, doubtless there would have been much bloodshed and damage, but nothing approaching the great human, physical, and human damage of the Korean war, or the distortion of the lives of both sides during the war and since: Left to themselves and (in comparison with what in fact occurred) given the fact that their available weaponry was minimal, it is quite simply inconceivable that their civil war would have killed the many millions it did on both sides, let alone have destroyed the cities of the North in any degree approximating our bombing of it.

Then there were—and are—the dangers and nastiness of the 50 years of "peace," including the USA-imposed fascist dictatorship beginning in 1948 with Syngman Rhee 1948-60, and continuing until 1980, the cruel dictatorship of the North, the insanely armed border from 1951 until today, with its 37,000 U.S. troops, and so on, and so on.

Ah! But wouldn't China and/or the USSR have intervened militarily? If the USA had stayed out, it is unlikely that the USSR would have/could have joined the war, given its still desperate situation at home in 1950, and their distant location. The Chinese did intervene, of course, well after the war had begun, and after General MacArthur had issued statements about the desirability not only of bombing China, but of "nuking" it. (SHERWIN; CUMINGS; WITTNER)

Now we'll never know, but it's a fair guess that the Koreans could not have been worse off had they been left alone to fight it out among themselves.

2. Indochina. Our involvements in Indochina started with Vietnam; before long its devastating effects took hold in Laos and Cambodia. When it started in Vietnam (as suggested above), the smoke of World War II had not faded. Earlier, the USA "deals" with the French were mentioned; a few more words about the French are in order here. Their Mme. de Stael made famous the notion that "to understand all is to forgive all." Perhaps so; not so for their—or

our—actions in Indo-China.

As Japan was consolidating its position there, it felt sure enough of the French to have them continue to administer the entire area until just before **Hiroshima**. When the war ended in Europe, the Vichy government of France—run by men who had been pro-fascist before the war and who had cooperated eagerly with the Nazis throughout the war (including the mass exportation of Jews to the death camps)—was soon displaced in France itself by the Gaullist government.

In Indochina, the French once again took charge; when French troops arrived in 1946 they immediately sought to put things back to their "normal" condition: brutal colonial rule.

But they were faced with a strong resistance movement, the Viet Minh. It had developed both its military and political strengths during the war. (In the South, as French repression mounted, there soon arose the National Liberation Front /NLF/.)

Because of the always rising strength of the resistance, the French moved into all-out war, shelling from the sea, bombing from the air—a preview of the **napalm** and "**carpet bombing** by the USA, whose **collateral damages** were meant to intimidate and to terrify.

By the end of 1946, the French were also dropping thousands of leaflets warning the Vietnamese to submit or else. On those leaflets (which I have seen) was printed a photograph of the entrance (roughly 15 x 15 feet) to a large building's from which was pouring a river of thousands of skulls: "mission civilisatrice" in action. The opposite of intimidation ensued, as signified by the thorough defeat of French troops at Dienbienphu in 1954, after six years of war. Those six years had been mostly financed and supplied by the USA—one of those "deals." In the name of "freedom" (or of stopping China) the USA was not going to let Indochina go down the drain. (YOUNG)

The history books date U.S. military involvement in Vietnam from the mendacious Tonkin Gulf Resolution of August, 1964; but (as noted above) the USA had entered, indeed had helped to create, the war 19 years earlier—beginning with the transportation of soldiers to the North and the financing of French war up to Dienbienphu. Then, after the French defeat, we assured a continuing war by creating the artificial division of Vietnam into North and

South at the Geneva Convention of 1954. Call it war or not, add in the numerous activities of our **Green Berets** and covert naval and army activities in and near Vietnam after 1954. (see **Vietnam**, ELLS-BERG /1972/; YOUNG)

That is only part of "the middle" of the cold war era. The rest may be found 1) in our **China** policies both before and after the 1949 Revolution; 2) in our (not the USSR's) managing to divide **Germany** in two (EISENBERG); 3) In our support of **fascism** in **Greece** right after the war and the distortion of the politics of **Italy** for decades after 1947, 4) in our support of fascism in **Chile** in the 1970s, and, among other bloody spots, 5) in our displacement of **Lumumba** in the Congo. (See **Africa**, **Asia**, **Europe,** and **Latin America**) A very fat middle.

And the end? The essence of the Cold War was its never-ending insistence on this, that, and/or another external threat, with its emerging corollary that anyone within the USA who objected to that rationale, and/or those who fought too strenuously for domestic reforms—strong unions, national health insurance, civil rights..., you name it—was either or just might be an external threat in disguise.

That "internal" threat and its constant din, beginning but not ending with McCarthyism, produced what came to be called the "cultural cold war." (See SAUNDERS, whose book's title is just that.) Its nature was to entice (and reward) leading intellectuals—poets, novelists, journalists, and academics—and even to finance and control the once highly-thought of journal Encounter (along with radio and other elements of the **media).** Those were its means; its ends were to win—by any means necessary—the Cold War we had created; its consequences were to corrupt and pollute the entire cultural operation in the USA and, to a certain extent, in Europe.

Back to external threats. They have now mutated from the USSR and China to the "axis of evil"—with, one may guess, more to come; now that the "communists" at home have been vanquished as the epitome of impermissible, it is the "liberals" who are brushed with the tar of odium. (see the ravings of COULTER)

It is has unfortunately become relevant to recall the admonition of the German Protestant minister of Hitler's time: "Today they come for the Jews; and tomorrow...?

That such an extension can be made—**Iraq** seen as a military threat, Chomsky as a domestic enemy for all that is sacred—has been but one of the horrible consequences of the Cold War. Whether in the universities, in the media, in unions, or in politics, dissent is rare and, when put forth, is rarely taken seriously; a mosquito's buzzing. If that.

But if what may be called the "official Cold War" ended in 1989, who lost and who won? It's easy to show who lost unquestionably: the many millions who were killed and otherwise harmed seriously over all those years. But there is much more to say:

1) As was publicly suspected throughout the Cold War days—and apart from other considerations noted earlier—the cold war militarization of the USA was designed specifically to make it impossible for the USSR to have a sound economy. Unlike the USA, indeed quite the opposite of the USA, the USSR had the opposite of widespread excess capacities in industry and agriculture; thus, when pressed by what it could reasonably see as its "external threat," it had to devote its limited production facilities to the arms, so the normal needs of its people and its society got short shrift; in turn that meant that dissent, always restricted, became more so. (see ELLSBERG, 2002)

2. The countries of East Europe under the control of the USSR were at least as much or more constrained and harmed in those regards. Less obviously, but just as true, was the damage done to West Europe, with large variations: Thus, a) **Germany**. Its division—deliberately brought by the USA (EISENBERG; KENNAN), was costly in many ways—economic, social, cultural, political—and continues to be so with the worst perhaps yet to come. (see BARBER) b) **Italy**. Of all the nations in Western Europe, Italy was the most likely to go left after the war, even if—very probably, especially if—their had never <u>been</u> a Soviet Union. The military threat from the USSR was non-existent; the political threat from within was great. So the USA went to work, using covert and open tactics without let-up for decades, beginning in 1947. The degrees of related **corruption** within both Italy and the USA, while not breaking any records, were substantial. c) In one degree or another, using diverse means, the USA did what it could, which was a lot, to distort in its favor the political lives of all the nations of Europe, east and west,

north and south, succeeding least in Scandinavia and the Netherlands: politicians bought off, media subsidized in one way or another, U.S. air and naval bases strewn all over the map, every one of them an economic source of corruption; and so it went, carrots and sticks, anything money could buy or pressure could force: the first grand wave of "americanization," for better and, more often, for worse.

3) Except for the wars, Asia has not been mentioned. The three most important nations in our efforts to win our way—positively or negatively—were China, Japan, and Indonesia (with India on the sidelines). Like all other nations noted, they are treated under their own headings. Here we note only the main effects of the Cold War.

a) **China**, of all nations, has probably benefited most from the Cold War (and, now, from **globalization**). First, its main rival, the USSR, was flattened by it, its army demoralized, its leadership chaotic, and its now "free" economy wracked by—and called—"Mafia capitalism."

China, on the other hand, and rightly or wrongly, is step by step taking back all the lands taken from it in the past; it is the fastest growing economy in the world and will be for some time to come, its economy already bigger than Italy or the UK, soon to surpass the gross production of Germany and Japan. It is able to do so by importing (and, slowly but surely, making its own) the latest technology and combining that with the lowest wages and probably the cruelest working conditions in the world: A horrifying combination of capitalism and totalitarian communism.

b) **Japan**'s economy has been stagnant for at least a decade, with its best hope now of settling in the mud rather than sinking into a black hole. It was a direct beneficiary of U.S. direct and indirect economic stimuli, beginning soon after the war, and continuing today (especially in the military realms). Perhaps it has come out even, "cold war-wise."

c) Not so, for the people of **Indonesia**. As is discussed in that essay, Indonesia was taking strong steps toward economic and social improvement in its post-war independence, led by Sukarno. The USA was critical in arranging the overthrow of Sukarno and supported the terrible violence involved (with as many as 1,000,000 killed). We wanted access to the resources of the area (not least, oil), and got it. What the Indonesians (and nearby East Timor) got was a merciless dictatorship.

So much for all those other countries and their people; what about the titular victor: the USA?

Well, the extraordinary **military expenditures** from 1946 to the present—something over 15 <u>trillion</u> dollars—was surely vital from 1946 on for staving off depression (as distinct from recession).

But our society steadily and, worse, unconsciously became militarized in the process—in its economy, its politics, its culture. What had once been seen as repellent, we came to take for granted. (see DOWD, 1981, "Militarized Economy, Brutalized Society.")

<u>If</u> the official Cold War is over, it is only because what C. Wright MILLS (1951) presciently saw as "the power elite" has won <u>its</u> war, at home and abroad: a world at home and abroad meeting the needs and wants of that "elite": of **big business**, the Pentagon, and the political establishment; a world learning to bend to the powerful combination of U.S. economic and military carrots-and-sticks; a world that has pushed all too many of the people of the USA toward a seemingly voluntary **dehumanization,** moving aimlessly toward a future that one dares not to contemplate more than fleetingly. (LEBOW)

That may be changing; as this is written, the always strong and now growing **arrogance** of the USA, symbolized but not confined to **Iraq** has created a rumbling dissent over the globe that <u>seems</u> to portend movements to weaken, even cut, "the ties that bind." Cross your fingers.

collateral damage: carpet bombing/ napalm/ cluster bombs/land mines

Massive "collateral damage" was done to civilians in the <u>millions</u> in World War II; however, because the war against the Axis powers was so popular, the <u>term</u> wasn't needed or used, despite that horrendous reality. Think only of the prolonged German bombing called "the Battle of Britain" and its 60,000 civilian deaths, and the "saturation" bombing of German cities with ten times that many deaths; add in Tokyo's fire bombing—and then **Hiroshima** and Nagasaki, with <u>their</u> hundreds of thousands burned to death, and some multiple of that seriously harmed. Plus so much else.

No, that Orwellian term came into being in and for the **Cold War**, itself a euphemism; now it has become a bureaucratic designation. What does the term mean?

It means that when something reprehensible happens—and in our era it happens a <u>lot</u>—it needs a **spin**. In the good old days, "collateral" meant something one put up to secure a loan; since **financialization** and its recklessness have come to be taken for granted, the use of the word in its original sense has vanished.

Now, it serves a political purpose. It has come to refer to what is <u>said</u> to be the unintentional killing of civilians: "We're sorry." "Couldn't be avoided." 'We had issued a warning." "The butler did it." But "unintentional" has lost <u>its</u> conventional meaning as much as "collateral" has: Several <u>millions</u> died in **Korea** and **Vietnam** and **Laos** from U.S. fire bombing, village strafing, Agent Orange, and other murderous ways (and that's not counting the effective destruction of the peoples and the society in **Cambodia**, for which we bear major responsibility). Those killing ways <u>inevitably</u>—and usually **deliberately**—killed civilians: Our form of "**terrorism**." (CUMINGS; YOUNG; SCOWCROFT)

Whether the German bombs dropped on London or the U.S. and British bombs dropped on Dresden, the harm done to civilians was not "collateral"; their aim was to break the morale of the civilian population. They had the opposite effect, as numerous studies show (including OSS research on the Dresden bombing). Naturally that would be so, when you think about it: If your family had been burned to death would you give in to the killers? Some would; most didn't.

Here I find it relevant to interject two such factual incidents of my own knowledge. The first I participated in myself in the Pacific, during World War II. I served there in a bomb group for bombing attacks and air-sea rescue. One mission over Formosa (now Taiwan) had to do with a major population area. Our group received the order (which I read) to "Burn Taegu." We bombed it with fire bombs, and literally burned it to the ground. Took almost an hour.

The second involved my friend Howard Zinn, when he was a bombardier in Europe. He tells us in his autobiography (ZINN, 1999) how, in the last three <u>weeks</u> of the war, his group was ordered to drop napalm on a <u>western</u> French village. It was the first time

napalm was used in war; there could not have been a strategic purpose, so one supposes they just wanted to see how it worked? It
worked very well: The village was destroyed—as did many of its
civilian population.

World War I was the worst horror story in history; until World
War II. Of course there were civilian casualties when the Germans
dropped their 50-lb. bombs on England from little canvas-winged
planes with engines weaker than those of today's motorcycles. But
most of the enormous horror by far was accomplished in the trench-
es. (FUSSELL)

Compared with what was to come, the ten million "or so" who
died, most of them soldiers, were rightly seen as the worst disaster
ever up to then. But in World War II, 60 million died in Europe
alone, most of them civilians. The quantum jump in numbers doubtless had to with the marvelous new technologies of warfare; but they
had much to do also with the effectively casual manner in which
killing had come to be treated—when it is "in a good cause." In that
the large numbers of people of all the nations participant in that and
subsequent wars were seldom if ever asked their opinion of the
"cause" for which they were killed, the phrase loses its meaning.

But it is in the wars of the Cold War era and its successor wars
against **terrorism** and the "axis of evil" that threaten to outdo all the
collateral damages of both the world wars. A reminder: the use of the
term collateral referring to civilian harm is meant to place it in contrast with the accepted military harm; but it is in the very nature of
the wars since Korea that their motivations are to be found not in
the realm of military but of political and economic threats and possibilities.

Thus, although it cannot be doubted that the Nazis and the
Japanese were involved in accelerating military aggression, the existence of any military threat can be and has been very much doubted as regards both Korea and Vietnam. (CUMINGS; YOUNG) To
say nothing of **Iraq**. That such is very much a minority opinion in
the USA is part and parcel of one of the major points of this book:
What the public of the USA thinks, does, and wants is very much a
product of a contrived reality. Here but a few instances of that reality:

1) Tens or hundreds of thousands of innocent civilians are killed

by the **carpet bombing** of **cluster bombs**; they are aimed at an area, not a target. Such bombs contain as many as 900 separate "bomblets" designed to be indiscriminate. In Iraq, 1 to 1.5 million were dropped. (*WSJ*, "Pentagon Rethinks Use of Cluster Bombs," 8-23-03. Sounds good, unless it means they're thinking of more and bigger bomblets?)

2) In recent decades <u>millions</u> of <u>land mines</u> have been planted on every continent except ours by the USA and others. Up to now, the USA has been resistant or less than cooperative in support of programs to rid the earth of them—as in, say Afghanistan.

3) <u>Napalm</u>, as noted above, was first used by us over France, experimentally (with some collateral damage). It became one of the weapons of choice in **Vietnam**. The closest to any realization of it for most of us came with that horrifying photo of the little Vietnamese girl running down a road, naked and shrieking, followed by an even smaller boy. There were some signs of repugnance in the USA at the time; soon it was shrugged off, forgotten. Mostly, we don't even need to shrug it off. It's somewhere else, where bad governments rule, where (in the long run) if we only persevere, there will be a better world, for us and for them. Those, that is, who had not been collateralized.

As will be discussed at greater length under **power**, those who are powerful are those who decide what will be done and what will <u>not</u> be done, in all realms of life. As the most powerful nation in history, the USA has greater abilities <u>and</u> responsibilities than any other nation to assist ourselves and others toward a better and safer world; more often than not, our power has deterred the better from occurring and allowed or hastened the worse. Collateral damage is a deadly disease; its spread will ultimately know no limits.

"America is the great policeman: Punish the thieves, quell the rebels, restore order, restore peace. There will be no war, but in the struggle for peace not a stone will remain standing." You remember that very funny joke from the Cold War? (LE CARRE')

colonialism (see anti-colonial imperialism and imperialism

commodification

We take for granted that land and labor—that is, natural and human resources—are commodities, to be sold at a price. "Twas not always thus, for either; that way of thinking coincided emerged hand-in-hand with **capitalism**; it became an onrushing process in Britain in the late 18th century, sped up by changing technologies and Adam Smith's *Wealth of Nations* (1776).

It was a tumultuous period; the commodification of land and labor required force and suppression and widespread misery. (MANTOUX; POLANYI; TAWNEY /1912/) The key development was what came to be called "the enclosure movement," which, although it had begun earlier and went on after, had its decisive victories in the 18th century. By the time the enclosures had done their job of transforming what had been a land of small free holdings into one of very large holdings owned—a preview of what happens today all over—80 percent of the land of England was held by 2-3,000 families. The fabled "yeomanry" of England who had farmed that land either starved or, to avoid that, had to sell their labor for semi-starvation wages. (MANTOUX)

The farmers and their families who had become commodities were at first confined to "workhouses." There, as with the slaves in the U.S. South, families were deliberately broken up; by the 1820s, men, women, and children were working in mines and mills for 12—14 hours a day, and—progress is <u>such</u> a complex process—their average life span <u>decreased</u> by 20 percent for the next generation or so. (HOBSBAWM, 1968)

That is, the once "proud yeomanry" had become the <u>lumpen-proletariat</u>; a many-dimensional tragedy. Our work lives are not the sum and substance of life, but in a sane society they can be a mainstay of that "substance"—as for the once free smallholders of England they had been. Then began the slow torture in what the poet Blake called "the dark satanic mills," ripping their humanity to shreds. (THOMPSON)

The Irish poet Oliver Goldsmith began his epic poem "The

Deserted Village" (1775) this way: "Ill fares the land / to hastening ills a prey / where wealth accumulates / and men decay." But that was just the painful beginnings of commodification.

Nowadays, not just land and labor, but everything has its price, or soon will: Everything for Sale (KUTTNER; HOCHSCHILD, A.R.)—where "everything" includes not just autos and TVs and blue jeans and food, etc., but health, education, housing, social security, and, along with what is becoming almost everything else, politicians, professors, doctors: everyone for sale.

Of the numerous negative consequences of the impoverization of workers, we shall note what is totally neglected by those who urge the commodification of everything—most famously, Professor Milton **Friedman** and his ilk. They are completely indifferent to what is now clear: commodification carried to its present extremes inexorably produces a society dominated by **corruption** and **decadence**, marching behind a banner shouting MORE!/NOW!/WHY NOT?/OUT OF MY WAY!!

Of course corruption and decadence go back to the beginnings of history, and have marked all societies to one degree or another. But the degree to which our and other contemporary societies are now dominated breaks all records, making Nero's Rome seem almost ascetic.

We humans contain two quite diverse sets of possibilities whose extremes are that we can be decent or just plain rotten; Eleanor Roosevelt and Joe **McCarthy** were both human beings. What we do or don't do is very much conditioned by the social process within which we live our lives. When that process is dominated by decadence and corruption, the very worst is brought out in us, and social relationships tend toward the condition where, as the elephant said when he danced among the chickens, "It's each for himself and God for all." Watch your back.

competition

Deeply embedded in our thoughts and feelings is the notion that competition is among the greater economic and personal virtues—for businesses in the economy, for individuals as athletes, students, job-seekers/holders, for "dates," you name it.

So embedded are these notions that even when we see clear

instances of the harms or dangers of competition—as noted below—
we shrug them off or attribute the negatives to something else:
including that there was not <u>enough</u> competition. Of the numerous
and complex aspects of economic competition, here we underscore
that under **capitalism** the society is in trouble both 1) when genuine
("Smithian") competition has been shoved aside by the growth of
big business and its market controls <u>and</u> 2) when genuine competition exists.

"<u>Competition" between giants</u>. The roots of competition as a
standard are several; for the modern era they may be traced directly
back to Adam Smith's <u>Wealth of Nations</u> and its offshoots. As noted
in **big business**, while Smith saw free market competition as "an
invisible hand" that would transform individual selfishness into
social wellbeing, he also saw businessmen

> as an order of men whose interest is never exactly the
> same with that of the public, who have generally an interest to
> deceive and even to oppress the public, and who have, upon
> many occasions, both deceived and oppressed it.

Nonetheless, Smith proposed the elimination of all institutions
and policies that might constrain the "deceptive and oppressive"
side of businessmen. He believed that competition, given a chance,
would prevail.

As noted in **big business**, his trust was badly misplaced; ironically so, for the very successes of the industrialization he hoped for
also gave birth to the giant business units that eliminated the very
possibility of market competition. Moreover, the first giants, those of
the late 19th century, were dwarfs compared with the behemoths of
today.

Also, if understandably, lacking in Smith's position was that
growing alongside the concentration of <u>economic</u> power would be
its Siamese twin of concentrated political **power**; that as the power
of the (monarchical) state withered the emerging business world
would both seek and gain that power—unless its power could be curtailed through democracy.

A large "unless," indeed. For there was a third element (understandably) not foreseen by Smith; namely, the role of the **media** and
of **lobbyists** in capturing "the hearts and minds" of the public and its
government; and, in doing so, replacing monarchy with plutocracy.

Wait, you may say, "Do we not have competition—between, e.g., Ford and **GM**, etc.?" No, not if by competition is meant what Smith meant; that is, that which drives down prices while at the same time increasing productive efficiency. The "competition" we have today is better seen as <u>rivalry</u>, through **advertising** and trivial product changes: keeping prices up and <u>increasing</u> costs; not what Smith had in mind, for these allow companies to control the market, rather than to be controlled by it.

Put differently, the competitive economy Smith hoped for— and which is still "the model" that sits in the center of the element of capitalist ideology called "**economics**"—has as its leading characteristics 1) that in each industry there would be so many firms that no one of them (or a few in agreement) could in any way influence prices: each seller had to take the market price as <u>given</u>; of lesser but also great importance, each seller would be producing a product essentially identical to all others'; and lastly, there would be nothing to keep new capital from entering an industry, and nothing to keep firms from leaving an industry when enduring losses were normal. What we have in all major industries are "markets" in which a handful of firms ("oligopolies") work together to manage prices, competing only in terms of advertising programs, superficial product variations, and the like: all increasing costs, not reducing them, as expected from competition.

2) Has Smithian competition ever been even approximated in the U.S. economy? Unfortunately, yes: In staple agriculture (corn, wheat, etc.), in cotton textiles, and in coal mining. Why "unfortunately"? Because in all those cases it meant one or more kinds of disaster: in agriculture, to most farmers and to the land (see **farmers** and **Dust Bowl**); in cotton textiles to the underpaid and overworked employees and to most of the companies; in coal mining (where once there were 5,000 + independent mines), to the miners (deadly low wages, injuries, deaths and disease), and bankruptcy for the owners. (see DU BOFF)

In all those areas, competition was brought to an end: in agriculture, by the farmers, through governmental intervention (quotas, price supports, subsidies); in cotton textiles by their absorption into giant companies, including chemical companies; for coal mines, absorption by the industries using coal (steel, chemicals) or by "energy" companies. In short, "real competition" was destructive of workers, resources, and businesses. (FAULNER; MITCHELL)

How could Smith have gotten it so wrong? Well, nobody can foresee the social process; in Smith's case, he couldn't foresee the technologies that would make possible (and, from capital's point of view, necessary) the <u>elimination</u> of competition; more subtly, but also important, great thinkers such as Smith (and Marx and Keynes and Freud, et al.), in concentrating on those matters they take to be absolutely crucial may be forgiven for not also concentrating on other matters that are or will become relevant—and, in doing so, very much affect social outcomes. (ROGIN) It is up to their followers to undertake those lesser, but vital, tasks. Which they have not always done.

There is much more to take into account in all these respects; some are discussed in other entries; some have been noted above. See also **CEOs, alienation, consumerism, advertising, commodification, unions.** Now we turn to competition among and between <u>persons</u>, as distinct from businesses.

<u>Non-economic competition</u>. Of course competition has been common in virtually all societies known to us; one need only mention the absurd to cruel Roman chariot races and gladiators to make that point. But in this respect as in so many others, the modern era seems to take first place, and the USA first among society of nations—understandably, for we are the most capitalist of all societies, and the "capitalist ethic" has had considerably less "competition" from other ways of thinking and behaving here than elsewhere—whether the reference is to the hold of political doctrines, or of socio-economic traditions. Usually those have all existed is some tight combination in virtually every society but the USA; for better and for worse.

So: Let us count (some of) the ways in which we compete with each other, openly and covertly. All animals compete with each other in order to survive; OK. But this animal, us, does so in such a way as to be self-destructive; we are a species that has stifled its natural propensity to <u>cooperate</u>.

In this matter, as in <u>all</u> others, we are not <u>born</u> to be this or that, we <u>learn</u> to be this or that. More exactly, as VEBLEN emphasized in his <u>Instinct of Workmanship</u>, we are creatures with both constructive and destructive possibilities; which of those tends to dominate us depends upon the time and the place and the social processes within which we live out our lives.

As was briefly noted in the <u>Foreword</u>, the social processes in which one grows up in the USA have been much conditioned by the interacting processes of militarism and violence, prejudice and racism, and an insatiable greed for money and power. Contained in all those ways of living and feeling are attitudes, beliefs, and behavior patterns that are <u>invidious</u> (that is, envious, hateful, ill-willed, disdainful, discriminatory). We pit ourselves against each other, come to see our wellbeing as being dependent upon others' illbeing: we become, first and foremost, <u>competitors</u>—for status, money, jobs, lovers, prizes, whatever. (KOHN)

It seems reasonable to believe that our species has only so much "room" in its thoughts and emotions; that if we use our mental and emotional energies in one set of ways regularly, we are at the same time reducing the likelihood of being either inclined or able to think and feel in another, conflicting set of ways. This does not mean to say that any of us is "all of a piece," monolithic; we all have moments when we "are not ourselves," so to speak. But the "selves" we learn to become in this very capitalistic society are, finally, competitive selves, and the motto with which we live, consciously or not, becomes "all against all."

Unsurprisingly, researchers in a recent study "found that when /the women studied/ chose mutualism over 'me-ism,' the mental circuitry normally associated with reward-seeking behavior swelled to life. And the longer the women engaged in cooperative strategy, the more strongly flowed the blood to the pathways of pleasure." (Natalie Angier, <u>NYT</u>, 7-23-2) "Why We're So Nice....")

Why unsurprisingly? Because it was women who were studied. And it is not a play on words to point out 1) that women are instinctively maternal and, 2) if they were not, our species would not have survived. And one need not specify the relationship between maternalism and a relative absence of "me-ism." (see **boys and girls....**)

In the long development of our species, as is well-known, men generally performed the function of hunters and warriors, women bore the children and, when a settled agriculture took hold, women did the farming.

Two mentalities are involved there. Of course there are cooperative and relatively "non-invidious" men, of which Gandhi is only the best-known (if not fully so). And of course there are combative and relatively heartless women (Margaret Thatcher pops to mind). But here, as often, it is the exception that proves the rule—which is: "It's a man's world."

Such a world is first and foremost competitive and combative; put differently, if women are to succeed in this world—as "success" is defined—they must take on "masculine," that is competitive and combative ways and means—whether on the playing field, in the classroom, the office, or in politics.

Again, to be sure there are significant instances where this has not been and is not so: they stand out etched against the sky in their loneliness.

Ah! It might be said, so there has been much competition, much combativeness; but without it would we have become economically so "developed," could we have gained and maintained our freedom? Although there is overlap, those are two very different questions, able to be discussed only with desperate brevity here.

First, our economic strength. That "strength," as will be seen in the discussion of **waste**, is more than a little illusory, and when seen in the context of the **environment**, the ways in which it has been gained have already caused terrible damage and now put all living species in peril. To say it is illusory means that the ways and means that have brought production of goods and services to their present levels have at the same time and for the same reasons weakened our ability to provide needed, useful, and satisfying goods and services that are not even attempted, let alone prized, in this competitive society.

To be sure, if—a very large "if"—the USA had moved on the quite different developmental path implicit in the foregoing, its growth and developmental processes would have proceeded more slowly than was the case. Had that been so, it would have/could have been friendly, rather than combative and destructive to the native **"Indian"** peoples. But if the reference points are the 18th and 19th centuries, the USA, of all the world's societies, had the resources and the geographic safety that would have made that feasible. What it didn't have was the outlook, the values, the impulse. Even less do we have them today.

Compromise of 1877 (see racism. slavery)

conformity

Perhaps the earliest, most enthusiastic and most studious admirer of the USA, after a prolonged visit in the early 19th century, was Alexis de TOCQUEVILLE, in his *Democracy in America*. But he had one major reservation: our tendency toward conformity.

He was not only a keen observer of the new USA, but also of his Europe, and he noted that the conformity of the USA was something different from the obeisance of the Europeans; it was voluntary and, as he saw it, at the same time both a comprehensible and an undesirable adjunct of U.S. democracy. He believed that though freedom was intensely desired by some (and quite apart from **slavery**) it was just as intimidating to perhaps a majority of others.

At the end of the century his position was echoed and extended by Thorstein VEBLEN (1899), with his concept of "**emulation**." Subsequently, in one variation or another, the tendency toward conformity in the USA was studied by many others, most notably in fiction by Sinclair LEWIS, in his *Main Street* (1920), in sociology by Robert and Helen LYND, in their *Middletown* (1937), by Phillip SLATER in his *The Pursuit of Loneliness* (1971), and in psychology by Erich FROMM, in his *Escape from Freedom* (1946). (Fromm, although transplanted from Germany and seeking to explain a critical element of the Nazi era was also writing to warn his adopted country.)

The tendencies toward conformity in one form or another, a trait which is a close cousin to fear, may be seen as both a weakness and a strength of our species, without which we are unlikely to have survived. There are indeed many reasons to be fearful today, as well; but conformity in today's world is likely to intensify, not to mitigate, our problems.

All the thinkers noted above were of course concerned with the modern era, but although the present is in many ways similar to theirs our times are also critically and worrisomely different.

Conformity in contemporary highly industrialized and democratic societies has become considerably more ubiquitous and more forbidding than even in 1971 (when Slater wrote); that is so most vividly in the most "modern" of all societies, the USA—where "modernity" <u>subsumes</u> conformity. Why?

Some of the several reasons for conformity's spread and intensification are an integral element of industrialization and democracy; others have been "orchestrated." In both cases, the results are alarming.

We look first at the "innocent" causes.

They are inherent in the very existence of industrialization under capitalist conditions, requiring conscious design from nobody. Industrialization brings with it <u>urbanization</u>, <u>standardization</u>, and <u>mass production</u>; all have both positive and negative possibilities. The U.S. democracy admired by Tocqueville was then and remains a <u>capitalist</u> democracy, unavoidably limited by its innately skewed pattern of power—not only the slavery of his time, but the ownership and control over the means of life by an always small and steadily shrinking minority.

Taken together, urbanization, standardization, mass production, and limited democracy would be sufficient to produce what is examined separately as conformity's close relatives, **alienation** and **dehumanization**; some degree of conformity is a natural outcome of such conditions, not requiring any additional stimuli.

But additional stimuli there have been, always increasing over time. In this age of **consumerism**, stimuli were first provided through **advertising**, always more powerful as **infotainment**, not least on **MTV**.

All this is channeled to us through the **media**, **TV** most of all; and the interlocking media themselves are owned and controlled by a very small and very powerful segment of the **big business** community. (see HERMAN and MCCHESNEY; BAGDIKIAN)

Whatever might have been disturbing to Tocqueville and those up to and including Slater, has in the past quarter century become considerably more so. It has been transformed from unsettling and worrisome to menacing: what 50 years ago was a rat racing around in the basement is now an 800-lb. gorilla in the living room.

It isn't just that we are all <u>un</u>consciously under pressure to dress, eat, behave, and think <u>alike</u>; rather it is that as products of the "consciousness industry" (ENSENZGERGER) we have learned to think and feel that what we do is, by golly, <u>our</u> idea; that we are dressing, eating, behaving, and thinking as sentient beings, as <u>free</u> individuals—and that anyone who wants to argue about that is some kind of nut; or worse. (see COULTER)

A reasonable response might well be that what here is considered as "conforming," something we do "under pressure," is, rather, done because in fact it makes sense; is, when all is said and done, good taste, good thinking, the good life.

Sure it is: Shop 'til you drop; go in **debt** as you and your family shred, parents seeing themselves as the kids' cash cows, kids seeing their parents as tightwads (and also as responsible for this <u>stupid</u> world). Sit in your **cars** (the bulk of U.S. families have at least two) fume at those (other) fools in all this goddamned traffic; follow your leader into senseless and obscene wars; glare helplessly at your kids and their ringed noses and bellybuttons (and who give you the finger when you're not watching); breathe in all that polluted air; worry about whether you'll be laid off; pay all those high and rising medical bills...: Hey! What more could you want? Just hang in there, pal; and stay in line! (FINNEGAN)

But, it may be said, so far as the "kids" are concerned adolescents have <u>always</u> been conformist: "Why I was myself when I was their age." True enough. But that's in the same family of arguments as saying that, hell, their have always been wars, there's always been sickness, always been.... But now those and other "always-es" are different, if also in different ways. (see, for example, **military expenditures, health care, preemption**).

And so is adolescence different now—for the adolescents themselves, <u>and</u> for the high percentage of our population being mesmerized so as to become permanently adolescent. In the past we have used "adolescent" as a metaphor to demean adults we don't like; now it's time to look in the mirror at the mote in our own eyes.

As is discussed in more detail in **TV** and **advertising**, the average adult watches TV at least four hours a day; the average youngster 5-6 hours; and "infomercials" are now watched more than the "regular programs." Note also the <u>content</u> of not only the ads but the "regular programs" and films; the violence, cheap sexuality, and fantasy that has come increasingly to dominate entertainment was originally "designed" for youngsters; now it is watched by all ages.

When mixed in with the open and covert advertising in almost all TV and films every day of the weeks, months, years, put it all together and what you get is a <u>society</u> of adolescent mentalities, spreading like an oil spill over all age groups.

Great for profits, great for tyrants; but for our children, the environment, peace, decency? Don't ask.

consumerism

When **economics** was "invented" by Adam Smith in 1776, there were no "consumers" in the modern sense of the term; nor were individuals seen as making "rational choices" about their purchases; nor did **advertising** as we know it exist at all. Close to 90 percent of the British were working for wages of "subsistence," as Smith put it; given their slave wages, they had little or no choices to make. (HOBSBAWM, 1968)

The remaining 10 percent or so—the landed gentry, merchants and financiers, the "ladies and gentlemen"—had incomes substantially above subsistence levels, and <u>could</u> make choices, of course; however, they and their successors were those who captured VEBLEN's attention and dispraise in his *Theory of the Leisure Class* (1899), calling their consumer "choices" a matter of "conspicuous consumption, display, and waste."

The latter were what economists would call "irrational" choices; what those few were doing then is now, in the age of consumerism, what the majority <u>wants</u> to do. They—we—are responding to massive and never-ending advertising designed specifically to <u>incite</u> irrational choices; designed, as BARAN (1969) put it, to lead people "to want what they don't need, and not to want what they do." And to borrow well beyond the point of rationality in order to so.

There can be and have been both beneficial and harmful consequences of the consumerism that originated in the USA in the 1920s, that took deep root in the 1950s, and that now marks much of the world. The beneficial effects are those which, in utilizing what otherwise would be unused or non-existent productive capacity, created jobs and profits and postponed economic stagnation while, at the same time, the majority's level of what is seen as material well-being increased.

That was generally so for about 25 years after World War II;

since the 1970s, however, consumerism's harmful consequences have come to dominate: widespread and massive amounts and kinds of **waste** (much of it destructive), accompanied by serious **environmental**, social, and political costs. (see **conformity, corruption, infotainment**).

Some important distinctions must be made between consumption and consumerism; they are species of the same genus, of course, but only as eating and gluttony are: we must eat in order to survive, but we fall into trouble if we are regularly gluttonous; similarly, eating is instinctive and essential, but habitual gluttony belongs in the realm of individual pathology. Consumerism is a social disease.

Throughout history, most people have been unable to meet their basic needs; today socioeconomies <u>could</u> meet those needs for all: Even at the pit of the 1930s depression, when **FDR** stated that in the USA "one-third of the nation is ill-clothed, ill-fed, and ill-housed," he was describing a tragedy (and understating it; half would have been more accurate); in terms of productive **capacities**, it was then possible for all in that same nation to have those needs met immediately or soon.

Today at more than one-half of all the <u>world's</u> people are desperately unable to meet their needs for nutrition, health, education, and housing, even though the agricultural and industrial capacities of the world would enable the "ill-fed and ill-clothed" to be lifted to decency in a year or so, and housing and health needs over about a decade. (see SEN; STREETEN; STRETTON)

Consumerism has done little or nothing to mitigate the problems noted by FDR, whether in the USA or elsewhere; indeed its side effects have exacerbated the problems of the poor in the rich countries, and deepened and multiplied the economic problems of the poor countries—processes accompanied and in significant part caused by the always more cacophonous "big sell." (see **globalization, free markets/trade, competition**)

Whatever its faults or its virtues, consumerism could not have come into being, let alone flourished as it has, without what ENSENZBERGER has called "the consciousness industry"—**advertising, public relations**, and the **media**. The people of the USA began to be the targets of sustained advertising back to the flash point of the 1920s; but advertising and consumerism took their giant leap forward with the 1950s.

Advertising's function is no more to provide information than consumerism's is to provide for people's needs; its main function is that of "mind management" (SCHILLER, 1973); the widespread "consumption" of **TV** programs and commercials that played the key role got their jump start in the 1950s.

As noted elsewhere, VEBLEN (1899) argued that our species has both benign and malign possibilities, but that **capitalism** brings out, indeed must bring out, the worst in us. BARAN made something of the same point and captured the essence of modern advertising when he noted:

> It is crucial to recognize that advertising and mass media programs sponsored by and related to it do not to any significant extent create values or produce attitudes but rather reflect existing and exploit prevailing attitudes. In so doing they undoubtedly re-enforce them and contribute to their propagation, but they cannot be considered to be their taproot.... Advertising campaigns succeed not if they seek to change people's attitudes but if they manage to find, by means of motivation research and similar procedures, a way of linking up with existing status-seeking and snobbery; social, racial, and sexual discrimination; egotism and unrelatedness to others; envy, gluttony, avarice, and ruthlessness in the drive for self-advancement—all of these attitudes are not generated by advertising but are made use of and appealed to in the contents of the advertising material. (1969)

Baran wrote that in the early 1960s (he died in 1964); since then, advertising has exploded quantitatively (about $500 billion yearly is spent worldwide now, half of it in the USA), and qualitatively has perfected its mesmerizing techniques in ways only dreamed of 40 years ago; but already in the 60s the late lamented Mort Sahl, while "riffing" on ostentatious **cars** (and before there were **SUV**s), asked "How else can you get sexual satisfaction?"

When consumerism first took hold in the 1920s, its fans were said to be "keeping up with the Joneses"; nowadays almost all have become its devotees, and the aim is to keep up with the advertising and to surpass the Joneses. The direct and indirect harmful effects of today's consumerism are many; they begin in the family, spill over into politics, and extend to the **environment**. A look first at the family.

Doubtless modern society with or without consumerism would

be more corrosive of the nuclear family than earlier times; in any case, perhaps the nuclear family is not the best of all worlds. Perhaps; but in western society we take it for granted that a healthy family is an essential part of the good life; be that as it may, consumerism's enticements are doing the family in.

Its insatiable spending and equally insatiable borrowing function act as a corrosive acid on family life. In the USA the spending and borrowing have made it necessary for two-thirds of families to have two (or more) wage-earners in order to maintain their "standard of living" and, more and more, to avoid bankruptcy. (see **debt, jobs, boys and girls, men and women,** and SCHOR, *The Overspent American*)

But, and going against good sense, supposing that both parents are more contented that way, and even supposing that all their purchases were sensible and that their mountainous **debt** will somehow take care of itself, then: who will take care of their children? Or has that suddenly ceased to be necessary in a "family"? Day care centers if you can afford them? And if not (and usually it is not)? Well, there's TV. There surely is; it is watched on the average of <u>six</u> hours a day by children. (see **TV**)

That would be disturbing enough even if the TV programs were just right for children; more often than not, they are just wrong— raw violence, raw sex, fantasies that cannot help but confuse children about realities—such as those of real fists, real knives, real guns, real relationships.

As for politics, consumerism promotes individualism, for which, in this case, barely one cheer. It is not individualism of the spirit but selfish individualism; nor could it come at a worse time— of always more large and small social problems requiring careful attention and thought <u>and</u> cooperative effort if they are to be resolved well and peaceably. But as Michael IGNATIEFF has warned,

> ... The allegiances that make the human world human must be beaten into our heads. We never know a thing till we have paid to know it, never know how much is enough until we have had much less than enough, never know what we need till we have been dispossessed.... Our education in the art of necessity cannot avoid tragedy.

A world addicted to consumerism is one in which the realm of politics—always and everywhere threatened by **corruption**—plunges into an always more precarious condition, marked by growing popular indifference and cynicism.

A major confirmation of that is what is now occurring in <u>all</u> the prosperous western nations. What were in the 1950s and 1960s strong trade unions and effective pushes for social democracy in Europe and the USA (bringing health care, pensions, and the like) are now being eroded. Why? Because those who had pushed hard for social benefits in the earlier years had, by the 1980s jumped on the bandwagon of becoming big time consumers—and indifferent citizens.

A few years ago, Europeans were shocked to learn that fewer than 40 percent of the USA's eligible voters in fact vote; then Europeans began to notice that their 80-90 percent voting rates had dropped toward 50-60 percent.

There is good reason for all to be cynical of contemporary political processes and politicians; but those who are cynical are too busy buying and borrowing to note that at least some of that is a consequence of a "life style" that centers upon looking at a TV screen and rushing off to shop. (BARBER)

Lastly, note the effects of consumerism and its by-product **waste** on our already severely damaged **environment,** discussed at length under those headings; here a mere highlighting. There are several dimensions. It is a commonplace that we live in the age of plastic and that commodities are used and disposed of just like that. Bless modern technology. Some of that may be classified as a kind of progress; most of it combines shoddy products with an ultimate waste of time and effort and human and natural resources— and an ever-more damaged environment.

Much of the waste, concerned with "use and throw-away" articles seems at first glance (and, sometimes even at second glance) to be a matter merely of garbage disposal—somewhere. That "somewhere" is becoming increasingly hard to find, whether for New York's garbage or for nuclear wastes; and no wonder, there is so much of it, most of it stinking, some of it lethal.

Those who read this who are, say, in their sixties or older, may remember when one had a small garbage can in the house and a larger one in a hallway or backyard, and that the garbage people came around and took it away once a week. Now it has become common in both the USA (and, increasingly, elsewhere) for there to be three very large common containers at several spots within a block—and/or to have a giant truck come to your residence where, outside, you have three separate containers (for dry, wet, hard, soft, whatever)—and that everything fills up quickly (to the profit of the generally **privatized** collectors).

But that's peanuts compared to the wastes and destructive wastes intrinsic to our major consumer and capital goods industries. It takes factories to produce all the stuff we buy, and other factories to produce their equipment. What we buy and use, often as not, either spews some kind of pollution into the air (**cars** among the worst, but not the only, offenders), or is indestructible junk, or odious, or...something. And the factories that produce our consumer goods, and the other factories that serve them, are energizing their production with carboniferous fuels —directly with coal or oil, indirectly with electricity, which depends upon coal or oil—unless its hydroelectric, which is rare. And so our atmosphere becomes warmer by the year, and our weather changes, and our agriculture, and the air we breathe, and..., and it's all good for business—not only for the businesses selling the consumer and capital goods, but those doing the cleanups in one way and another. And anyway, didn't President Coolidge teach us that "What's good for business is good for America"?

corporate welfare

In recent decades, and especially since the **Reagan** era, we have been taught to see welfare as a dirty word; something given to the poor (especially, as Reagan always hinted) the black poor: Bad for them, bad for everyone; costs too much. In the discussions of **poverty** and **inequality**, it will be argued that such teachings should be seen for what they are, ways of deepening prejudice and facilitating other governmental expenditures, among them, not least those constituting welfare for the rich.

"Corporate welfare" does not refer to all governmental expenditures in favor of business, only those without reasonable justification—where "reasonable" means the expenditure is for the benefit of society which, without such an expenditure (and the uses to which it is put) would leave the society worse off, or miss an opportunity for it to be better off. That it also benefits the company, under such circumstances, is acceptable—at least up to a point.

From our first years as a nation there have been many such expenditures; indeed, one of Treasury Secretary Alexander Hamilton's great virtues was his understanding of the need for such grants—for the building of roads and canals and (among other projects) the subsidization of Eli Whitney's inventions (except, perhaps, muskets). Then there was the government's subsidization of the building of the transcontinental railroad. Great to have the railroads; necessary for the government to pay for two-thirds of their construction, and to do so with enormous land grants? Not quite. The end was admirable, the means were one of U.S. history's larger instances of **corruption** with, in addition terrible consequences up to this day. Why?

Because those lands were rich in forests and mineral deposits, and would become valuable real estate as their millions of acres became populated. The land grants were a simple give-away, the result of the ability of a few companies to become extraordinarily rich and powerful—and to continue to control a large percentage of U.S. resources and possibilities. (PHILLIPS, 2002)

In today's world, and especially in the past two decades or so, corporate welfare has become almost entirely a form of thievery for businesses, notably those able to keep a stable of **lobbyists** in permanent residence in the hallways and waiting rooms and offices of local, state, and federal legislatures—90,000 in D.C. alone. (PHILLIPS, 1994, 2002)

What the lobbyists seek to accomplish in the way of corporate welfare has several dimensions: the reduction of corporate capital-gains **taxes**, with resulting **tax expenditures**; those in turn mean an increase in <u>our</u> taxes, assuming governmental expenditures to remain steady or to rise. Then there is the creation of or increase in subsidies, whether for domestic or global trade or production. Add to that legislation for particular kinds of production with built-in cost plus contracts that insure exorbitant profits (see **military-industrial complex**), the initiation or extension of patent rights, allowing exorbitant monopoly profits for decades, most disgustingly for **pharmaceuticals**); and so the list goes.

That "list" has been put forth in extraordinary and fully documented detail in the 1996 book of ZEPEZAUR/NAIMAN. Note here merely the headings of their list: in the book, each heading is followed by several <u>pages</u> of details, including the costs to the taxpayer in descending order of the billions involved, most of them understatements, most of all that of the leader of the pack, **military expenditures** ($172 <u>billion</u> in 1995), least to "Ozone tax exemptions ($320 <u>million</u>):

- Military waste and fraud
- Social Security Tax Inequities
- Accelerated Depreciation
- Lower Taxes on Capital Gains
- The S&L Bailout
- Homeowners' Tax Breaks
- Agribusiness Subsidies
- Tax Avoidance by Transnationals
- Tax-Free Muni Bonds
- Media Handouts
- Excessive Government Pensions
- Insurance Loopholes
- Nuclear Subsidies
- Aviation Subsidies
- Business Meals and Entertainment
- Mining Subsidies
- Oil and Gas Tax Breaks
- Export Subsidies
- Synfuel Tax Credits
- Timber Subsidies
- Ozone Tax Exemptions

<u>Total</u> of the money handed out to wealthy individuals and corporations: $448 <u>billion</u> a year, at least 3 1/2 times that spent on welfare for the poor—itself subsequently reduced drastically by the **welfare** reform bill passed after the book was published.

There is great injustice in making the rich richer; but injustice is transformed into viciousness and deepening social harm when it is made easier by decades of snide campaigns that make the poor poorer, the rich disgustingly richer and, at the same time, feed our always deep **racism**.

corruption

That term usually signifies the betrayal of function—of one's self as a person, of a public or private office, of a process, of an institution; it is another name for succumbing to temptation for sexual, monetary, political, or other forms of anticipated advantage; for "selling out." It has existed in all known societies.

But to say that corruption has been timeless, ubiquitous, and multi-dimensional should not suggest that we shrug it off; as with polluted air, unless we try to rid ourselves of it, we can be done in by it. Not least is this so when we find it among individuals or institutions or nations that portray themselves as exemplars of all that is good: whether politicians, or companies or... the USA.

The ensuing discussion of the corruption of U.S. politicians, companies, and the nation does not mean to be comprehensive; see also, for example, **education, health care, pharmaceuticals, J. Edgar Hoover, Nixon, Bushes I** and **II, ADM, GM** and the USA's actions in **Latin America.**

If it is true that corruption has marked all societies, it is equally so that its intensity and its spread differ from time to time and place to place, in response to the equally diverse patterns of opportunities, rewards, and punishments for corrupt behavior.

The USA, home of "rugged individualism" and the richest ever of all nations, has offered very great opportunities and rewards along with the mildest of punishments in these respects. Writing just a century ago, VEBLEN (in his *Theory of Business Enterprise*) summed it up, in his customary wry manner:

> It seldom happens, if at all, that the government of a civilized nation will persist in a course of action detrimental to or not ostensibly subservient to the interests of the more conspicuous body of the community's businessmen.... There is a naive, unquestioning persuasion abroad among the body of the people to the effect that, in some occult way, the material interests of the populace coincide with the pecuniary interests of those businessmen who live within the scope of the same set of governmental contrivances. /And "corruption" is beside the point:/ In the nature of the case, the owner alone has, ordinarily, any standing in court. All of which argues that there are probably very few courts that are in any degree corrupt or biased... Efforts to corrupt them would be a work of supererogation, besides being immoral.

Before the modern era, few indeed were those who had an opportunity to become corrupt; such openings were confined largely to the very small percentage of those who sat at or near the apex of power—the top political (usually military) and religious functionaries. On the other hand, whatever the rewards for becoming corrupt, the punishments—real or imagined (as in the case of consignment to Hell) were severe, including a rather freer and terrifying use of executions (by fire, being torn asunder, beheading) than in our day.

Taking a long leap up to our own time and place, the opportunities have been, so to speak, "democratized," are no longer confined to the powerful. Individuals of merely comfortable (or even average) incomes can corrupt themselves—e.g., university professors (in refraining from writing or teaching in ways that might hold back their careers; or the opposite, doing work without merit except for its benign effect on career); doctors (in attaching more importance to their incomes than their patients' health, and doing so, ultimately, unconsciously); businessmen, in cutting corners qualitatively, engaging in "planned obsolescence," as with **cars** and computers) as a means of enhancing profits), **CEOs** lying about their companies' earnings; professional athletes (in taking strength-enhancing drugs), and so on: truly democratic corruption.

Of course, the higher one's place in the strata of power, the greater the opportunity and the reward for corruption: the prime example at the moment being our **CEOs** and top politicians, with the biz execs coming out on top. Ponder this quotation from the *Financial Times*:

> "Corporate insiders from the top 25 bankrupt companies (my emphasis) took $3.3 billion in stock sales, bonuses, and other compensation, even as their firms were spiraling into insolvency." (NORDHAUS) Good thinking.

All this is another way of pointing to two of the dominating characteristics of the USA: **commodification** and **competition**. If almost everything has a price, it is likely that almost everyone will have a price—whether in the realms of **education, health care**, business, politics—tutto. And if we all come to believe and to act upon **competition** as an acceptable basis, and, in any case, the ongoing basis of social existence—come to accept that "It's each for himself and God for all"—then each of us is more likely than not to see others as opponents: in the office, the classroom, in sports, business, politics—wherever. And   let   our   moral   standards   drop. (HOCHSCHILD, A.R.)

It was one of the most popular professional football coaches (Vince Lombardi) who added to his fame <u>and</u> his popularity when he said to his team (the Green Bay Packers): "Winning isn't <u>every</u>-thing; it's the <u>only</u> thing!"

But to say that **commodification** and **competition** feed the processes of corruption points to another set of tightly interacting processes: **decadence.** What has decayed in a decadent society are its functioning ideals and principles and the traditional constraints within which they exist. In brief, commodification puts a price on goods and services that should be provided on the basis of human **needs** rather than income; competition sets us against one another when, instead, mutually beneficial cooperation would be best for all. Not least is all this so when we comprehend the commodification of politics through **lobbyists** and of culture through **advertising** and the **media.**

What is common to all of the foregoing is a form of individualism that emphasizes personal gain or status, and lets social wellbeing take care of itself. Thus it is that competition and commodification contaminate and erode our humanity and the traditions that support it.

Our focus is, of course, the USA. As a nation <u>founded</u> on the rock of idealism—and which sees itself as a paragon of virtue in a debauched world—the degrees and kinds of corruption here have a special meaning.

Corruption in "America!" took hold as we became a nation. Those who first settled and developed the original colonies were Christians, the Puritans devoutly so: Their treatment of the native tribes ("**Indians**") was from the first a murderous corruption of anything to be found in the Gospel of Christ.

Nor can anything better be said for the almost immediate adoption of **slavery** as a crucial basis for the colonial and national economies. How great the inspiration of the words of our famed "Declaration of Independence": "We find these truths to be self-evident, that all men are created equal, that they are endowed by their

Creator with certain unalienable Rights, that among these are Life, Liberty, and the pursuit of Happiness...."—inspiring then here, and since then, everywhere.

How reconcile those words with the fact that so many of its signers held slaves, Jefferson and Washington among them. We may set aside the limits of the word "men" and attribute it to the historical context; but there is no way to set aside the meaning of slavery. The colonists (and those who practiced or abided in slavery up into the Civil War) were at least as aware of what slavery meant to those enslaved as were the "Good Germans" who watched the departing trains of the Holocaust. Nor has the many-headed racism in this nation been unknown or entirely unwelcomed by most.

That is but one of the almost innumerable dimensions of corruption in the USA—past and present. In our recent history, political corruption was fabled: Already in the late 19th century, Mark Twain famously saw it as "The Gilded Age"; the historian Vernon Parrington called it "The Great Barbecue." (PHILLIPS, 2002)

What was golden and being barbecued were the resources and economic possibilities of the USA. In those same years, the U.S. Senate was called "a rich man's club," for the office was bought and paid for; now <u>all</u> political offices (and most policies) are bought and paid for, through **campaign finance** and **lobbyists**; now it has become virtually impossible to find a candidate for any office, or any proposed policy, who has not been "on the market"—all of which is enhanced by the always more powerful and tightly-controlled **media**.

But corruption is not limited to politicians and policies; it is not limited at all. It exists in our attitudes both as "leaders" and "citizens," when, for example, we acquiesce in the deaths of 3 million or more Vietnamese in our war for their presumed freedom, in the deaths of hundreds of thousands of children in **Iraq** as a direct result of our 1990s embargo; meanwhile, we condemn the killings— assuredly horrific—of thousands at the hands of Serbs. If (and when) others behave like us in these and other respects, we accuse them of employing a **double standard**, which indeed they are; as indeed are we. Corruption of course extends well beyond the political sphere, most famously at present in widening scandals concerning **CEOs** and their companies (Enron, Tyco, Citigroup, MCI/WorldCom,

Martha Stewart, ad infinitum), and in our **health care** system, and in our universities (see BOK), etc.

But surely, all the fuss and feathers have put an end to the dirty doings? Not quite: Enron was given a large slap on the hand by the General Services Administration in 2001, when it suspended it from further federal contracts," and its travails are not yet over; it could yet get a slap on the other hand.

However. MCI/WorldCom's frauds caused their investors to lose $180 billion (three times more than Enron); yet the Bush administration, now MCI/WorldCom's biggest customer, has upped its business with them by over half since their scandal broke, with $772 million in contracts. (FM, "Well Connected, 5-28-03, WP, "MCI to begin rebuilding Iraq Phones, 5-15-03) Crime pays.

It is easy to say, "'twas ever thus"; however, there are different degrees of corruption, as well as different kinds and degrees of damage. As one who has spent over half a century teaching in the universities of this country (and Italy), I have seen both the degrees and the kinds of corruption intensify with each passing decade. I provide one telling illustration: In 1951, I was teaching at the University of California, Berkeley, on a joint appointment in the School of Business Administration and the Department of Economics. At a Biz Ad faculty meeting, a proposal came up to be voted upon: A well-known corporation (XYZ, here) had offered to pay an annual stipend that would entirely subsidize a full professorship; what it wanted in return, it said, was simply that the professor would be called the "XYZ Professor of Biz Ad." Of the 25 faculty members, only one voted in favor; the rest, after a vigorous set of denunciations, voted against it. Today, in contrast, many (perhaps most) of the professorships are in a corporate-named "chair"; and all Bus. Ad. profs teach in The University of California Haas School of Business. (Haas is the family that owns Levi's.) It is hard to believe, one would have to be a fool to believe, that School and its designated "chair" professors, are unaffected by such funding. Money talks; and silences. Not just universities, but all educational institutions, K-12 on up—are now being gamed. As **education** is turned over to profit-makers and advertisers. Neither least nor most, but perhaps most famously is that so for the corruption of high school and college sports. Once upon a time, or so they say, sports served as icons of purity and earnest dedication. No more, as shown in an article whose title is apt: "Something is very rotten in U.S. college sports," (George Vecsey, NYT, 10-19-02).

The tales told range from the use of free sex to entice athletes to many universities, to uniforms with ads on them, to the dependence upon TV revenue to finance sports teams and, inter alia, to the binge-drinking associated with college sports fans. "In the United States," Vecsey laments, "people know all about the corruption, the phony admissions standards, the payoffs, the boosters that permeate college sports. School administrators know. Fans know. We all go along." Wotthehell, everyone's doing it, no? Or, as the saying now goes, "If everybody is corrupt, nobody is corrupt."

Already back in the 1920s, the poet Robinson JEFFERS saw what was on its way:

While this America settles in the mould of its vulgarity,
Heavily thickening to empire,
And protest, only a bubble in the molten mass, pops and sighs out,
        and the mass hardens,
I sadly remember that the flower fades
To make fruit,
The fruit rots to make earth,
Out of the mother, and through the spring exultances,
Ripeness and decadence, and home to the mother.

credit cards (see debt)

crime and punishment

As with so many of the matters discussed in this book, the USA is by no means the only or the worst offender as regards <u>what</u> is considered a crime (as distinct from a civil offense), <u>who</u> is most likely (or unlikely) to be charged with it (whether or not one has committed it), and what the <u>penalties</u> are over the broad range of crimes (and civil offenses).

What does set the USA apart from other countries are the <u>bases</u> for the injustices regarding the foregoing questions and, among other matters, how highly we tend to regard ourselves regarding questions of justice. As the self-styled "land of the free and the home of the brave," we are also the land which carries a heavier burden of hypocrisy than any other on this matter.

In what follows no more than a representative sample of these questions will be examined; there is much more to be learned from the relevant bibliographical references. I begin with a brief look at the quantitative and qualitative aspects of crime and punishment in the USA.

First, some numbers: "Record-setting 6.6 million Americans behind bars or on parole," was a headline in the SFC (8-26-02). That amounts to one of every 32 adults in our country. In 2003, a third of those—2.2 million—were behind bars in prisons and jails, an increase of 30 percent since 1995, "even though crime, including violent crime, is down sharply." (NYT, editorial, 8-1-03)

No problem, those who are not uneasy with such numbers might say; we're a very big country, with almost 300 million inhabitants. Right. But it's the relative numbers comparing ourselves with other rich nations that should make one sit up and wonder. Compare the number of prisoners per 100,000 inhabitants:

> The USA has 702/100,000. The only country that comes close is Russia, with 664; then, Portugal, 131; Britain, 126; Italy, 93; Ireland, 78; France, 75; Sweden, 64; and the winner (loser, we in the USA might say), is Finland, 52. (NYT, 1-3-03)

How explain the difference between that Finland's 52 and our 702 (= 13.5 times as many prisoners, in relative terms)? Are the Finns stupid? Are their houses and banks being robbed, their children kidnapped, their stores broken into? Etc.? Not quite:

> Thirty years ago, Finland had a rigid model, inherited from neighbor Russia, and one of the highest rates of imprisonment in Europe. But then academics /those ninnies?/ provoked a thoroughgoing rethinking of penal policy... "Finnish criminal policy is exceptionally expert-oriented /says the head of their National Research Institute of Legal Policy/; we believe in the moral-creating and value-shaping effects of punishment instead of punishment as retribution."

As will be seen in **prison-industrial complex**—and in addition what will soon be noted below—the increase in the number of those imprisoned has coincided with the prison construction boom that began in the 1980s. ("Study Finds Big Increase in Black Men as

Inmates Since 1980," *NYT*, 8-28-02) The article goes on to show that in 1980 three times more black men were enrolled in institutions of higher learning than behind bars," but that now /20 years later/ there are "more black men behind bars than in colleges."

It is thus no surprise to learn that of those incarcerated (as distinct from on parole or probation), 46 percent were black, 36 percent were white; although blacks were about 11 percent and whites about 80 percent of our adult population. The foregoing "quantitative" statements require a "qualitative" explanation. As of April, 2003. "An estimated 12 percent of African-American men ages 20-34 are in jail or prison.... the highest rate ever measured...; by comparison, 1.6 percent of white men in the same age group.... (*NYT*, "Prison Rates Among Blacks Reach a Peak, Report Finds.)

The explanation the foregoing data that would first come to mind to a majority of our people would be that blacks are more prone to crime than whites. To the degree that such an assertion has any accuracy, it is made so because of the **racism** and the discrimination barring them from equal **education** and job opportunities and their consequent higher rates of **poverty** than whites. However, to that must be added that blacks are more likely to be arrested than whites for the same actions (whether as regards drugs or driving), more likely to be arrested when entirely innocent of any relevant action, and much more likely to be convicted and sentenced heavily when charged: guilty until proved innocent. All the elements noted in **bold** above are examined in their own place—as will be another literally deadly matter; namely, the inordinate and all too often eager resort to the **death penalty** against blacks.

The ways in which this has happened since the slowed rate of lynching early in the 20th century, may be viewed as "legal lynchings" conducted in police stations and courtrooms. Consider only the most recent instance of 110 cases of exoneration of death row inmates on DNA evidence. In the *NYT* articles "Confession Had His Signature; DNA Did Not," and "Man Freed After DNA Clears Him of Murder," (8-26/8-27-02), the case of Eddie Joe Lloyd—who had been in prison for 17 years—is revealed.

Mr. Lloyd, a black man, was in a mental hospital at the time of his arrest and confession. The confession was something he signed, but it was written by the Detroit Police Department. The

Department is now under investigation for "using excessive force, for prisoner deaths, for the widespread detention of witnesses..., and for at least one other case of a confession." (8-26-02) Mr. Lloyd is still alive and able to <u>be</u> exonerated only because Michigan does not <u>have</u> the death penalty—which, however, the presiding judge at the time thought was "the only justifiable sentence." And, upon the news of the exoneration, that judge—still "presiding"—remarked the "the fault lies upon /Lloyd/, no one else." (8-27-02) Say again, Your Honor; did I miss something? More on these and related matters is discussed under **racism;** what about <u>some</u> "whites" and crime? They too receive unequal treatment, depending not on color but class: To oversimplify somewhat but not too much, one may say that someone who "breaks and enters" to steal from a home or a shop may find himself with a prison sentence counted in years. In those years, he will be treated in such fashion—by guards and fellow inmates— that more often than not he will be scarred for life and, as often as not, become more hardened than reformed in his ways. And if he is caught doing the same in California (or New York, et al.), it's "three strikes" and a life sentence. (A law upheld by the Supreme Court, 5-4, March, 2003.)

Suppose, however, that a **CEO** is caught at having defrauded his stockholders and, because of employee stock options and 401(k)s, his employees; that while doing so he accumulated a fortune measured in tens of millions of dollars (or, as we have seen, oodles more); <u>and</u> that his employees have been cheated on their actual and expected incomes, their pensions, their jobs. Then what?

That **CEO** might be accused and convicted of a civil or of a criminal act. If the former, no prison, perhaps some unpleasant publicity, perhaps no more CEO offers. If convicted of a crime, he may have a prison sentence of a few years, maximum; more likely it will be a few months—probably in a minimum-security prison. And, when he emerges, he will still possess some or most of the millions he stole.

Those who mete out such "justice" are not blind; they have been led to do so by <u>very</u> expensive lawyers ($600-1000 an hour) and judges from the same class; both the judges and the jurors (if it is a jury trial) are more likely than not to be prejudiced against the black and the poor, and envious of the rich and the powerful.

What about the many <u>middle</u>-class whites who are caught at something other than a capital crime? Are their convictions and sentences likely to be as severe as those for blacks who have committed the same crime? Guess.

To all this two other serious matters need adding: 1) that imprisonment is a big business for a large number of companies and their teams; concerning which, see **prison-industrial complex**; 2) how prisoners are treated.

Their treatment, as with their sentences, depends upon whether they are in maximum or minimum security prisons, their age and gender, their class, and their color—and, more recently, upon the fiscal conditions of their state. Given what has been said above (and their REFERENCES), suffice it to say here 1) that maximum security prisons are hell for everyone, no matter what, if a bit less so if and when you get in with the relevant gang and that not only the prisoners but the guards help to create and maintain that hell; 2) that conditions are severe and maddening even in minimum security prisons (as I discovered when I taught in one for a year, in the 1960s); 3) that from their beginnings they have served to provide cheap—usually unpaid—labor for road building, agriculture, and industry, and now serve as one of several devices to keep the official **unemployment** rate beneath the real rate (HALLINAN); and, finally, with the fiscal crisis of all 50 states now well underway:

> State corrections departments are cutting costs and making prison life harsher. A few examples: in South Carolina, prisoners must now pay $2 to visit the infirmary and one-cell bunks now have 2 or 3, so close together cannot actually sit on their beds, and 87 prison educators have been laid off; Texas has cut its dietary requirements from 2700 to 2500 daily; Minnesota has cut meals to two a day on weekends and holidays; California now keep prisoners in their cells on 24-hour-a-day lockdowns to save money on overtime pay for guards; Pennsylvania has seven institutions already operating at 130 percent of capacity, and one at 163 percent. (*D&S*, "Fiscal Lockdown," 7/8-03)

It is—sort of—comforting to know that the prisons will not become even <u>more</u> crowded in consequence of the **CEO** scandals of late—as indicated by this headline of August 14, 2003: "Big names in corporate fraud go free: No indictments in sight for controversial CEOs." (*Bloomberg News*) The "big names" in this case were the execs caught with their fingers in the jam in two of the largest fraud scams of all: Bernard Ebbers of WorldCom and Ken Lay and Jeffrey Skilling of Enron.

In addition to what their shareholders lost ($50 <u>billion</u> + at Enron, alone), 35,000 jobs and $1 <u>billion</u> in worker pensions were lost by the two firms combined. Ebbers, Lay and Skilling, the three stooges of this unfunny show, will not only get off scot-free, but will be rolling in the riches they stole. That Ken Lay—until exposed—was **Bush II**'s number one buddy is, or course, totally irrelevant; nor is it relevant that **Cheney** held a big confab with the energy gang(sters) at the White House <u>before</u> all hell broke loose, and will not allow any peeking into the minutes of that meeting.

It's a good thing those guys didn't rob a service station; then they would have been in deep you know what. Moral: If you're gonna be a crook, be <u>white</u> and go <u>big</u> time.

Justice has <u>never</u> been blind regarding class or color; when it also applies the **death penalty** it has often been an accessory to murder. (See next entry.)

death penalty

Except for Russia and China, the USA stands alone among the world's major and most of its minor nations in having a death penalty. We stand entirely alone in another sense: In 1972 the Supreme Court deemed it unconstitutional, and it was <u>abolished</u>; sort of.

In 1976, the Court reversed itself, permitting states in effect to decide for themselves; 12 decided to leave well enough alone, the rest went back to savagery. Since then there have been over 700 executions (nearly one-third of them in Texas); and more than three thousand are sitting on death row.

Even those in favor of the death penalty, despite all, have reason to have second thoughts. What "all"? Here's some of it: As a result of DNA findings, as of 2002, <u>106</u> of current death row inmates had been found to be innocent. Then there are those juveniles and retarded who would <u>not</u> have been executed had they been sentenced after 1988; that was the year in which the Court ruled the death penalty could not be meted to those who were not yet 16 at the time of their crime. (The Court later refused to extend that to those 16 and 17, of which there are now 80 on death row. Too bad also for the retarded who were executed before June, when the Court exempted the retarded. (BANNER, *NYT* /6-22-02/)

Setting aside questions of errors and sadism, let us assume for a moment that the death penalty exists because it will <u>deter</u> the most violent of crimes. But it hasn't. Of the 27 states with the highest homicide rates, 25 have the death penalty; for the past 20 years, the homicide rate in states <u>with</u> the death penalty has been 50-100 percent higher than in those <u>without</u> it; Iowa, which doesn't have it, has the lowest homicide rate in the USA. (*NYT* 7-22-01) Go figure; but don't you <u>dare</u> say that the death penalty <u>causes</u> some to commit capital crimes.

Those who most vigorously support the death penalty don't seem to care about the data on errors, etc.; nor upon reason; indeed, something less easy to dignify with words seems to be operative:

> In all too many cases, defendants are convicted of serious crimes on the flimsiest of evidence. Juries often hang guilty verdicts on the word of a single witness, despite numerous academic studies showing that witnesses are frequently unreliable. Courts admit evidence of dubious quality at trials and send defendants to prison—or to death—on the basis of it." (*NYT*, editorial, 4-10-02)

Ponder the meaning of the recent flurries of DNA-based reversals of convictions, including many with death penalties (and some too late): as noted, 106 convictions have been reversed (on the grounds of wrongful grounds); 12 of them entailed the death penalty on grounds of DNA alone. Extrapolate that appalling finding backward into time. Scott Turow, noted novelist and criminal courts lawyer, has no moral compunctions about the death penalty, but he now supports its abolition, on grounds quite simply that it cannot "be fairly administered." (*NYT*, 4-28-02)

Add to all this the role of **racism**. <u>Of course</u> many more people of color have been executed than whites, not only in keeping with faulty evidence but without <u>any</u> evidence, all too often with an obscene enthusiasm, whether in the innumerable lynchings of the past or of their occasional repetition in the subsequent years.

The bare facts in Maryland alone would seem to indicate the need for extensive second thoughts. Consider 1) that 28 percent of that state's population is African-American; 2) that blacks represent 70 percent of the death-row population and 80 percent of its murder victims; yet, 3) "when prosecutors seek the death penalty, more than 90 percent of the victims have been white." (*NYT*, 5-5-02)

Enough already; but not for **Bush II.** In February, 2000 he proclaimed "I'm confident that every person that has been put to death in Texas, under my watch, has been guilty of the crime charged and has had full access to the court.") (*SFC*, 5-4-02) And that's that: As he said on another occasion (see **Bush II**) "I believe what I believe and that's what I believe." We're in good hands.

I prefer the position taken in 1994 by the late Supreme Court Justice Harry A. Blackmun: "The death penalty experiment has failed; I no longer shall tinker with the machinery of death."

The good news is that opinion is coming back to life, slowly, but one may hope, surely. So it was that in May of 2002, Governor Ryan of Illinois ordered a moratorium on executions and commissioned a special study on whether or not minority defendants are singled out for the death penalty. In January of 2003, as he was preparing to leave office, and after concluding that the death penalty is "arbitrary and capricious, and therefore immoral," he commuted the sentences of 167 death row inmates; "the broadest attack on the death penalty in decades," that is, since 1972 when the **U.S. Supreme Court** temporarily declared it unconstitutional.

In a speech Ryan made the same day at Northwestern University (to a group of whose faculty and students have taken the lead in investigating the injustices of the death penalty), Governor Ryan stated that,

> ...the number of /shown to have been/ innocent men freed from our death row now stands at 17.... If you really want to know what's outrageous and unconscionable, 17 exonerated death row inmates is nothing short of a catastrophic failure. (*NYT*, 1-12-03)

To which it may be added, that <u>one</u> would be plenty catastrophic enough for the dead man, and that although out of death row, the commuted prisoners will serve life sentences without parole—leaving open the question of the justice of the guilty verdict that sent them there. Could Illinois be the re-start, finally, of something good? Maybe. <u>Postscript</u>: While Governor Ryan was making his efforts, this headline appeared in the *NYT*: "State Can Make Inmate Sane Enough to Execute":

> The federal appeals court in St. Louis ruled yesterday that officials in Arkansas can force a prisoner on death row to take antipsychotic medication to make him sane enough to execute.... "Eligibility for execution is the only unwanted consequence of the medication," wrote the judge. (2-11-02)

Now who's insane?

debt

Historians often quarrel as to just when and just where **capitalism** was born; for present purposes, that discussion may be set aside. But one thing is clear, there has been no capitalism without debt.

The institutionalization of debt seems to have begun in Genoa in the 16th century—no surprise, given that the cities of Italy in the medieval era had been very much involved in trade and pre-modern industry.

Capitalism <u>requires</u> indebtedness in various forms. Central both to the birth and to the vitality of capitalism is "capital accumulation." That process first began to take hold in the era of what Marx called "primitive accumulation"—where capital expanded almost entirely from gains made from trade with—or, in the case of slaves, <u>of</u>—others, not, as would be so later, through industrialization and direct worker exploitation, as well as through trade and finance.

> The beginnings and spread of colonialism involved trading companies (the East India Company, most famously), which generally required naval protection and "merchant bankers." The bankers served as agents of various forms of borrowing. Marx's characterization of that era is worth quoting, both for its eloquence and for what it reveals:

> The discovery of gold and silver in America, the extirpation, enslavement and entombment in mines of the aboriginal population, the beginnings of the conquest and looting of the East Indies, the turning of Africa into a warren for the hunting of black-skins, signalized the dawn of the era of capitalist production. These idyllic proceedings are the chief momenta of primitive accumulation. (MARX, 1867/1967)

However, to say that the accumulation of capital has always gone hand in hand with the accumulation of debt does little to suggest the quantitative and qualitative dimensions of debt in today's world, led by the USA. Debt had grown and its forms had altered greatly in the 19th and early 20th centuries, but it entered an entirely new phase from the 1950s on, and then again from 1980s to the present.

Now debt has become something else; what once was incurred as a necessity has now become an addiction. It is an increasingly <u>dangerous</u> addiction for several reasons, not least because of the socioeconomic <u>fragility</u> it creates; withal, it is difficult to see that capitalism could survive without it.

Now an elaboration of that sweeping generalization (in addition to what is put forth under **capitalism** and **financialization**).

Nowadays, most especially but not only in the USA, debt, once engaged in only by businesses and nations, has become considerably more complex both in structure and function and is incurred by virtually everyone for almost everything; and recklessly so. The composition and nature of debt will be examined in what follows under the headings of a) <u>government</u> debt, b) <u>business</u> debt (with separate discussions of 1) <u>non-financial</u> corporations' debt and 2) the debt of <u>financial institutions</u>, c) the <u>foreign</u> debt of the USA, and d) <u>household</u> (mortgage and credit-card) debt.

a) <u>Government debt</u>. This will be dispensed with quickly here with a generalization as to why, and the reader directed to further discussion under **deficits and surpluses**.

"Governmental debt" refers to that which a nation usually "owes to itself," a result of it having spent more than it has taxed over time; it takes the form of government bonds. Although foreigners may and do hold such bonds, only for weaker nations is that of importance—except in extraordinary instances—such as, perhaps, could face the USA in the future because of its equally extraordinary <u>foreign</u> debt (now close to $7 <u>trillion</u> and rising by over $500 billion a year).

National debt is different from the other forms of debt discussed here precisely because it <u>is</u> a debt largely owed by the nation to itself. The rise in such debt <u>can</u> lead to a variety of socioeconomic problems and has done so; but, unlike other forms of debt, a relatively strong nation—as distinct from an Argentina, for example, has means at its disposal to resolve its debt problems—by raising taxes, and/or lowering expenditures, and or "printing money." One or all of these may or may not lead to <u>other</u> problems. Be that as it may, other forms of debt do not have the same options.

b.1) <u>Non-financial corporations' debt</u>. The principal function of capitalists' debt accumulation up to the early 20th century was to finance production and trade. What could or should not be accomplished through selling shares (equities) was taken care of by long-term borrowing for expansion and short-term borrowing for the purchase of raw materials, building inventories, and paying wages. Rarely is it either possible or desirable for a business to fund its operations <u>without</u> indebtedness.

For both lender and borrower, until the late 19th century that was a generally positive set of processes. When, however, industrialization came to mean <u>over</u>-industrialization—i.e., a persistent tendency for supply to exceed demand—the entire world economy moved toward deep economic and associated political crises; they did not end until the upheavals of World War I, depression, revolution and counter-revolution and World War II had run their course. At least for a while.

Beginning already in the late 19th century, a principal consequence of those emerging and negatively interacting processes was to transform the role of finance, beginning with the intervention of financial companies into the mergers of once-separate industrial companies as the 20th century was dawning. In the USA, the key figure in that process was J.P. Morgan; relevantly, his namesake financial giant of a company is now one of those in deep do-do (as **Bush I** was wont to put it.)

That movement was the infancy of what has become the **M&A**s of today: Between 1897 and 1905, over 5,300 industrial firms came under the control of only 318 corporations. J.P. Morgan engineered the mergers of what once had been 750 and then became 12 steel companies into one, the U.S. Steel Corporation: the first billion dollar company in history. Then as now, the "engineer" was among the prime gainers: Morgan collected over $1 million in fees (which, in today's terms, would be at least a billion). (JOSEPHSON, ADAMS & BROCK)

In those days, such processes were like a long night of fireworks; but they were soon outdone in numbers and effects in the 1920s. In its turn the 1920s were dwarfed by their counterparts in the 1960s:

the highest number of mergers in single <u>year</u> as the 19th century ended was about 1,200; and it was about that in 1929, just before the Crash—except a) the number for the entire <u>decade</u> was more than twice that of the earlier decade, b) the average <u>size</u> was larger, and c) the mergers were also different in their sweep: not just "<u>horizontal</u>" mergers within a given industry as earlier, but also "<u>vertical</u>" mergers, of firms at different levels from the merging company—its suppliers and its customers (a steel company buying up a coal and a bridge building companies), plus "<u>conglomerate</u>" mergers, where an electrical products company (**GE**) buys an airplane engine company and a media company (inter alia).

Any one of these kinds of mergers increases the concentration of economic power; when all three kinds take hold, such concentration is much heightened and tends to increase the concentration of political and social power as well.

Striking as the numbers and kinds of the mergers were up through the 1960s, they were soon dwarfed by the rampage of combinations of the 1980s; and they in turn were outdone by the whoop-de-doo of the 1990s. (**M&As.**)

Returning to J.P. Morgan and his 'engineering" of the U.S. Steel Company (in whose "Research and Strategy Department" I worked before World War II), one can without too much difficulty comprehend how the role of the financial world has necessarily been enlarged and transformed over time, most especially after the 1960s. Those thousands of M&As required the intervention of countless financial and accounting companies of diverse function—none including production, all having to be paid for, and handsomely.

Whatever else was happening, borrowing was much expanded and it too was transformed. The 1980s and 1990s were the years in which the aptly-titled "junk bonds" and raging corporate buy-outs, then "derivatives" and "hedge funds" became the vogue. Those activities, taken together or separately, provided fortunes for some (and short and minimum-security prison terms, as well, for a few, such as Ivan Boesky and Michael Milken). (**financialization**).

Little or none of this could have occurred as easily as it did—or at all—had those same years not been the main take-off years for **downsizing and outsourcing**, an orchestrated weakening of **unions**, and the **deregulation** of the financial realm, overturning the reforms in banking and corporate finance—most notably, the **Glass-Steagall Act**—that had been painfully established in consequence of the Wall Street-as-Las Vegas of the 1920s.

Among the several quantitative and qualitative differences between all earlier periods and now, one is struck by the widespread behavior of corporations that borrowed substantially in order to buy back their own stock—mostly to provide for stock options and to raise their stock prices: In 1999, at least 3.6 percent of GDP went into stock buybacks (among other scams; see **deregulation**).

The past quarter century that produced the socioeonomic framework allowing **financialization** to supersede production and trade as the critical center of the economic process also created the conditions by which **speculation** became the critical center of finance; that takes us to examine the financial sector itself.

b.2) <u>Financial institutions' debt</u>. The debt of "Wall Street" companies neither begins nor ends with banks and stock brokers (nor are they all on Wall Street). It has now come to resemble a very complicated gambling casino whose elements are scrutinized under **financialization**. One of its recent innovations is called "securitized lending." The term refers to lending activities of financial companies that "spread the risk" (to themselves, not us) of lending by joining together on a given loan. Fine. But in recent years those same companies have <u>borrowed</u> on the loans they have granted: from $2.4 <u>trillion</u> in 1989 to over $7 <u>trillion</u> by 1999—an amount bigger than household debt and almost double the size of nonfinancial corporate debt. Remember when "banker" meant "conservative"?

In 1999, *Business Week* asked, "Is the United States Building a Debt Bomb?" (11-20-99) By 2002 (as will be seen) it was asking even more dire questions; and answering in the affirmative.

c(<u>U.S. foreign debt</u>. During and partially because of World War I, the USA ceased being a debtor nation and began its move toward becoming the world's and history's largest creditor: from 1915 to 1980 we went from <u>owing</u> some millions to being <u>owed</u> $1 <u>trillion</u>. **Reaganomics** combined with a changing world economy managed to turn that number inside out: When **Reagan** left office our debt to the rest of the world was $1 <u>trillion</u>. As noted earlier, now we owe about 7 <u>trillion</u>, rising by at least $500 billion yearly.

That foreign debt arose for several reasons: 1) because of our dominating economic strength, we had become the world's savings bank, whether literally or as a seller of corporate and U.S. government bonds; for that and related reasons, 2) our corporate stocks were also the most sought after, globally. Because for foreigners to buy our bonds and our stocks they had to buy dollars, the dollar soared against all other currencies; which, 3) meant other countries' products (imports) were cheaper for us and that ours (exports) were more expensive for them: the USA became what it remains, "the consumer of last resort."

Sounds fine, until you think about its implications—which neither Reagan and his advisers did nor the Bushies do: "The strong dollar means a strong country," said Reagan. That it does; but it also carries with it more than a few warnings: 1) For many U.S. companies it meant more competition at home, fewer sales abroad (Item; In 2003, 40 percent of all cars purchased in the USA were produced abroad); 2) and that (among other "causes") meant continuing "**downsizing and outsourcing**," which 3) brought the slow but sure descent of production and the rise of services (not least financial services), that is, 4) as our manufacturing center (also the home of the strongest unions) shrinks, there are fewer good jobs with their higher incomes at home, and thus an average decrease in purchasing power—except through more borrowing and more in the family having to take **jobs**; and, neither last nor least, 5) it meant an increasingly fragile global and national economy.

It could not be otherwise for the global economy, dependent as it has become on the U.S. borrowing always more in order to buy always more, while business also borrows always more in order to make always higher gains through their own and others' debts—a process all too suggestive of the fabled "house of cards." As 2003 became 2004, that fable could be seen as coming around the corner as a reality: the dollar having lost more than a third of its value against the Euro (for instance), and foreigners beginning to shrink their purchases of our securities rather than, as had bee so for decades, to increase them; fragility on the rise

Next, considering that it is now generally agreed that **consumerism** is the driving force of the U.S. and therefore the global economies, as we examine household debt, we shall see just how shaky all this has become.

d) <u>Household debt</u>. "Consumer Credit: A Crunch May Be Coming," was <u>BW</u>'s lament of 8-12-02, wherein two tables of consumer debt had as their heading "Reaching the Breaking Point?" There are various attitudes towards indebtedness, and various measures of it. As noted under **decadence**, the attitude that held sway until a century ago was that expressed by Benjamin Franklin: "A penny saved is a penny earned." Saying such in the USA as the 1980s ended, and even more today, could lead to a spell in an asylum for the demented:

> "From 1950 to 1992, households saved about 9 percent of their after-tax income. In 1993 the savings rate began a long slide, going negative (meaning that people were spending more than their incomes) last year for the first time since 1933." (*LBO*, 5-24-01)

That note was followed by the quoted comment of Standard & Poor's economist David Wyss: "The only thing keeping the economy afloat is the willingness of American consumers to live beyond their means." (ibid.) Here some of the bare bones of the transformation, taking only the last 25 years: In 1978, household debt (= mortgage + all other consumer debt) as a percentage of after-tax income was 62 percent; in 1992 it was 75 percent; as of now it is well over 100 percent and, both because and despite relatively hard times, rising.

But the bones don't tell all; here a bit of flesh and muscle. First <u>who</u> is borrowing, and <u>how</u>, <u>what</u>, and <u>why</u> are they doing so? And what are they borrowing for, <u>now</u>, as compared with earlier?

The answers are a great mix, with here only suggestive responses: 1) the well-off to rich are often refinancing their homes to purchase stocks and bonds, to take fancy trips and other luxurious forms of consumption: "In nearly two-thirds of recent refinancing of loans owned by Freddie Mac Corp., people took out bigger loans than the ones they paid off, freeing up cash for more spending." (*BW*, 8-12-02)

2) Then there are those in the middle, neither well-off nor poor (called "<u>subprime</u>") in the industry.

Some of the middle-level folks (myself included), use their credit cards only as "check cards," and <u>never</u> to borrow. We are a minority. The others are borrowing, but not necessarily knowing what it costs them in "interest." They don't know they are not just paying a monthly rate for purchases but, as well, a daily rate on unpaid balances that are increasingly common (if only because such cards are merchandised increasingly—and for their victims, confusingly).

Among the most easily fooled in that group are the young, not least the college-going young. They may be innocent, but their "captors" are not. Seventy-seven percent of full-time undergraduates at 4-year schools have credit cards; 32 percent of college students have four or more cards; 41 percent of graduating seniors have an average debt of $3,000. (And now you will see banks advertising to parents: "You can open a checking account for your children.")

No surprise there when one learns, for example, that one credit card company pays the University of Oklahoma a percentage of every purchase made on its university "affinity" card: In 13 years, the U. of O. has "earned" $13 million for such dubious practices. (NYT, 7-21-02, Abby Ellin, "Creditworthy? Be Credit-Wary.") (I remember being shocked in 1971 while teaching at a state university in California, to see card tables outside many of the buildings, enticing students to take on a credit card with this enticement: "No references necessary; just get one." Just do it! And then pay an average of 14.5 (+) percent on your balance, 'til death do you part. 3. And now, the cruelest cut of all: the subprime borrowers. These are those who would otherwise be rejected by major banks; such borrowers naturally pay a premium for a home equity, a personal or an auto loan, from 5 to 8 percent more than the non-subprimers. The subprime market grew quickly in the 1990s, from insignificant to more than a third of credit-card loans (WSJ, 8-19-02) Alongside that development, and helping to explain it, is that credit card solicitations rose by about six times in the same years (from just under 1 billion to over 6 billion, and as the default rate rose almost exactly in proportion. (ibid.)

Subprime loans "begin to exhibit predatory characteristics when the interest rate has no relation to actual risk..., is whatever the lender can get away with. Other predatory red flags include 'packing' the loan with unwarranted fees, 'flipping' the loan or attaching a 'balloon' payment to the loan. All of these red flags allow predatory lenders to evade state usury laws, which only cap interest rates." (ZM, 9/2002)

In a *NYT* story headlined "Minefields Abound in Attempts to Reduce Debts," (9-22-02) we read another instance of the plumbing of depths below depths: "With consumer debt at an all-time high, people... are being deluged with phone calls, e-mail messages, television and radio commercials and letters peddling various forms of credit repair, credit consolidation and debt counseling..., which experts warn... can lead already desperate consumers into deeper financial problems." The story goes on to tell the story of the hard-working Mrs. H., who paid a "credit-repair" company $4,000 but found a year later that none of her debt had been cut; after interest and late charges, indeed, it had more than doubled.

Nor is Mrs. H. unique: personal debt as a percentage of personal income has risen steadily for the past twenty years; already in 2000 it stood at 110 percent of income, and has risen since. Credit-repair, anyone?

These practices, usually imposed upon people whose English is poor, and/or who are desperate, routinely result in ongoing debts and effectively exorbitant interest rates that create a lifelong burden for the borrower: very much akin to the neighborhood loans from gangsters that were common in the first decades of the 20th century. They were crooks; what are the credit-card companies who follow in their tracks today?

But the accumulation of household debt was not, and could not have been accomplished by the financial world alone; it came to be in an economy which was increasingly guided by and dependent upon **consumerism** which, in turn (and apart from homes), was centered first and foremost on **cars** and **TVs**, and other assorted durable goods, the combination of which has had fearsome consequences in the realms not only of political and economic **corruption** and social **decadence** but in the **environment** and **waste**.

> Here a household debt warning: If you have an ongoing debt balance of $5,000 and you are making the usual minimum payment, with an effective annual interest rate of 17 percent it will take you 40 years to pay it off—and you will have paid the company $16,305 for the privilege of being preyed upon.

But there's one dead broke guy who doesn't have to worry: Rep. James P. Moran (Dem., VA). He voted for the bankruptcy bill of

2002 that makes it <u>very</u> difficult for poor people to file for bankruptcy (and thus save some of their property). He voted for that very tough bill, despite being up to his neck in debt himself. Well, not <u>quite</u> despite; easily understandable in fact, given (as the <u>NYT</u> reported, 8-9-02) that the world's largest credit card company MBNA (a main sponsor of the legislation) "...loaned him $475,000 in 1998, just a month before he became a supporter of the law for which they were among the principal **lobbyists**... 'The timing of my loan was wholly coincidental with the co-sponsorship of bankruptcy reform,' said Mr. Moran." Maybe so; on the other hand, "...in 1999 he took a $25,000 loan from a pharmaceutical company lobbyist shortly before he /became/ a sponsor of a bill to help the company maintain its patent on an allergy drug." <u>Another</u> coincidence! After that, in 2002, one more loan, this time for $50,000 from the CEO emeritus of AOL. But hey! He's Congressman, Moran is; after all, a Representative; and someone has to represent companies, too. Something wrong with that?

<u>Postscript</u>: This has to do with borrowing—lots—to spend on weddings.

> More people are seeking credit counseling, citing wedding expenses as a contributor to their financial troubles. According to a survey of bridal magazine readers by Conde Nast, the average spent for a wedding totaled more than $22,000 /in 2002/, or about 22 weeks of the median family income /$52,000/. (NYT, 7-1-03)

More than a third of that 22 grand for conspicuous consumption was for the reception, a tenth for photographs. If they're like more than half of us, in a few years they'll have to borrow again for the divorce. C'est la vie, nezpa?

Enough fun and games; the latest news on household debt is not only sad for the folks involved, but ominous for the "consumer of last resort" economy. In a NYT essay by Jeff Madrick of 9-4-03 ("Necessities, not luxuries, are driving Americans into debt...). Set aside that what are called luxuries are the things the average household <u>thinks</u> it needs (**cars**, **TV**, and other durables):

> The costs of what it really takes to be middle class today—education, health care, housing, pharmaceuticals—rose much faster than median family incomes."

Madrick goes on to show that although between 1973 and 2000 incomes rose about 5.5 percent, health care costs went up by 8 percent and those for education by 6.5 percent; and then there are the costs of the two-income family, which must pay for day care and pre-school and, usually have to have two cars. (see **health care, education, cars, pharmaceuticals, jobs**)

Meanwhile, there is a teensy percentage of us—10 percent maximum—getting tired as they seek out $10,000 watches, $6,000 shower curtains (for the Tyco boss), third, fourth, and fifth homes somewhere, and all that jazz. It would be nice to think, well, after all, when the economy begins its slide down into the mud, they'll go, too; except most of them don't, and almost all of us <u>do</u>. Time for a change.

decadence

In its literal sense, "decadence" refers to <u>physical</u> degeneration: plants, buildings, bodies, and the like.; in social commentary, as here, it is used metaphorically: it was what Yeats had in mind in his famous "The Second Coming": "Things fall apart, the centre cannot hold..." It has been among the most ubiquitous of social diseases, knowing no limits in time or space. Even in the relatively brief history of the USA, decadence has taken hold several times, finding its place in both fiction and nonfiction: The novels of Edith Wharton bridging the 19th and 20th centuries —most famously, the ironically titled *Age of Innocence*—were at least somewhat influenced by VEBLEN's *Theory of the Leisure Class* (1899).

Another roll in the hay began in the 1920s (see among other books Sinclair Lewis's *Babbitt* and *Main Street*, and F. Scott Fitzgerald's *Great Gatsby*,) and it was of course rampant in the broader popular culture of both those periods, as exemplified in clothing, dancing, drinking, gambling, vulgar display.

But, <u>what</u> was being decayed <u>from</u> in the 1880s/1890s and once more, in the 1920s? Lots, but more than anything else it was the most prominent set of beliefs accompanying the founding of this society; namely Puritanism. Its firm base was religion, from which sprang its social principles. Their effects were both potent and, for a while, enduring.

Sitting at Puritanism's center was its obsession with sin. It was defined very broadly, beginning with sexual activities, going on to "excess consumption," and setting the need for self-discipline. Its canons of <u>social</u> uptightness came to be replaced by Ben Franklin's <u>economic</u> uptightness: "A penny saved is a penny earned." "Neither a borrower nor a lender be" "**Waste** not, want not." (This guy is crazy; lock him up.)

Puritanism took hold with a social framework coming to be dominated by early **capitalism**; as the 17th century gave way to the 18th, the socioeconomic dicta of Puritanism came to be ever stronger and ever more serviceable to capitalist political economy.

However, as the 18th century rolled on, the descendants of the Puritans were less likely to be found in the ministry than in the fur trade, fisheries, lumbering, <u>and</u> the slave trade—as in the "economic Calvinism" of Franklin; let sin take care of itself.

However, as the 19th century drew to its end with explosive industrialization, such notions had became problematic, at best; in our time, if lived up to, the socioeconomic process would grind to a halt.

By the 1880s, U.S. industry—mining, manufacturing, railroads—had been roaring long enough to find it itself with too much to go around—too much, not for the people in general, but for the businesses trying to sell at a profit; from 1873 until 1895, there was what was called "the great depression": **competition** had come to be called "destructive," savings were seen as excessive, and, with what was called "the combination movement" (nowadays called **mergers and acquisitions /M&As/**), competition was shoved aside by the first steps toward the giant companies of today.

Thus had Puritanism yielded economically to the "Robber Barons" and "the great barbecue," and "The Gilded Age." The time for decadence to become socioeconomically useful had arrived. So it went up into and beyond World War I. <u>Arrivederci</u>, Ben.

The decadence of the 1920s was a continuation but also a deepening and spread of its prewar nature, with its own discrete—which is not to say "discreet"—origins. It was a period of widespread disillusionment, not least but not only with the war—a war whose length, bloodshed, deaths (10,000,000, in Europe, 250,000 U.S. soldiers) and downright insanity was unprecedented; the foolishness of the (Puritanical) Volstead Act of 1919—which illegalized the sale and use of alcoholic beverages—didn't help: it led not only to massive lawbreaking by perhaps a majority of the people, but to the connected rise of gangsterism, and to the combination of drinking with a loosening of sexual standards.

All this (and more) took place in a world in which mass communications and entertainment were just a-bornin': film, radio, magazines, tabloids, larger and more crowded cities, mass-produced cars..., you name it. If there was a heroine of the time, it was the scantily-clad and sexy Clara Bow, the "It Girl," while the sports hero Babe Ruth was equally renowned for over-eating and over-drinking. (The only "clean" hero was Lindy—whose name was got more than a little mud on it in the late 1930s when it came out that he was a be-medalled Nazi sympathizer. Where are the heroes of yesteryear? *NYT*, 8-2-03)

Then the Crash of '29 and our Great Depression hit, and the excesses of the Twenties were no longer affordable, either in their spirit or at their price. Try to imagine: 25 percent unemployed; no unemployment insurance; no social security; virtually no unions; no health insurance; no wage and hour laws; no **SEC;** widespread legal child labor. *Hard Times.* (Read Studs TERKEL's marvelous book of that name.)

All that meant that the average person would spend more time thinking about how to survive than where to get a drink. (And anyway, Prohibition had been repealed in 1933.) And then there was World War II, whose timing was just what the doctor had ordered (except for the bloodshed).

The years 1930-1945 shoved decadence into history's wastebasket and, in doing so, allowed socioeconomic reform to get on stage. Except for a handful of localities and a small percentage of the people, both Puritanism and decadence were memories, at most—except for the uncool and uptight who saw the 1960s (several of whom became President of the USA, later).

The complex, even contradictory socioeconomic processes of the Seventies and Eighties set the stage and put into play the latest and longest period of U.S. decadence. It was a strange period with many seeming contradictions: serious inflation and serious employment in the 70s and, in the early 80s, the worst recession since the 30s; the beginnings and worsening of **downsizing and outsourcing** and **globalization** and their accompaniment of permanent losses of good jobs for workers.

All that occurred while, at the same time, **consumerism** was expanding exponentially—a seeming contradiction made explicable by the extraordinary increase in household **debt** that would take the average household from owing under 70 percent of its income to over 100 percent by 2000, itself explained by the always improving techniques of **advertising** and the **media**.

Out of which, the new decadence: in the economy, in politics, in popular culture, in education, in every walk of life. Meaning what? Meaning an era of always spreading and deepening institutional and personal **corruption**, the decay of remaining sensibilities and ethical standards, the deepening of social indifference and the fanning of individual **greed**. (HOCHSCHILD, A.R.)

The good people of the USA have never been much interested in working toward a society whose people would be seriously concerned with each other's wellbeing; now most of us are plumbing always lower depths as, for all too many, desperation combines with socialized greed to keep us hustling to the tune of "Anything goes."

The slogans on our coins are "<u>E pluribus unum</u>" and "<u>Liberty</u>." From never having been representative of our realities, they have now become embarrassing. How about we change them to "<u>More!</u>" and "<u>Why Not?</u>," and get real?

deficits and surpluses

Those who read the economic and business news regularly—and especially those who have majored in **economics**—will see my treatment of this topic as sheer nuttiness. The reasons are several: 1) It goes against the teaching and preaching of mainstream economists for the past 25 years or so (as compared with the 25 years preceding them); 2) the permanent fog of confusion created by public officials and financial journalists, with Milton **Friedman** and Alan **Greenspan** the main foghorns; and 3) the natural tendency to think of governmental deficits as one does household debt (there being few with the occasion to think of household surpluses).

The conventional (and applied) wisdom today is very much what it was before the mid-1930s: It is a sin to run a governmental deficit (which increases its debt), a virtue to accumulate a surplus (which reduces it). Think of deficits and surpluses as rivers running into or out of a lake, causing debt to rise or fall (setting aside rainstorms, very hot weather, etc.).

In the USA, local and state governments are <u>forbidden</u> to run deficits without voter confirmation of a bond issue and accompanying tax increases. The federal government, on the other hand, may run a deficit and sell bonds to finance it merely by getting congressional approval—a process which can and often has had the effect of "printing money."

Before World Wars I and II, the **economics** profession divided its analyses and theory of the national economy into micro and macro, the former referring to the behavior of individual markets (for commodities, labor, etc.), the latter to the behavior of the economy as a whole. But until the ideas of Keynes were put forth in 1936 and put into practice in the 1940s, <u>macro</u>economics didn't really exist, except as **monetarism.** (see the excellent, easily read introductions to macro and micro /respectively/ in the <u>D&S</u> books by MILLER, et al., and OFFNER, et al.)

The essential ideas of monetarism were first put into practice by the Bank of England throughout the 19th and into the 20th century. "The Little Old Lady of Threadneedle Street" was a privately-owned (but no longer is) and controlled bank, something of a model for our Federal Reserve System, which also began as and is still privately-owned and controlled by its governors who, in turn are appointed by the White House, which wouldn't <u>think</u> of appointing anyone not approved by—guess who?—the private banks; otherwise known as the fox guarding the chicken coop. Which reminds me:

> Item: When Clinton was elected in 1992, he saw himself and was seen by others as a "New Deal liberal." Late in his first year, seeking to explain to his inner circle why he could not pursue certain policies, he muttered "It's the f.....g bond market!" Somewhat more politely, his first campaign manager, James Carville mused "I used to think if there were a reincarnation, I wanted to come back as the President or the Pope or a .400 baseball hitter. But now I want to come back as the bond market. You can intimidate everyone. (NORHAUS)

Until the past few years, banks have always had as their first concern protecting their loans: that is, <u>THERE SHALL BE NO INFLATION</u>. Why all the fuss? Because when there <u>is</u> inflation, the value of a loan decreases proportionately: If I borrow $10,000 and the price level is at an index of 100, and it rises to 150, the cost of the loan to me, the borrower, has decreased by 50 percent, for money is "cheaper." And the lender has lost proportionately.

So bankers staunchly oppose government spending on anything that might stimulate the economy; it might raise prices, which might reduce the real value of bonds and other loans. It is not that they are entirely wrong; stimulative spending, precisely because it is stimulative will contribute to some degree of inflation. That it might do lots of other things that would be valuable for the economy, the society, and the bankers—who, after all, lose when their borrowers go bankrupt in bad times—seems to have been beyond the comprehension of the banking world. It isn't as though bankers are stupid (although that, too, is possible), it's that their focus has the width of a needle's eye. One of the interesting things about what is now going on with the **Bush II** and its record-breaking deficits is how and why he retains the—albeit queasy—support of Wall Street.

In his *General Theory....* (1936), KEYNES argued that price inflation of three percent or a bit more is in fact essential to a healthy capitalist economy; that when the economy is in decline, let alone stuck in the mud (as when he wrote), the government should initiate projects of "social consumption" and "social investment" which would be useful for the society and its people and which, because they would add public to private demand for labor and resources and commodities, would be good for the economy as a whole—including, of course, businesses that didn't have enough buyers and banks that didn't have enough borrowers.

His position came to be called "functional finance": it says that whether the government should run a deficit or a surplus depends upon whether the economy is too cold or too hot: if it's cold, warm it up by spending (without raising taxes); when it's too hot and threatening to inflate too much, the government should decrease its expenditures and raise taxes, and use monetary policy to raise interest rates: Make it harder for people to buy and for businesses to borrow. There is neither virtue nor sin in either deficits or surpluses; it depends upon the context.

When his ideas were applied in the USA and elsewhere in the 1930s and again after World War II, Keynes was shown to have been right. A significant part of the business world in the USA saw that, helped to so by the massive **military expenditures** which alone took us out of the depression; shown again by their counterpart in the **Cold War.**

The number of sane businesses has diminished greatly in the past quarter century (with mainstream economists trotting alongside). Moreover, as the structure of business power in the past quarter century has shifted toward finance, the banker mentality has come to dominate our economic policies always more (see **financialization**). Raise high the banner: NO deficits; only surpluses.

But WOW!, has that and they changed. Starting with **Reagan**, and renewed with **Bush II**, the slogan became no old-fashioned deficits; only those birthed by the "supply-side economics" of Reagan and the Alice Through the Looking Glass econ of the Bushies.

What actually happened in Reagan's years were persisting budget deficits, averaging 3.5 percent of GDP, going up to 5 percent in 1992; then, under Clinton, the deficits went down and the budget went into a surplus of 2 percent of GDP in 2000. "Since then, the federal budget has moved toward the red by more than $700 billion..., a fiscal reversal /that is/ the largest four-year deterioration in the federal budget in American history. (NORDHAUS)

How could it not have been? Massive reductions of the **taxes** of the rich and very rich and of corporate income taxes, expansion of **milex** over the record-breaking levels of Reagan (which benefit mostly the rich), and while not even counting the war expenditures in **Afghanistan** and **Iraq**, using all that as an excuse to cut back on grants to states for their social expenditures while cutting back those of the federal government: Praise the Lord, pass the ammunition— and, find some nice little islet in the Caribbean to flub up your finances.

The **Bush II** budget proposal for fiscal 2004 (which took hold October 2003) asked for $2.3 trillion, with an expected deficit of $450 billion (when Iraq is counted), compared with a surplus of $127 billion for 2001. But the deficit as such isn't the problem now, nor was it with the Reagan crazies; it's what it is and is not paying for; put differently, who benefits from, and who pays for that budget?

The recent recession, declared to be over some six months after it began, may be over for some but it sure as hell isn't for the nine or so million officially unemployed and another nine or so million who are <u>also</u> unemployed: The lousy times that continue have the Bushspun name of a "jobless recovery" more likely than not to worsen <u>because</u> of what Bush's budget does and does not do. (see below, and **unemployment** and **jobs**)

According to Keynes (and me), now is just the time for the federal government to stimulate the economy by spending more than it's taking in; what the society needs most are jobs and more purchasing power for the bottom 80 percent of the people; and the kinds of jobs that could/should be provided—in health care, education, public transportation—society and we need most.

To the degree current governmental thinking touches any of the relevant bases, it is the realm of **taxes**. However, not only does the lion's share of tax cuts go to the rich, but the deficits are used to cut direct federal social expenditures and payments to the 50 states for <u>their</u> social expenditures in education, Medicaid, and among other areas, safety.

<u>Item</u>: " 1.2 to 1.6 million poor people have lost their health benefits as a result of cuts /over the past three years/ at the state level."

<u>Item</u>: "... state troopers have gone to a four-day workweek, and schools have run out of money for textbooks and computers."

<u>Item</u>: "State officials have had to contend with a cumulative $200 billion in budget shortfalls." (*NYT*. "Hints of fiscal upturn for crisis-weary states," 1-6-04) What Bush II is doing now is a deliberate rebirth of the conscious program of the Reagan years; it was called "Starve the Beast." (STOCKMAN) The "beast" was the set of social expenditures <u>hated</u> by those right of center: health, education, social security, public transportation, welfare. How does one "starve" that particular beast? By cutting governmental income (by reducing the taxes of, mostly, the rich) while, simultaneously, increasing military expenditures and subsidies for big business (especially for agribusinesses). The result? Well, folks, there just ain't no money left for those other things; and besides, those "other things" are bad for our national character.

And so it has gone with Bush II's fiscal policies. (also see

taxes/tax expenditures): <u>direct</u> (personal and corporate income) taxes have been cut, so <u>indirect</u> federal <u>and</u> state taxes must <u>rise</u> while (as noted above) states' social expenditures must <u>fall</u>. That causes after-tax incomes (and purchasing power) of the majority to fall while, <u>also</u>, they fall because of the many job losses thus incurred.

Are there alternatives? You bet; we know because some were tried and got fine results in the late 1930s—right here in the U. S. of A. They came to be called "alphabet soup," because of their acronyms: WPA (Works Progress Administration); PWA (Public Works Administration); CCC: (Civilian Conservation Corps); NYA (National Youth Administration); TVA (Tennessee Valley Authority). That's the short list of the best part; the worst part included NRA and AAA (see **FDR, farmers**). Just a few words about the good ones.

The WPA was wonderful, as note some of its programs: Writers Project; Musicians Project; Actors Project...: get it? There were more than 6000 who got a "subsidized" start in the Writers Project, including Richard Wright, Saul Bellow, John Cheever, Conrad Aiken, Nelson Algren, Malcolm Cowley, Studs Terkel, Ralph Ellison, Zora Neale Hurston.... Read any good books lately? They got $20-25 a week. ("Unmasking Writers of the W.P.A.," *NYT*, 8-2-03)

Doesn't sound like much, but it was, then; nor, ultimately, was money the most important part. I was in a related project for students, the NYA, while going to San Francisco Junior College, 1936-38 (itself a creation of the New Deal): Tuition $1 year, 40 cents an hour ($20/week) to help a history prof's research. I don't know if it helped her, but it certainly made a <u>very</u> big difference for my life (and you are now paying the price.

As for PWA, when you cross a bridge, drive on a road, look at a dam, chances are it got its start by the PWA. The CCC helped some, mostly young, from starving while also helping nature along. In the Tennessee Valley, the region's economy and its families' lives were changed for the better by the TVA.

Those who worked in any of those agencies were not only getting what was an almost livable income then, but in spending it they were also helping to maintain or increase jobs for others; at least as important, they were doing something noticeably useful with their lives and for their society.

Unfortunately, in that <u>everything</u> is just hunky-dory today, we have no use for such social expenditures, right? There is <u>no</u> reason to repeat the errors of those bad old days. At least, so they say.

During the **Vietnam** protests, there was a song we used to sing against that war; now's the time to sing it again, loud and clear, against this economy: "When will we ever learn?" (Actually it was "they" not we; but it is <u>we</u> who must learn; <u>they</u> are doing just fine.)

dehumanization/alienation

Because those two words are rarely heard and are very controversial when they are, and because their reality is at the heart of what this book is about, it is advisable to attempt some clarification of terms.

First, what is the "humanity" that is being "dehumanized"; from what are we being "alienated"? To be a human being is to be a mammalian biped, with many structural and physiological features we share with other mammals; it is the characteristics we do <u>not</u> share with them that makes us human.

All animals must breathe and eat and procreate, and in comparison with humans, when most animals' characteristics change, they do so <u>very slowly</u>. That we are very much <u>unlike</u> all other living creatures in that respect (among others) is the focus of the ensuing discussion.

Our consciousness and our character and, most relevantly, the whys and wherefores and the <u>speed</u> with which both can be and have been altered over time is the core of that discussion.

Consciousness is shaped from two sources: 1) from the larger social process within which we live—in this case those of **capitalism**; and 2) by our personal "character," with great variations for different people, depending upon class, gender, "race," parents, time and place. (LICHTMAN)

Character and its central "self" serve as a sentinel at the gate of consciousness. The sentinel allows selective entry to the many types of "information" confronting the passive being and issues "passports" for the inquiries of the active being. Character is shaped both in the family and the larger society in processes of mutual interaction of different degrees of intensity consequent upon our "education" at home, in school, and in our daily lives as shaped by our jobs, the

media, war or peace, and so on.

The social process and its structures provide us with the full panoply of matters to be perceived, but our character selects out what matters we will or <u>can</u> perceive, and how we will respond to what we have perceived.

<u>Given</u> the social process, character is decisive for consciousness; <u>given</u> our character, the social process is decisive. But the complexity is greater still, for consciousness is itself a shaping force on both the social and personal processes; there are no one-way streets of causation in society.

The gist of this discussion will be that the capitalist process from its beginning has had a deleterious, draining influence on the positive elements of what it means to be human, and necessarily so. For intrinsic to the satisfactory functioning of capitalism is 1) the concentration of socioeconomic <u>power</u> that <u>requires</u> workers—almost everyone—to be economically powerless and with reduced dignity at work, and 2) that it <u>requires</u> and seeks always to increase the **commodification** and the **corruption** of everything and everyone (see **jobs, education, health care**) and, neither least nor last, politicians. (POLANYI, VEBLEN, BARBER, KUTTNER, PHILLIPS).

It was Marx who launched the main attack on capitalism as a system that necessarily "alienates" its people. He borrowed the term from Hegel, but as with so much else from his education, he turned it on its head. The German word for alienation means "estrangement." Marx saw capitalism as entailing workers' estrangement from themselves as human beings—and though he cared less, <u>also</u> of capitalists: the "Messrs. Moneybags."

It is relevant here to point out that as the discipline of psychiatry evolved, those who practiced it were called "alienists"—FREUD most famously. (see his *Civilization and Its Discontents*)

From his start as capitalism's critic to his last words, Marx's critique of capitalism was aimed at its ruination of our species' wonderful possibilities; TUCKER summarizes it that view succinctly:

> The basis of /Marx's/ moral condemnation of wage labour
> is not that wages are too low, but that wage labour by its very
> nature dehumanizes man. This means, for Marx, that it defeats
> his natural human urge toward spontaneous productive activity,
> converts his free creativity into forced labour and drudgery, and

frustrates his human need for a variety of occupations.

Marx's first writings in what became his lifelong condemnation of capitalism are found in the *Economic and Philosophic Manuscripts of 1844*; that is, four years before the *Communist Manifesto*. His analysis of workers' lives deserves sustained quotation: (his emphases)

> What constitutes the alienation of labour? First, that the work is <u>external</u> to the worker, that it is not part of his nature; and that, consequently, he does not fulfil himself in his work but denies himself, has a feeling of misery rather than well-being, does not develop freely his mental and physical energies but is physically exhausted and mentally debased. The worker, therefore, feels himself at home only during his leisure time, whereas at work he feels himself homeless. His work is not voluntary but imposed, <u>forced labour</u>. It is not the satisfaction of a need, but only a <u>means</u> for satisfying other needs. Its alien character is clearly shown by the fact that as soon as there is no physical or other compulsion it is avoided at all costs. External labour, labour in which man alienates himself, is a labour of self-sacrifice, of mortification... not his own work but work for someone else...In work he does not belong to himself but to another person... /The/ worker feels himself to be freely active only in his animal functions—eating, drinking and procreating, or at most also in his dwelling and personal adornment—while in his human functions he is reduced to an animal. (in BOTTOMORE)

But what about the substantial increases in the level of material well-being since 1844? In that same manuscript, and as though he had anticipated the age of **consumerism**, Marx went on to say that the capitalist "system of private property, just as it increases

> the mass of private objects, therefore the realm of alien entities to which man is subjected also increases. Every new product is a new potentiality of mutual deceit and robbery. Man becomes increasingly poor as a man; he has increasing need of money in order to take possession of the hostile being. The power of his money diminishes directly with the growth of the quantity of production, i.e., his need increases with increasing power of money. The need for money is, therefore, the real need created by the modern economic system, and the only need which it creates.... Excess and immoderation become /the/ true standard. This is shown subjectively, partly in the fact that the expansion of production of needs becomes an ingenious and always calculating subservience to inhuman, depraved, unnatu-

ral, and imaginary appetites. (ibid., his emphases)

Marx was of course writing more than 150 years ago, in the era of competitive, not **monopoly capitalism**, before the average worker could even <u>think</u> of having decent food, clothing, or shelter, let alone a **car** and a **TV**—or an **education**. As all that was coming into being, so also was what Marx had expected in the way of alienation. (POTTER, MARCUSE) This is how the Marxist Paul BARAN saw those matters in an essay of 1959:

> At no time in history has this power over the vast and growing productive forces been to such an extent power over life and death of millions of men, women, and children everywhere. But the most insidious, and at the same time the most portentous, aspect of this overwhelming power of the objectified productive relations over the life of the individual is the capacity to determine his psychic structure. (BARAN, 1969)

Thorstein VEBLEN was as severe a critic of capitalism as Marx but, because born and raised in the USA and writing half a century after Marx, he found many reasons to bring additional dimensions into his analyses; in doing so, he developed a substantially different critique, one paying more attention to the socio-psychological consequences of capitalism's functioning. *The Theory of the Leisure Class* (1899), his first book, was much concerned with what he called "**emulation**."

To emulate is to strive to be seen as belonging to a social class of higher rank than one's own; in Veblen's analysis, it was the working class "emulating" the "leisure," that is, the capitalist class. Marx's saw workers' solidarity as the mark of their humanity, and saw it as leading them to overthrow their oppressors. Veblen saw emulation as more likely to lead them to seek to be <u>like</u> their oppressors.

Worse, because Veblen saw that which is "emulated" as referring not just to matters of "conspicuous consumption," but those also those in the realm of **nationalism,** the depraved offspring of patriotism. That was the central theme of his study of the German working class before World War I. It had produced the strongest socialist movement in the world with significant power in the government. However, it "emulated" its rulers; in the Reichstag, its members were easily seduced into supporting "war credits" in 1914. In so doing, workers offered themselves up to slaughter: alienation as suicide.

(VEBLEN, 1919)

In the ensuing decades that take us to the present, all of what Veblen saw as "imbecile institutions"—unfettered business greed, nationalism, emulative consumption, not least—have penetrated and shaped our consciousness and character to degrees Veblen had feared. In his book that focuses most squarely on "human nature and conduct," *The Instinct of Workmanship* (1914), these were his dour conclusions:

> In those cases where... those instincts which make directly for the material welfare of the community, such as the parental bent and the instinct of workmanship, have been present in such potent force..., there the bonds of custom, prescription, principles, and precedent have been broken—or loosened and shifted so as to let the current of life and cultural growth go on, with or without substantial retardation.
>
> But history records more frequent and more spectacular instances of the triumph of imbecile institutions over life and culture than of peoples who have by force of instinctive insight saved themselves alive out of a desperately precarious institutional situation, such, for instance, as now faces the people of Christendom.

That was written with regard to the "imbecile institutions" of 1914; now, as these words are written, our social condition is surely no less "desperately precarious," and the institutions are at least as imbecilic. Shall we "save ourselves alive"?

deliberate obsolescence (see cars, waste)

deregulation

The history of regulation/deregulation in the USA has been and remains one of a long-running carnival act with lotsa laughs, but only for the crooks:

> Act I: The excesses of business cowboys and sharpies take good parts of the economy toward or over a cliff. Act II: Congress is persuaded to do something about it and institutes some regulation. Act III: Time passes, memories fade, the good times roll, **lobbyists** get to work, and back to Act I we go, spectacularly so, with the Blackout Follies of 2003 that provide the Curtain for this discussion.

The first inaugural show began in the late 19th century, also the first of three "new eras," each more disastrous than the other: 1) the 1880s up to World War I, 2) the 1920s, 3) and the one we are mired in now. 1. The period from the 1880s on was called "the second industrial revolution" because of its mass production, its continental railroads, its expanding (pre-**cars**) oil, steel and machinery industries—dependent upon the technologies linked to physics and chemistry rather than "mechanics." (VEBLEN /1904/; DU BOFF; FAULKNER)

Out of all that arose the first major "combination movement" (**mergers and acquisitions**). **Big business** and high finance moved on stage and "rugged individualists" such as Carnegie, Gary, Rockefeller, Du Pont and Morgan became household names, and dubbed "robber barons" by JOSEPHSON.

The raw deals of that period produced critics who, taken together, came to be called "the Muckrakers." Best-known were Ida Tarbell (on Standard Oil), Lincoln Steffens on **corruption** and **poverty** (*The Shame of the Cities*), Upton Sinclair on the meatpackers (*The Jungle*); and those years prompted the first overall critique of U.S. capitalism, VEBLEN's *Theory of Business Enterprise*—as also the first move toward <u>some</u> kind of regulation as the 20th century began, led politically by Theodore Roosevelt.

Preceding Roosevelt was the Sherman Antitrust Act of 1890, often seen as an anti-monopoly law. It had that potential in that it made it illegal for companies in the same industry to make agreements restricting competition, and (25 years later) set up the Federal Trade Commission (FTC) to police it; until 1911 the Sherman Act was used instead to hold back **unions**, in order to maintain what is now a unidirectional "<u>flexible</u> labor market," one in which, that is, wages and working conditions are "flexible" downward, easy to worsen, very hard to improve.

As consequence of Tarbell's Standard Oil expose', and in part because President "Teddy" Roosevelt was at times a charismatic populist in a time of rugged business "individualism," Rockefeller's giant Standard Oil Trust was taken to court in 1911 and, at least on the surface, lost: It was required to split into 29 parts, resulting in six still <u>very</u> big companies.

They have managed to find their way home again, resulting in

EXXON MOBIL (once Standard of N.J. and Mobil of N.Y.) and CHEVRON TEXACO (once Standard of CA and its Texan copy). Over time the tightly-knit global **oil** industry of "seven sisters" (see SAMPSON) has continued to run a smoothly controlled market, at home and abroad, all the more dangerous because its separate members can <u>seem</u> to be competing. (BLAIR; ENGLER)

The only other action that is often seen as a major reform was the creation of the Federal Reserve System (1913). Modeled on the Bank of England and, like it, owned and designed to be effectively controlled by bankers, it became the apple of the eye for monetarists—for the same reason that others (myself included) see it as a major gift to financiers and something like the opposite of a reform. (see **economics** and **monetarism**)

But at least there was that moment. Soon after, the distractions and increased concentration of economic power attending World War I propelled the USA into the "Roaring 'Twenties"—in many ways a precursor of *The Roaring Nineties* (STIGLITZ, 2003): A "new economy" of **cars**, electric light and power and telephones, consumer durables, soaps and cigarettes, the beginnings of mass **advertising**—and a soaring stock market.

Business prospered, fortunes were made, there was a new, more widespread <u>and</u> more penetrating combination movement, <u>and</u> the first conclusive steps toward **financialization** (itself dominated by speculation) were implanted. While all that was going on it is estimated that **unemployment** averaged 5 to 13 percent, and (by today's measures) **poverty** afflicted at least half of the population. (MILLER, H.) Their problem; not to worry. There were also regulatory agencies in existence, not only the Fed and the FTC, but, in response to the enormous expansion of public utilities (gas, electricity, telephones), the separate states legislated public utility commissions (under one name or another) to control what were "natural monopolies"—"natural" because it is integral to the production and distribution in those industries that in order to function at all efficiently, they must be so large as to be able to serve a proportionately large market: market "competition" is thus precluded.

The regulatory commissions came into existence in the separate states. Which meant something, but not much, unless the state legislatures and commissions were free of **corruption**: That's a joke, folks: state regulatory agencies worked hand-in-glove with private utility giants to fix rates at such a level as to assure high profits for the companies while providing the appearance of fairness to the public: the best of all possible worlds. Until, that is, Enron (et. al.).

The "fix" from the 20s on was arranged, so to speak, through agreements. But as the 80s ended and the latest "new economy" took hold and, along with it as political corruption spread and deepened, deregulation also spread. In 2001, Enron showed California just what that means when aided and abetted by today's instantaneous communications: a gas and electricity market turned into a chaotic gambling casino, with big millions to be raked in from enormous "buys" and "sells" from Texas to California.

Billions of dollars in increased rates—up 40 percent in 2001—and increased taxes were the first result; following them, cutbacks in education and other state programs. Three billion cheers for the free market. The whole sordid Enron tale has been put together in SMITH/EMSH-WILLER in their *24 Days*. Read it and gnash your teeth.

The whoop-de-doo business practices of the "prosperity decade" of the 20s were great for the top companies and the incomes of the top 10 percent; but hard times for the unemployed and the poor as income **inequality**, always high, shot up. (SOULE, MILLER, H., DU BOFF)

2. The excesses of the 1920s in the USA, joined to the long-standing and deep-seated economic and political crises over the globe, produced the worst depression ever and made World War II unavoidable; in the USA it also produced the most sweeping socioeconomic reforms and regulations of our history.

The reforms concerned both the misbehavior of finance and **big business** and, as well, the unmet needs of what **FDR** called "the ill-fed, ill-clothed, ill-housed" in his inaugural address in 1933. After World War II, along an erratic path, still other socioeconomic reforms meant to meet human and social **needs** were added: for **health care, housing, social security, unions,** and **education.** (MITCHELL, B.)

However, and as will be examined both here and elsewhere, all the reforms enacted after 1935 began to be deliberately eroded as the 1970s unrolled. Their swansong was provided by **Milton FRIED-MAN** throughout the 60s and subsequently. His crusade against regulation was first expressed fully in his *Capitalism and Freedom*.

Because the 1960s were years in which political discourse tended to be significantly influenced by liberal/left discourse, Friedman was more ridiculed than influential—until the 1970s. Since then his arguments have been the analytical basis for the wiping out of the social reforms that began in the late 1930s and anything since then.

Sitting at the hard center of Friedman's position is that all goods and services **commodities** and should be treated as such: or, as Kuttner has put in his book: *Everything for Sale*. Everything? Right, says Friedman, His position was aptly summarized by E.K. Hunt:

> Milton Friedman advocates the elimination /my emphasis/ of 1) taxes on corporations, 2) the graduated income tax, 3) free public education, 4) social security, 5) regulation of the purity of food and drugs, 6) the licensing of doctors and dentists, 7) the post office monopoly, 8) government relief from natural disasters, 9) minimum wage laws, 10) ceilings on interest rates charged by usurious lenders, 11) laws prohibiting heroin sales, and nearly every form of government intervention that goes beyond the enforcement of property rights and contract laws and the provision of national defense.

Friedman didn't advocate the elimination of Medicare, for it didn't exist until 1965. He's gotten around to it since, as he has to the early 1970s' Clean Air and Water legislation, while supporting the privatization of "national defense" (now underway in Iraq: SINGER). Since the late 1970s, and at an always increasing rate and severity, Friedman has had his way to one degree or another—except in #11, the elimination of the laws prohibiting heroin sales; the only one that for which one can make a plausible case.

A lot of people just plain laughed at Friedman in the 'Sixties; since then, as with a clutch of others of his ilk, he's gotten the Nobel for Economics, and his spirit has come to dominate legislation across the nation—including that which in the past quarter century has been harmful to 1) at least 80 percent of our people in the realms of income inequality, health, education, housing, and social security, 2) all of our people in the realm of infrastructure (most damagingly public transportation) and 3) again to all of our people (and those over the globe) in the diminution of our always inadequate environmental policies. What was still left in 2000 was placed or is being placed on **Bush II**'s chopping block. Who's Number One? Prof.

Friedman.

The reforms from 1935 through 1972 were very mild as regards regulating business, of meeting unmet human and social needs, and for protecting the environment; but they went **too** far so far as the business community was concerned. In what follows we trace out was attempted in the way of regulation and how and when it was undone.

In the financial sector the **Glass-Steagall Act** of 1933 and the **SEC** (Securities and Exchange) Act of 1934 were passed to control speculation and to separate short-term from long-term lending, and the Federal Deposit Insurance Corporation /FDIC/) to protect small depositors. In general those reforms were meant to minimize the ways and degrees by and to which ordinary people could be harmed by the ravages of speculative finance. And they worked reasonably well; for a while. Glass-Steagall was repealed by Congress in 1998; but already in the **Reagan** years it was in fact becoming defunct, as was the original meaning of the FDIC. In the 1980s, the perversion of the **S&Ls** was accompanied by their being taken over by "financiers" (many of whom were quite simply gangsters) and, instead of the FDIC protecting the small depositor it began to (and still does) protect the large financial speculators. (MAYER, NAYLOR, PIZZO): The scandals from 1999 to the present are evidence of just how well the SEC has done its job (as STIGLITZ was quoted as saying above).

The torrid combination movement of the 1920s was hot not only in its record-breaking numbers but as well in its new <u>kinds</u> of mergers: not just one company in a given industry buying up a competitor ("horizontal" mergers), but buying up its suppliers and customers ("vertical")—as when steel buys up a coal company <u>and</u> a bridge building company); or when a steel company buys an oil company and a bank, that is, all <u>sorts</u> of companies ("conglomerate"). In doing their doing this, they were also greatly increasing the concentration of economic power, to degrees that made the 1880s et seq. seem pale in comparison. (As seen in **big business**, in the past 20 years or so, conglomerate **M&As** not only have a **GE** buying up an NBC, but going global as **TNCs**, buying up companies of all sorts in other countries.)

Despite what the 20s had produced in the way of increased concentrated business power, FDR's reformers didn't get around to doing more than investigate (as with the TNEC: Temporary National Economic Committee). The TNEC studies produced 40 volumes on various industries and problems, showing who owned what, how economic power was being misused, and how the socioeconomy was being harmed. (SWEEZY, in NATIONAL RESOURCES COMMITTEE, 1939): But the investigations, begun in the late 1930s, ended abruptly as war began.

Thus, far from the reforms of the 1930s having their effects on business power, something like the opposite occurred. Facilitated by the war's pressures for even <u>more</u> "cooperation" among and between business giants, new heights of concentration occurred: 100 companies received two-thirds of <u>all</u> war contracts, which they doled out to tens of thousands of smaller companies who then became beholden to them, and usually stayed that way after the war; by the 1990s, the amounts spent had gone up and the number of companies dominating them had gone down, as the **Cold War** was taking on new dimensions:

> Over 130,000 separate firms contract with the Pentagon; 25 of those firms receive about half of all contracts and farm them out to still other thousands of firms—which, along with about 3 million civilian arms plant workers, over 1 million civilian workers on the Pentagon payroll, and over 1 million reservists (with income supplements), constitute a formidable political support system for military expenditures. (CYPHER /1991/)

After World War II, a new "combination movement" took off, reaching <u>its</u> peak in the 1960s; or so it was thought; after a hiccough in the 70s, all that was surpassed in the wild and woolly 80s and then again in the even wilder 90s (**big business**; (RAVENSCRAFT; DU BOFF)

In short, there has been <u>nothing</u> done to slow, let alone to reverse, the massive pressures toward ever-greater size, along with the always broader national and global scope of giant companies; meanwhile, always more concentrated <u>economic</u> power becomes always considerably more concentrated <u>political</u> and <u>social</u> power.

Socieconomic reforms accomplished from 1935 up through the 'Sixties included those in the realms of **social security, unions, health care, housing,** and **education**. Created with great difficulty and never fully satisfactory, they are easily sundered and weakened.

Herewith some of that history.

1) In 1935, and in addition to the Social Security Act, the Wagner Act was enacted; the latter provided that workers must be able to form and use unions without coercive acts against them by employers; 2) in 1937, legislation provided subsidized housing for the poor; then, 3) in 1938, Congress enacted legislation prohibiting child labor, setting a minimum wage, the 8-hour day and the 40-hour week—with pay for overtime. What needs remarking first is how inadequate they were to begin with and how late in our history they all came: Germany's social security system started half a century earlier; second is that all such legislation departed from a base of compromise that virtually insured malignant weaknesses: **Social Security**, though much better than nothing, is <u>not</u> providing security (and is now threatened with "**privatization**"; the Wagner Act was followed in 1947 by the **Taft-Hartley Act**, whose weakening consequences endure; the **housing** act was never reasonably financed and, in recent years, has been transformed into subsidies for <u>middle</u>-income, not low-income families; except for members of Congress, the military, and other governmental beneficiaries, <u>no</u> governmental health care except Medicare (for the old) and Medicaid for (some of) the poor in the mid-19<u>60</u>s, both—again, better than nothing—inadequate; the law against child labor—it was about time!—defied still and on a rising scale; the minimum wage amounting to an income well <u>under</u> the poverty line; and the 40-hour week—that is, requiring overtime to be paid for more than that—now increasingly violated: "... in 1999, the <u>average</u> U.S. worker put in 260 hours more work than in 1989, that is six weeks work without extra pay." (*BW*, 12-6-99)

That was the same decade in which worker productivity was regularly reported as wonderfully rising. In <u>this</u> decade, the decade with the new phenomenon of "jobless recovery," once more we are supposed to cheer reports such as "Productivity Jumps Again," until we note the rest of the story, "As Job Creation Remains Slow" (<u>NYT</u>, 8-8-03). What is actually going on is indicated in a small paragraph toward the end: (and see **jobs**)

> .... Technology spending has been weak since the stock market bubble burst three years ago, and business investment over all has been the weakest segment of the economy for the last several years. Instead, companies have shifted strategy and hunted relentlessly for every possible way to squeeze more pro-

duction out of the remaining workers.

Another way of putting that would be to say that **exploitation** is rising and easy to bring about because **unions** are at their weakest since the 1930s—with the additional note that when businesses invest, they create jobs and help to stimulate expansion; now they are **downsizing and outsourcing**: dynamite when added to **Bush II's** version of "Reagonomics.

As regards deregulation and the **environment**, although **Nixon** is usually thought of as being very conservative, even reactionary, he was not so in the realm of the economy. He was even daring, one may say when, in the early 70s, faced with emerging deficits in our international balances, and with both prices and unemployment rising, he was quick to enact not only wage and price controls and tariffs on imports and effectively to go off the gold standard but, as well, it was in his administration that the **Clean Water** and **Clean Air Acts** were put in place and that OSHA (Office of Safety and Health Administration) was created for worker safety.

As the **Nixon** entry shows, his behavior in those regards were not a consequence of his generous heart, but that he only really gave a damn about his own power; as **Haldeman** (his Chief of Staff) reports, his concerns with economic matters (in this case, foreign trade) were nicely expressed when in a related discussion he expostulated "I don't give a shit about the lira." Cattivo.

None of our regulatory agencies are ever adequately financed—least of all the **SEC**, OSHA, or the Environmental Protection Agency: On their office doors should hang signs: "Do Not Disturb. Lobbyists at Work." The low comedy suggested at the beginning of this discussion has provided little to smile about—except for those who should be regulated and who have had their **lobbyists** buy their way out or get deregulation.

Meanwhile, **big biz** laughs all the way to the bank. As they do that, the rest of us have to recognize that the domination of our economy and our society by a few is tighter now than ever before; precisely because of that, there is a greater need for regulation than ever before. Putting their domination and our **needs** side by side tells us something else: We have a very large problem on our hands; it will only become more severe unless it is dealt with politically.

It will not be dealt with by those who created it, except by making it worse. We cannot expect much help from a bought and sold Congress and White House and State legislatures, nor from the media; they are part of the problem, not the solution. So are we, unless we recognize that the solution is ours, not theirs, to construct. Of which, more will be said in the <u>Afterword</u>. <u>Postscript</u>: Shortly after the foregoing was written, the Blackout Follies came to town. Endless discussions of its whys and wherefores took place in print, on TV, and on the Internet. After many hours of silent meditation, **Bush II** interrupted his fund-raising to assure us that everything would be OK as soon as we built some new facilities. Period. Only a few voices even suggested that the cause of both the Enron scandal and of this blackout were the same: deregulation.

Robert KUTTNER (of *Everything for Sale: The Virtues and Limits of Free Markets*) put the whole matter clearly and well in his Op-ed essay in the *NYT*, "An Industry Trapped by a Theory" (8-16-03). Some excerpts:

> Deregulation of the power industry was supposed to use the discipline of free markets to generate just the right amount of electricity at the right price. But electricity... is not like ordinary commodities...: /It/ can't be stored in large quantities..., it needs a lot of spare generating and transmission capacity...; it requires a great deal of planning and coordination, and it needs incentives for somebody to maintain and upgrade transmission lines. Deregulation failed on all these grounds; yet it has few critics.

> Ten years ago, most public utilities were regulated monopolies..., guaranteed a fair rate of return..., compensated for building spare generating capacity...; /and/ in the half century before deregulation, productivity in the electric power industry increased at about triple the rate of the economy as a whole.

He goes on to show <u>why</u> regulation is essential to prevent gouging, witless speculation—and blackouts, pointing to Enron, which cost Californians "tens of <u>billions</u> of dollars," adding that "a generating company needs to control only 3 percent of the state's supply to set a monopoly price." And he concludes with this astute observation:

> When the blackout hit on Thursday /8-14-03/, many of us first thought of terrorists. What hit us may be equally dangerous. We are hostage to a delusional view of economics that allowed much of the Northeast to go dark without an enemy lifting a finger.

dictators

The 20th century was littered with them, all over the globe. Something of why that was so is at least touched upon in the relevant regional/national discussions. Here we ask: what were the relationships of the USA with dictators; what was the "pattern" of those relationships?

There were <u>lots</u> of them; for perspective, we merely list merely the best-known in the five regions:

Europe: Hitler, Stalin, Mussolini, Franco, Salazar, Ataturk, the Greek "Colonels."
Middle East: the Shah of Iran, Hussein of Iraq.
Africa: Mobutu.
Asia: Chiang Kai-shek, Mao Tse-tung, Rhee, Diem, Ky, Souvanna Phouma, Sukarno, Suharto, Marcos.
Latin America: Batista, Castro, Somoza, Pinochet, Peron, Vargas, Duvalier, Stroessner, Noriega.

Even a cursory, let alone a thorough study, shows that virtually without exceptions (to be noted), the pattern was to fight against, blockade, or isolate those left of center while actively supporting or giving critical assistance to those right of center. Freedom and democracy? Are you kidding?

Europe. There was a sharp contrast between our responses to dictators in Nazi Germany and Communist USSR. **Germany**: We intervened in the Germany economy in the early 1920s, when its horrendous inflation —prices rose four <u>trillion</u> times, 1918-1923— threatened not only the stability of Germany (which had strengthening left <u>and</u> right movements) but, as well, our investments there and in connected European economies.

From 1925 to 1933, as the Nazis gained in strength and then took over, we looked the other way. Despite Hitler's unspeakable ferocities, we remained aloof until the outbreak of war in 1939, with some notable exceptions. Most glaring among them was

1) In 1938 at Dusseldorf, the largest steel companies in the world—my then employer U.S. Steel the largest—met to form a global steel cartel. It was designed to keep prices up by sharing the market in an "orderly manner." They did so, until war broke out.

2) In 1936, the Popular Front in Spain won a free election.

Immediately after, Generalissimo Franco initiated his military effort to overthrow the Loyalist government. In the process, he gained the substantial military support of Italy (ground troops) and Germany (aerial bombing).

As the Italian and German fascists assisted the Spanish fascists, we were shipping them oil and metals while, at the same time, a White House decree denied Spanish Loyalist ships the right to even enter N.Y. harbor: the "Mar Cantabrico" incident.

During World War II, Fascist Spain's troops fought side-by-side with the Germans in the Russian campaign. After that war, and as the **Cold War** took hold, our good friend Franco gave us all the air bases we wanted.

3) When we finally did join the war against Germany in 1942, it was after Germany had declared war against us; that is, after we had declared war on Japan.

On the other hand, our opposition to the Soviet Revolution began immediately as it succeeded in 1917 and took military form soon after World War I when 1) we sent troops to fight against their Red Army in Vladivostok, and 2) we supplied the White Army with materiel by sea from the Baltic. (see **USSR**)

Our opposition continued in one form or another up to and through 1941; then, in 1942, with a common military enemy, we began to work with them in terms of supply. But already in 1945, the European war over and that in the Pacific continuing, we resumed our anti-Soviet efforts. (see **Cold War**)

Whether Hitler's dictatorship was worse than Stalin's or vice versa is not at issue here; both were horrendous. The point is that the efforts of the USA against neither Germany nor the USSR were concerned with freedom or dictatorship.

As for Mussolini, we entered the Italian peninsula in 1943 in order to push the Germans out. In the process Mussolini was found and killed by the anti-fascist Italian partigiani. From late 1943 on, for almost half a century (see **Italy**), we worked to assure that the rightwing Christian Democrats would rule, while also protecting known fascist military groups (most notoriously Decima Mas) from arrest and capture. Those U.S. processes were directed by the notorious James Angleton of the OSS/**CIA**. Our energetic and many-faceted campaign to assure that the left would be kept out of the

Italian government succeeded for decades, with still persisting consequences.

As fascist governments rose to power in Portugal and Turkey, we were at best indifferent, while with Greece, as with Spain, we were "helpful" in getting "the /fascist/ Colonels" aboard and keeping them there. (The 1960s process in Greece is dramatically portrayed in the film "**Z**".)

Middle East. In **Iran**, a major oil country, a democratic government had come into being as the 1950s began, led by President Mossadegh. It is no longer disputed that the **CIA** was instrumental in overthrowing him and, soon after, in elevating to power and then "guiding" "the Shah of Iran" (whose father had been an active sympathizer of the Nazis). (BLUM; POWERS, 2002)

The Shah's hard-nosed regime was bitterly-contested and extremely unpopular on both political and religious grounds; in the 70s it was overthrown from within, yielding the religious dictatorship of Khomeini, hostile to the USA from the beginning—one of many instances detailed by Chalmers JOHNSON in his *Blowback*.

Our present attempts to unseat **Iraq**'s Saddam Hussein were in the 1980s preceded by substantial acts of military assistance to him during the Iran-Iraq wars. As will be seen under Iraq, many of the now infamous "weapons of mass destruction" were furnished to Saddam by the USA, presumably on the principle that my enemy's enemy is my friend. And Iran was then our enemy.

Africa. The USA was not the originator of the devastation of Africa; that began no later than the 16th century. But once we began to flex our muscles there in the 60s we initiated our own inglorious history, worsening the always-desperate conditions of newly-independent African nations. Here we pay brief attention only to the **Congo**. (see HOCHSCHILD)

As will be elaborated upon in its own discussion, although the history of **imperialism** is engorged with tragedy for the imperialized and dishonor for the imperializing nations, the behavior of the Belgians (or more accurately, of their King Leopold) in the Congo was probably the most despicable.

Withal, by 1960, the Congo had won its independence. Patrice Lumumba, who had been most effective in their struggle, became their very popular—and non-dictatorial—leader; but not for long.

He was assassinated with the vital cooperation and financing of the **CIA**. (see the **Congo**).

By the choice of the USA, Mobuto was installed. Of all the terrible dictatorships suffered by the ex-colonial nations—themselves requiring explanation (see **imperialism**)—Mobutu's was among the very worst: repressive, exploitative, and decadent beyond description.

That the vast Congo region is the richest of all in resources in Africa meant that the USA's interest was, and remains, great. Not that we <u>need</u> their resources, but that the world has great use for them, so it is a fine place to make very profitable investments in precious minerals at low cost. As for the people of the Congo and the rest of Central Africa? Don't be silly.

Asia. China has perhaps the longest experience of any society with tight control, so it is not surprising that in the tumultuous 20th century, the era of dictatorship, both its right and its left would continue that history.

The struggle between Chiang Kai-shek and Mao Tse-tung goes back at least to the appallingly bloody 1920s (see MALRAUX, *Man's Fate*) and continued as, after 1931 the Japanese made a slaughterhouse of Manchuria and China. Then, during World War II, what occurred in China was to happen elsewhere in **Vietnam** and the **Philippines**: Chiang's government did little to resist the Japanese, while the revolutionary forces of Mao, growing always larger in the hinterland, fought back and, ultimately, became important allies of the USA in the war. Like the Viet Minh of North Vietnam and the Hukbalahap in the Philippines, Mao's troops allied with us but with war's end were treated as our enemies. (see **Cold War**)

What happened in **Indonesia** was similar. Sukarno was very popular and independent (it was he who organized the conference of newly-independent countries in the 1950s (the origin of "Third World"). He was overthrown in the early 60s by Suharto who, supported by the USA, promptly imposed a ferocious dictatorship.

It is relevant to repeat here what is noted under the appropriate headings elsewhere: The governments we <u>supported</u> in Vietnam, in Laos, Cambodia, the Philippines, Indonesia, and Korea, because they were oppressive and extremely unpopular, had to and did rule by force and violence; in opposing Ho Chi Minh and Sukarno, we were opposing very popular leaders. (Laos, the Philippines and Korea didn't have a chance to <u>have</u> a popular government in the critical years right after independence.)

Latin America. Just a brief look at two of the many countries there; in connection with the matter of "dictators" it is difficult not to discuss at least **Cuba** and **Chile**.

For the average U.S. citizen, the immediate response would be, Ah! Castro. Not quite. Castro rules with a firm hand, but just as Cuba is not a full-fledged democracy neither is Castro a full-fledged dictator (see below); but Fulgencio Batista, placed in power by the USA, was a <u>very</u> full-fledged dictator.

No sooner had Cuba gotten the Spanish off their backs in 1898 than they found Uncle Sam standing over them; as, a century later we still do, with the embargo and our control of Guantanamo. Our troops and navy did not leave Cuba until 1916, more than a handful of years after 1898—except for Guantanamo, the ongoing home of "Camp X-Ray."

From then until 1959, Cuba remained under our economic, military, and political control. Batista, who had been a sergeant in the army, was put in charge. He remained so, like a cheap imitation of Mobutu. (see above) Batista was in effect the manager of our hotel: he saw to it that there would be no interference with the U.S. companies that owned and ran the sugar plantations and utilities (including telephones), or with the gambling casinos and houses of prostitution (with their very young girls for tourists); no problem. Batista himself was a drunk and a brute; had he any politics but brute force, they would have been—in practice, were—fascist. But he was <u>our</u> fascist; sit back and relax.

The whole world should have breathed a sigh of relief when he was—easily—knocked over by Castro; as, indeed, most of it did; as a good part of it still finds what Castro has done for education, health care, average incomes in Cuba much more on the positive than on the negative side; nor is it foolish to believe that the negative aspects of Castro's rule would have been considerably lessened or nonexistent had his country been allowed to be free and unthreatened. (see **Cuba**)

Chile. Of all the nations of South America, Chile has been the most advanced economically and politically the most democratic. Thus when Salvador Allende came to be its president as the 70s began, it was in an utterly free election. He was a Marxist, and a true democrat. So? So we helped the fascists in Chile to get rid of him; natcherly.

When Allende was overthrown and killed in a coup d'etat in 1973 it was a general who took over: Augusto Pinochet. Even to look at him makes one shiver; as the saying goes, had there not been fascism, he would have invented it. He presided over the capture and imprisonment of tens of thousands of Chileans, at least 40,000 of whom were never seen alive again.

Pinochet would not have gotten into that office had it not been for the active and substantial assistance of the government of the Nixon administration, the **CIA**, and at least one major U.S. corporation. (BLUM; HERSH)

Absolutely horrifying, disgusting, and inexcusable; see **Chile** for details; and I wouldn't advise reading about **Nicaragua, El Salvador, Panama**, et al., at the same sitting if you have a weak stomach.

In sum, for the USA, the position on dictators is: We can take 'em or leave 'em; it depends.

discrimination (see racism, boys and girls...)

Disney, Walt (see FBI, Reagan)

domino theory (see Asia...Vietnam)

double standard (see corruption, Cold War, arrogance)

downsizing and outsourcing (see big business, free trade, globalization)

Dust Bowl

The USA has had a unique history in many ways, not least in its ability to expand its boundaries over a vast and resource-rich continent against only minimal resistance from indigenous peoples—

"minimal," given the respective military strengths of the invaders and the defenders' forces. (see **"Indians"/"Indian removal"**)

The role of **farmers** in that long process was substantial, for it was they who settled on the conquered lands or, having ventured into those still under tribal control, were ultimately able to remain through U.S. Army support; with diverse consequences in the enormous areas to the west of the original colonies, for better and for worse.

In the Great Plains region, it was mostly for the worse, and in the states ranging south from the Dakotas to Texas, worst of all. Throughout that region there was recurrent drought. Its first serious appearance in the 20th century was 1930-31; it became more than serious beginning in January 1933, yielding intermittent and disastrous droughts up through 1937. Their most feared and frequently recurring manifestation were the dirt storms with winds up to 60 mph and high temperatures. Thus did the area come to be called "The Dust Bowl." (BONNIFIELD)

It was easy and common to see those disasters as the fault of Mother Nature, for the vast region between the Mississippi and the Rockies is known for its relative lack of humidity. But the fault lay less in nature than in the farmers' indifference to both the possibilities and the limitations of natural grasslands. Thus, where grazing might have continued indefinitely and successfully, instead (or in addition) the farmers almost universally created an economy dependent upon corn and wheat, raised for sale as such and as feed for the livestock.

Even without human activities, droughts are normal in that area; so, when droughts occurred after a long interval in the early 1930s, the earth, exhausted by the crops borne over the years, simply dried up and blew away. Weather conditions came to be reported in terms of <u>visibility</u>—one block, a quarter mile or, on good days, a mile. The loose soil was drifted against fences and half buried buildings. Even if the people who did not move managed to survive somehow, their cattle could not live without water and feed. (CALLENBACH; B. MITCHELL)

Notwithstanding, through it all too many people were confident that a normal season of rain would "restore the area to its customary pursuits and productivity"—until 1937, when it all happened again, more drastically.

The Department of Agriculture concluded its investigations of this prolonged disaster with an analysis blaming "... the attempt to impose on the Great Plains a system of agriculture not adapted to the region..., the outcome of a mistaken public policy." (ibid.)

The "mistaken policy" was the still much-lauded Homestead Act of 1862; lauded because, in principle providing 160 acres of free land, it was seen as a main basis for helping to create a nation of small and independent farmers. There was much wrong with that understanding; most relevantly for present purposes is that the small allotments of the Act required that "part of each be plowed, causing immeasurable harm in overcultivation, overcropping and overgrazing." (ibid.)

The result in the 1930s was hundreds of thousands of desperate farmers; all the more so because this occurred in an era of general economic desperation. Among the most desperate were those in Oklahoma, one of the most arid of the states of the Plains. Their plight was immortalized in Steinbeck's *Grapes of Wrath*, and the film based on it; both are very much worth reading and/or watching for understanding how badly those who had left their dead farms were treated in California; instead of finding something better, their lives became similar to those of the desperate **immigrants** now flowing over the globe (until World War II's **milex** jobs).

In part because of Steinbeck, those best known to us are the "Okies" induced by thousands of leaflets to leave for California with the promise of jobs. The number of leaflets distributed was systematically a great multiple of the number of jobs available. A wise move on the part of the large California farmers responsible, a cruel move for the victims. Not only were there few jobs, there were many police awaiting them, herding them, beating them, mistreating them; their children treated like dirt in the public schools. (GREGORY)

Perhaps the most memorable moment in *Grapes of Wrath* (film version) is when Muley, whose farm and home is being "tractored out" (that is, bulldozed over), aims his shotgun at the tractor driver, and the latter informs him that he too was tractored out and is just doing this for a living, working for a local bank. Then, Muley says, he'll shoot them. But, the driver says, that company is just a bitty part of a big bank back east. "Then who'm I gonna shoot?" asks Muley, collapsing as his house is bulldozed down.

And now, as the 21st century begins, the droughts are once more becoming common in the Plains states, and not only there: "Much of the West, and especially the region running from eastern Montana south through the High Plains, is entering its fourth straight year of drought, and in places the dust has begun to blow again. (*NYT*, 5-22-02) This time, however, it is not only due to the historically mistaken ways of farming but in the ever-more destructive impact of **global warming**, everywhere; the whole world as a dust bowl.

In his essay "The Oil We Eat" (*Harper's*, 2/2004), the "agro-environmetalist Richard MANNING provides a blunt summing up:

> The Dust Bowl was no accident of nature. A functioning grassland prairie produces more biomass each year than does even the most technologically advanced wheat field. The problem is, it's mostly a form of grass and grass roots that humans can't eat. So we replace the prairie with our own preferred grass, wheat. Never mind that we feed most of our grain to livestock, and that livestock is perfectly content to eat native grass. And never mind that there likely were more bison (see **buffalo**) produced naturally on the Great Plains before farming than all of beef farming raises in the same area today.

Progress is our most important product; a little dusty and deadly but, wotthehell, ya can't have it all.

"earnings"

This will be short. In the sweet bye and bye that word, whether as used by almost everyone or by economists, referred to the income one received for a contribution to production or the provision of services (teaching, medicine, etc.). Now it means whatever any company or executive or stockholder gets, no matter how, when, why, or for what.

Along with "investor" and "investment," such changes in the usage of important words are what Orwell was warning about in 1948, when he published his *1984*. We have come to call it **spin**, the fine art of advertisers, politicians, PR folks, the **media**. For a fine analysis of how far the **corruption** of our language had gone already by the early 1970s, see SCHILLER, *The Mind Managers*.

economics

What's wrong with economics? Plenty. But we focus here on only two of the major problem areas: 1) its methodology; 2) its social function. (Other areas would include "It's boring!")

1. "Methodology" is one of those off-putting words that refer to matters much simpler than the term itself; in this case, to the aims and means and validity of economic <u>theory</u>. (see ROGIN; DOWD /2000/)

Methodology is not directly concerned with the <u>content</u> of an analysis, but with how and why that particular content was selected, dealt with, and used to construct; specifically, for economics, its theories and, by extension, the manner in which such theories lead to or support associated socioeconomic policies. (See SACKREY, et al. for an extended and excellent review.)

Among the key matters relevant to methodological inquiry are those entailing questions of abstraction, factuality, and focus; <u>what</u> is abstracted from and <u>why</u>, and what <u>is</u> and is <u>not</u> focussed upon (and why), such that they become the theory's "variables" or shunted aside. Both the whats and the whys are vital.

All theory is and must be <u>abstract</u>; abstraction from reality is essential to understand both nature and society. As Marx put it, if appearance and reality were the same, there would be no need for theory. But they are <u>not</u> the same. Consider, for example, what appearance tells us about the universe: It's so lovely to see the sun rise and set, as it goes 'round and 'round our world; except that it doesn't; just as wrong (and for closely-related reasons) as the appearances that tell us, on a star-filled night, that the ground upon which we stand is the flat part of an over-arching dome. Astronomic <u>theory</u> (beginning with Copernicus) was essential if we were to know what lies behind and <u>creates</u> those appearances.

That is, the problem of abstract theorizing is not abstraction as such, but what is abstracted <u>from</u>—what is taken as "given," what is or is <u>not</u> examined—and what is focussed <u>upon</u>. For example: Newton's theory of gravity, $S = gt2$, abstracted from (among other things) friction. He knew well that a body's weight (which is in his equation) is not its only property; it also has girth which, if slender will allow an object of the same weight to fall faster than one "fatter." Utilizing his theory for practical purposes (which, in economics points to economic policy), requires "relaxing" its assumptions as to friction; as an aeronautical engineer does in making decisions about engine strength and wings. (OK; I may be wrong about that example, but who's counting?)

As will be noted later, mainstream economic theory is even more abstract than Newton's, but its economic policy recommendations do not take the abstracted-from-reality back into consideration; the reason is that, whether or not economists know it or not (and most don't) economic theory is ideological in nature, not scientific. A thoroughgoing analysis of economic theory also speaks to our second concern: the social function of economics. That takes us to two more terms that are too often taken for granted: objectivity and neutrality. Mainstream economists assert or assume that they are both objective and neutral in their analyses: that they are "scientific." They are not.

Even if we "assume" that most economists are objective, that they pay due respect to fact and to logic, we are left with the question of neutrality. If "neutrality" signifies disinterest in the outcome or implications of an analysis, it is implausible to believe there are such economists; or, rather, spare us the social analysts who don't give a damn about the social implications of their analyses.

It would seem clear that neutrality is muddled by the analyst's very choice as to what to study, and how. To which it may be added that even though "neutrality" in the natural sciences may be possible, it is likely that at least in some cases (or, more likely, in most) scientists do have preferences regarding the implications of their findings (re: research grants, Nobels, etc.)

Adam Smith and David Ricardo, usually seen as the founders of "classical political economy," explicitly cared about the policy implications of their works; that degree of self-conscious honesty began to diminish after the 1860s as contemporary—"neoclassical economics"—took the place of "political economy."

By the last quarter of the 19th century the neoclassical economics had come to dominate; its "textbook" was MARSHALL's *Principles of Economics*—still required required reading after World War II.

The defining difference between that economics and classical political economy was that the latter openly advocated socieconomic change, whereas the neoclassicists are implicit advocates for the status quo: their abstract analyses always explicitly or implicitly assume that nothing but the few "variables" under examination need to be considered; all else is taken as "given," "other things being equal": "ceteris paribus." Among the other things dropped into that wastebasket are human needs. (ROGIN; DOWD /2000/)

Such analytical procedures and assumptions were consciously and even sensibly made by those who brought neoclassical economics into the forefront, as was true of MARSHALL. But Marshall and many of those on whose work he built had studied economic realities and were self-conscious concerning the policies their theories implied. Not so, nowadays. (see HUNT)

In the 1930s and into the 1960s, the depression and other harsh realities forced at least some economists to look out the window at the world; so, to become an economist one was often required to become proficient in a) the history of economic thought, and b) economic history. The study of the two provided the budding economist with a sense of the relativity of economic analysis to time and place and, at the same time, much about the complexity of socioeconomic life. A study of economic history means a study of the interaction of the economy with the rest of the social process over time.

Nowadays, all one needs know up to and beyond the Ph.D. in Economics is undergraduate math, abstract economic theory, and when to keep your trap shut. "Economics" has little or nothing to do with "economies," but it has much to do with providing rationales for keeping the economy functioning within the status quo of income, power and ideology. (SACKREY, et al.)

Now some elaboration and support for the foregoing generalizations.

For present purposes, Economics may be seen as being divided into four spheres: microeconomics (the theory of specific labor, commodity, and service) markets; macroeconomics (the theory of the expansion/contraction of the overall economy, inflation/deflation;); trade theory (the theory of economic relations between nations; see **free trade; globalization**); and distribution theory (the theory of who gets what and (presumably) why. The latter, which purports to be saying that one's income varies in proportion to one's contribution to production, is taken up under **capitalism, profits, inequality** and **exploitation**).

It is in the very nature of the profession that those who are experts in one of those areas need not and normally do not have any but a passing interest or competence in the others—although reflection tells us that of course the four areas in reality are in constant interaction with each other and with the entire framework of the larger society at home and abroad.

However, and as VEBLEN (1919) noted long ago, economists have "a trained incapacity" to understand the economy, let alone its connections with pertinent "non-economic" realities. Of course there are mainstream economists (many of whom have been cited in this work) who do know something or a lot about socioeconomic reality; however a) what understanding they have they did not achieve because, but despite, their training; b) and that understanding, the stronger that understanding the greater the likelihood they will cease to be "mainstream economists"; it is to become "heterodox" (or a scoundrel).

A good recent example of this has been the evolution of Paul Krugman, always prof at one or another of the top universities and mow NYT Op-ed columnist. Even better examples are KEYNES (1883-1946), in the realm of macroecon and SCITOVSKY in microecon.

Keynes, bless him, was the leading monetarist—i.e., conventional macro—economist in the world in the 1920s; however, struck by the enduring stagnation of his (UK) economy throughout the 20s and the deep and persisting global depression of the 1930s, KEYNES (1936) underwent some very large second thoughts: he showed why **monetarism** was at best inadequate for recovery and might well exacerbate the problem; his policy recommendations were distinctly non-conservative, although he was in fact seeking to conserve what he saw as a self-destroying capitalism (very much as Kevin PHILLIPS has done in his recent books with empirical rather than theoretical works combining political with economic materials).

Except for a few, Keynes's fellow economists were not instructed by but appalled by him, and he and his ideas came to be ostracized. No surprise to Keynes: In the Preface to his *General Theory*, he noted that those least likely to understand his (very abstract) theory were precisely those fellow economists. He agreed with Veblen: they suffered from a <u>trained</u> incapacity.

Scitovsky was primarily a <u>micro</u> economist. But, as **big business** and **consumerism** took hold after World War II, he too had second thoughts. In his *Joyless Economy* (1976) he not only deplored what was happening to the consciousness and character of the socioeconomy, but also the virtual irrelevance of mainstream micro theory. As with Keynes decades earlier, Scitovsky found himself ignored or ostracized by all but a few of his one-time colleagues. Now we turn to the three worlds of the ostracizers—my polite term for ideologues.

<u>Microeconomic theory</u>. It is the heart and soul of "neoclassical economics." That is, although the latter presumably comprises what came to be <u>macroeconomics</u>, functioned in effect as though attention need not be paid to the overall functioning of the economy; the free market and the interest rate take care of that.

It was when it took care of itself disastrously after World War I that Keynes, himself a neoclassicist, had his second thoughts (of which, more below). No matter what, his fellow economists were undeterred; they stood by the convictions of their field, a conviction based upon "Say's Law," uttered just a century before the Great Depression of the 1930s: "supply creates its own demand." We can all sit back and relax.

What J.B. Say means was that there can never <u>be</u> a depression; were there to be one, it would signify that a lot of supply wasn't being demanded: thus, falling profits, layoffs of workers, falling demand, collapsed banks. As will be seen when we look at macro, Mr. Say took as "given" what was central; with aggressive stupidity, his ideas were resurrected in the 1980s under **Reagan**, and came to be called "supply-side economics:" Fools in economists' clothing.

The heart of neoclassical micro has its two sides. Theory and policy. The theory works within a framework of assumptions specifying competitive markets functioning in a timeless context, with all participants—businesses, consumers, and workers—behaving "rationally." That "rationality" in turn was based upon the 19th century psychological notion of hedonism (which time and FREUD have undone). VEBLEN's mockery of the economists of all that (1919) was so funny that one thinks it must be a caricature; it was not:

> The hedonistic conception of man is that of a lightning calculator of pleasures and pains, who oscillates like a homogeneous globule desire of happiness under the impulse of stimuli that shift him about the area, but leave him intact. He has neither antecedent nor consequent. He is an isolated, definitive human datum, in stable equilibrium except for the buffets of the impinging forces that displace him in one direction or another. Self-imposed in elemental space, he spins symmetrically about his own spiritual axis until the parallelogram of force bears down upon him, whereupon he follows the line of the resultant. When the force of the impact is spent, he comes to rest, a self-contained globule of desire as before.

Tell it to the **advertising** honchos, whose very existence depends upon manipulating our several irrationalities. But that is only one nutty and vital element of mainstream economics; serving as the vital core of its "market analysis" is its "theory of the firm." Despite all, that theory clings to the basic "model" put forth by MARSHALL, more than a century ago.

The analytical center of the model was "the representative firm." The size and power of such a firm would be found today, if anywhere, in your neighborhood small grocery, in the shoemaker down the street, or the garden shop a few blocks away; that is, a tiny firm, owned and operated by a person or family, with absolutely <u>no</u> market power, one of many such in your community; except that Marshall had in mind small manufacturing companies with, say, 50-100 workers, companies in an industry with many hundreds of virtually identical (usually textile) companies producing absolutely identical products. (OFFNER, TILLY, et al.)

The kind of thing Adam Smith had in mind (and that Marshall assumed) was what <u>could</u> happen once state restrictions were removed. It <u>did</u> happen, when in keeping with "<u>laissez-faire</u>" restrictions on new entrants and on movement began to be dismantled as the 19th century began, a process completed by mid-century.

However, at the very moment when Marshall was writing, mergers of those small companies had already initiated a process that would make **big business** common in all industries. They would be called **oligopolies** (= a few sellers). Now typical, their means of doing business include making (usually illegal) agreements and <u>not</u> competing with other companies in the same business. (see DU BOFF)

What is called "competition" in **cars** and computers, and **oil**, etc., is more accurately seen as "rivalry." To be sure, each company is trying to get as large a share of its market as possible; but not by doing what Smith hoped for and that neoclassical theory assumes; namely, by maximum cost reduction and minimum prices. Just the opposite: except rarely (during crises, for example), prices are never lowered and, when raised (which means a relative lowering of the others') they are raised in tandem. Moreover, for most durable goods, successful rivalry has come to depend upon always increasing unit costs, because of **advertising** and product variation ("**deliberate obsolescence**"); which, taken together, raise do not lower costs. (see **cars**, and ADAMS/BROCK, RAVENSCRAFT)

As all of that was becoming universal in the 20th century, economists were becoming always more abstract, more mathematical (which means more abstract), and more removed from anything having to with a real economy; least of all that of the USA, champ of all that game.

Except for 15-20 years right after World War II, those who studied economics have been "educated" solely along neoclassical lines. Those who walked away in boredom or disgust left behind them those who now constitute the economics profession—most of them totally unaware that there is an alternative way of being an economist: a way that involves studying the actual economy, rather than economics.

Macroeconomics. As suggested above, it came into being in consequence of the 30s depression and Keynesian economic theory. As may be inferred from the earlier discussion of Say's Law, the economics profession—despite the agonizing depression—steadfastly refused to shed its conventional analyses. Indeed, with numberless factories shut down, thousands of banks with closed doors, millions of workers unemployed, the off-stated "analysis" of mainstream economists in the USA—I am not making this up—was that "workers are demanding too high wages."

It would have been lovely for an economist or two to tell that to the innumerable workers who were in fact standing in "breadlines" all over the country, unable to demand anything, given that almost to the end of the 30s, very few of them were in unions. What may be seen as the moronic obtuseness of mainstream economists

led to the emergence of a group of economists with alternative
views, from the 30s through the 40s and 50s; some were Marxists,
some followers of Veblen (and called "institutionalists"), some just
sensible students of the socioeconomy; some, myself among them,
combined all three ways of trying to understand. Now the "some"
has been reduced to "few"—with some cheering signs that their
numbers are on the rise.

So what was Keynes all about? Interestingly (and, ultimately,
harmfully, as will be seen), Keynes's theory accepted the "micro"
assumptions of neoclassical economics; that is, Keynes also assumed
rationality and competition. Where he differed was on Say's Law:
Supply does <u>not</u> always create its own demand, Keynes argued; it
depends. (MILLER, J., OFFNER, et al.)

His theory was highly abstract; so abstract it can be explained
in terms of a very few and very simple "equations" whose terms are
Y (income), C (consumption), I (investment) and S (savings).
Here we go:

1. $Y = C + I$. So,
2. $Y—C = I$, and
3. $Y—C =$ Sand therefore
4. $I = S$.

"Income" (Y) can mean individuals' or the sum of all incomes
(the national income); "consumption" (C) is what we buy with our
incomes; "investment" (I) stands for what businesses spend on productive capacity (<u>not</u> with what "**investors**" do when they buy
stocks and bonds), that is, when businesses expand productive
capacities.

"I" was the key for Keynes; it constitutes an increase in the
demand for materials and labor and transportation in order to
increase productive capacities; in turn, those who provide all that
receive incomes for doing so, all or some of which they will spend.
When they do, incomes for others (who produced or sold what was
bought) rise. The initial increase in "I" thus leads to a multiple
increase in spending and incomes: Keynes called it "the multiplier
effect).

But all along the way, some of the increase in incomes is <u>not</u>
spent, but <u>saved</u> (S); the percentage of S to Y rises as (personal and

national) income rises. Keynes' major point was that, given that I = S, when Y rises and S also rises, that means that I must rise, or that Y will fall.

Of vital importance In the theory is that "I" is the "independent" variable; that is, C and S are both a function of (that is, a result of) Y, but Y is a function of I—of capital accumulation. Which makes sense in a capitalist society.

Remember, Keynes was working on a very high level of abstraction, assuming away any and all changes except in Y, C, I, and S. But, for his purposes (and, up to a point, for ours), his theory was as valid as Newton's; that is, the "relaxation" of the assumptions would not change his main point. Which was?

That as a capitalist economy expands over time (other things being equal: no technological change, no structural changes in demand and tastes, no wars, etc.), Y will rise and C will rise, but not as fast as Y; that is, S will rise more rapidly than Y, unless I also rises. But I rises in anticipation of an increased in C: why else increase productive capacities?

Note also this: the greater the **inequality** of income distribution—that is, the greater the gap between the top and bottom levels of income—the more likely that increases in the national income will lead to increases in savings and therefore a reduced incentive to invest. Look closely, and you will see the problem: capitalist economic expansion builds a trap for itself.

Keynes observed that the period after World War I was one in which there was general excess productive capacity, and that therefore there was no likelihood that economies would pull themselves out of recessions as they had in the 19th century: the 19th century was one of always spreading global industrialization with an accompanying growing demand for more investment goods; whereas World War I was in significant part a consequence of pervasive excess productive capacities.

Thus Keynes argued "demand" had to be created by public policy. Governments had to make substantial expenditures on what he called "social consumption" (housing, education, health care, and the like) and "social investment" (what today we call "infrastructure"—dams, public transportation, etc.). That would not only provide needed goods and services, but would also increase national and personal incomes and, thus, consumption—and thus utilize productive facilities.

All that of course raised the question of **deficits and surpluses**. The pre-World War II conventional wisdom (the wisdom of bankers and mainstream economists, that is) was that governments should never run deficits; that would amount to placing a serpent in paradise. If nothing else, World War II and its massive expenditures taught the U.S. business establishment the wrong-headedness of that: the war lifted the USA (and both its businesses its workers) out of endless depression: there had still been 10 percent unemployment in 1941.

So, in the postwar years of **Cold War**, business became enthusiastic supporters of "military Keynesianism"—or, as Joan Robinson, a member of Keynes's theory circle, called it "bastard Keynesianism." (see TURGEON)

Despite all, the financial community never got it; what they did get, as **financialization** came to dominate the economy, was **power**. And that power, from the 1980s on, was very much behind the "rediscovery" of Say's Law, the birth of "supply-side economics" and its predictable re-acceptance by mainstream economists. It was akin to a bunch of modern scientists "rediscovering alchemy.) (see **Reagan**, King of Alchemy)

Trade theory. David Ricardo (1772-1823)—note the dates— was the creator in Great Britain of what, despite intervening hell and high water, stands still as the basis for trade theory, and its policies called "free trade." Ricardo put forth his arguments in his *Principles of Political Economy and Taxation* (1817): note "political" and "taxation." (BLOCK)

Like Smith, Ricardo was trying to get rid of the economic encumbrances inherited from preceding centuries; in his case, mostly, tariffs on imports. He was not prompted by a generosity of spirit toward those selling those imports from other countries; not at all. Again, like Smith, Ricardo was keen on enhancing the economic strength of Britain. As will be seen below (and in **free trade...**), he made some arguments which are being made still today—with much the same reasoning, and much the same questionable—conscious or unconscious—aims.

Ricardo made them on a highly abstract level, and with many

specified assumptions; they became, over time, the methodological framework and procedures of all of neoclassical economics, not just trade theory; and they endure in both content and form to this day—with, it seems, most economists having forgotten the assumptions. Given the enormous kinds and quantities of change of the intervening almost-two centuries, either his theory was stunningly brilliant, or the economists who still depend upon it are some combination of thick-headed and thick-skinned. You're paying your money; take your choice.

What were his arguments? To begin with, his policy aim was the enhanced industrialization of Britain. That was just beginning as he wrote (the first factory was in 1815). Like Adam Smith (and, subsequently, Marx) Ricardo accepted the "labor theory of value," and he posited an inverse relationship between wages and profits: Other things being equal, when money wages rise, profits decline, and the incentive and ability to expand investment will also decline. (And vice versa, if money wages decline.)

But what would make wages rise, in a period when unions did not exist? Ricardo's accurate answer was tariffs (i.e., taxes) on imported grains—at a time when the working class was not able to buy much more than food (and too little of that). Those tariffs, in raising the price of imported grains, allowed the landed gentry in England, producers of domestic grains, to raise their prices—and to receive what Ricardo called a "rent" or "unearned income." The undesirable by-product was the necessity to raise the money—not the real—wages of workers; and thus to lower profits and hold back industrialization.

Workers' wages, Ricardo, Smith, and Marx all agreed, were at the subsistence level: lower them, and the workers die off; raise them, and profits go down. But the tariff-induced increased cost of food meant a deadly lowering of real wages for workers, unless they had a proportionate increase in money wages. That is, the landed gentry were benefiting at the expense of the rising industrial capitalists and of Britain's strength.

Three cheers for free trade—for Britain and its capitalists, that is. In 1817 it was the only seriously industrializing nation. Ricardo knew that his policies of free trade for all—in an era in which Britain was becoming in its time what the USA in this time—also meant that Britain would <u>remain</u> the only industrial nation: it would have the advantage of getting the cheapest rates on all of its food and raw material imports, with no way for other countries to become industrialized—unless, that is, they didn't go along. Which, in fact, is what all the countries that were thus able to <u>become</u> industrial did do; the USA, Germany, France, and Japan, the largest, and the Low Countries and Scandinavians, the lesser, all pursued nationalistic economic policies, protecting their "infant industries" (as Alexander Hamilton called ours) from the more efficient British exports. The others remained weak and/or colonized, hewers of wood and drawers of water economically, their cultures and resources devastated, their politics determined elsewhere. (see **imperialism**) The theory behind today's **globalization** policies has barely budged more than an inch or two from Ricardo; it has the same intent, unspoken by Ricardo, denied by the bigwigs of today: Genuine "free trade" would be bad enough for the poor countries; the free trade preached but not practiced by the rich countries (see, e.g., **farmers**) makes them richer and the already poor desperately poorer.

But that's not the way mainstream economists (or the **IMF, WTO, World Bank** see things. Since World War II, the principal source of the latter's "economics" has been "the Chicago School." In the 50s and 60s, when (as noted above) economics and economic policy had ceased for a while to be single-mindedly "neoclassicist," the Chicago School came to be seen as extreme advocates of <u>laissez-faire</u>.

Its main thinker in the 30s had been Frank H. Knight; by the 40s, however, his views were supplemented (and pushed to the right) by the Austrian members of the Chicago faculty, Ludwig von Mises and Friedrich A, Hayek; and their star pupil was **Milton Friedman**. (HUNT)

Von Mises had been, above all, an abstract theorist; HAYEK was a policy wonk. He became famous in 1945 when *Reader's Digest* published a condensed version of his *The Road to Serfdome*. It sold 600,000 copies. The book itself came out in 1952. What "serfdom" was he talking about? Why, you idiot, **FDR**'s New Deal, that's what. And star pupil Friedman came out with <u>his</u> manifesto (written with his wife Rose Friedman) in 1962: *Capitalism and Freedom*—which some of us thought should be called *Capitalism **or** Freedom*.

Friedman was mostly sneered at in the 60s; since the 70s he's been doing the sneering. "Freedom" is a lovely word, but not as Friedman means it. For him, if the economy is completely free from any and all governmental intrusion, if there is no regulation of any kind, no governmental ownership of control of any kind—you get the idea—then and only then can there and will there be freedom for everything and everyone.

Mind you, he means get the government (local, state, federal) out of education, prisons, parks, the military, transport, health care... everything. Stop smiling: he means it. What's wrong with the world? Government. What will save the world? Free markets. What are free markets? Markets in which buyers and sellers meet without any other presence, presided over by 'the invisible hand" of the "free" market: that is, by a few **TNCs**. Tell it to the U.S, Marines; with today's **globalization** they're needed always more to pick up the pieces. (see **deregulation**)

Funny thing about that serfdom of FDR's; it provided jobs, it provided for the first time in our history at least some kind of social security, it prohibited child labor and set the 8-hour working day, provided better schools, some housing for the poor, a big cultural lift through the WPA, and a lot more. (see **deficits and surpluses**) Moreover, people were pulled up and out of the almost universal despair of the ineffably lovely free market depression.

I can't resist a story about Friedman and me. You will know there was a man named Ray Croc, the genius behind McDonald's. He got VERY rich making kids and their parents fat; by the 70s, with little to do but bank his millions, he began to dabble in politics. He built a huge estate over the hills east of Santa Barbara, CA. It had a big auditorium with about 100 really cushy black leather seats, each with its own consoles, plus a beaut of a swimming pool: Every penny of it tax deductible of course. (After all!)

I forget the exact year, but Ray called together a conference with 60 execs, half from Coca-Cola, half from McDonalds, all of them VPs except the two Ps. The handful of economist speakers included Uncle Miltie and yours truly. (How I was invited is another story.) The focus of the conference was "Ethics in Business."

I spoke, others spoke, Uncle Miltie spoke. My position was that ethics in business is an oxymoron (you could look it up), and that to discuss it didn't make sense; the only ethics practiced in business had to do with employees not stealing from the cash register, and other such naughtiness. Friedman, on the other hand, also thought it a foolish discussion: There was no <u>need</u> to discuss it because a free market <u>as such</u> made for the best ethic.

Later, we were at a dinner table, facing each other. He didn't even look at me; but I was watching as he pocketed some of Kroc's silver. It was <u>free</u>. Because we now live a couple of blocks from each other in San Francisco we have finally found something to agree upon: The neighborhood is <u>spoiled</u>—by him as I see it, vice versa as he sees it. So move already, Uncle Miltie; it's a <u>free</u> country.

Back to economics. Implicit in all the foregoing is the wrong-headed focus of the discipline. The question that "economics" should start with is "What do we need to know about the economy, and how can we find out?" Having studied out that realm, we then go on to the next essential question: "What policies are necessary if the economy is to serve the **needs** and possibilities of our people and our society?" The resulting political economy would be an unrecognizably different "economics."

You may have noticed the word "need" in the second question. If you are momentarily foolish enough to look through economic <u>theory</u> you will <u>never</u> find the word <u>need</u>; for mainstream econ it is <u>the</u> four-letter word. However, IF economic studies and analyses were to start there, and IF we were to study the matter of <u>possibilities</u>, the discipline would necessarily become <u>less</u> abstract <u>and</u> interdisciplinary; it would develop questions and answers requiring an understanding of the constant and mutually transforming interactions between "economic" and "social" and "cultural" and "historical" and "environmental" processes—just as a medical doctor <u>must</u> know of the interactions between the heart and the lungs and the kneebone and the thigh bone and... That just like a body, a society is an <u>organic</u>, not a mechanical, entity.

If, as, and when economics became part of a larger <u>social</u> discipline, we could then drop all those "quote" marks in the previous paragraph. (It may be noted that in this respect, as in many others, the social "sciences" are lagging the natural sciences; in the latter, it has now become common to study as a <u>bio</u>chemist, an <u>eco</u>biologist, a <u>palio</u>biologist, a <u>physio</u>chemist)

The whole matter of "needs and possibilities" will be taken up more systematically in the <u>Afterword</u>. In addition to a summary criticism, there will be found suggestions as to next steps regarding "basic needs" and alternative possibilities within our reach—if, not yet, our grasp.

Meanwhile, for a fuller grasp on what's wrong with economics and what it could/should be, see ROBINSON's *Economic Philosophy* for a fine introduction, and STRETTON's *A New Introduction...* for every jot and tittle. Bon voyage.

education

All agree that a good education is essential for a good life; but what kind of education and for whom? And what is meant by "a good education" or, for that matter, "a good life"? The answers to those questions have of course varied very much from time to time, place to place, and over time in any given place. Here we examine only the educational system of the USA in our time, for elementary school, high school, and the university.

In the educational realms, as with so much else treated in these pages, the USA has had every opportunity to develop an excellent system for all at every level. Never have we realized those possibilities; even worse, by any reasonable measure, and in keeping with a general rightward political shift, our <u>entire</u> educational system has undergone an accelerating deterioration since the late 1970s. Support for those generalizations occupy the rest of this discussion.

In the 1920s the poet Vachel LINDSAY (in RODMAN) admonished us,

Let not young souls be smothered out before
They do quaint deeds and fully flaunt their pride.
It is the world's one crime its babes grow dull,
Its poor are ox-like, limp and leaden-eyed.

About 80 years later, the late biologist/ paleontologist Stephen Gould observed that he was

>...somehow less interested in the weight and convolutions
>of Einstein's brain than in the near certainty that people of
>equal talent have lived and died in cotton fields and sweatshops.

In their different ways, the poet and the scientist were concerned with the same matters: that is, the aims and the availability of a decent education, and the social circumstances that have precluded it for almost all, everywhere; and both knew that the responsibility for those who are poorly educated lies in our social institutions, not in the genes of their victims.

That certainly refers to the plight of the poor in a society where access to what passes for a good education is effectively rationed in terms of income and wealth, color and, more subtly, gender. (see **inequality, racism, affirmative action, boys and girls...,** and **poverty.**) But the reference is also to those lucky enough to be exempt from such discrimination: our educational system is woefully inadequate for <u>all</u>.

Indisputably, educational systems function first and foremost to strengthen the status quo of their societies; the core of that status quo in the USA stands is **capitalism + nationalism.** Beginning in grammar school and lasting through the Ph.D. the central point of reference is that status quo; although, of course, that is rarely made explicit.

That the young—whether 7 or 17—can and do have additional or other needs and possibilities is—one may say <u>naturally</u>—given short shrift at all levels, except by an always small and now shrinking number of teachers.

All education in the USA, even for the well-off, is not only defective but mutilating; and to point out that 80 percent of the world's people would be eager to have access to our education is at the same time a comment on how unnecessarily desperate their societies are—and for which the realities of **imperialism** and **globalization** are principally responsible.

The worst aspect of all of this in the USA affects those <u>not</u> "well-off, those who are poor. Whatever might be wrong with even the best schools when set against sensible criteria, <u>everything</u> is wrong for poor children.

Now a look at some of the defects of education at each of the three levels.

<u>K through 12</u>: This is the level where "young souls are smothered out" for both rich and poor. All three levels are vital to us, but because we are at our most vulnerable and susceptible when children it is at elementary school where we can be hurt or helped most. If we

are hurt sufficiently there (and setting aside other relevancies), we must be <u>very</u> fortunate at the later stages to recover and go on to becoming our realizable selves.

It is necessary to distinguish between <u>training</u> and <u>learning</u>. As the words are used here, the former is a top-down process suiting a curriculum delivered by teachers who—and quite apart from having also been "educated" in the same manner—need to follow the rules in order to keep their jobs: both pupils and teachers are fitted into an educational status quo, itself accommodating the larger socio-economic system—symbolized by the common practice of small children beginning the day by singing the national anthem and saluting the flag; as common in the USA as it is rare elsewhere.

If there is to be hope for this or other societies to wrench ourselves loose from the commissions and omissions that constitute the dangerously imperfect status quo, it resides in each generation having the opportunity to think for itself: to <u>learn</u>. That means to ask and to seek answers to questions, more than to prepare for college entrance exams—now disgustingly common even at the <u>elementary</u> level.

DICKENS devoted a considerable part of his *Hard Times* (1854) to the tendency to squelch learning, through the persona of Schoolmaster Gradgrind. The book opens with him:

> Now, what I want is, Facts. Teach these boys and girls nothing but Facts. Facts alone are wanted in life. Plant nothing else, and root out everything else. You can only form the minds of reasoning animals upon Facts, nothing else will ever be of service to them.... Stick to Facts, sir!

Except that we don't even get many honest "Facts" in elementary school. The best that can be said for most "education" is that it might prepare one for a **job**, help one to become able to do what is <u>being</u> done: No questions asked, except "how?" Hardly ever are students led to ask "why?", or "for whom?", or "are there alternatives?"

That is bad enough; it is worse that the average youngster spends 4-6 hours a day watching **TV**. Nor does it stop there: something truly rotten is added by the commercialization of school space, in and outside the classroom. Consider these data compiled by Michael MOORE (derived mostly from studies by the Center for the Analysis of Commercialism in Education):

Item: The National Geography Spelling Bee now has a corporate sponsor; book covers are distributed free to students with ads for various companies; sports shoes companies "sponsor" inner-city high school teams; two large companies have programs rewarding schools for getting parents to buy their products (e.g., General Mills gives a school ten cents for each box top logo sent in, up to $10,000 a year (= 100,000 boxes of their product sold); in the 1990s, 241 school districts sold exclusive rights to one of the big three soda companies (Coca-Cola, Pepsi, Dr. Pepper), perhaps the grossest offender being Colorado Springs: the school district will receive $8 million + over ten years from its deal with Coca-Cola. And so it goes—coupons for Burger Kings handed out in nutrition classes, ads on school buses, on school rooftops, GM's supplying to many schools the economics course GM writes and for which it provides the textbooks.

Item: And then there are the electronic marketers in the classroom, the kingpin of which is Channel One Television, presumably there in the name of better education: Eight million students in 12,000 grade school classrooms watch Channel One, an in-school news and advertising program every day. Of the daily 12-minute programs, 80 percent of the time is devoted to advertising, the rest to non-commercial matters. And Channel One is shown predominantly in low-income communities with minority populations, where the least public money is devoted to schools. (MOORE)

Item: "Neediest Schools Receive Less Money, Report Finds": "As schools enter a new era of tough federal demands to raise achievements among poor and minority students, a report /by Education Trust/ shows that in most states, school districts with the neediest students receive far less state and local tax money—an average of just under $1,000 per student—than school with the fewest poor children." (NYT, 8-9-02)

But what about the much-touted school voucher program, touted not least for poor and minority children? Item: Referring to the recent Supreme Court decision upholding Cleveland's voucher program, heralded as "the second coming of Brown v. Board of Education," Brent Staples (in his "School Vouchers: A Small Tool for a Very Big Problem" (NYT, 8-5-02) writes that "The voucher program serves only about 3,700 of the public school system's 75,000 children. Chosen by lottery, the children from the poorest families are provided a maximum of $2,250—less than a third of the cost of educating a public school student—if they wish to move out of the public school program."

Staples goes on to note that of the three possibilities for their attendance—suburban schools, non-religious private schools, and a religious school—"the religious schools enrolled 96 percent of the eligible students, with the others being too costly or too crowded." Thus the present tendency to violate the separation of church and state is intensified, as is the tendency to neglect public schools.

There are some who have given up on our public schools, and others who never cared about them in the first place. Those who have "given up" include a lot of hard-working not very well-off people who scrimp and sacrifice to get their kids into a school that will give them a chance to have a decent life; and it includes some who simply have enough money without having to sacrifice.

As well, there are a few who will not only pay to see that their child gets into a good private school, but have enough muscle to do almost anything to assure it. One of those is Wall Street's famous Jack Grubman, star stock analyst now with legal difficulties because he gave out optimistic forecasts to potential buyers, having been hugely bribed to do so by corporate sellers. But Jack had more than one trick in his basket.

He has two children, 3 and 4 in years, and he wanted VERY much to get them into Manhattan's most prestigious nursery school (the "92nd St. Y"). Because he is good friends with another heavy in the financial realm, Sanford Weill (also under scrutiny), he agreed to put a big buy on AT&T (of which Weill is a Director), if Sandy would use his substantial weight with the 92nd St. Y. Weill did, the kids got in, the stock's sales and price went up and then—way down. Business is business. (*NYT*, 11-16-02, "How an analyst 'fiddled' with stock rating" and *WP*, same date, "Getting into pre-school: Top-tier clout helps.")

For most of the little ones, in sum, grammar and middle schools are where they spend too much time learning to be obedient drudges, to be "boys and girls" and "Americans"; it could instead be a place where we got all excited about nature's mysteries and beauty, and books, and <u>life</u>, rather than how to take tests and what to buy.

<u>High school</u>. It is difficult enough to be a **teenager** without having to spend four years in a school where, rather than our education doing something to ease our tensions and fears and to give us some insights about our hopes, the wrongs done to us in grade school are given wings. More's the worse, as adolescents we are more than ever prone to **conformism**, and more than ever likely to be punished by our peers if we don't. In high school the damage done by an assembly-line education has more fertile soil in which to flourish, for in those years we have already begun to lose much of whatever individuality we had as a child. (DENNISON, KOZOL)

To repeat, the fault is not simply or mostly that of teachers, whether for small children or adolescents. Some teachers, it may be assumed, see their jobs simply as jobs; most, it may also be assumed, first decided to become teachers mostly to get a job doing something useful, interesting, challenging—possibly even beautiful. But the bureaucracy wears them down, as does the working atmosphere where the children steadily lose the possibilities they were born with, to become cogs in a dehumanizing machine.

<u>The higher learning</u>. Thorstein VEBLEN (1908) wrote a book with that title concerning the university. Its original subtitle was "A Study in Total Depravity." The publisher found that undesirable, but settled for something he should have seen as equally derogatory: "On the Conduct of Universities by Businessmen." That was almost a century ago. If Veblen (d. 1929) were around today, so much have the universities degenerated since then that he wouldn't even bother to write on the subject. "Degenerated" in what ways?

Under **corruption** a story is told about an attempt on the part of a corporation to corrupt the Business School at U.C. Berkeley in 1951, on whose faculty I then sat. And how it was defeated 25 to 1; and how today, in contrast, the corporatization of the university has come to be taken for granted.

But that is only one form of corruption in the universities; as business was increasing its always-excessive role after World War II, so was the Pentagon—by its subsidies and its "constraints."

The subsidies have been numerous, mostly in those realms which directly or indirectly contribute to military strength in chemistry, engineering, and physics, as is—or should be—well-known.

The "constraints" are as subtle as they are important. For example, in a *NYT* Op-ed piece "Power Over Principle: How the military bullied its way into law schools" (9-7-02), Professor George Fisher (of the Stanford Law School) states that "this year there will be a new team of recruiters at many law schools: those from the Judge Advocate General's Corps of the United States military. "

This is not something entirely new; but a decade or so ago, most of the leading law schools ceased to allow it, mostly because the military rejects qualified students who wish to serve if they are <u>openly</u> gay or lesbian or bisexual: "Dishonesty is the best policy." But now the universities have begun to relent, beginning with the "top two": Harvard (East); Stanford (West).

So <u>why</u> have /they/ and other American law schools changed their policy? "The reason, almost everywhere, is money," the professor reports.

> In 2000, The Department of Defense issued regulations reinterpreting federal law, so that: If any part of a university denies access to military recruiters, the entire university will lose an array of federal funds.... For years law schools have stood in defense of the anti-discrimination principles they teach. Now the military is forcing them to bend their principles—and the cost falls not on the schools but on their students." (ibid.)

Derek BOK, long-time former president of Harvard, knows just how bad it is; the title of his recent book tells at least some of it: *Universities in the Marketplace: The Commercialization of Higher Education.* He sees the purposes and the consequences as many. Among the former are the "hunt for profits," through "anti-educational" sports programs, collaboration with corporations to find and patent scientific discoveries (with biased research and testing), corporate subsidized executive training programs (for their own specialties), grade inflation to attract and retain satisfied student "consumers"—and so it goes, ad nauseum. And the consequences?

The competition for the "best" students and faculty has produced anxiety among students and those "best" faculty not only use up funds (and deepen the corruption) but increasingly exempt the "stars" from teaching; also, and in the long run (which has arrived), Bok makes it clear that these tendencies also exacerbate the already appalling division of the society into an already rich minority to become richer and an already poor majority to become poorer. (see **inequality, poverty**)

So it is that in the universities, as elsewhere, **corruption**—that is, the betrayal of function—spreads and thickens, taking so many forms that it is barely noticed. The function of college professors is twofold: to teach, and through their research and writing to expand the frontiers of understanding and appreciation (and thus, also, to become a better teacher).

"In the old days," by which I mean until the last 30-40 years, to become a part of "the higher learning," one gained an M.A. or Ph.D., began to teach (and study further) and, if competent, moved from being an Instructor to Assistant Professor to Associate Professor (with tenure) to Professor. In 1970, 78 percent of university level teachers had received tenure (which meant your job was secure, even if you were a social critic). But by 1999, those tenured had dropped to less than one-third. (USDE) What are the others two-thirds doing?

Called "part-time temps" in the rest of the service sector, in academia they are euphemistically called "adjunct professors." If they are teaching two courses, they are paid at poverty income levels ($12-14,000/year), usually with a maximum of $3,000 a course—with no benefits nor, usually, even an office in which to speak to students.

Whatever the reality at the colleges and universities, it is considerably worse at community colleges—many of which, according to a Harvard University report of 1995, have no tenured teachers, and where over two-thirds are part-time temps. (TAIRA)

So what? So, the teachers thus affected (exploited would be more accurate) 1) often must work at more than one institution at a time, commuting from place to place (not always in the same town), 2) are unable to even think of doing serious research or writing, 3) are thus deprived of even a slim chance at a permanent job, 4) learn to keep their mouths shut on any kind of controversial matter, within or outside the school, 5) are ruled over by the small percentage of tenured profs most of whom got theirs 30 years ago, and 6) are stuck with their very low pay and those non-existent health benefits, pensions, disappointment, and frustration.

Imagine how much time they are able to give their students—

and imagine how little time those with tenure give their students, if any. In short, the line between a university and a department store or a tool factory, as with any other business, has become hard to find: a business is a business is a business. (NELSON)

As the selling of the university has gone from the attempts of corporations to have as many "chairs" in a university department as they please, and as the out-and-out corporatization of the universities has come to be orchestrated from the top down, another tendency has emerged from the bottom up, namely, the attempts of what has become an academic proletariat to form unions. As has always been true for industrial and other workers, those attempts are fraught with difficulty.

To be an organizer of "adjunct professors," or even to support the effort, is often to get fired; moreover, as blue collar and service workers have discovered and the companies well know, there are always other workers who badly need and want the vacated jobs: "the reserve army of the unemployed" has many Ph.D.s nowadays.

But there is a subtle something else that other workers, however difficult their lives, have not had as a problem: When university teachers seek to form themselves into a union, they have to deal with the not entirely attractive thought that being a prof was different from working in a factory or a mine. Still, organizing is now the only way to keep the "higher learning" from becoming just another source of **profits** (although the word is verboten in academe; there they use one or more Latin or Greek terms).

By way of conclusion, and as someone who has observed education's ups and downs from both bottom and top since the 1920s, I cannot help but feel strongly about what those ups and downs. The "ups" included a handful of dedicated teachers along the way, the expansion of access to university education provided to millions (including myself) by the GI Bill after World War II, the great satisfaction derived from teaching both in the USA and Italy and, among other matters, the enlarged access to previously denied children to Headstart, improved urban schools and, after the 1960s to universities through **affirmative action**.

When the "downs" began to take hold in education in the late 1970s, it was not from a high peak, but a low hill. The improvements made in the educational realm in years after World War II could be seen as only first steps, as was true also for other changes involving **health care, social security**, and the like. Put differently, the deterioration of education—on all levels—was part and parcel of a general deterioration, part of that "rightward shift."

Among the most sickening developments of those years, and one that continues to be more so, is the relationship between the decline of public moneys spent on schools and the meteoric rise of expenditures on prisons (see **crime and punishment, prison-industrial complex**). Both sets of those public expenditures are largely financed by the individual states; they must be approved, directly or indirectly, by voters approving bond issues (and the taxes to pay for them). As such, they compete with each other.

It is a competition loaded in favor of prisons. In the recent decades in which the schools' loss and the prisons' gains have occurred there have been at least three background developments goading them on: 1) a "flight to the suburbs" and to private schools for middle and upper income families, 2) a continuing—usually racist—din about crime and violence from politicians and the media, and 3) the intensification of the borrowing and spending habits intrinsic to **consumerism**. The consequences include a growing resentment of taxes for education and a grudging acceptance of those for incarceration—in which we lead the world.

There is so much wrong with all that, so much that is harmful not just to its victims but, as well, its (conscious or unconscious) perpetrators and to the society as a whole, it is difficult to know where to begin in response. But one indisputably major consequence is what we have lost along the way, and for the future: a realization of the positive human potentialities for all concerned.

Those potentialities are discussed elsewhere in this work (**inequality, environment, racism**, among other subjects); here let me concentrate on what is least obvious and, at the same time, most important, and which distinguishes us from all other species: our minds and our imagination.

Whether as children or as adults, our minds never do stop working, and never can. Whether they will function in ways lively or dull, in constructive and positive or destructive and negative ways, depends less upon innate abilities than upon our formal and informal educational experiences.

This discussion of education began with the poet Lindsay's appeal "Let not young souls be smothered out...," and the scientist Gould's lament concerning those who have lived and died and in the fields and factories, with never a chance to move toward, let alone reach their possibilities. Massive and tragic indeed have those losses been for "the young" and those confined to Spartan lives, whether because of being poor, or of the "wrong" color or gender..., or something. But they have been massive and tragic for everyone, if in different or lesser degrees.

Not everybody can become an Einstein or a Beethoven or a Roualt, no matter what their social circumstances; but everybody's mind <u>could</u> be more fully and richly used and developed in a formal educational process devoted to facilitating that instead of to maintaining the status quo. In the modern era, and in the richest countries, we have always possessed the <u>resources</u> to do just that; but not the will.

Our schooling is meant to serve the existing society, not its or our possibilities. There has been little inclination even to consider that society would be better served were education to be directed to learning, to understanding, to the cultivation and enhancement of human possibilities—which, finally, are also human <u>needs</u>. Mr. Gradgrind has won.

embedded

The policy of "embedding" reporters with a particular military unit was introduced (or renewed in more highly controlled ways) as the war in **Iraq** was on its way; the idea was that of Victoria Clarke, the Defense Department's aggressive voice. On June 18, 2003, the AP reported her as saying that "Pentagon officials were so pleased with the results of embedding about 700 journalists with troops in Iraq war that they wanted the program expanded in future conflicts."

Why was the Pentagon so pleased? And what does "embedding" mean? And, by the way, <u>which</u> future conflicts?

The answer to the first question is made easier by the answer to the second, looking first for the accepted meaning of "to embed." Dictionaries do (and must) keep up with the times; in that our times are ever more Orwellian in terms of language (among other matters), I turn to the classic 1911 *Webster's New International Dictionary* for a non-*1984* definition: "**em-bed**, <u>v.t.</u> To lay as in a bed; to lay in surrounding matter; to place (a substance) in a mass of wax...." Hmmm.

Military journalism did not, of course, begin with the war in Iraq. Such reporting goes back at least to the Civil War, with Ambrose Bierce's bitter *In the Midst of Life*; some of journalism's sorriest history gave rise to the expression "yellow journalism" in reaction to Hearst's reporting of the Spanish-American War); and war reporting has always tended to have a glorifying and patriotic stance.

All that said, embedding, like so much else in our time that connects with the **media,** represents a big jump, if not yet a quantum leap; we may expect those "future conflicts" to be more and more like a TV series: Maybe with Martha Stewart in the role of star reporter?

If we can rarely expect <u>neutrality</u> in war reports, we may at least hope for <u>objectivity</u> the latter refers to reporting the facts as clearly as possible. But that does not dispense with the problem: <u>Which</u> facts are reported and which are <u>not</u>? It takes a very good reporter indeed, with or without embedding, to report facts that redound to the disfavor of one's side, even though doing so may be essential to preventing such facts from recurring; may be essential, indeed, to the long-run wellbeing of "one's side."

It is worth remembering that the slaughter at My Lai 4 in the **Vietnam** war was not brought to light by journalists then reporting the war but by Seymour HERSH; and that required a year of traveling tens of thousands of miles in the USA to track down its GI participants. I doubt that Hersh was invited to be one the 700 "embedded" in the Iraq war. (see **Vietnam** for recent revelations about "hundreds of My Lai's.)

The pressures on the **media** to soften or ignore "bad news" is most especially great when it comes to news concerning the major corporations, the White House, and the military in wartime: the media require access to the sources, where access itself is the <u>privilege</u> granted by the government to be present at the "newsroom conferences" (and much more, if one is scheduled to be called upon), of corporations, of the White House, and of the Pentagon.

It is difficult enough under the best of circumstances to gain such access; and perilously simple to lose it by "misdeed." Ask any White House reporter.

The privilege is not, of course, just the reporter's but her/his organization's; the reporter gets pressured from two sides. In the past century, a large percentage of the best-known (and most highly-paid) reporters reached that status in conjunction with their wartime reporting, most especially during World War II, and the Korean and Vietnam wars, with TV reporting becoming always more important as we approach present.

Now, imagine yourself to be a reporter who, knowing and caring about all of this travail much better than yours truly, is embedded with the some infantry battalion in Iraq during the "main fighting." As anyone who has been present knows, combat conditions are always chaotic in their several dimensions—all of them worthy of being reported. To which one or more of those "dimensions" shall you react with a story? The one that will get you into trouble? Let's see, now.

All reporting, all <u>writing</u>, is selective, whether that of journalists or professors..., of everyone. The selections that constitute this book were determined by my values; others by their values; a war reporter must consider how the values of his military group <u>and</u> of his employer would lead to the selection or neglect of a particular story; and, when selected, how to frame it, decide on its tone. If one is doing that from afar it is difficult; "embedded"? Considerably more difficult.

Put differently, if Victoria Clarke and the Pentagon are "pleased" with the embedding experiment, We the People should be worried.

emulation

The 20th century was shot full with paradox: <u>technologically</u>, it saw the greatest quantitative and qualitative advances ever in the realms of communication, production, and transportation while, at the same time, more human beings worked harder than ever before (HOBSBAWM/1968/; GORDON, D.); <u>economically</u>, it brought development and growth to more people than ever while, at the same time, more people and societies became economically devastated (STAVRIANOS); <u>culturally</u>, greater numbers of people became able and inclined to appreciate and enjoy all levels of learning, of art, music, and literature while, at the same time, popular culture became ever more degraded with violence and vulgarity (BAR-

BER); politically, democracy in some degree came to mark a large and always increasing number of societies; but it was also the century in which totalitarianism oppressed more millions than ever in history; and, finally, although there were more sustained and organized institutions for keeping or bringing peace, militarily the 20th century was the most disastrous ever.

Such wild contrasts beg for explanations that would fill many volumes. That said, surely one of the explanatory factors would be irrationality: in a reasonable world, "paradoxes" with such ghastly consequences could not occur, let alone persist and worsen.

Irrationality alone is not the answer, of course; and irrationality itself has many dimensions; here we examine only one of those, itself multi-dimensional: emulation. In doing so, I shall depend mostly on its treatment by Veblen.

Before proceeding further, a note on Veblen's use of language. It was frequently ironic, often ambiguous, and systematically illusive: camouflaged. Veblen was a severe critic of the status quo and wary of the price to be paid for such a stance. So it was that even for the title of his first book, a study first and foremost of the ruling class of his day—the capitalist class—he found an almost whimsically ironic title: The Theory of the Leisure Class (1899). In the same spirit the working class became "the underlying population."

(DOWD /1964/2000)

Veblen was born in 1857 and was reaching adulthood in the same period in which Marxism and related socialist movements were swelling. Veblen was critical of Marx, but it was the criticism of an ally in disguise: like Marx, profoundly anti-capitalist; unlike Marx, not at all optimistic. The principal difference for Veblen had to do with the emulative component of "human nature."

Marx believed that workers, in order to preserve their humanity in the face of devastating working conditions (see **dehumanization/alienation** and OLLMAN) must and would organize themselves, revolt, and overthrow capitalism. He expected that to occur first in Britain, the Netherlands, and the USA, then the most capitalist, advanced, and democratic of nations. Instead, tragically—but for Veblen, understandably—revolution occurred first in Russia, a society more imperialized than capitalist, socioeconomically backward, and not at all democratic.

Veblen began his writing in the USA after Marx's death (1883), a country very different from Marx's mid-19th century Great Britain and its "first industrial revolution." As the 19th century was ending and the 20th beginning, the USA (along with Germany) had taken the lead in a "second" industrial revolution; also, it had just begun its overseas expansion and wars in the Caribbean and the Pacific—to the eager accompaniment of nationalistic support from, among others, the working class.

By 1910, as the drums were pounding for World War I in Europe, Germany's "underlying population" had created the most powerful socialist movement in the world. Veblen wrote an essay anticipating the eagerness with which <u>that</u> movement also would support war and give itself up in eager and self-destructive sacrifice to it. (The essay is found in the 1919 collection of VEBLEN.)

In the USA at that same time, the "Gay Nineties" were peaking. "Gay" they may have been for perhaps 10 percent of the people of the USA; the rest were at best comfortable and at worst desperate. (FAULKNER).

A larger minority would benefit materially from the postwar "new era" of the 1920s, when the first blush of **consumerism** took hold, perhaps doubling the percentage of gainers. What was new about that economy was that it was the first to begin to center upon mass-produced consumer <u>durable</u> goods and, thus, upon modern **advertising**. (SOULE) Those two processes—one greasing the path to war the other to consumerism—both hinged upon <u>emulation</u>. What did Veblen mean by that term, and why did he give it such analytical importance?

<u>Human nature and conduct</u>. Some of what is relevant was discussed under **dehumanization/alienation**, and will not be repeated here, except in summary form. Suffice it to say that Veblen (simultaneously with philosopher John DEWEY, whom he knew and worked with) made the then novel argument that human beings adapt to, are changed by, and change the always evolving processes of history; that human nature is not "given" but responsive, functioning with always differing means and ends, shaping and being shaped by social "institutions" (= customary ways of behaving, feeling, thinking).

Our constructive and destructive tendencies and what inclines us to respond to and utilize them in one degree or another (or not at all) is vitally consequent upon time and place and an always changing social system. The "social system" of Veblen's time, as he saw it, was dominated by "the system of business enterprise and absentee ownership" (i.e., **capitalism**) and by "the patriotic spirit" (embodied in **nationalism** and **imperialism**).

They themselves were an outgrowth of centuries of evolution from <u>always</u> class-dominated and militaristic societies, from Ancient Egypt to Ancient Rome to the feudal and early modern monarchies, and up to the present. The rulers of the pre-modern worlds, some combination of military and religious functionaries, gained and held their power through force and violence—or, as Veblen put it, "force and fraud" (where "fraud" included all ideology, whether political, economic, or religious in nature, or some combination of them).

In such a world of past and present, what is the common human response? Veblen begins with the importance of self-respect (or felt dignity) and its shaping by society: without self-respect we "go to pieces."

That is true not just of us but of many mammals—most clearly observable when it is lost by animals in **zoos**. One cannot sensibly observe a tiger going compulsively back and forth in its cage without seeing it as deranged and being so because it has lost what may be seen as its dignity. As noted in **racism** and **slavery** and **dehumanization**, much the same is true for us, when we are treated as inferior, as stupid, as <u>things</u>. (OLLMAN)

In being demeaned, we lose our self-respect. With such matters in mind, Veblen wrote

> The usual basis of self-respect is the respect accorded by one's neighbors. Only individuals with an aberrant temperament can in the long run retain their self-esteem in the face of the disesteem of their fellows. Apparent exceptions to the rule are met with, especially among people with strong religious convictions. But these apparent exceptions are scarcely real exceptions, since such persons commonly fall back on the putative approbation of some supernatural witness of those deeds. (1899)

Which takes us to "the leisure class." It is the class of property owners, those who control the means of production, the means of life; the class with claims upon the labor of others. Here we must oversimplify the long process from our beginnings as a species to the present; doing so, it is reasonable to state that the first "leisure class" was made up of those who with the violence of hunting and "warlike exploit" contributed to the "survival of the fittest" while, at the same time, ruling over their groups.

There is no straight line from the prehistoric millennia to the present, but it may be asserted 1) That those who held power and prestige in the prehistoric era gained it through sheer violence, and 2) that in the ancient, medieval and early periods, still very violent (the 17th century had only four years <u>without</u> war), force was institutionalized through serfdom, the Church, and the State to provide both power and prestige.

In the modern era of capitalism and political democracy, given the continuation of violence through intermittent wars, the principal source of both power and prestige was shifted to those who dominate the economy and, thus, the society: those who own and control the means of production: What the ideology of the Church meant in the pre-capitalist era has been replaced by the ideology of capitalism-<u>cum</u>-nationalism in our time.

Or, as Veblen put it, the sources of "esteem" and power in the modern world combine military with economic "prowess." (The quoted words are Veblen's) He saw the modern business leader as essentially a latter-day predatory warrior—transformed, armed, and clothed in a fashion enabling him to dominate modern society:

> The relation of the leisure... class to the economic process is a pecuniary relation—a relation of acquisition, not production; of exploitation, not of serviceability... Their office is of a parasitic character, and their interest is to divert what substance they may to their own use... The conventions of the business world... have grown up under the selective surveillance of this principle of predation, or parasitism. They are conventions of ownership; derivatives, more or less remote, of the ancient predatory /i.e., hunter and warrior/ culture. (ibid.)

Putting his analysis forth in an anthropological framework, Veblen saw our evolution from prehistoric to modern times as a continuity with temporal variation:

> When a /primitive/ group emerges into the predatory stage, the employments which most occupy men's attention are employments that involve exploit; the assertion of the strong hand, successful aggression... becomes the basis of repute..., the

conventional ground of invidious comparison between individuals, and repute comes to rest on prowess. /That/ virtue par excellence gains in scope and consistency until prowess comes near being recognized as the sole virtue.... The tame employments, those that involve no obvious destruction of life and no spectacular coercion of refractory antagonisms, fall into disrepute....

In the further cultural development, when some wealth has been accumulated and the members of the community fall into a servile class on the one hand and a leisure class on the other, the tradition that labor is ignoble gains an added significance, not only a mark of inferior force, but also a perquisite of the poor. This is the situation today: Labor is indecorous. (1934)

The foregoing has been concerned with the "emulation" that underlies nationalism and warlike tendencies; equally or more important for Veblen was "pecuniary emulation" which, indeed may be seen as the main theme of *The Theory of the Leisure Class*. It is central to Veblen's analysis that there are not just the "leisure class" and the "underlying population," but many strata <u>within</u> each grouping: within the leisure class proper there are the settled aristocracy and the <u>nouveau riche</u>. The latter emulate and gradually replace the former, and the former despise the pretensions and usually greater wealth of the latter. (see Edith Wharton's novels of turn-of-the-century New York for a delicious pairing of those gradations.)

Within the "underlying population" there is an even more considerable stratification. Veblen saw the members of each sub-group straining to be identified with the group <u>at least</u> immediately "above," that is, next closest to the leisure class proper. The result is thus one of pervasive discontent and striving, where the most relevant <u>standard</u> of living is the visible level of those above one's own "social class"—a standard functioning much the same as the legendary carrot placed in front of a donkey's nose, providing the motive for unremitting effort to change one's life, no matter how comfortable or adequate it might be in the absence of pecuniary emulation:

> The standard of expenditure which commonly guides our efforts is not the average, ordinary expenditure already achieved; it is an ideal of consumption that lies just beyond our reach, or to reach which requires some strain. The motive is emulation—the stimulus of an invidious comparison which

prompts us to outdo those with whom we are in the habit of classing ourselves.

But that's not all:

> The standard is flexible; and especially it is indefinitely extensible, if only time is allowed for habituation to any increase in pecuniary ability and for acquiring facility in the new and larger scale of expenditure that follows with such an increase. It is much more difficult to recede from a scale of expenditure once adopted than it is to extend the accustomed scale in response to an accession of wealth.... With the exception of the instinct of self-preservation, the propensity for emulation is probably the strongest and most alert and persistent of the economic motives proper..., and as regards the Western civilized communities of the present, is virtually equivalent to saying that it expresses itself in some form of conspicuous **waste**. (my **bold**)

Mind you, those quotations are all from a book written in 1899. Quite apart from the extraordinary insights and foresight involved, and that modern advertising wasn't even invented for another two decades or more without, even then, anyone foreseeing its present powers of manipulation, Veblen's way of thinking must be seen as phenomenal. I say that here because, as noted in the Foreword, it is my hope that readers of this book will be stimulated to work their way through at least some of the many bibliographical references: Veblen (who wrote another ten books until he died in 1929) should be high on any such reading list.

Read him and weep; and smile; and weep some more.

Enron (see deregulation)

entertainment (see TV, media)

environment

Introduction. Going back at least as far as Ancient Greece, it has been recognized that the bases for our and all other species' existence are "earth, air, fire, and water." From their interaction, all of life was created and sustained and—if "fire" includes household heating and cooking, explosives, and internal combustion—together they enabled life to become more comfortable, more complicated, <u>and</u> more dangerous.

All species have had both an adversarial and a sustaining relationship with some or all of the four interacting life elements; only ours has been able to transform the problems and possibilities of "raw" nature in our favor and, more's the worse, to wreak permanent damage and destruction upon the whole of nature—including ourselves. Both the useful and the harmful have evolved at an always-accelerating rate.

Many of the harmful results—such as overcrowded cities, intermittent famine, even air pollution—are all too often seen as caused by "too many people," made possible by lowering death rates and longer life expectancies. It is surely desirable to halt or reverse global population increases but to do so acceptably requires progressive social policies—the very policies usually opposed by those who see rapid population growth as the fault of the people themselves—the <u>poor</u> people, that is.

As with many other daunting problems, however, the explanation for the "population surplus" is to be found in the larger social realm. For the past two centuries that has been the realm of **capitalism**, neither least nor only because its history is coincident with the rapid advances of both the population surge and the **technology** accompanying it: It is more than coincidence that when the world's first factory opened in 1815 there were fewer than one billion people in the world, and that today there are over six billion. (BRAUDEL)

It was not the <u>existence</u> of new technologies that caused the problem, but the ways in which they were and were <u>not</u> used from the time that both capitalism and industrial technology took firm hold in Britain in the late 18th century, along with the beginnings of modern agriculture.

Those changes carried with them social disruptions of unprecedented kinds, amounts, and rapidity; they transformed countless thousands of families on the land from having been "a proud peasantry" to becoming increasing desperate people who, unless fed by their townships, would have starved to death. One reaction to that was the famous epic poem of 1770 by Irish poet Oliver Goldsmith, "The Deserted Village." It begins this way:

Ill fares the land, to hastening ills a prey,
Where wealth accumulates. And men decay:
Princes and lords may flourish, or may fade;
A breath can make them, as a breath has made;
But a bold peasantry, their country's pride,
When once destroyed, can never be supplied.

However, those same conditions subsequently prompted the Rev. Thomas MALTHUS to develop his even more famous and considerably more influential "theory" of population. Malthus and his family were among the landed gentry who, because of the "Poor Laws" (lingering from medieval and Elizabethan times) had to pay taxes to feed the starving peasantry. Thus provoked, in 1798 Malthus wrote his still circulating *Essay on the Principle of Population*.

There he raised the specter of "too many people": The Poor Laws, he wrote, allow the number of people to rise "geometrically" over time (1, 2, 4, 8, 16, 32...), but food supplies can only increase "arithmetically" (1, 2, 3, 4....). He was dead wrong; since 1798 global per capita food production has <u>always</u> exceeded the number of people. As a leading authority has written, "Starvation is the characteristic of some people not <u>having</u> enough food to eat. It is not the characteristic of there not <u>being</u> enough food to eat." (SEN, 1981)

That Malthus made such a gross error of judgment <u>could</u> be explained by his (and others') inability to foresee the technologies allowing always more food than people—except that the relevant processes had been well under way well before he was born, and were speeding up as he wrote. His "error" was due to something else, one that permeates much otherwise inexplicably wrong-headed thinking.

Malthus was intent on doing away with the predecessors of modern welfare programs—"those damnable Poor Laws," he called them—and their taxes on the well-off. He chose to see them as harming both the poor and the comfortable; and he was strikingly blunt and cruel in his solution, the era of euphemisms yet to come:

> To act consistently, therefore, we should facilitate, instead of foolishly and vainly endeavoring to impede, the operation of nature in producing this mortality /induced by starvation/; and if we dread the too frequent visitation of... famine, we should sedulously encourage the other forms of destruction.... Instead of recommending cleanliness to the poor, we should encourage

contrary habits. In our towns we should make the streets narrower, crowd more people into the houses, and court the return of the plague..., we should build our villages near stagnant pools, and particularly encourage settlements in all marshy and unwholesome situations.... (MALTHUS)

It would be pleasant to think that the good Reverend was being ironic; not at all. He goes on in like manner, bringing to mind the last words of Kurtz, in Conrad's *Heart of Darkness*: "Exterminate the brutes!"

Fortunately, others see the solution as eliminating the thoroughly substantiated causes of over-population: tightly linked poverty, insufficient education, and the oppression of women. The areas of most rapid population growth are also those of the greatest poverty; the same areas are also characterized by the highest degrees of oppression of women, not least as concerns their inability to decide whether or not to have children, and their connected lack of education.

The Nobel economist/philosopher SEN has made those arguments solidly and eloquently; in addition, as the biologist Josue' DE CASTRO has shown, still today, as in the deeper past, the agricultural poor have children because they are poor, for they function as "hands" in the field.

Nowadays, because of the millions continually forced off the land by "modern agriculture, those "hands" are more likely to be held out asking for money in city streets (or serving as prostitutes); there are not enough agricultural or other jobs for them in their own or other countries. (See **globalization, farmers**, BOUCHER, /ed./)

Those on the path toward becoming emerging industrial capitalists were rarely from the landed gentry; unlike the gentry, they didn't wish to see the poor and the weak "exterminated." They preferred to have them available—especially desperately so—to work 12-16 hours a day in their mines and factories as the world's first capitalist working class: children, men, and women, powerless and easily exploitable.

That has not changed: relevant businesses encourage immigration, both legal and illegal while, at the same time **racism** rises among workers in the rich countries, as they see their wages being pulled down by the same process. (MCWILLIAMS)

It is of course technological change that brings the greater productivity in food production <u>and</u> the improved health conditions that allows population to grow. As will be discussed further under **capitalism**, the accelerating technologies from the seventeenth century on served as a set of stimuli and opportunities for the birth and subsequent life of <u>industrial</u> capitalism; and, as that new socioeconomic system appeared and grew, it in turn always stimulated the speeding up of <u>more</u> technological change—among many other changes. MARX and ENGELS caught these inter-acting processes vividly in the *Manifesto*:

> The bourgeoisie cannot exist without constantly revolutionizing the instruments of production, and thereby the relations of production, and with them the whole relations of society. Conservation of the old modes of production in unaltered form, was on the contrary, the first condition of existence for all earlier industrial classes. Constant revolutionizing of production, uninterrupted disturbance of all social conditions, everlasting uncertainty and agitation distinguish the bourgeois epoch from all earlier ones. All fixed, fast-frozen relations, with their train of ancient and venerable prejudices and opinions, are swept away; all new-formed ones become antiquated before they can ossify. All that is solid melts into air; all that is holy is profaned, and man is at last compelled to face with sober senses his real conditions of life and his relations with his kind. The need of a constantly expanding market for its products chases the bourgeoisie over the whole surface of the globe. It must nestle everywhere, settle everywhere, establish connections everywhere. (1848/1967)

As capitalist institutions inexorably took hold, so too did the **exploitation** of all of nature—nonhuman and human—in a destructive and tragic interaction.

> In modern agriculture, as in the urban industries, the increased productiveness and quantity of the labor set in motion are bought at the cost of laying waste and consuming by disease labor-power itself. Moreover, all progress in the art, not only of robbing the laborer, but of robbing the soil; all progress in increasing the fertility of the soil for a given time, is a progress towards ruining the lasting sources of that fertility. The more a country starts its development on the foundations of modern industry, like the United States, for example, the more rapid is this process of destruction. Capitalist production, therefore, develops technology, and the combining together of various processes into a social whole, only by sapping the original

sources of all wealth—the soil and the laborer. (MARX, 1867/1967)

But the full meaning of the degradation of the "soil and the laborer" goes beyond and deeper than what are often seen as its "economic" consequences to poison and our air, our water, our social and political existences—where "our" is itself an **arrogance**, in seeing (at least some) human beings as precious, and the rest of the flora and fauna (except, perhaps, pets) as grist for our mills.

Up Against the Wall, Mother Nature! Some of those with a scientific bent excluded, in the "advanced" societies it is a common conceit to see nature as something to exploit (the term long used, without second thought), rather than as that of which we are a dependent part—uniquely different though we may be. That has had both positive and negative consequences, almost entirely positive for us as we have seen things, almost entirely negative for the rest of nature.

In what ways are we "uniquely different"? First, all species may be seen to depend—or prey —upon one or more of the other elements of nature: animals upon other animals, plants, and upon the air and water; similarly with plants, etc. And some animals other than ourselves—beavers, for example—also transform nature through their "constructions."

However, after all is said and done regarding all species but ourselves, we have been both constructive and destructive in ways utterly beyond all others: beavers gnaw down trees and make dams to hold back water; they can do so in only in their tiny "neighborhood." Sharks eat other fish, lions eat other mammals; etc. All very local, all contained by natural reproductive forces and basically unchanging mortality rates. Not so for us.

What sets us apart from all other species is our ability to imagine; indeed, our inability not to do so. From our imaginations rise our hopes and fears, our rationality and irrationality, our skepticism and fanaticism, our music and literature, our science and technology—and, thus, our ability to destroy each other in the millions in wars.

But the most insane and threatening of our proclivities is to destroy the environment that gave us life and sustains us. Except for lemmings, we are the only self-destructive species. But lemmings are not dangerous to other species, or even to lemmings in other "neigh-borhoods"; we are dangerous to all and everything.

'Twas not always thus, at least not in today's dimensions, nor with their probable outcomes. What our species does now in both its positive and negative ways <u>could</u> not be done until modern science-cum-technology provided the chemistry, the physics, and the engineering which made possible today's far-flung rapid transportation and instantaneous communications, mass production and consumption, and the like: Attila the Hun was perhaps no less ruthless than Hitler, but he had only horses, spears, and swords with which to wreak his horrors; Hitler was more of a monster than Truman; but Hitler did not have **nukes**. What hath man wrought?

The full answer is not only nukes, but global warming, defor-estation, polluted and lethal air, dead and dying lakes, oceans, and rivers, melting Alps, <u>thousands</u> of disappearing faunal and floral species each year, cities on every continent moving relentlessly toward gridlock and gas masks. That's the short list.

But, and as with almost all desirable and undesirable sets of consequences, technology <u>alone</u> was not, cannot be, the cause of the good <u>or</u> the bad; the answer lies in what those with ruling socioeco-nomic power see fit to have technology <u>do</u> and <u>not</u> do: what is encouraged, what stifled.

The social structures associated with modern technology, as with so much else explored in this work, have been those of **capital-ism, imperialism, industrialism,** and **nationalism**—each feeding upon and feeding the others in a mutually transforming set of processes as they took hold, slowly or rapidly, from the 17th century to the present.

Except for a rare and unheard voice, it was not until after World War II that social thinkers began to sound environmental alarms. That is not surprising; although all the processes that would take us toward environmental catastrophe were in place <u>before</u> World War II, they had not reached their "critical mass" until the late 1940s and beyond; were not yet obvious.

That they were becoming increasing so after the war was due in part 1) to the swift acceleration of technological advances of—and for—the two world wars. They laid the technological basis for the post-World War II socioeconomic developments whose rapidity and spread were qualitatively different from anything earlier; and 2) given the weakening of <u>all</u> other nations but our own, due also to the easy global predominance and associated strategies of the USA, most capitalist of all nations. (FOSTER /1999/; O'NEILL)

That technology, taken together with U.S. means and ends, may be seen as having "transported" the elements of the U.S. socioeconomy over the globe: not just its mass production, but its mass consumption and **consumerism**, and its undisputed "free market" ideology.

Among the first works to point to the implications of these developments was K. William Kapp's *The Social Costs of Private Enterprise* (1950). Although Kapp's work was readable and he was a reputable economist, its audience was never more than minimal: It may be asserted that not more than a handful of mainstream economists of the past half century have read or sent their students to that book; unsurprisingly: had his analysis been taken seriously and pursued further and been translated into social reality, both business and governmental policies would have been required to change drastically so as to limit the power of business, and, as they would see it, to reduce their profits.

Kapp's analytical base was one he borrowed from 19th century economic thought, that of "external costs." Those are costs caused by producers, but not paid for by them—for example, the costs of cleaning up a factory's polluted air (and the costs of <u>not</u> cleaning it up); and so on, for poisoned lakes, rivers, seas...; you name it. As the ways of producing and much of what we consume have increasingly incurred such "external" costs, the economics profession has remained in its lockstep with business by losing interest in the matter—except as revived by some on the fringe of the profession and, more recently, by the emerging environmental crisis. (see ULL-MAN)

Among the best known and earliest of those was the natural scientist Rachel CARSON, with her *Silent Spring* (1962). She turned attention to the broader costs to Mother Nature of technological "progress": the silence of her book's title referred to the disappearance of birds because of the chemical killing off of insects and, as well, by poisoned soil, water, and plants. But 1962 was birds' paradise, compared with today. (MANNING)

In a subsequent comment on her book, Carson noted that even ten years earlier she had not worried that "nature... actually needed protection from man." But, she adds,

> I was wrong. Even those things that seemed to belong to the eternal verities, are not only threatened but have already felt the destroying hand of man. Today we use the sea as a dumping ground for radioactive wastes, which then enter the vast and uncontrollable movements of ocean water through the deep basins, to turn up no one knows where... The once beneficent rains are now an instrument to bring down from the atmosphere the deadly products of nuclear explosions. Water, perhaps our most precious natural resource, is used and misused at a reckless rate. Our streams are fouled with an incredible assortment of wastes—domestic, chemical, radioactive, so that our planet, though dominated by seas that envelop three-quarters of its surface, is rapidly becoming a thirsty world. We now wage war on other organisms, turning against them all the terrible armaments of modern chemistry, and assume a right to push whole species over the brink of extinction. (quoted in HAYNES)

That was written several decades ago; since then, everything that concerned her—and more—has multiplied and intensified, in the ways in which and what we produce and consume, in their quantities, and in their geographic spread and impact. Meanwhile, what little progress was made in environmental protections in earlier years has undergone deliberate reversal, now speeding up under **Bush II** (see below).

Among the principal causes of high and increasing environmental destruction are the also increasing ways in which modern economies **waste** natural (and human) resources, most clearly and vividly—but by no means only—in the production and use of **cars**, and in **milex**. Much is said of those and other wasteful processes— and, as well, of <u>destructive waste</u> (that which is environmentally harmful) under the three "entries" just noted; here a few brief comments on only some of the relevant and major environmental disasters well under way: those causing air pollution, global warming, rapidly shrinking glaciers, depletion of water supplies, and the destruction of forests.

They are all connected and interacting, and there is a critical causal link between them and today's obsession with economic growth (see below), which, like its cousin the **free market**, has become an ideology. Aided and abetted by "educational campaigns" against environmental safeguards by its "institutional **advertising** and its bought and paid for legislators, the businesses most responsible for environmental damage have managed not only to weaken or prevent regulation, but to deflect attention away from the fact that programs of environmentally "sustainable development" could at the same time lift real per capita incomes for all. (see Afterword; DALY /1996/)

Instead, as though crazed, we continue to destroy the sources of our wellbeing. Now some short discussions of the main areas of the environment under attack.

The air. It has become dangerous to our and the rest of nature's health in numerous ways: by the spewing into the skies of industrial contaminants from products using rising numbers of new chemical combinations; by leaks large and small of all too many contaminants; by the continuing and insane decline of public transportation as there are always more gas-guzzling, air polluting **cars** per capita; the proliferating uses of internal combustion engines, and the rising number of sales of the more dangerous and much more profitable SUVs; by the increased use of synthetic products made from petrochemicals, with plastic junk proliferating everywhere, providing the waste and dusts which foul both air and water. Etc.

Whatever else all that entails in terms of lung and heart disease, in conjunction with the rising use of chlorofluorocarbons (CFCs) it has already created a large and rapidly growing "hole" in the ozone layer, and initiated climate change toward global warming. Because of environmental rules seeking to control the use of CFCs, there has been some progress in that respect; but the **lobbyists** and neocon thinktanks are working on that, cheered along by, among others, **Bush II & Co.**

As the polluters have their way with Congress and the White House, it is well to pay attention to the fact that the already very damaging processes of global warming are becoming worse, faster. In the respected scientific journal *Nature* (January, 2003), a new report "whose level of certainty is far higher than earlier," posits projections of global warming by year 2100 by 2.5 to 10 degrees (Fahrenheit), should concentrations of carbon dioxide and other heat-trapping gases continue to rise. The gases flow mainly from smokestacks and

/**cars'**/ tailpipes. By comparison, the world took about 10,000 years to climb out of the depths of the last Ice Age and warm from 5 to 9 degrees to current conditions." (*NYT*, 1-3-03)

That had to do with "projections"; here are some frightening realities expressed in recent headlines or short statements: "Thinning Ice" (*NYT*, editorial, 9-25-03). "Huge Ice Shelf Is Reported to Break Up in Canada" (*NYT*, 9-23-03). "Warming Doubles Glacier Melt," (*Guardian* /UK/, 10-17-03). "Antarctica ozone hole now larger than North America," (*IHT*, 9-20-03) Then, as noted by Nicholas D. Kristof in his "Baked Alaska on the Menu: Bad News (*NYT*, 9-1`3-03):

> The U.S. Navy reports that in areas traversed by its submarines, Arctic ice volume decreased 42 percent over the last 35 years, and the average thickness of ice below water declined 4.3 feet. The Office of Naval Research warns that "one plausible outcome" is that the summer Arctic ice cap will disappear by 2050.

And,

> Global warming could wipe out a quarter of all species of plants and animals by 2050 in one of the biggest mass extinctions since the dinosaurs, according to an international study. The UN said the report... showed the need for the world to back the Kyoto Protocol, an agreement meant to curb rising temperatures linked to human pollution. (*IHT*, 1-8-9=04) /Which we won't sign; see below)

So? We're not plants or animals or dinosaurs. Anyway, the ice melt only hits coastal cities. On to Iowa!

Trees. The Europeans and we have done a lot to use up the forests in our own countries; more recently, we have been hard at work destroying those of the rest of the earth, most notably those of Brazil. Quite apart from all else—which includes the linked tragedies of the "forest people"—those southern forests have always had the function of "cleaning" the air of the northern hemisphere: as our air becomes always dirtier because of what we do up here, we are also destroying what alleviation we might receive from the south. Self-destruction, Inc.

A not so funny element in this process is that **Bush II**'s people, in response to customary business pressures, have proposed that we can offset our non-participation in the Kyoto Pact (see below) by "planting trees as carbon sinks" here and there in the USA. Good idea in itself, but it would take a minimum of a century or so for such trees to have an effect—assuming their quantities would be more substantial than has been proposed <u>and</u> that current cutting would be reduced. Don't hold your breath; in fact, if you can handle it, don't breathe.

<u>Water</u>. We can't survive for long with always dirtier air; nor can we survive with always less water—clean <u>or</u> dirty. With an already large and always rising global population it might seem that adequate water supplies would be a problem, no matter what. Perhaps; probably not. As with other problems noted earlier, water pollution and shortages are not caused by too many people drinking and washing but by the misuse and overuse of water supplies from streams, lakes, oceans and the rain, directly and indirectly. How so?

The villains are many and closely-related: the ways we produce and clean ourselves and our possessions, the disposal of industrial and bodily wastes and cleansers, the washing away of agricultural, industrial, and urban-applied insecticides and herbicides, the increased runoffs of water from filled-in swamps and denuded hillsides, the closing off of local for distant water supplies as major cities become overcrowded and extended into suburbs. As that dirge resounds and swells, we are all—including the poorest people in the poorest countries—being asked to begin to pay, or to pay more, for water. (MANNING; O'NEILL; FOSTER /2002/

As early as 1967, this and more led **LBJ** to declare that "every major river system in the country is polluted." But he was only talking about dirty and dangerous river waters. Now the apprehension is widespread and growing among scientists that water—not oil or gold or titanium—will soon become the scarcest of resources. That is not, however, true of mainstream economists: despite all, **economics** textbooks continue to cite air and water—and markets—as "free goods." <u>Nuclear wastes</u>. In the separate discussion of **nukes**, it will be seen that something more than environmental degradation is at stake, with or without more Three Mile Islands and Chernobyls: Here then, setting aside the likelihood that nuclear <u>weapons</u> will be used again, some time—what about plain old nuclear <u>waste</u>?

It would be amusing, except that it isn't, that for the USA and the other countries using nuclear energy—all the big ones and some of the little ones—the problem of disposal has produced a merry-go-round of schemes and scams to dispose of the innumerable tons of the deadly stuff: in the USA, bury them in Nevada, say the other 49 states; bury them in Montana says Nevada; up yours, says Montana.

All of the rich countries say pay the poor countries—that is, their corrupt rulers—enough to allow us to bury the stuff there. Put them on always moving ships in the Atlantic Ocean, say the Chinese and the Japanese; in the Pacific say we (except for those on the Pacific Coast and Hawaii): In a word, "NIMBY" = not in my backyard. Maybe we should never have started with the weaponry or with nuclear energy? Grow up!, say the kingpins.

It is, however, encouraging to learn that five European countries—Belgium, Germany, the Netherlands, Spain, and Sweden—have pledged to close all of their nuclear power plants by 2005; however, they have not specified what they will do with their accumulated nuclear wastes. Like Scarlett O'Hara, they'll think about that tomorrow.

But at least some Europeans are closing nuclear plants; in the USA, one of the **Bush II** "solutions" for our energy needs is to have more of those plants. Just how carefully his administration has thought these things through was indicated in May, 2001 by then Treasury Secretary O'Neill: When the safety record of nuclear power plants was queried by someone in an audience of businessmen, O'Neill responded by saying that "If you set aside Three Mile Island and Chernobyl, the record is really very good." ("O'Neill's Outspokenness..., NYT, 12-7-02) OK, now, gang, get ready: "One, two, three, Set 'em aside!"

Demon growth. What is it about our "civilization" that it finds so many ingenious ways to harm itself? What is it, that when the harms have been explained, have even happened, that those with power sail blithely on, denying the harm or explaining it away, even lying about it? What is it that ensures that when a problem has been recognized and, if rarely, laws passed to contain it (as with the EPA and **OSHA**, for example), there are insufficient personnel to enforce those laws, which frequently face repeal?

Setting aside corruption and dishonesty and lobbying—and they can't be set aside—part of the answer lies in our cultivated obsession with economic growth. Whether in the university, by the Federal Reserve Board or by corporate **CEOs**—whoever, whatever—we have learned to believe that the source of economic "wellbeing" and, as well, the solution to all socioeconomic problems is a "healthy" rate of growth. That is, the satisfactory resolution of complex human and social problems as presently pursued is seen as quantitative in its nature. Arising from, compounding, and supporting that set of notions is our equally socialized belief that the main basis for personal satisfaction is to have MORE!—a four-letter-word summing up of the consumeristic lust for buying and having; and borrowing. (SCITOVSKY; SCHOR /1998/)

Because a socioeconomic system such as capitalism depends upon expansion for its viability, it must also find ways to have it occur globally. Seen as the only basis for the profitable production of both producer and consumer goods—by any means at hand, and have someone pick up the pieces later.

But—as is pursued further in other discussions (**cars, capitalism, waste**)—whether or not desirable, it is quite simply impossible for all the world's countries, or even most of them, to live as those in the richer countries now do—led by the USA, where "led" refers to both our quantitative position and our influential role in the world's economic, political and, not least, cultural trends. (BARBER)

China is the clearest (but by no means the only) example of the literally dead end of this notion. China 1.2 billion people. Its GDP is already beyond that of Italy's. In the foreseeable future, it is probable that per capita purchasing power could equal that of, say, Italy today. It is inconceivable, however, that the levels and the patterns of consumption of China could reach those of today's Italy without an environmental catastrophe for the entire world: China's urban (and some of its rural) air is already among the most deadly in the world (nor do they show any signs of doing anything about it); even if their present population were to remain constant—most unlikely—what that pattern of elevated consumption would mean to their already polluted air and water (and to the globe) is not pleasant to contemplate. Then there is good neighbor India, with another billion people. Between them, China and India account for a third of the world's people, and they are adopting, adapting, and using the most modern technologies at an accelerating rate—reminiscent, with variations, of what the USA and Germany did when they caught up and passed Great Britain. (see **globalization, jobs**)

Is it implicit in the foregoing that the Chinese and Indian peoples should/must remain stuck at their present average real income levels? Not at all. Instead, if there is to be a substantial and lasting improvement in their (and others') lives, what is essential is to develop and employ economic development (as distinct from growth) strategies which will simultaneously protect the environment and raise the levels of comfort, safety, and decency for all.

That could not be done overnight, but some of it could be within a decade, the rest in two to five more. What cannot be done is to create the rest of the world in the economic image of the USA; nor can the USA continue on its present path without it disaster to itself and the world. (DALY /1996/)

What is being done; and undone. Despite all, the **Bush II** administration pushes along the destructive path; and let the devil take the hindmost.

Bush portrays himself as a "compassionate conservative": neither he nor those who advise him on domestic, foreign, and environmental issues are either "compassionate" or "conservative"; they are heartless, ruthless reactionaries. So what are they doing for—or, more relevantly, against—"earth, air, fire, and water"?

Here now a representative sample of their environmentally harmful "commissions and omissions." "Earth" The focus here will be separately on the soil, forests, and mining—remembering, however, that environmental relationships are organic in nature; what happens in each interacts and overlaps with the others in minor or major ways—e.g., both forests and mining with "fire," and it with air pollution. But we have to start somewhere.

Soil The soils of what became the USA are quite probably the richest in quantity and quality in the world. But, as noted in **dust bowl**, the long-standing and reckless use of the soil in (especially, but not only) the Plains States directly caused decades of environmental deterioration up to and beyond the 1930s.

The focus here is upon the equally reckless and at least as dangerous applications of chemical combinations in industrial or agricultural production, of which the best-known are insecticides which have poisoned both the soil and the surrounding flora and fauna.

The dire effects of "toxic sites" on human health and the larger environment has long been recognized. As the problem's intensity and damage spread and deepened and most dramatically produced the "Love Canal disaster" of the 1970s, Congress and President Carter joined hands in 1980 to create the "Superfund" program: better late than never.

The legislation meant to make those pay who were responsible and to induce them and others to take care

Administered by the EPA, its aim is totally to clean up toxic sites and to minimize their future existence.

The law's original provisions were that taxes on (or lawsuits against) the polluters would pay the Superfund's annual costs of $1-1.5 billion. Very much in the spirit of Kapp's Social Costs of Private Enterprise.

Naturally, the polluting companies hated that law.

So, they did what comes naturally: they financed individual politicians' campaigns and paid lobbyists sufficiently to induce the GOP-controlled Congress in 1995 to do their wish; since that year, the federal budget has not continued or reinstated the toxic site tax.

In consequence the Superfund not only isn't "super" anymore, it's only barely a "fund." Like other regulatory agencies (**SEC**, **OSHA**, EPA, IRS) it's running out of money. Since 1995, the needed funds have had to be taken increasingly from the general tax fund; that is, paid by you and me. The Bush administration proposes to keep that up and something more. ("Bush Slashing Aid for EPA Cleanup at 33 Toxic Sites," NYT, 7-1-02) It's bad enough to have an inadequate **health care** system; isn't it a bit worse to have to pay taxes to subsidize the companies who are helping to make us sick?

Because of the Superfund, between 1980 and the present almost 800 toxic sites have been cleaned up. That leaves a lot of places you wouldn't want to have in your county (or even the next one over). But better than nothing; and nothing is what we're headed for. What polluters wants, polluters gets.

Forests. 1995 was a good year for the environmentally dangerous: the pro-loggers bought enough allies in Congress to pass the "salvage logging rider."

It suspended all federal environmental laws, thus allowing

> unrestrained logging of healthy, green old-growth forests on fed-
> eral lands under the guise of 'forest health' and 'fire risk reduc-
> tion.' This despite overwhelming scientific evidence that log-
> ging increases fire conditions. (SFC, 8-2-02: Chad Hanson,
> "The Myth of 'Thinning Forests.")

Reminds one of that U.S. Army Colonel in **Vietnam** who informed us that he was destroying the village of Ben Suc "in order to save it." Be that as it may, in that same week of August, 2002, Bush II announced the "Healthy Forests Initiative." (ibid.) If—that is, when—the announcement becomes law, it will provide for the curtailment of environmental reviews and legal challenges to loggers and accelerate what Bush II called "mechanical thinning"—once called logging—on 190 million acres of federal land. And he and his GOP Congress still have two years in which to think up other ways to make loggers smile, in addition to the jest of "planting trees" in order not to have to sign the Kyoto Pact. Where is Mort Sahl, now that we need him?

Mining. That can mean drilling for oil, digging or clearing for coal and other minerals. What follows is confined to coal. In the deep past, coal mining meant digging holes and tunnels in the ground. More recently it has come to mean shaving off or blowing up the tops of hills and mountains: Poisons the water, wrecks the valleys, but saves a lot of time. No problem. Here some reportage:

> Soil and rock are blasted and scraped away by enormous
> machines, then dumped down the mountainside into adjacent
> valleys and streams that run through them....
> The Bush administration's motives also appear largely
> political. West Virginia /where this is happening/ is an impor-
> tant swing state, and the mining companies and coal-burning
> utilities contributed heavily to Mr. Bush's campaign. The new
> rule was signed by Christie Whitman /head of EPA/... as eco-
> nomically necessary and environmentally manageable.... The
> Army Corps of Engineers /will/ be instructed to minimize the
> damage... (Editorial: " Burying Valleys, Poisoning Streams,"
> NYT, 4-4-02.)

To be sure, the continuation of coal mining and many other environmentally disastrous activities makes money for the business-es, keeps jobs for some workers, and helps politicians to get or stay in office. Worth it to them in the short-run, harmful to all in the long run. And unnecessary. As will be seen in the concluding portion of this essay, there are workable and desirable alternatives that can protect the environment <u>and</u> provide for a better economy for all. Even ex-polluters. (DALY)

<u>Air</u>. You're lucky if you have to read this to know that the air is dirty and dangerous; not just in cities like New York and Chicago and L.A. and New Orleans and..., but even in unlikely very high-up places like Denver or at Lake Tahoe, everyone is breathing contaminated air, a little or a lot; in any case, always more so. The cause is mostly from carbon dioxide in the air; in turn, that comes from factories and **cars** using fossil fuels: coal and oil.

All this has been known for decades; over 30 years ago, it led to the passage of the 1970 Clean Air Act (along with the Clean Water Act, when Nixon was President, but indifferent to anything but Vietnam at the time).

In addition to there having been lax application of those and all other regulatory laws, Bush II in mid-2002 submitted to Congress his "Clear Skies Initiative." He claims it would "reduce most power plant emissions by 70 percent by 2018, using market incentives.... Scott Segal, a spokesman for the Electric Reliability Coordinating Council, a consortium of power companies, praised the plan..." ("Bush Energy Proposal...," <u>NYT</u>, 7-30-02) Perhaps by "clear skies" Bush II means getting rid of that pesky ozone layer? After all, it gets in the way, doesn't it?

Setting aside that Bush's skies don't have to get "clear" until 2018, must get that way in terms that satisfy the polluters, and that nothing at all is said about car and truck emissions—setting those details aside, the whole matter seems subsequently to have been made moot by:

> Washington: The Bush Administration moved /November 22, 2002/ to loosen federal air pollution standards that must be met by electric utilities, oil refineries and other heavy industries that modernize their plants. California, whose air pollution standards have long been more stringent than the federal government's, would be forced to comply with the mandatory new rules, potentially reducing the state's air quality... ("EPA relaxes rules...." SFC, 11-23-02)

Air pollution is bad enough, but what pollutes the air often also contributes to what is probably the most ominous of all environmental deteriorations: global warming and "and climate change."

These are not problems whose effects lie in the future; the damage is already well under way: such as, significant rises in average daily temperatures, melting glaciers, rising tides and, in coastal areas, always more flooding (best known, that of Venice, whose main square is flooded over 100 times annually, at higher levels); increased severity and irregularity of harsh weather (both colder and hotter, when and where it isn't supposed to be); droughts here, prolonged rain there: A lengthening and melancholy list. Been reading the papers?

In the face of this, as a *NYT* editorial put it ("Crossroads on Global Warming (6-5-02"), "President Bush has no serious strategies for climate change.... It appears /from Bush's report to the UN/ that he is largely finding ways to <u>adapt</u> to warming instead of preventing it." (emphasis added)

That may be too positive a response for what is going on: If the Bush administration has its way in dumping prior policies and replacing them with those advocated by the major polluters, we shall not be adapting, but <u>exacerbating</u> conditions—the causes for which the USA is more responsible for than any other nation. Which takes us to,

<u>Fire</u>. As noted earlier, "fire" here is meant to apply to the realms not only of heating and cooking but, as well, of internal combustion and explosives. The Bush administration is allowing and encouraging almost everything that increases "fire." No surprise there, given that its chief supporters and key cabinet members are disproportionately drawn from the energy, auto, airplane, and military-industrial complexes. That support is given with the hope (and payoffs) and, we may assume, the understanding that the easing of environmental restraints is what they have paid for.

Moreover, as is discussed under **militarism...**, military actions and production are among the most wasteful and environmentally (as well as humanly) destructive of any industry, "collateral" though the damages may be; and this is the most militaristic administration of memory. With Bush himself and his V.P. Cheney (et al.) having been executives in the oil industry, it would seem unnecessary to discuss the influence of oil on related policies (including those involving war).

Nor should it be forgotten that the auto and airplane industries are integral and powerful parts of the military-industrial complex, none of which can function non-destructively even <u>without</u> war; and that all of them are unsurprisingly more prone than the rest of us to find reasons to <u>support</u> war.

Taken together, the foregoing are among the principal villains in the warming of the globe. They profit from, indeed <u>need</u> the activities that do so. And they have paid well to sit in the front seats where the decision-makers in D.C. can hear them. Beware.

<u>Water.</u> We have to drink it, use it in cooking, bathe in it, use it for industrial and agricultural production and, among other things, swim in it. We need it, and we need it clean. "U.S. water growing foul, warns EPA. Reports cite runoffs from farms and sewage plants as causes." (*SFC*, 10—-02): "More than a third of surveyed rivers, and about half of all lakes and estuaries are too polluted for swimming or fishing..." And if the water is no good for that, who would want to drink it? And then there are the oceans, especially the shores—whether polluted by oil tankers' accidents or by offshore drilling.

Something <u>is</u> being done about all of this, by the EPA and other regulatory agencies, of course; but very little, and damned little when set against the problem: meanwhile, water pollution is rising, not falling.

Almost all of the above has been concerned with water in the USA; but our **globalization** agenda by definition encompasses the entire globe. Most of the people on earth are poor, 1.2 <u>billion</u> live on less than what $1 a day would buy in the USA, 2 <u>billion</u> are miserably to deathly poor—where deathly is descriptive, not a metaphor. Why?

Because the policies to "modernize" and make "free" the resources and production of the entire world have meant just that for water supplies (to mention only them, here)—whether through the ways in which such policies have diverted, eliminated, dried up, or poisoned streams, or flooded lands while, at the same time, in all those lands once ample and free water supplies have been or are being privatized: water for profit, irrespective of the human consequences. What's good for business....

According to a UN report, by the year 2020, <u>half</u> of the world's peoples—three billion+—will live in "water-stressed" conditions unless significant changes in water management are made by government, private industry, and consumers. (*Guardian*, 12-18-02). The problem is that significant changes <u>are</u> being made; but they're all going in the wrong direction.

At the Earth Summit at Johannesburg in September, 2002, Nelson Mandela declared that "Access to water is a human right, and those countries, like the US, that are trying actively to prevent a world commitment to improve sanitation were shamed." (ibid.)

What is imperative for the preservation and enhancement of water supplies and all other environmental conditions is immediate and substantial action; what the Bush government is doing is immediate enough, but worse than nothing—the sum and substance of which was aptly symbolized by its behavior with respect to the Kyoto Protocol.

<u>Kyoto</u>. That agreement was produced in 1997 at a global conference. Its aim was to reduce greenhouse gases, the main cause of global warming, by 20 percent by the year 2010. Much more than that is needed; still...; But the USA, with less than five percent of the world's people but producing 25 percent of those greenhouse gases, won't sign.

To repeat some of what has been stated earlier, rising global temperatures raise sea levels, change precipitation and other climate conditions, alter forests, crop yields, and water supplies, and threaten human health, the lives of birds, fish and many types of ecosystems while threatening both floods and expanding deserts. Pretty serious stuff.

Not enough evidence, says the USA. So, although the USA participated in a cooperative manner at Kyoto in 1997, the Bush II administration has made it clear that it matters not that 160 other countries have signed it, the USA will not. Haste makes waste.

Bush says he thinks it exaggerates the nature of the problem and..., Oh yeah, it would be hard on business, and anyway.... Hey! We don't have to sign any stinkin' prodelecall. Next question?

<u>Late Bulletins</u>: "Critics Say E.P.A. Won't Analyze Clean Air Proposals Conflicting with President's Policies." (*NYT*, 7-`4-03. "Bush orders speed-up of energy extraction." (*SFC*, 8-8-03):

> The Bush administration on August 7 directed government land managers to remove environmental and procedural

obstacles that are slowing development of oil and gas resources in several areas of the West... The new policies do not require congressional review, and are the latest in a series of administrative initiatives aimed at increasing oil and gas production on federal lands.

"Draft of Air Rule Is Said To Exempt Many Old Plants: A Victory for Industry." (*NYT, 8-22-03*)

> After more than two years of internal deliberation and intense pressure from industry, the Bush administration has settled on a regulation that would allow thousands of older power plants, oil refineries, and industrial units to make extensive upgrades without having to install new anti-pollution devices... /which/ would let industrial plants to continue to emit hundreds of thousands of tons of pollutants into the atmosphere and could save the companies millions, if not billions, of dollars in pollution equipment costs, even if they increase the amount of pollutants they emit. "This makes it clear that the Bush administration has meant all along to repeal the Clean Air Act by administrative fiat," commented New York's Attorney General. ("Air Rule Said to Exempt Many Older Plants....; A Victory for Industry," *NYT*, 8-22-03)

"Ground zero air quality was 'brutal' for months; EPA reports misled the public." (*SFC*, 9-10-03).

> A UC Davis scientist who led the air monitoring of the smoldering ruins of the World Trade Center said dangerous levels of pollutants were swirling about the site at the same time the U.S. Environmental Protection Agency assured the public that the air was safe to breathe.

Who said Bush II doesn't have an environmental policy?

Do we have to sacrifice to live safely? The answer is both simple and complicated. We have to change, to begin to live differently, yes. But the ways in which we must live differently could well be ways of living better, not worse. If so, "sacrifice" is irrelevant. To which must added, it should be clear that if we do not change, we will have to sacrifice: our health, our comfort, our pleasures, while, at the same time, finding ourselves paying more for less, spending more time on simply getting by (and getting to work or shopping or play) and, to cut it short, to go down with our planet as a species. That might not happen "soon enough" to affect those reading this; but how about your children, their children, their childrens'? Or have we just been kidding about all this family stuff? That's the simple part.

The complicated part has two sides to it: one is a specific set of interacting proposals to change our systems of production and consumption to equate not just with our, but with nature's needs. The first step there is to understand that there is no conflict between them, except insofar as we have been socialized to believe otherwise.

But even that "complicated" part has already been discussed and proposed in many books, among others and most readably, Herman DALY's *Beyond Growth: The Economics of Sustainable Development*. What is <u>really</u> complicated is to develop the politics that can break through the high walls now separating common sense from good sense. The first steps that can and should be made for climbing that steep and slippery slope are discussed in the <u>Afterword</u>.

A few pages back the distinction was made between the words "growth" and "development." The former is measured in quantitative terms: 3 percent annually, etc. Development cannot be "measured" that way, for it refers to qualitative changes—in the structures of production, consumption, trade, income and wealth, education, health care, transportation—that is, in social wellbeing, the quality of our lives.

It is not difficult to posit the various types of change that are needed and possible. They have been discussed in a happily growing literature over recent decades, under a heading that has come to be called "sustainable development." (DALY, DALY & COBB, and see their references.)

What <u>is</u> difficult is to stir ourselves to become as actively involved in rescuing the environment as those with economic and political power have been in making profits from destroying it.

Europe

As with the all the categories dealt with in this book, "Europe" is meant to deal with only those matters that reveal one aspect or another of the behavior betraying what the USA presumably stands for at home and abroad. Much of such behavior is discussed for the countries listed under other headings, such as **Cold War, arrogance, globalization,** and **militarism.** The separate country discussions here are extremely brief; those readers who seek a useful/essential pre-World War II background may find it in two excellent histories: 1) BOWDEN, KARPOVITCH, and USHER, _Economic History of Europe Since 1750_ and 2) for the economic history of the interwar period, W.A. LEWIS, _Economic Survey, 1919-1939_. And there will be references for more recent matters.

The first years of the 20th century ushered in an always more explosive chaos in almost all corners of the globe. That chaos, soon to be followed by decades of social disaster and military destruction, was an outcome of the overlapping processes of **capitalism, nationalism**, and **imperialism.**

They in turn had their origins in the also disruptive era of "the discoveries" and European expansion, with its subsequent and never-ending intrusions into all the world's societies. What roils the world still today are the continuing consequence of that history and of the two world wars emerging from it; and so it goes, still.

It has been the universal habit of the major powers to pursue economic and strategic gains and power in all quarters of the world and, in doing so, to impose their institutions upon the peoples of the invaded societies. As one studies the persisting, even worsening upheavals in those regions (see **Africa, et al.**), what stands out is not just the cruelty, social devastation, and ferociousness of European and U.S. behavior, but the patent irresponsibility of those who caused it—like that of children who trample a garden while playing, and race away without looking back—or stay and keep it up.

What is less obvious is the manner in which the "progress" of the past several centuries also depended upon the disruption of the entire continent of Europe and, as well, of the tens of millions of "**Indians**" of the western hemisphere).

To be sure, there was progress in the levels of material and social wellbeing for many; but in one set of ugly developments or another the peoples of what were to become Great Britain, Germany, France, Russia, et al., lost their identity in favor of some more powerful intruder—artificial new boundaries created, economic and political and cultural institutions wiped out or turned upside down.

Today those disruptive processes continue in "Europe," whether in "ex-Yugoslavia" (itself an artifice meant to impose order on chaos), or in "ex-USSR/Russia," or in Turkey, or in...; and, of course, beyond Europe.

That said, the totally destabilizing effects of the two world wars and the intervening 1930s depression left a Europe in ashes—economically, politically, militarily; humanly. Only the USA had the power and the prestige to seek remedies for that devastation.

What we did after the war was not entirely negative, but much of it was; our power and prestige were used and misused in order to serve the narrow interests of what C. Wright MILLS aptly called *The Power Elite*: **big business, the military industrial complex**, and the **corrupt** politicians beholden to them; and the **Cold War** served as an over-arching means of doing so.

Ah! Some reading that will say, another "conspiracy theorist." Not at all. There was no conspiracy, nor was there a need for one. The three groups just noted were already powerful as World War II ended, and had been working together for many years; perforce. The needs and desires of each member of that "elite" merged easily with those of the others; indeed, a course other than that of the Cold War would have met with considerable opposition: the Cold War was "functional," a "natural."

In some cases our actions during the Cold War were a continuation of processes preceding World War II (as noted under **dictators**); others awaited the end of the war. I begin with France, which, for reasons now to be discussed, was importantly different from the others.

France

Until World War II the USA and France had a largely amiable relationship. It dates back to our and their revolutionary periods, when the French assisted us against the Brits, because of their hatred of their then military enemy Britain in Europe and North America: Thus, "Lafayette, we are here!" when our troops arrived to assist them in World War I. Since World War II, however, our relationship has been one combining distrust with anger.

Between the two world wars, France, like most of Europe, was immersed in socio-economic and political turbulence. In the 30s, it veered to the left with the Popular Front and then to the right as war approached. Its rightwing tendencies were strong enough so that after the 1940 "armistice" with the Nazis, the Vichy government ruling over "unoccupied France" enthusiastically rounded and shipped thousands of Jews to the Nazi death camps; they also cooperated with Germany against the valiant underground French resistance movement the "maquis."

The external resistance was headed by General de Gaulle. He was very much the nationalist, with an unmistakable nostalgia for France's past greatness in the Napoleonic era. He held the presidency for a decade or so after 1958, during which he had the sense and decency to give up its Algerian colony—having learned something from the humiliating and painful experience of the 1954 French defeat at Dienbienphu.

Thus it was, in 1965, that de Gaulle advised the USA to get out of **Vietnam** as it was sinking into the "quagmire." Our "best and brightest" were not smart to enough listen.

That alone sufficed to give De Gaulle's a bad name in the USA; but his main claim to ill-fame here was that as a French nationalist he deemed it essential that Europe remain European, in order that it not be (as he nicely put it) "Coca-colonized."

To be sure, de Gaulle hoped to see France itself as the main player in Europe, himself as its coach. His tradition goes on; even since his death in 1970 the USA has always had trouble on its hands in dealing with the still significant "Gaullist" camp in France, most recently as regards Iraq.

Merci beaucoup, mon general, especially for the Coca-Cola jab. French fries with a glass of Beaujolais to wash them down, anyone?

Germany
The USA began to become involved in Germany in a serious way in the early 1920s. Then and there, as noted under **fascism**, history's most spectacular inflation ever had taken hold: from 1918 to 1923, prices rose 4 trillion times. Germany was then (as now) the strongest of the European economies; because U.S. banks and industrialists had substantial investments there, the USA took steps to protect those investments. It did so with the Dawes Plan, which retired the worthless currency and replaced it with one backed by the USA.

That was our first but not our last big jump into Germany's

affairs. The friendly relationship carried over into Hitler's rule—
openly or covertly, up to, through, and beyond the outbreak of the
European war, and was officially resumed as the war ended. (BRADY
/1933, 1937, 1943; EISENBERG; WITTNER)

"Officially" suggests there was an "unoffical" period in which
contacts continued even into the war; as they did: Not only was the
USA willfully and obscenely indifferent to the death camps, but
seems also to have spared at least some "investments" from U.S.
bombing during the war: OSS bombing surveys showed that at least
some facilities owned by U.S. companies (among them GM, producing trucks and tanks) remained undamaged. Plain good luck or
tainted collateral non-damage? (BREITMAN)

After the war, the USA quickly and secretly both protected
Nazis who stayed in Europe and whose "anti-communism" was useful for cold war political aims, while we also imported Nazi scientists
to assist us in our rapidly developing missile and space age technology for cold war military needs and possibilities.

But Germany had still another vital role to play for the USA;
namely, to be divided. Immediately after the war, Germany was
occupied by French, British, Soviet and U.S. troops and divided into
four zones, as was Berlin: By 1949, there were only two zones and
two Germanys, with a wall dividing them. The consequences were
many, all of them negative. (EISENBERG; LAFEBER; LEFFNER;
WITTNER)

Damn the Soviets, we have learned to think, they wanted
Germany divided, and they got their way, and put up the Berlin Wall
to make their point. Right? Wrong. There was one really useful by-
product of **Nixon**'s Watergate screw-up; it led to the Freedom of
Information Act of 1975. The Act provided that once secret documents must be released upon request; many have been and are being
released, with tons still kept under lock and key. Here an excerpt
from some of those concerning Germany. A statement the U.S.
Ambassador to Germany made to U.S. President Eisenhower in the
period leading up to the official division of Germany: (my emphasis)

> The difficulty under which we labor is that in spite of our
> announced position /for a united Germany/ we really do not
> intend to accept German unification in any terms that the
> Russians might agree to—even though they seemed to meet
> most of our requirements. (EISENBERG)

No small difficulty, that. However, no problem, not in the age of **spin**: It would be difficult to find all but a handful of people in the USA who believe that the USA, not the USSR, wanted Germany divided—even though division served many useful purposes for the USA and relatively few for the USSR throughout the entire Cold War. Great for our purposes, hell on earth for countless Germans. So long as the people of the USA went along, what's the diff?

Greece

As with so many of the hot spots searing Europe after World War II, Greece became so because the war shattered the political foundations of the pre-war status quo. Greece, long a de facto colony of the British, had been formally ruled by the latter's chosen despots. The war itself, however (and as in Italy) had given rise to local resistance forces led and dominated by the left. (CLOGG)

When the war ended, Britain was so weak as to be helpless to maintain its prior dominance over the area stretching from Greece and Turkey to Egypt without force and violence; it no longer had the resources for anything like that. As elsewhere in Europe, most notably **Italy**. With the prewar and wartime rulers in disgrace, the way was open in Greece for the left to gain power in free elections.

So, in 1947, the Truman Doctrine. In Greece, as elsewhere, any threat to the status quo from the left was automatically seen by the USA as being engineered by the **USSR**. Doubtless the USSR would have liked to shake things up in their favor wherever possible; but it was even weaker when the war ended than the losers—Germany, Italy, and Japan. (see below)

What the USA was <u>not</u> willing to accept publicly was why the prewar status quo was unable to keep order without military; force which none possessed. The Truman doctrine was designed to provide them with such force and, when necessary, violence. On May 15, 1947, Congress appropriated $400 million (=many <u>billions</u>, now) for the USA to use its resources to that end; no holds barred. (FREELAND)

So, in the name of holding back Soviet communism, Greek fascism was put in place under Karamanlis; he was replaced in the 60s by a non-dictatorial regime; it was overthrown by fascist "Colonels" (whistling "I'm a Yankee Doodle Dandy"), for whom rule equated with violence. (WOODHOUSE; and look for the DVD/VCR film "Z", for a great film about a disgraceful episode in both Greek and U.S. history.)

At the same time in neighboring territory, the USA began its policies of taking over Britain's role in Palestine; it started with assisting the Israeli's to overthrow the British and, at the same time, to hold back the in-no-way-communist Palestinians.

Nobody dared suggest a Soviet plot at work there; the emphasis was placed on the area's strategic importance (including Greece and Turkey) for the Cold War and, with less fanfare, its possession of the largest part of the world's oil resources in its front and backyards. Greece and Turkey may—or may not—have recovered; it is doubtful that **Israel/Palestine** ever can.

Italy

The intervention in Italy was treated at some length in **Cold War**; herewith no more than a few additional words. When the **CIA** was still the OSS, its efforts in Italy began in 1943; indeed its many-sided and successful efforts to shape postwar Italy to fit U.S. plans served as a boot camp for the CIA; and, unfortunately for Italy and future efforts of the CIA, it was a pushover.

The reasons for the "unfortunately" are that Italy, like Germany and Japan, had been a) fascist, and b) defeated in the war. The populations of all three nations were severely damaged, demoralized and needy; in addition, they tended to look upon the USA with friendly eyes (which was not so for their attitudes toward the British, French, or Soviets); thus, "pushover." One unfortunate result of our easy successes in Italy was that it fed our normal over-confidence in subsequent efforts in Indochina, Cuba, and Central America (and **Iraq**).

As in Germany and Japan, the USA was able with relative ease to distort Italy's entire postwar history. Violence was minimal there; not so, elsewhere: Our twisted efforts to prevent the peoples of all too many other countries from finding their own ways have been accompanied by the deaths of many millions of mainly civilians, and the ravaging of their cultures, economies, and politics—while, at the same time, gutting the possibilities of a meaningful democracy here in the USA. (see the lengthy discussions of Italy in **Cold War, McCarthyism, corruption**)

Italy remains Italy, the *bel paese* (I have happily lived and worked there for decades); but though its Italian heart is still beating it does so with a pacemaker marked "Made in USA."

Spain

As noted under **fascism**, the U.S. relationship with Spain began in the period of its civil war (1936-39). Here some added comments on that war are pertinent.

From the medieval era until the 1920s, Spain was ruled over by a monarchy. It was replaced by the dictatorship of Primo de Rivera in 1923. But in 1931, in Spain's first democratic election, it became a republic, leaning to left of center. Two years later that was succeeded by a rightwing government which, in 1936, was ousted by the second democratically elected "Popular Front" government.

It was at then that Generalissimo Francisco Franco organized his fascist army to overthrow the Republican ("Loyalist") government by force. The also fascist German and Italian governments soon provided substantial military support for Franco: the Germans supplying bombing from the air (as a training ground for the Stuka bombing in northern Europe in 1939), the Italians furnishing thousands of mostly reluctant infantrymen.

As that counter-revolutionary war unrolled, the British and the French shrugged their shoulders and looked the other way; what about the USA? Well, we participated, but contemptibly. Throughout the civil war the USA not only continued to trade with Franco's principal allies (Nazi Germany and Fascist Italy), but knowingly sold them materials directly or indirectly used by Franco's army. At the same time we disallowed the trade of the Republican government, most evidently when in 1938, a Spanish government's cargo ship—the *Mar Cantabrico*—was refused entrance to New York harbor upon the direct orders of **FDR**. The principle invoked was that the USA wished to remain neutral in the conflict. Of such principles are rubber bands made.

(There are many books on that war. Among the best non-fiction books are those of BRENAN (*Spanish Labyrinth*) and ORWELL (*Homage to Catalonia*). Having fought and been wounded in that war on the Loyalist side, Orwell's book has a special quality to it. Also, see the fine novel of Ramon SENDER. *Seven Red Sundays.*

Our dubious relationships with fascist societies were underscored when, after the civil war, Franco, although he had declared
Spain to be neutral, nevertheless sent a Spanish division to fight
alongside the Germans on the Russian front in World War II.
Despite that, after the war the USA saw Franco's—still fascist—
Spain as an ally in the Cold War's struggle for global freedom: We
placed several important air and naval bases there, as Franco continued his savage rule. They are probably still there.

How does that old saying go? Ah yes; the end justifies the
means.

Turkey

The USA had little or no interest in Turkey until after World
War II. Then, as with all the countries on the northern and eastern
coasts of the Mediterranean, the USA's interest became intense. We
planted our feet easily and solidly on Greek, Spanish, and Italian soil
(as discussed), but our interests were greatest at the eastern end of
"the fertile crescent." Why?

Because inland were the greatest oil deposits in the world, and
northward was our declared enemy, the **USSR**. **Israel** proceeded to
become the lynchpin for the most eastern part of the crescent from
1948 on; earlier, with the Truman—Greece-Turkey—Doctrine, the
USA began its long and deep financial and military connections
with Turkey. The two countries receiving the most financial and
military aid from the USA from 1947 on, and to this day, have been
our good buddies #1 Israel and #2 Turkey.

Considering the who knows how many billions handed over to
Germany and Japan in the past half century, friends, that is saying a
lot. But for the supporters of the **Cold War** and Israel, and, of course,
the **lobbyists** for the oil companies, it was worth every penny of the
your taxes. Right?

As noted in the discussion of **Greece**, our interest in Turkey
had nothing to do with the presence or absence of democracy (that
would be intruding); good thing, for Turkey, like Greece, was fascist
more or often than not as it was counting our $$$. Almost despite
us, Turkey, measled with our air, army, and naval bases and the rot-
ten governments who had been rewarded for going along with them,
nevertheless worked its way up a very steep slope and, later rather

than sooner, found its way toward something like democracy (with a <u>very</u> strong military component keeping its eye on parliament).

Shucks! The USA must now think; ingrates: In March of 2003, as we were preparing to brave weapons of mass destruction to bring freedom and democracy to **Iraq**, we wanted to use Turkish territory for the effort. But the Turkish Parliament voted (faced with 90 percent against participation) voted down <u>any</u> participation in the Iraqi war; although, as is customary in such deals, the Prime Minister supported their intervention. ("Make a note of that Condi and Rummy; we may have to take care of those terrorists one day soon.")

Turkey has a long way to go to make up for the cruelties of its Ottoman days and on up to its treatments of the **Kurds** in our time; perhaps it has taken the most important first steps. Perhaps not. Cross fingers.

USSR/Russia

The Russian revolution was in 1917, World War I still underway. The Russians had fought on the eastern front on the Allied side, and had lost at least a million soldiers in the process.

Russia was then ruled over by the Czar, that is, by a hereditary dictator. It is hard these days even to imagine what kind of society the Russian Empire was. By any sensible measure, it was in no way "modern"—economically, politically, culturally, or militarily.

The Czar's court was a model of old-fashioned **corruption**; the economy, where it wasn't agricultural (and backwardly so), was a <u>de facto</u> colony of some combination of British, German, and French companies; its transportation system was largely rivers going in the wrong directions (that is, if coal was found "here," it had to be shipped <u>upstream</u> to "there"—a thousand miles away); its overwhelmingly rural population was also over-whelmingly illiterate (80 percent); its army was great on flags and swords and Cossacks, and duels...; and so on. (BOWDEN...)

Not exactly what Marx had in mind when he anticipated a workers' socialist revolution. Nor is that what Russia got. It got *"The Ten Days that Shook the World"* (REED). A reading of that book (made into a not-so-accurate film a few years ago), shows just how nip-and-tuck the process was that produced the "Bolshevik

Revolution." Lenin was a superb tactician, without doubt; but no matter how superb the tactics might be, if one is trying to move up a steep and slippery slope, it's essential to get a little help from up above. And Lenin's "Bolsheviks" (majority) got it, in the form of sheer political chaos within the czar's circle and wobbly leadership from the liberal "Mensheviks" (minority).

He also got undying enmity from the major European powers and the USA. Part of the reason was that Lenin took Russia out of the war six months before it ended, requiring the large numbers of earlier slaughtered Russian peasants to be replaced entirely by the western powers.

The larger reason, that which propelled the anti-Soviet efforts from 1918 up to 1989, was that the Soviet Union had opted out of the capitalist world (while also taking over French, German, and British assets).

Lenin died in 1924; there ensued a power struggle (to oversimplify) between Trotsky and Stalin, won by Stalin in 1927—10 years after the revolution. The path followed (by what came to be named the Soviet Union in 1922) changed markedly in the few years following 1917, then again from 1921 to 1924, and then again after Stalin's accession to power in 1927—with, of course, many alterations from then until his death in 1953. (see DOBB, 1966)

There is no knowing what might have become of the Soviet Union had Lenin not died when he was only 54. What can be said is that while Lenin was still alive—and even though he was no Boy Scout—the policies he pursued had more of a pragmatic than ideological quality to them, such that one can believe that even <u>given</u> the external pressures (soon to be discussed), Lenin's policies would very probably have been wiser <u>and</u> less harsh than Stalin's.

> Under Lenin, revolutionary Russia first lived within "war communism," a system of extreme constraints essential quite simply for material survival. In 1921, with continuing poor but less desperate conditions, Lenin devised the NEP (New Economic Policy). It provided a good deal of flexibility in terms of ownership, decision-making, and decentralization (all in sharp contrast with both war communism and with Stalin's subsequent policies). What that might have led to, had it not been abruptly ended by Stalin in 1928, cannot now be said. (<u>News flash</u>: One of the sweet things in our history is that **Nixon**, faced with an economic crisis in the early 1970s, devised a set of poli-

cies whose initials were "NEP." A Leninist in the White House!
McCarthy was right.)

A moment ago, a generalization was made that set aside external pressures on the USSR; they cannot be set aside of course. From 1917 on they were constant. That being so, the question arises of just how much Lenin might or might not have differed from Stalin and the ironclad rule that accompanied the latter's "Five-year plans" after 1928. Although one may conjecture that Stalin's totalitarian tendencies would in any case have taken hold, the never-ending economic and military interventions and other efforts from the West to undo the revolution prohibited any substantial degree of economic or political relaxation.

As noted, the "interventions" almost in step with the revolution (involving, among other matters, U.S. as well as others' troops). Before proceeding further with the emergence and nature of Stalin's Soviet Union, it is worth recalling the view of KEYNES in 1925— preceded by a relevant note about his position on the behavior of World War I's victors—Britain, France, Italy, and the USA—at Versailles.

As noted under **economics**, Keynes was a conservative; but an "enlightened" one. During the dealings for the Versailles Peace Treaty, he represented the British Exchequer (our Treasury Department). He was dismayed sufficiently with the greedy and spiteful goings-on to write a damning book concerning it: *The Economic Consequences of the Peace* (1919). It all too accurately predicted that the Treaty could not help but lead to chaos and a second world war.

KEYNES's wife was Russian, (and a well-known ballerina). In 1925, Keynes went to the USSR on an official visit for the Britain. Putting together what he knew with what he saw and what the western powers (including the USA) were doing, upon his return to Britain he wrote this (KEYNES /1931/):

> So, now the deeds are done and there is no going back, I should like to give Russia her chance. For how much rather, even after allowing for everything, if I were a Russian, would I contribute my activity to Soviet Russia than to Tsarist Russia! I could not subscribe to the new official faith any more than to the old. I should detest the actions of the new tyrants no less than those of the old. But I should feel that my eyes were turned

towards, and no longer away from, the possibilities of things; that out of the cruelty and stupidity of Old Russia nothing ever could emerge, but beneath the cruelty and stupidity of New Russia some speck of the ideal may lie hid.

Underlying Keynes's desire to "give Russia her chance" were the possibilities of a decent society for the peoples of the Soviet Union; there is no reason whatsoever to believe that such was ever the concern of the major European powers or of the USA, either in the interwar period nor the decades of **Cold War**. (OGLESBY) The endless attempts to throttle the Soviet economy, along with related direct and indirect military interventions—independently of a Stalin—would quite reasonably have led leaders of the Soviet Union to believe they <u>must</u> have a strong economy, and <u>must</u> arm themselves. Put differently, from 1918 on, the Soviet Union was effectively living under the threat of overthrow from outside, by any means necessary; facing threats, to put it in the present context, considerably greater than those of 9/11 and after for the USA.

The "chance" Keynes hoped for the Soviet Union never had; instead, it <u>had</u> to become a militarized society in some significant degree; Stalin went overboard in that respect, but he was given ample excuse by the capitalist democracies, helped along by their behavior during the Spanish Civil War and their indifference to or cooperation with vigorously anti-Soviet Nazi Germany.

When the Nazi-Soviet non-aggression pact of 1939 was signed, the Nazis were freeing their eastern flank from attack as they went into Poland, while the Soviet Union was freeing its western flank to give it time to arm itself further for the attack from Germany that came in 1941. Sounds awful, and was; who was it who said "Judge not, that ye not be judged?"

Now we turn to the decades after World War II. Under the headings of 1) **Cold War** and **Hiroshima** the reader will find much that is relevant here, regarding U.S. activities <u>during</u> the late stages of still ongoing World War II (the USSR our ally), 2) under **Germany** and **Italy**, and **Spain** above (and, regarding them, also under **Cold War**), and 3) under **military expenditures**.

Taken together, those activities went beyond intimidation into the realm of actually <u>shaping</u> Soviet development. By the latter is meant that what the Soviet Union became after World War <u>I</u> was clearly influenced by the incessantly hostile actions of the major European powers (Britain, France, Germany) with the intermittent cooperation of the USA.

But after World War II, that aggressive hostility and its attendant manipulation were greatly overshadowed, institutionalized, and much deepened by the U.S.-created Cold War. The USSR was cast into a mirror-image arms race with the USA's **military-industrial complex** —itself a dominating influence in shaping the USA.

What is discussed at length under **military....** bears repeating here in part as regards the double-digit <u>trillions</u> of $$$ spent on **milex** by the USA from 1946 to the present. Manna from heaven for U.S. industrial corporations and lots of workers, of course; however, at the same time such militarization sounded the death knell for anything even remotely resembling a democratic socialist society for the USSR.

It is useful to echo Keynes (as above) once more: From its beginnings, Russia had been an autocratic, exploitative, and repressive society; the social raw material with which the Soviet Union began was daunting, especially if traditional socialist ideals—democracy, equality, general wellbeing—were to be realized.

Many of the early leaders of the revolution were firm supporters in those ideals; they never had a chance. Those who survived the intense political conflicts of the 1920s (of which Trotsky is only the best-known figure) were fated to be executed by the infamous trials of the 1930s (or, in the case of the exiled Trotsky, murdered in 1940 in Mexico).

The rationalization for the depths to which Soviet injustice and mistreatment went they justified before World War II by the hostility of the West; with even more obvious justification, that rationalization continued to be used. In recent years, the **CIA** has not only admitted but boasted that the conscious <u>intention</u> of the USA was to <u>force</u> the Soviet Union to push itself to socioeconomic disaster on the wall of militarism and its expenditures. We won.

Hooray. Now the Soviet Union is in the free world: Putin, their leader, used to run <u>their</u> **FBI/CIA**, the KGB; their economy (it is widely-agreed) is run by "Mafia capitalists"; their lives suffer from unemployment at 1930s depression levels, while education, health care, and housing have fall to disastrously low levels; their corrup-

tion breaks new records; their politics now vacillate between a growing fascist and a growing communist movement. (BARBER, LA
FEBER)

In addition to accomplishing that great feat for the people of
the Soviet Union, what have we done for ourselves in the same
process? Well, the militarization of our <u>own</u> economy certainly pre-
vented us from having a serious recession/depression and, in the
same years, provided more jobs and higher incomes for a large percentage of the population. Here we set aside until the <u>Afterword</u> a
discussion of the alternative possibilities that <u>could</u> have generated
just as many jobs and a qualitatively much better social existence,
and ask another question: What did our "successful" effort to affect
Soviet politics and society do to <u>our</u> politics and society?

Some responses to that will be found under **corruption,
McCarthyism, decadence** and other entries; here a summary comment only. The combination of the **Red Scare** of the 1920s and its
1930s follow-up with the dirty games of the **House un-American
Activities Committee,** plus their Cold War intensifications, could
not help but pollute the cultural, educational, and political life of
the USA.

The "life" just noted had never in the USA come close to meeting our social needs and possibilities; but, after World War II, they
just <u>might</u> have begun a successful journey in those directions.
Those who were in their 20s or older as World War II ended (as I
was), may remember that there was something in the "cultural and
political air" that had a much sweeter smell to it than before the war.

It wasn't just that—once more—"the war to end all wars" had
ended. Much more than that. There was a celebratory attitude
toward <u>peace</u>; there was a noticeable stir toward something that
could be called solidarity afoot, whether as regards fellow ex-GIs, fellow workers, or fellow human beings irrespective of "race, creed, or
color"—wasn't that, after all, what the war was <u>about</u>? There was a
down-to-earth major development in education: Every GI was able
to go back to school, at whatever level—high school, college, grad-
uate school—with tuition paid, <u>and</u> with a living stipend (on which
one could in fact live); myself a beneficiary.

And all that—<u>all</u> of that—slowly but surely began to change
already in 1947, changes that accelerated over time. The Cold War

had "officially" begun; as had the new anti-unionism (**Taft-Hartley Act**), loyalty oaths, inquisitions in Hollywood, in D.C., everywhere. And, to cut this dismal tale short, by the time we arrived at the 1980s, virtually all that "sweet spirit" was souring in favor of **Reagan**'s militarism, anti-poor, anti-black, anti-environment ("See one redwood, and you've seen 'em all," he chortled), anti-education, pro-military, pro-big business and high finance, all of it playing games with truth and decency. Hooray; again.

The Soviet Union—and Vietnam, and Cuba, and Germany, and Italy and so on—paid a high price for the Cold War. So did we. But now our hearts and minds have been so thoroughly injected with institutionalized fear and loathing—and anaesthetized by **consumerism**—that we wouldn't know a decent society if it came up and smiled in our face. What price victory?

exploitation

The word itself has a revealing history; it is used with both a negative and a positive meaning: the exploitation of workers, as Marx used the term, was seen as meaning the <u>abuse</u> by the powerful of the powerless; the exploitation of nature, as used conventionally, was used to refer to the desirable <u>use</u> of natural resources. In consequence, in conventional usage the exploitation of workers was denied, and that of natural resources applauded. Today, as worries concerning the **environment** multiply, mainstream spokespeople deny that <u>either</u> exploitation occurs. But both do and, indeed, increase (as noted in **environment, jobs, big business,** and **globalization,** and **inequality**).

Marx (among other critics) did not of course employ "conventional" usage. As quoted elsewhere, already in mid-19 century MARX saw that <u>universal</u> exploitation was intrinsic to capitalism:

> The more a country starts its development on the foundation of modern industry, like the United States, for example, the more rapid is this process of destruction. Capitalist production, therefore, develops technology, and the combining together of various processes into a social whole, only by sapping the original sources of all wealth—the soil and the labourer. (1867/1967)

In the discussion of **environment**, ample attention is paid to the exploitative destruction of natural resources; what follows now will be concerned with the exploitation of workers as explained by their <u>economic</u> powerlessness; under **inequality** that will be pursued at greater length, as will exploitation's <u>social</u> bases; namely, **racism** and gender and **poverty**. All these elements interact and feed each other and aid the exploiters, for they set workers against one another. (see ROEDIGER)

We start with **profits** (which see). **Economics** provides no plausible explanation for the question—a rather large one—"Where do profits come from?" Instead, <u>all</u> recipients of incomes—interest, profits, rents, and wages—are seen as receiving a return for their "contribution to production": profits are normally discussed as "**earnings**."

That notion was refined into a "marginal productivity theory of income distribution." Each income recipient gets what he/she deserves; that is, as determined by their marginal (or last increment of) contribution to production.

So, as the productivity of labor rises, so too will wages—until recently, if ever. (see **jobs, deregulation, unemployment**) Similarly with the marginal productivity of capital. (To save space and keep a good temper, we won't pursue what those who receive interest and rents—"<u>rentiers</u>"—have done to "earn" their incomes; the cause(s) are so mysteriously determined as to be, how shall I put it: <u>ineffable</u>.)

We can test the productivity argument empirically for our time. The years after 1995 were officially described as providing substantial and rapid rises in labor productivity, measured in terms of volume of production divided by number of workers. In those same years, wages either remained stagnant or rose only slightly; meanwhile, profits rose dramatically (as did interest and rents). (see **jobs** for more recent data)

Profits, interest, and rents go to one element or another of those who own and control <u>property</u>—whether that means machinery, equipment, finance, or real estate—or money. All of them, now so much richer than they were a decade or so ago, must have really been working HARD (some of them at large-scale robbery; but who's perfect?) If mainstream economists noticed anything peculiar about the "disequilibria" of those relationships, it hasn't become public.

Worth noting is that both Adam Smith and David Ricardo, the

"founders" of economics, saw worker exploitation as both normal and necessary, although they did not use the naughty word "exploitation." What <u>was</u> used was the presumption that workers ought <u>naturally</u> to receive only subsistence wages, the level of which (as they saw it) is determined <u>not</u> by their production or productivity but by what it takes to keep them alive and working. Hard words, but accurate.

What Smith took for granted, Ricardo pursued further (though not for present purposes)): As noted earlier (**economics**), Ricardo saw wages and profits as having an inverse, seesaw, relationship—if one went up the other must go down—and argued that existing protective tariffs on imported foodstuffs, by raising the price of bread (and workers ate little else in addition) <u>therefore</u> raised wages, and <u>therefore</u> lowered profits—the gain going to the landed gentry, to the loss of budding industrial capitalists. He, and economists ever since (although the youngies today probably have not been informed of it) called them "unearned incomes" "<u>rents</u>." (Today's <u>rentier</u> class, however, refers to those who take in money for lending and speculating.)

Marx took Ricardo's reasoning and applied it rigorously to profits. If we put his argument in modern terminology, it was that aside from the work of managing (a form of work) the returns going to capitalists were nothing more than a return to **power**, based on their ownership and control of the means of production.

But surely the exploitation that Smith, Ricardo, and Marx saw as essential and ubiquitous in the 19th century was much lowered in the 20th century and today? Not quite. Contemporary data (see references to **jobs**, etc. above) reveal that in the USA, although there was a substantial <u>reduction</u> of worker exploitation in the 50s and 60s, since then it has steadily and pervasively <u>increased</u> in both the commodity and service sectors: to repeat what was noted elsewhere, *Business Week* (12-6-99) reported that the <u>average</u> worker put in 260 more hours in 1999 than in 1989, with no overtime pay, with wages mostly stagnant; and average workers in the USA work 350 hours more every year than their European counterparts.

All that says nothing of the much larger number of people and harsher exploitation occurring in the poorer countries as **globalization** has spread and deepened in the past 2-3 decades—exploitation as bad as or worse than that common during the 19th century "industrial revolution" in Britain.

Now it is necessary to broaden the scope of what is meant by "exploitation" in today's world. Marx focussed "only" on workers and resources. In the decades since World War II, two additional forms of "exploitation" have become common. The "quote " marks are used, for the tern "exploitation" is not commonly used with respect to what is now discussed; namely, that of consumers and of taxpayers (discussed more fully under the headings of **consumerism** and **taxes/tax expenditures**). Here a short summary statement, supported in the relevant references.

"Consumer exploitation" refers to the interaction of three processes: the artificial stimuli for buying, its associated and essential **debt**, and the quality of the products bought. The annual expenditures on **advertising** in the USA are about $250 <u>billion</u>; they must be so if the productive capacities of the economy are to be profitable. As BARAN put it (1969), "we are taught to want what we don't need, and not to want what we do." Can that be seen as "exploitation"?

Effectively yes. Just as workers and nature are "abused" to suit the interests of those who control economic processes, so are consumers; that is, the quantities and functions of our consumption provide always decreasing satisfaction per dollar. (see SCITOVSKY, *Joyless Economy*)

With the average parent spending four and their children six hours in front of **TV** (with children watching 40,000 commercials a year /*IHT*, 2-18-03/), and with ads skillfully wrought to excite purchasers, the consequence has become the transformation of human beings into frenzied consumers—who, in order to buy beyond their means have now accumulated mountainous debt: the average household now carries household debt well over 100% of household income (see POSTMAN, and **debt**).

Whether called consumer exploitation or exhilaration it is a condition created to the benefit of those who pay for the advertising, and to the harm of those who—themselves or their nagging children—pay for it.

What are they getting for their pains? As discussed in **consumerism** and **cars**, what they are getting all too frequently are products deliberately designed to wear out soon or to be used and thrown away, which not only adds to the enormous **waste** and **environmental** damage of our times but, at the same time, reduces the population to a mass of foolish and greedy individualists—while allowing an always smaller number of those on the top to get richer and rule.

That always smaller number is also the prime beneficiary of **tax expenditures** which simultaneously need to be seen as "tax exploitation" for at least 80 percent of the population. Note first that federal expenditures have risen without interruption since World War II. On the other hand, as a result of intense and persistent **lobbying**, taxes on corporate profits and the income tax for the rich have both declined precipitously since the 1960s while, at the same time subsidies for businesses (owned by those at the top of the income scale, not the middle or bottom) have also risen.

Put all this together and ask who is to pay for the always rising governmental expenditures. The answer is simple, those who are <u>not</u> on the top; that is, the bottom 80 percent of taxpayers. (see **taxes/tax expenditures**) Call it what you will, exploitation, robbery, sleight-of-hand.... Them what has, gits. Unless the rest of us wake up and outdo the lobbyists.

Exxon-Mobil (see oil, cars, big business)

farmers

If one were to rank what and who in our history we have held most dear—other than movie stars and military and sports heroes—linked together at the top would be the cowboy, the farmer, and the country town. The fearless cowboy and the hardworking farmer are the pioneer spirit embodied; they (together with soldiers, of course) were the agents of our continental grabs. And the country town—not the city—has been seen as the civilizing process of what were viewed as empty lands, except insofar as occupied by those we deemed savages.

Though most of us are city slickers, those attitudes guide us still without our being conscious of it.

> It has come to be recognized that the country town situation of the nineteenth century is now by way of being left

> behind; and so it is now recognized, or at least acted on, that the
> salvation of the twentieth century democracy is best to be
> worked out by making the world safe for Big Business and then
> let Big Business take care of the interests of the retail trade and
> the country town, together with much else. But it should not be
> overlooked that in and through all this it is the soul of the coun-
> try town that goes marching on. (VEBLEN, 1923)

Put differently, the veneration of that rustic trio reverberates still as the heartbeat of "America," whether in the popularity of a film such as "Shane" (where farmer and the gunslinging cowboy are enshrined together), what is seen as the surprising popularity of country and western music, or, more importantly, in the easy affection gained by "down home" politicians of all political stripes— **Truman**, George Wallace, Eisenhower, Carter, **Reagan**, Gerald Ford, McGovern, **LBJ**, Strom Thurmond or, among others, **Bush II** and Clinton—all with their real or contrived country twang.

The "rugged individualism" which has been so much esteemed in the USA has its roots in that rural trio, despite all. Individualism is to be treasured, of course; our fabled individualism, more often than not, was manifested in ruthlessness, cupidity and violence.

Those same processes, in both their positive and negative moments, meant something else: they militated against the emergence of a meaningful role of any sense of community as our nation evolved: a hallmark of U.S. history. Veblen again (himself son of a farm family):

> Their community spirit has been quite notably scant and
> precarious...; they stand still by the timeworn make-believe they
> still are individually self-sufficient masterless men. (Ibid.)

Such illusions had to be set aside or altered by farmers toward the close of the 19th century when falling prices, rate-gouging railroads and speculators combined to produce widespread economic depression for them (among others); in consequence they organized themselves into what became the Populist Movement; fittingly, its titular head (and failed presidential candidate) became William Jennings Bryan, a noisy portent of Huey Long-cum-George Wallace.

That anti-big business movement quickly lost whatever virtues it possessed when, at the turn of the century, the farmers, once spirited "anti-colonials," joined hands with their political enemies in the business world to become "**anti-colonial imperialists** in foreign affairs "… as a strategy of becoming equals at home" by finding expanding markets abroad for their products. (WILLIAMS, 1969)

From then to the present, the dog-eat-dog circumstances of advancing capitalism have required farmers to suppress their much-vaunted independence in practice, if not in rhetoric; they have become "political," one set of lobbyists among many.

But, like farming and so much else, the meaning of their politicization has changed greatly in the past century as 1) they have gone from being a majority to a tiny minority of our population, 2) the economic significance of agriculture has decreased, and as 3) the impact of technology and national socioeconomic policies have transformed farming into globalized agribusiness.

A quick glance at some relevant numbers sets the stage for understanding those shifts: (USDA)

	1850	1900	1950	1990
U.S. population (millions)	23	76	151	266
Farm population "	12	29	25	5
Number of farms "	1.4	5.7	5.3	2
Farmers as percent of the labor force	64	38	12	2

The great quantitative decline of farmers was due to an agricultural technology that greatly increased productivity, of course; it was due also to two negative factors: 1) the combination of the disastrous "**dust bowls**" of the 1930s with the contracted markets for staples (corn, wheat, cotton, and rice), 1920-1941, plus 2) the growth of giantism in agriculture after World War II.

The Populist Movement faded into memory with the onset of World War I. That war was a great boon for all of agriculture and of industry as well; but the economic buoyancy thus provided was short-lived for the farmers who produced staple crops (corn, wheat, etc.) as distinct from dairyists, cattlemen, and fruit and vegetable growers. The latter four did relatively well in the so-called **prosperity decade**; not so, the staple farmers.

By the end of the 1920s, farmers had become an organized **lobby** pushing for the maintenance and support of agricultural prices; if with little positive effect. From the 1930s to the present, however, they have been successful in one form or another up to the present. But who "they" are has changed and has to be defined.

From the AAA (see below) to the present, what has been achieved in agricultural policy has been inversely related to need: The smaller the farm the less the help and vice versa, always more blatantly, represented most scandalously in recent years by **Archer Daniels Midland**, Meanwhile, as though by divine intervention, the average family has had to pay higher prices because of farm subsidies (see below) and more in **taxes/tax expenditures**, as the rich sit back and chuckle.

Now a quick review and some substantiation of the foregoing. The reality behind <u>all</u> farm policies is that they are <u>meant</u> to maintain high prices by restricting production—in a world where most people have always needed food at lower prices. (For the history and some analysis of what is now to be unfolded, see USDA; SCHEIBER; HIGBEE; SOULE; MITCHELL, B.)

<u>The Twenties and Thirties.</u> After much debate and a series of ineffectual agricultural policies, in 1929 the Federal Farm Board was created. Its principal aim was the setting a platform beneath which farm prices would not fall—based on the false expectation that farmers would reduce their production. Naturally, the opposite happened: farm output rose in response to "satisfactory" prices; the whole program "ran out of money" and went <u>kaput</u> coinciding, as it did, with the onset of the Great Depression.

Such policies, much modified, were brought back again with the AAA (Agricultural Adjustment Act) of 1933. This effectively guaranteed a maintained price <u>if and only if</u> the benefiting farmer restricted output to an assigned level; <u>then</u> what one received was in proportion to one's output. Thus, a small farmer with a few hundred acres of wheat would receive support payments a mere fraction of those going to a giant farm of many thousands of acres. Notwithstanding the always rising concentration of landholding in the hands of agribusiness, their **lobbyists** continue to phrase their calls for assistance in the language of the family farm. Wouldn't you? Among the very largest of these is Archer Daniels Midland; its affairs—one of which led to its being fined $100 million recently—are such that it has an entry unto itself in this work.

<u>The 1960s to the present</u> For two decades or so after World War II, agricultural policy underwent many congressional debates. Some of them resulted in genuinely beneficial programs, such as using food

surpluses for serving the needy at home and abroad, and supplying Food Stamp programs. However.

Meanwhile, the largest "farms" grew to monstrous size, and what are now called "family farms" could survive only by adopting the latest technologies. That meant capital expenditures in the hundreds of thousands of dollars which, for a farm family, meant heavy bank indebtedness and dependence upon governmental largesse in times of inadequate demand.

Already in the 1960s, the family farm was more a memory than a reality: In 1972, less than 1 percent of farms (mostly Agribusiness, Inc.) produced a quarter of total farm output; by 1987, about half of farms had sales of $10,000 or less, and sold but 2.5 percent of total farm sales, while 0.5 percent, with sales more than $1 million annually sold almost 30 percent. (DU BOFF)

That brings us to the present. After a brief period in which farmers were told they could no longer count on governmental supports, lo and behold! New legislation was passed in 2002; it goes back to a combination of the principles of the Federal Farm Board of 1929 and the AAA of 1933: except with the bounty falling squarely into the laps of the very, very rich giant agricultural companies who dominate the production and the sale of the staples (now including soybeans), plus some largesse for dairies and peanut growers (and their **lobbyists**).

The legislation was supported with equal enthusiasm by both political parties, for a large number of states in the USA continue to have a critical "farm vote," though not a large number of family farms.

The bill passed in 2002 will cost about $180 billion over ten years; about 100,000 of the 2 million farmers, particularly the large agribusinesses among them, will take in at least two-thirds of that $180 billion. (*NYT*, 8-25-02) That was in 2002; more than a year later, its "Weaning U.S. farmers off aid," the *NYT* editorialized

> Even though the farm subsidies are fraudulently sold to the public as a way of propping up the small family farm, in reality they only accelerate the concentration of farming in the United States. Taxpayer handouts amount to almost <u>half</u> of the total net income for American farmers, but <u>two-thirds</u> get <u>no</u> subsidy. (my emphasis)

Withal, as the debates over these issues go on over the globe, the Bush administration is "pushing European and Asian nations to reduce subsidies to their farmers." (*NYT* 5-14-02) (The European Union provides annual subsidies of $60 billion, and Japan subsidizes its rice growers.) Meanwhile, we raised import tariffs on steel and heckled the rest of the world for not trading "freely."

According to the USDA, "big farmers use their subsidy checks to expand their acreage, buying small neighborhood farms, and increase their production, which pushes down the world market price." A major consequence for the small farmers in the poor countries—who have <u>no</u> subsidies—"is that they have no defense against world grain markets, which are at historic lows. In poorer countries, where two-thirds of the people still live on farms, America's grain subsidies are seen as equivalent of a declaration of war." (ibid.)

So, the USA, not only the cheerleader for "free trade," but the director of **IMF** policies that chasten and punish the "developing countries" for not having entirely open markets, punishes the small farmers who <u>have</u> free markets, while rewarding our own rich "farmers"—if indeed Archer Daniels Midland and Cargill can be called "farmers."

But then, as Emerson pointed out long ago, "a foolish consistency is the hobgoblin of little minds."

fascism

World War II began in September, 1939, when fascist Germany invaded Poland and began its march across Western Europe, soon joined by fascist Italy. Two years later, the USA entered the war when fascist Japan bombed Pearl Harbor. Understandably, World War II came to be called "the war against fascism."

But fascism did not end with the defeat of Italy, Germany, and Japan; not only did it continue in Spain and Portugal for another quarter century, but it was born anew, as when (for example) we gave a leg up to Pinochet's murderous 1973 coup in Chile.

Moreover, there is reason to fear that it might reappear in new forms not only in, say Russia, Austria, and Eastern Germany (BARBER) but also in the USA, dressed in sheep's clothing: "compassionate fascism." (GROSS) Fascism's horrifying nature and consequences and its still beating pulse provide good reason to take a long look at what it has been and how and why it came to be. The word itself didn't exist until 1922, when Italy became the first fascist society. Like many "big words," fascism has come to be used in so many different ways that confusion concerning it is inevitable. Contributing to the confusion is that the main <u>elements</u> of a fascist society have partially existed (and do, still) in many non-fascist societies; they are:

1) Severe political repression,
2) authoritarian/ totalitarian government,
3) fervid militarism,
4) Persecution on ethnic and religious grounds, and
5) suppression, imprisonment, and/or execution of specified political and "racial" groups.

One can locate one or more of those elements in many <u>non</u>-fascist societies, even in the pre-modern world. Thus, for example, Venice, a strong medieval city-state republic, had early traces of capitalism and democracy and racism <u>and</u> was noticeably authoritarian, militaristic, and repressive; but it was not fascist. Its capitalism, although among the most advanced of its era, was still in seed, with nothing like an anti-capitalist working class <u>requiring</u> political repression; its racism prompted Shakespeare to underscore it in at least two of his plays—in "Othello" against a black, and in "The Merchant of Venice" against a Jew (who felt compelled to demand "And if you prick me, do I not bleed?"). But it was not of <u>major</u> social consequence, and although the militarism of Venice was vital for its commercial strength, it had no need to infiltrate the social process for mass approval. (LANE)

The term fascism is applied appropriately only to societies combining a maturing combination of capitalism, industrialism, and democracy. The British historian/ philosopher Harold LASKI neatly defined fascism as "capitalism with the gloves off," where the "gloves" were those of political democracy.

Robert A. BRADY, in his *Business as a System of Power* (1943), went beyond epigram to provide extensive socioeconomic and political analysis. In that book he studied the six leading capitalist nations between the two world wars —Italy, Germany, Japan, Vichy France, Britain, and the USA—of which the first four became fascist.

Brady showed that fascism was an outcome of capitalist <u>crisis</u>; that the interactions of **capitalism, imperialism,** and **nationalism** that had produced the two world wars and global depression had also, in the four "have-not" capitalist countries, also produced fascism. (What they did not "have" was an empire sufficient to provide access to vital resources.)

We now examine the whys and wherefores of fascism as it took hold in the first major fascist nations. First, a brief sketch. (for **France**, see **Europe....**)

<u>Italy</u>'s capitalism and industry were considerably less developed than Germany's; however, its working class was at least as militant as World War I approached. As far back as far as the 16th century, Italy's "free" agricultural workers in the North labored as though in factories; by 1918 Italy possessed a long-standing and well-organized agricultural/industrial, socialist-oriented working class.

<u>Japan</u> had a strong military tradition, an advanced industrial economy, inadequate natural resources and little in the way of democracy; in the 1920s it was confronted with the beginnings of a strong and left-leaning working class and, as the 20s were ending, a slowing economy; by 1928, it was effectively fascist.

<u>Germany</u>, along with the USA the most advanced industrial society, had a highly-organized socialist/ communist working class before and after World War I, <u>and</u> by 1929-30 a deep depression <u>and</u> inadequate resources. In what follows, detailed attention is given only to Italy and Germany.

<u>Italy</u>. For two or three years after World War I, organized workers occupied <u>thousands</u> of factories and fields in the "industrial triangle" of the North (the world's first "sit-ins"). Its working class was strongly organized, but because Italy was not yet a fully-industrialized society wage-workers were also a distinct minority; the Italians who were <u>not</u> agricultural or industrial wage-workers were effectively appealed to by industrialists, bankers and farm owners, and by the military (especially the bitter war veterans), the ruling royalty, and the Church. (SALVEMINI)

The autocratic democracy of Italy fell all too easily into the hands of Mussolini in 1922. (BOGGS; HOARE /in re: GRAMSCI/) Benito Mussolini, "*Il Duce*," was a braggart and what we would call a "blowhard"; a bone-deep militarist exuding nostalgia for Imperial Rome.

Italy had suffered enormous casualties from the war and, to make matters worse, was treated shabbily by its fellow victors at Versailles; there were ample grounds for bitterness. Mussolini and his "black shirts" (the Nazis' shirts would be brown) were able to transform that into political fervor and violence—breaking up union meetings and threatening and beating up journalists and politicians, up to and including murder.

As would occur once more in Germany, all that happened with the indifference or active cooperation of the powers at the top. The result was the spoliation of Italian culture, the ruination of its economy, the death of its emerging democracy and two decades of a devastating war. (see SCHMIDT; SALVEMINI; and the heart-wrenching novel of SILONE, *Fontamara*, as well as anything you can find of the late Primo LEVI.)

As World War II approached, Mussolini joined Hitler in every way (including, by 1938, the deportation of Jews to the death camps), and became Germany's first ally. (Vichy France would be the second, Japan the third.)

World War II, to repeat, had entirely negative and self-destructive consequences for Italy—except, politically, for the left: During the war the numerous and courageous *partigiani* showed that Italy had not entirely lost its admirable virtues; after the war the widely-popular left of center forces began to regenerate the "Italian" qualities not yet forgotten. However, the USA saw all this as a threat to be contained in Europe and, as well as a threat to its aim of controlling the Mediterranean. (see **Cold War**) We won; Italy lost.

Germany. Hitler was handed the Chancellorship of Germany after the election of 1933 in which his party received but a third of the vote; it was "handed" to him, unsurprisingly, by President/General Hindenburg, hero of World War, in a process not entirely unlike that in which **Bush II** was "handed" the presidency by the Supreme Court of the USA.

As German fascism came took power and strengthened in the 30s, and except for a small minority, the people and the government of the USA were unconcerned with Hitler and his doings within and outside Germany. (see **dictators**) Subsequent events showed how dangerous our indifference had been; current tendencies here suggest that we should do all we can to understand how and why such a reprehensible social system came to be in, of all places, Germany.

To which most people in the USA would respond, why "of all places"? What more could one expect from such a barbaric nation? The answer is that Germany, far from being a barbaric land before the Nazis, for most of its history, and especially in the 1920s, was seen as a—even <u>the</u>—cultural and scientific center of the world; and, if anything, politically more democratic than most countries. With reason.

In addition to Germany's many "greats" in art, literature, music, philosophy, and science, it probably possessed the best educational system in the world after the 17th century; by the early 20th century its economy was accurately viewed as the world's engineering and technological leader: in the late 1920s Berlin was the magnet for cultural, scientific, and technological leaders and students.

Even more relevant as regards fascism is that once Germany had effectively recovered from both World War I and its horrendous price inflation of 1918-1923)—when prices rose four <u>trillion</u> times—it not only regained its prewar economic strength and enjoyed prosperity until 1929, but did this within the democratic political system of the Weimar Republic—while, at the same time, the prewar vigorous left of center movements came back into life. (NEUMANN; BRADY /1943/; GERSCHENKRON)

Those same years also produced the Nazis. Their path to power after 1918 owed its beginnings to a horrendous period of bitterness, disillusionment, and material desperation, aided and abetted by the vindictive spirit and greedy practices of the Treaty of Versailles.

> It deprived Germany of 13 percent of her /European/ territory... and population, and 14.3 percent of her arable land;... 19 percent of her coke, 74.5 percent of her iron ore, 16.6 percent of her blast furnaces, 19.2 percent of her raw iron and steel...., 12 percent of her livestock, her entire ocean-going merchant marine, 5,000 locomotives, 40,000 box cars.... /and a good deal more, in the way of resources and productive capacities/, plus heavy reparations. (BRADY /1937/; KEYNES /1919/)

The post-inflation revival and prosperity of the late 1920s was assisted in 1924 by the intervention of the USA's "Dawes Plan" (KEYNES /1919/) which both extended loans <u>and</u> effectively cancelled punitive reparations. The Allies did this for reasons of self-interest, not decency, when they realized "that every conceivable kind of reparations must inevitably compete with domestic production /in England and France/." (BRADY /1937/)

So if the good times were finally rolling in Germany, whence the catastrophe of fascism? Brady was there to see it happen, and subsequently wrote *The Spirit and Structure of German Fascism*, the definitive study of that time, place, and phenomenon:

> /What/ most forcibly struck the observer of the German scene in 1930... was that underneath all this one sensed a certain lurking fear, a certain undefinable and not-to-be-forgotten dread. Deeply rooted as were the traditions out of which the resurgence came, the tone and mood seemed nervous and somehow unreal. Much of it had a note of artificiality and make-believe about it; much of it seemed sickeningly combative; all of it seemed to be conducted in a mood compounded of desire to forget and a haste to enjoy before some new and nameless horror should sweep away what little there was left. (ibid.)

While Brady was doing his investigations for his earlier and path-breaking *Rationalization Movement in German Industry* (1933), the poet Christopher Isherwood was eyeing the culture. His *Berlin Stories* were set there in 1930 (and were the source first for the play "I Am A Camera" and its musical comedy film version, the simultaneously funny and unsettling "Cabaret").

What was shocking for both of those acute but quite different observers was the end of the road for "laissez-faire capitalism": The political situation in Germany from 1918 on was one simultaneously of always more concentrated economic power and of always greater polarization politically between left and right which, as a consequent trend, ineluctably vacated the middle ground and forbade either politics or business "as usual." (GERSCHENKRON)

That the Nazis won out in that struggle was despite the fact that, by 1933, the left of center groups taken together constituted a clear majority; however, as has all too often been so, the struggle between them absorbed their energies more than that with their mutual enemy; both they and democracy were crushed.

In Germany (as in Italy and Japan, and elsewhere), when the left anti-capitalist forces gained strength, the capitalist status quo found it easy to abandon whatever principles of democracy they might once have held and to allow the courts, the police, and the streets to be taken over by swastika-ed brutes. As cruel beatings, book burnings, harassment, and murders increased, they were decreasingly reported in the news or to the police, and seldom prosecuted.

The ferocity of German fascism may be seen as proportionate to the threat of German socialism. The "gloves of political democracy" were thick in Germany in the 1920s, but its concentration of economic power combined with its bitter nationalism proved to be eve "thicker." Its capitalist industrialism was the world's most advanced, but so too was the political cynicism and sophistication of its business leaders in industry and finance. (BRADY /1933/)

All that—class struggle, highly concentrated economy and hard-headed business politics, and a population bleary with disillusionment—made for an unstable society which, in retrospect, seems to have been designed for the fire-eating bombast of an Adolf Hitler who, in a sane society, would be seen as clinically insane. (see FROMM)

In the interwar period, several other nations plunged into fascism, Spain, Portugal, Hungary, Poland, Rumania, and Turkey among them. They were not industrial capitalist countries reacting self-destructively to capitalist crisis, but largely traditional autocratic countries reacting to chaos and political crisis. No comfort to their stricken populations, that.

Among the lessons to be learned from Germany's experience with fascism most important today is that the admirable qualities of democracy and freedom of a country—those of the USA, as much as those of Germany—can be extinguished, and quickly: Germany, having represented the peak of western civilization in 1928 had become its pit by 1933. A transformation to be heeded.

One important means of understanding how swiftly and horribly a presumably decent society can become utterly vile is revealed by the Holocaust. It entailed the systematic murder of, among many others, millions of Jews. It is seldom understood now that Germany was by no means the most anti-Semitic of European nations; Poland was much more so, as were Russia and France. Where Germany did take the lead was in the ability of its fascists to turn customary prejudice into mass slaughter, while the bulk of the population—the "Good Germans"—feigned ignorance.

As is discussed at length under **racism** and **slavery** and, with a political focus, under **McCarthyism** and related matters, the USA has anything but a reassuring history in these realms. But surely we have gone above and beyond that sordid past?

Surely not, if one takes account of the indisputable continuation of racism in its many forms, now made feverish by 9/11 and its systematic, indiscriminate, and cultivated fears and prejudices; not if one takes account of the repression and suppression made easy by the Patriot Act (see **Ashcroft**); not if one adds to that scary mix our traditional militarism and the ideological/ religious fervor now emanating from the White House. In taking account of that and our general political apathy and disinformation, and what one sees are warning signals flashing: IT CAN HAPPEN HERE. Only if we allow it.

FBI

The history, nature, and functioning of the FBI are incomprehensible unless it is understood that from the early 1920s until 1974—half a century—it was a one-man show. In that year **J. Edgar Hoover,** the "one man," died: the saints preserve us.

The origins of the FBI were a portent of just how misguided governmental policies can be or become. In 1919, the 18th Amendment, expanded by the Volstead Act, was passed; it made illegal the sale or use of intoxicating liquors (defined as one-half of one percent alcohol in a beverage). It was called prohibition, and lasted until repealed by the 21st amendment in 1933.

Its main consequences were: 1) to heighten the charms of drinking by making it glamorous, 2) to create the new industry of "bootlegging," within the USA and as between us and Canada, the West Indies, Mexico, etc. 3) to create the FBI, whose mission was to investigate (those) interstate crimes.

Prohibition was a man-made social disaster, father of a long crime wave, gangsterism (and a U.S. Mafia that endures to this day), and the ruination of innumerable lives caught up in its created illegalities and passions. Its offspring the FBI multiplied all of that, thus creating new problems.

The FBI did work away on "interstate crime," of course, and Hoover saw to it that the FBI received a great deal of publicity, including many films, to help us know about it: we may be sure that many FBI personnel worked hard, well, and honorably. However.

However, Hoover saw to it that the burden of the FBI's efforts would be on political and social matters having little or nothing to do with "interstate crime." As noted under **J. Edgar Hoover**, he was obsessed with lefties, gays, and blacks; he <u>hounded</u> them (or those he presumed to be "them"; no holds barred. And while doing that, he became the USA's prime blackmailer, insuring that the FBI would be generously-funded and that he would remain its Director for 50 years, until death did us part.

A principal instrument for the achievement of his goals (as noted) was the blackmail of members of Congress, of media personalities, and of anyone else who might stand in his way. It is a shameful tale, ludicrous but never funny. (MILLER; SUMMERS) Herewith a true story, the documentation for which will be provided.

It begins, in a sense, after **Nixon** was forced to leave the White House. Up to—and after—that, he had done a lot to suppress all kinds of information; which led to congressional passage of the Freedom of Information Act. It required that anyone could demand of any governmental intelligence office (of which there are many) that it provide documents on those individuals or groups surveilled.

A politically active professor at U.C. Berkeley was asked by his politically active son (who had been imprisoned on a political charge) to ask for the father's FBI file, the son believing that perhaps there might be indications concerning his own situation: he had been imprisoned with a sentence of one year in a maximum security prison (along with six others) for "having crossed state lines in order to create a violent disturbance."

Prison is a very dangerous place for a young person; he survived his time there only because he was released early on appeal, when he and his friends were found innocent. The government was the guilty party, for under the "Houston/Nixon Plan" the disturbance at the relevant demonstration had in fact been arranged by the U.S. government. Not for nothing was Nixon called "Tricky Dick."

Even though having been freed (but jailed again on contempt of court charges), the son wanted to know as much as he could, and thought that his father's file might contain relevant information. So the professor wrote to the FBI and asked for his own file. The FBI wrote back and said he could have it, that it was 2,500 pages, and it would cost the prof 10 cents a page. He sent a check for $25 saying he would sample 250 pages. When the pages arrived, this is what he saw: 250 pages with his name on top of the page, and every line blacked out, except for one page where a public speech against the war in Vietnam was summarized.

Lots of surveillance, 2,500 pages. (Multiply that by some thousands of surveilled, and figure the taxes paid for it—by us.) What had this professor done to warrant such attention? He had made speeches in <u>public</u>, he had worked <u>openly</u> in civil rights efforts 1964-66 in the South for voter registration (denied the blacks at that time), he had run for <u>public</u> office on third party tickets more than once. Everything he had done had been in the open for all to see; as was also true for almost all others being followed around by the Feds.

So, where is the documentation? It is contained in the fact that I was that professor; to be sure, a critical one, as this book shows. But lawbreaker? Dangerous? Not for the "America!" I was taught to admire and love.

Due to the FBI, my son's life was seriously, almost irrevocably, damaged; I was just bothered and, to put it bluntly, pissed off. But many lost their careers, their families, their opportunities, their real freedom to be; and "America!" lost a great deal along the way.

The USA lost—and has yet to recover fully—the kinds and amounts of political dissent essential to the life of a genuine democracy, as distinct from a bought-and-sold "democracy" whose sources of information and understanding have been dammed up and diverted and polluted. (PHILLIPS /2002/)

That loss has been one of the many ingredients making it possible for a **Bush II** to rule over this country, combining arrogance with ignorance with venality, among other obscene to frightening qualities, bringing back to life many the nightmares of the Hoover/McCarthy years; now as then, in the name of defending "America."

For those who find the foregoing to be dubious it would be useful to search out a recent 8-page study entitled "**Reagan**, Hoover and the UC Red Scare," *San Francisco Chronicle* (6-9-02). There you will read not only of the manner in which the FBI conspired with the

CIA and the University's Board of Regents to "harass" the faculty (among them, myself) and students involved in protests, campaigned successfully to destroy the career of the moderately liberal UC President Clark Kerr (whose sin was to criticize the FBI), and "forged a relationship with Reagan /a loyal informant for the FBI/... catalyzing his transformation from liberal movie star to the staunch conservative he became."

With such friends, who needs enemies?

financialization

Banks served a merely "lubricating" function in the medieval period, as simpler lending did at least as long ago as the ancient world; but modern economies are inconceivable without enormous networks of financial institutions and instruments. As used here, however, the term financialization refers to the <u>domination</u> of an economy by finance.

Financial—as distinct from agricultural, trade, or industrial—domination has existed before for particular national economies: for the Dutch in the 18th century, and the British as the 19th century ended; and finance played an important <u>inter</u>national role in both cases. (BOXER; FEIS)

But never have the leading economies <u>and</u> the entire global economy been dominated by finance as they came to be at least a decade ago, and which is always both broader and deeper—and more fragile, more explosive. There are many dimensions, problems, and prospects in that domination; what follows will deal with only three of them: 1) how and why the present situation came to be; 2) its present importance and functions; and 3) its already great and always increasing fragility.

1. <u>The sources of today's financialization</u>. For **capitalism** to come into existence and grow, two conditions were fundamental: a) the creation of a propertyless and therefore powerless working class—achieved in Britain by the "enclosure movements of the 18th-19th centuries (MANTOUX); b) the birth and maturation of the processes of trade and finance—achieved through processes of interaction with economic and geographic (colonial) expansion <u>outside</u> of Europe.

Trade, in the form of the simple exchange of goods for goods ("barter") goes back to time immemorial. When the scope and content of trade expanded beyond a certain quantitative and geographical point, it produced "traders"; that is, those who <u>only</u> traded.

When the volume and geographic scope of their trade expanded much further, it became essential for "trading companies"—the best known of which were the "East India Companies" of the Dutch, the British, and the French—in which risks and costs could be spread <u>among</u> traders and, ultimately, could be and <u>had</u> to be financed not by the traders themselves, but by financial companies: banks.

Traders specialize in buying and selling commodities; banks specialize in borrowing (others' savings) and lending. It is in the economic sectors of agriculture and industry that production occurs. Although traders and financiers may perform a useful function, they do not <u>produce</u> anything to <u>be</u> traded or financed. They are "intermediaries."

However, because in a capitalist world nothing ever stays the same, economies least of all, under certain conditions the "intermediaries" come to control those whom they "mediate"; that is, to control one or more of the other three sectors: agriculture, industry, and trade (and now, services /which includes finance/).

That has happened only and always at the "mature" stage of economic development—that is, when a leading nation, or the world economy has entered a prolonged slowdown.

Thus the Dutch were the most progressive and active traders and producers and successful colonialists of the commerce-based economies of the 17th century; by the 18th century, Holland (a <u>very</u> small country, with <u>no</u> resources other than water) depended for its continuing prosperity upon its lending to the British and the other countries that were moving toward industrialization.

By the 19th century, Britain was the leader of the industrial revolution. Already by the end of that century, the baton of industrial strength was being passed to—or taken by—the USA and Germany, and Britain's dependence was on finance for its continuing prosperity. (BOWDEN, et al.; BOXER; VEBLEN /1915/)

Out of the chaos of the 20th century, the USA's great industrial power, much aided by war and **Cold War**, was able to perservere from the 1930s into the 1970s; from that point on, finance began to strengthen until, by no later than the 1990s, it had become dominant. (BARAN & SWEEZY; PHILLIPS /2002/; DOWD /2000/)

Those have been very broad generalizations; the interested reader is advised to consult the references noted above (and the sources noted in them). Among the many important matters left aside, one deserves attention before we proceed; namely, given that traders and bankers provide a service but do not produce anything, does that suggest that those in agriculture and industry do? Yes, but most of U.S. agricultural production is done not by **farmers** but by farm workers, and no industrialists produce anything at all—except management, as distinct from rule.

That, of course, is a "Marxian" observation; but one need not be a Marxist to agree. Industrialists and today's dominating "agribusinesses" (see **Archer, Daniels, Midland**) receive incomes almost entirely due to their ownership and their associated **power** over those who do the actual work—under conditions and for wages which are set by their powerlessness and their employers' wishes.

It is of course true that there are numerous and ongoing decisions that must be made, and that those who make them are contributing to production. But the incomes of **CEO**s and other executives and owners are only in a small percentage set by that "work."

Indeed, and setting aside those who merely own stocks and receive dividends, it may be said that the closer to the contemporary era we come, the managerial functions of owners have been greatly overshadowed by the functionaries of quasi-political strategy.

The early capitalist Richard Arkwright, and those a century or more later such as Alexander Graham Bell and even Henry Ford were indispensable to the technology and/or the creative nature of their enterprises. (I say "even" as regards Ford, because his talent was in borrowing ideas, not forming them. /see SWARD/)

But the "creative" functions of those following them in their industries—textiles, communications, **cars**—are more accurately seen as those of "operators," adept at putting together giant companies by any means necessary, barely distinguishable from a military general or Mafia leaders who let others do the "work." Which takes us to the next realm of financialization.

2. How it functions today. Our focus is the USA, but in this as in so much else, our ways and means (and their consequences) are

becoming "**globalized**." The financialization of today gained its first impetus in the late 1960s.

Although generally and with reason seen as a prosperous period, the 1960s were also the years in which the West European and Japanese economies' reconstruction had made them not only competitive with U.S. production—most dramatically in **cars** at first—but did so in a world economy slowly but surely moving into global excess productive capacities.

Those developments gave rise to the most dazzling round of **mergers and acquisitions** ever—until, that is, the 80s and 90s—while, at the same time, reducing the incentive for <u>real</u> investment in new productive facilities. The financial world is the prime beneficiary of **M&A**s, at least at first and, often, enduringly.

(<u>Item</u>: When U.S. Steel became the first billion dollar company in history as measured in assets, J.P. Morgan took a million dollars as a fee for organizing the financial details, giving rise to the term "big deal.") One need not be enamored of business profits to believe that within the capitalist framework profits going to those involved in production are more likely to be useful for the economy than those derived from the ownership of purely financial assets—let alone speculation in them (see below).

The incomes of financial companies fall under the categories of both "interest" and "profits," but what is more important are its quantitative and qualitative meanings. In that connection, the statistical tendency after 1949 is illuminating, even riveting:

> In 1949, corporate profits (of non-financial companies) were ten times as high as interest (for financial companies); in 1959, ten years later the ratio was five to one; in 1969, that had dropped to two-and-a-half times; by 1979, at one-quarter of interest, it was less than double; and since 1989 corporate profits have always been <u>less than</u> interest. (*Economic Report of the President*, various years)

As that process was unfolding the traditional role of interest in the economy was "going the way of all flesh"; in doing so it signified a major transformation in the overall functioning of capitalism—something like the difference between having some good wine to round off a fine dinner and becoming a drunk. The latter carries danger with it. Here some details:

First, from the 1960s on, corporate profits themselves have included large gobs of interest, not only because the number of financial corporations as a percentage of all corporations has risen greatly, but because an always rising percentage of the giant producing corporations have themselves merged with or created their own large financial institutions. Item: both **GM** and **GE** are giant money lenders.

Second, Wall Street has increased its size, its scope and, greatly, its political power since the 1970s, in leaps and bounds:

> In the early 1970s... the financial sector was subordinate to Congress and the White House, and the total of financial trades conducted by American firms or on American exchanges over an entire year was a dollar amount less than the gross national product. By the 1990s, however, through a twenty-four hour-a-day cascade of electronic hedging and speculation, the financial sector had swollen to an annual volume of trading thirty or forty times greater than the dollar turnover of the "real economy".... Each month, several dozen huge domestic financial firms and exchanges... electronically trade a sum in currencies, futures, derivative instruments, stocks, and bonds that exceeds the entire annual gross national product of the United States. /PHILLIPS /1994/, his emphases and exclamation point)

In addition to the stimuli noted earlier, the financial sector grew mightily in response to an interacting set of stimuli: the emerging importance of money, equity, and pension funds, the enormous increase of household, business, and governmental **debt**, the spread and strengthening of insurance companies and their mergers with other financial companies, the expansion of individual and professional financial speculators, and the dazzling growth of international **speculation** in the vast and explosive derivative markets. (see HENWOOD)

Then there is something else, disgraceful as much in its origin as in its consequence. The reference is to the savings and loan (S&L) scandals of the 1980s. The S&Ls were legislated in the 1920s and flowered in the 1930s and into the 1960s.

Their stated purpose was to create regulated neighborhood "thrift banks" which, through ceilings on their interest charges, would enable middle-income and working class families to purchase a home. And, with the help of a buoyant economy after World War

II, the result was as hoped: by the end of the 1960s, two-thirds of all U.S. families were "homeowners," most (myself included) having financed their homes at the "neighborhood" S&L.

Enter Ronald **Reagan**, stage right. One of his first triumphs was **deregulation** of the "thrifts" by the Garn-St. Germain bill (1981). In doing so, it served as an invitation to reckless financial practices for households and all financial institutions, among them and leading the pact, the S&Ls; worse, and predictably, their ownership and control were increasingly taken over by sharpies, fools, and downright crooks, getting their capital in every which way, with always rising interest rates, and careless lending, not least for "junk bonds." By 1984, one after another, they collapsed. The Federal Deposit Insurance Corporation (FDIC) guaranteed all depositors up to a maximum of $10,000 of their savings. Even that (nowadays seemingly small) amount far exceeded the possibilities of middle or low-income depositors. But under Reagan the limit was lifted to <u>ten</u> times that, and—naturally—the crooked or just plain reckless people who had taken them over used this to make S&Ls into sedate gambling casinos, playing with "hot money." (see POZZI, et al.)

Because the S&Ls' deposits were guaranteed and, nationwide, enormous, and because the Reagan folks saw to it that the people who <u>caused</u> the debacle were <u>not</u> to lose any money, they were "bailed out." The cost to you taxpayers will be in the hundreds of billions; the lowest estimate I have seen has been $200 billion, the average estimate is $500 billion.

A new government agency was created to handle the problem, with the finely-spun name Resolution Trust Corporation, composed of lawyers and accountants. To give you an idea of what you are paying for, the lawyers are paid $600 per <u>hour</u>. How many <u>days</u> do you have to work for that amount? "Your" government at work.

What is striking is that the foregoing, which should have served as a warning of financial hocus-pocus and fragility, led to something like the opposite. The presumed "disciplinary function" of **free markets** would have left reckless financial institutions to drown in their own failed investments; instead

> the national power structure bailed out the shaky financial sector, and on a large enough scale that in the end the banks and S&Ls rescued through federal insurance payouts represent-

ed a higher share of the nation's deposits than the institutions forced to close their doors in the economic hurricane of the late 1920s and early 1930s.... Financed by massive borrowing and further enlargement of the federal deficit, the bailout served largely to safeguard bank investors and assets. The result was not just to prop up the stock market but to allow it to keep hitting new highs, while Wall Street firms achieved new record earnings.... and the financial economy... continued to eat the real economy. (PHILLIPS /1994/)

All of the foregoing, taken together with the mountains of all kinds of **debt** and the need for it to <u>increase</u> if national and global economic collapse are to be avoided, becomes fraught with dire meanings when we recognize the highly speculative quality of the entire financial system, and its implications; which is next.

<u>Fragility</u>. Debt and speculation have always been part of modern economies; stock and bond exchanges were built at least in part to accommodate both. Until recently, the 1920s were seen as the height of insane speculation and associated debt. But neither was more than a babe-in-arms compared to the Godzilla twins of the 1990s and now.

The consequence has been not just that finance dominates the economy but that, in addition, speculation dominates finance. The "Crash of '29" it may be feared, could one day be seen as a gentle tremor compared with the massive national and global earthquake potential now possible.

Debt is discussed at length under that heading, as is **speculation**. Remembering that the two are intertwined in a dangerous dance, here we treat only summarily of speculation.

In the realms of finance, speculation is now ubiquitous; in is a recognized or hidden part of every variety of financial instrument (and, as well in commodities: wheat, tobacco, etc.). It used to be that almost all of the speculators were "pros." The late 1920s saw a jump of the innocents into the ring, but they were shortly knocked out—and, it seemed, never to return.

But in the 1990s a tidal wave of new innocents e-mailed their way into the ring, accompanied by a group of pros well outnumbering anything seen in the 1920s. In short, speculation came to be the biggest game in town, even sucking in countless hopefuls going so far as to take out second mortgages out on their homes in order to bet on those sure things. Sitting in the wings humming to itself is now a "housing bubble" that brings to mind the "tulip mania" of the 17th century (in Holland, of course). (BOXER)

One of the most popular speculator sports is that of foreign currencies. The triumph of the giddy free market ideology that has spread like a fever was linked to **Nixon**'s end of fixed exchange rates in the early 1970s (He endeared himself to me when, asked by his right-hand man HALDEMAN what he was going to do about some rapid changes in the Italian lira he spat out "I don't give a shit about the lira." It may have been the only time he spoke the truth.)

When currencies began to exchange freely the door is opened to always rising speculation. The Bank of International Settlements, as its name suggests, keeps track of the buying and selling of all currencies. Already in 1986 it was startling to read that daily "forex" transactions amounted to $186 billion, and that no more than ten percent of that was for trade and investment; the rest was speculation. Wow.

Peanuts. Five years later it had jumped to $800 billion daily, only three percent of which was for trade and investment. Now it flits back and forth between $1.5 and $2 trillion in daily transactions with barely one percent of that for trade and investment; that is, 99 percent is speculation. (STIGLITZ /2002/)

All speculation is in the nature of gambling, of course; but some of it is virtually unavoidable: the giant transnational companies (TNCs) must deal in various foreign currencies every day: they are constantly having to buy and sell this and that and pay workers; if they don't speculate (that is, buy and or sell more than their ongoing trade and investment needs) they stand to lose and/or to forego a profit they might make by guessing right. Apart from that, most of the rest is sheer speculation.

Item: One of the most respected and longest-standing banks in the world is Baring Brothers of London. They were the most important creditor of the USA for much of the 19th century. And they were very conservative. A few years ago one of their employees in Singapore (I think it was), was absolutely certain that the Japanese yen was going to go down (or up) by this or that amount, so he went big on it for Baring. And lost one billion dollars for them and, in the process, dragged them into bankruptcy. He guessed wrong; can't win 'em all.

That sort of thing, usually with less severe effects, is going on everywhere, 24/7, most famously bringing on the "Asian financial crisis" of 1997. It started in Thailand—for purely speculative reasons. It spread like SARS throughout the East, bringing otherwise healthy economies like Korea's to their knees. (And, not so incidentally, causing many of their companies to sell out to always observant "vulture capitalists" from the West.) (HENWOOD)

It is worth noting that much of the whiz bang talk about the need for and benefits of "free markets" has as its center the virtues of "transparency," and that the most "transparent" of all markets are (supposed to be) those of finance. They are the least regulated or constrained, the most accessible to instantaneous communications (and buying and selling), the most "globalized," the most competitive, and the most integrated of all; indeed, they represent to a "T" the mainstream economists' "perfectly competitive market."

For the second and third-tier economies, however, those markets have meant something like handing thieves the key to the front door. The rich countries, not least the USA, are the thieves. Frequently they function with the help of our con man the **IMF**, and its gunsels the **WTO** and **World Bank** and **NAFTA** and **GATT**.

It may be said with full assurance that the USA in its non-dominating 19th century would never, that is NEVER, have allowed any, let alone all, of those institutions to darken our door, which was in no way "transparent": it was covered with tariffs, subsidies, and where necessary (or convenient), gunboat diplomacy.

As suggested earlier, the "roaring 20s" were, in comparison with the "new economy" of the 90s, as a kitten is to a tiger. But KEYNES (as quoted in another context) was famously alarmed even by that kitten:

> Speculators may do no harm as bubbles on a steady stream of enterprise. But the position is serious when enterprise becomes the bubble on a whirlpool of speculation. When the capital development of a country becomes a by-product of the activities of a casino, the job is likely to be ill done. The measure of success of Wall Street, regarded as an institution of which the proper social purpose is to direct new investment into the most profitable channels in terms of future yield, cannot be claimed as one of he outstanding triumphs of laissez-faire capitalism—which is not surprising, if I am right in thinking that the best brains of Wall Street have been in fact directed towards a different object. (1936)

Now that "enterprise" <u>has</u> "become the bubble on a whirlpool of speculation" it seems necessary to ask, if Keynes was rightly fearful of that kitten's meow what would his response be to the tiger <u>roaring</u> in our living room; or, more to the point, what should <u>our</u> response be?

free markets/free trade

"Free" is a most appealing adjective. Who could be against anything prefaced by "free," no matter the context—free tickets, free as a breeze, free spirits, free citizens..., free markets, free trade; the very word wins consent, if only because its implicit opposite—unfree—sounds ugly.

But as is often so for more than a few of the nouns modified by "free" there is a catch; many more than one catch when applied to markets and trade.

As is discussed more fully under **big business** and **globalization**, free markets and trade were first effectively argued for at the dawn of industrial capitalism, by Adam Smith and David Ricardo. Their overlapping aims, respectively, were to enhance the then infant processes of industrialization within Britain and to secure its global economic supremacy.

Those clarion calls in their own time and again today have served and serve to distract attention from the hard-nosed policies meant to secure the opposite of "freedom," and/or whose ramifications act to prevent rather than to create the desirable world posited by the slogans of freedom.

Though Smith's focus was national and Ricardo's both national and international, the ultimate meaning of free <u>markets</u> and free <u>trade</u> merge to become the dominant force in all social realms, not just the economy:

> Markets not only allocate resources and distribute income, they also shape our culture, foster or thwart desirable forms of human development, and support a well-defined structure of power. (BOWLES)

Smith well understood that freedom for new businesses to build factories and run them as they wished—as Ricardo did regarding freedom from protective tariffs in international trade— would entail disadvantages for others, both at home and abroad. Among many examples: "Free" markets for labor in practice means no **unions** to protect or advance workers; absence of protection for newly-emerging economies means they will <u>never</u> be able to compete, never have their own industries. And those constraints, among others, have not just economic but, as Bowles pointed out, can and have had harmful non-economic consequences in political, cultural and military realms. All that is completely unacknowledged by mainstream economists still today, after centuries of accumulating evidence.

Notwithstanding, this <u>was</u> understood and acted upon early on by the nations following along in Britain's path, first and foremost in the USA. As the 19th century and the new USA began, Alexander Hamilton argued effectively for a set of national policies that would both protect and finance the industry and transportation essential to industrialization. He was famously opposed by Thomas Jefferson, a devotee both of agrarian democracy <u>and</u> of Adam Smith; Hamilton and industrialization won—for better and for worse.

So the USA began its national economic history as a protectionist and statist society. In doing so successfully it brought into being an ever-sharper conflict between the industrializing North and slavery-dependent agricultural South. More than any other single factor, this it was in this arena that the civil war was born.

It is in some sense reassuring to see the Civil War and its hundreds of thousands of dead as having been fought to abolish **slavery**; it was not. That was but one of the issues—concerning which there was by no means total agreement in the North; as indicated, for example, by the large number of northerners who refused to fight or bought their way out of the army. The main issue was connected but different: Who would rule?

Up into the 1850s, the South ruled: Of the 12 presidents 1789-1850, 8 were from the South; for the same reasons, the South dominated the Senate and congressional committees and held a majority on the Supreme Court for at least as many years.

The South was against protective tariffs and all attempts to favor industry through subsidization and tariffs. Why not? The South exported most of its products—cotton, tobacco, sugar and rice—to Britain, in exchange for the latter's relatively cheap manufactures (and loans).

Also, there were two main factions in the North that leaned to the southern position: the New England traders in slaves and rum. Here Veblen, with his usual irony:

> The slave trade was never a "nice" occupation or an alto-gether unexceptionable investment... But even though it may have been distasteful to one and another of its New England men of affairs, and though there was always a suspicion of moral obliquity attached to the slave trade, yet it had the good fortune to be drawn into the service of the greater good. In conjunction with its running mate, the rum trade, it laid the foundations of some very respectable fortunes at the focus of commercial enter-prise that presently became the center of American culture, and so gave rise to some of the country's Best People. At least so they say. Perhaps also it was...in the early pursuit of gain in this moral penumbra that American business enterprise learned how not to let its right hand know what its left hand is doing; and there is always something to be done that is best done with the left hand. (VEBLEN, 1923)

Some of the traders also became involved in finance and indus-try as the 1850s moved on; in any case, the industrial sector was enlarging rapidly as was, in tandem, its political power: up to a point. From the viewpoint of emerging industrial capitalism, the political power of the South <u>had</u> to be subdued, whatever the issue, whatev-er the means. For the South the issue was slavery <u>and</u> power; for the North, power. (SCHEIBER; WILLIAMS, W.A., 1961)

A sad corollary of the foregoing is that no modern war can be fought by anything resembling a democratic society in the crass terms of power; idealism and/or morality are essential: the abolition of slavery for the Civil War, the end of war itself for World War I, the defeat of **fascism** for World War II, the achievement of freedom for **Vietnam**. Such issues have seldom been <u>entirely</u> irrelevant; nor have they <u>ever</u> been central.

In the era of spreading industrialization that ended as World War I erupted, the USA's departure from free markets and free trade was the motif also for Germany, France, Italy, and Japan; and they, plus the British and ourselves thus became and still are the major powers of the world (with China and, perhaps, India coming up from behind; see **globalization**).

The focus up to here has been on the more distant past. Shifting the focus to the first half of the 20th century, it was then discovered that whatever else might be wrong with free markets/free trade, the freer they were, the more destructive. How and why?

There is much to say; here we note only that already by 1900 markets had begun to be flooded by excess industrial capacities to produce—"excess" meaning there was inadequate global demand to meet the global supply that could get a profitable price: Germany alone, for example, could meet the capital goods needs of <u>all</u> of Europe by 1910. Thus an intensified scramble for markets (and the **imperialist** scramble for assured territories and their resources); and World War I. (BOWDEN, et al.)

In the USA, at war's end there ensued a decade of wild **corruption** and **speculation**, assuring that if and when trouble came around the corner it would be carrying economic explosives.

The ensuing Great Depression convinced a sufficient majority of the electorate that <u>laissez-faire</u> free markets were not for them, that businesses required rules to protect both us and them through governmental regulations and interventions in the economy.

Out of this emerged the New Deal and not only its rules (**SEC**, **Glass-Steagall**, etc.) but also its actions "outside" the market: the enabling of **unions**, the creation of **social security**, the prohibition of child labor, the Tennessee Valley Authority, and so on

But after World War II, and in the midst of two decades or so of governmental rule-making and actions lifting "the social wage," the free marketers began to gain their voice again; more specifically, they began to listen to the voice of the economist **Milton Friedman** and a rising number of mainstream economists advocating total free marketry: for Friedman, that means that <u>everything</u> should be commodified: a **free** labor market (i.e., no unions), a completely privatized health care and retirement system, privatized education at all levels, privatized national parks and prisons, a privatized—i.e.,. mercenary—military (as in Europe, centuries ago): <u>everything</u>. (see **deregulation**)

And as he and his big business supporters have increasingly won their way, society has found itself paying increasingly high costs—human, economic and political costs: they spill the oil and we must try to swim in it—most painfully, but by no means only, in **health care**.

The cracks in the dam of mildly reformed capitalism began to widen as **Reagan** entered the White House; now the waters runneth over as "free market" capitalism at home and abroad is allowed to rule—heedless of the damaging consequences to weaker countries, the global poor, or to **jobs** and **inequality** here at home.

"It's each for himself and God for all," as the elephant said when he danced among the chickens.

Friedman, Milton
(see deregulation, commodification, privatization)

BIBLIOGRAPHY

An Introductory Note

The aim of this small encyclopedia is to provide readers with brief discussions of many important matters generally treated blandly or misleadingly in the media, most books, and in schools—when they are not ignored.

It is hoped that those who read this will take it upon themselves to deepen their understanding by going on to other books more conventional in <u>form</u> that can be found in the following listing.

Some of those books can serve as a set of substantial introductions for more sustained study; to assist in that, the following few books are now singled out. All of them provide broad perspectives on areas of vital relevance; in their own turn they might send readers to still more books. If such efforts are made by those who read book, its main hope will be fulfilled.

1. The most useful and, happily, most readable of all histories of the USA is Howard Zinn's <u>A People's History of the United States</u>.

2. Kevin Phillips, a self-styled Republican conservative, has in recent years written several books exploring what he sees as the dangerous depths to which political corruption and economic autocracy have gone, so far as now to threaten the society he wishes to see "conserved." See especially his <u>Arrogant Capital</u> and <u>Wealth and Democracy in the United States</u>.

3. The scope, penetration, and consequences of U.S. economic, military, political, and cultural dominance over the globe are well-treated in Noam Chomsky, <u>Year 501: The Conquest Continues</u>, William Greider, <u>One World, Ready or Not</u>, and Benjamin Barber, <u>Jihad vs. McWorld</u>.

4. In the past century, the media and advertising in newspapers and magazines, radio, TV, and film have gained always more importance and sway in the entirety of our existence; that being so, those with already substantial power outside the media world have acted so as to gain control over and increase the concentration of media ownership. See Edward S. Herman and Robert McChesney, <u>Global Media</u> and Ben Bagdikian, <u>Media Monopoly</u>.

5. All of the foregoing developments have emerged within the always strengthening socioeconomic, cultural and political frame-

work of capitalism, with the early and continuing assistance of the economics profession that came into existence as it did. My <u>Capitalism and Its Economics</u> seeks to illuminate their mutually supportive interactions, from Adam Smith and the industrial revolution to the present.

All of the just noted books and the hundreds that follow (both new and used) are to be found for sale easily and, often, cheaply on the Internet, with listings of relevant used book shops over the country and ways of ordering. See, for example, <www.abebooks.com>, or <www.google.com>. On the Web site for my community classes in the San Francisco area are also many suggested articles: <www.dougdowd.org>. Now the books used and cited for this work.

ADAMS, N.S., MCCOY, A.W. (eds.) 1970. *Laos: War and Revolution*. New York: Harper & Row.

ADAMS, W., BROCK, J. 1986. *The Bigness Complex: Industry, Labor, and Government in the American Economy*. New York: Pantheon.

AGEE, P. 1975. *Inside the Company: CIA Diary*. New York: Bantam.

ALBELDA, R. DRAGO, R., SHULMAN, S. 2001. *Unlevel Playing Fields: Understanding Wage Inequality and Discrimination*. Cambridge, MA: Dollars & Sense.

____WITHORN, A., (eds.). 2002. *Lost Ground: Welfare Reform, Poverty, and Beyond*. Cambridge, MA: South End Press.

ALLEN, G.C. 1946. *A Short Economic History of Modern Japan: 1867-1937*. London: Macmillan.

ALPEROVITZ, G. 1965. *Atomic Diplomacy: Hiroshima and Potsdam*. New York: Vintage Books.

ALTERMAN, E. 2003. *What Liberal Media?* New York: The Nation.

ALTMAN, D. 2002. "Ensuring Competition for Military Contracts," *NYT*, 9-15-02.

ANDERSON, S., CAVANAGH, J., LEE, T. 2000. *Field Guide to the Global Economy*. New York: The New Press.

ARONSON, J. 1970. *The Press and Cold War*. Indianapolis: Bobbs-Merrill.

ASHWORTH. W. 1987. *A Short History of the World Economy Since 1950*. London: Longman.

AUDEN, W.H. (see RODMAN, *Modern Poetry*)

AUSTIN, J. 1990. FOCUS: *America's Growing Correctional-Industrial Complex* (San Francisco: National Council on Crime and Delinquency.

____IRWIN, J. 1990. *Who Goes to Prison?* San Francisco: NCCD.

BAGDIKIAN, B. 1983. *The Media Monopoly*. Boston: Beacon Press.

BALIBAR, E., WALLERSTEIN, I. 1991. *Race, Nation, Class: Ambiguous Identities*. New York: Verso.

BANKS, J. 1996. *Monopoly Television: MTV's Quest to Control the Music*. Boulder, CO: Westview Press.

BANNER, S. 2002. *The Death Penalty: An American History*. Cambridge: Harvard

Univ. Press.

BARAN, P., SWEEZY, P. 1966. *Monopoly Capital: An Essay on the American Economic and Social Order*. New York: Monthly Review Press.

_____1957. *The Political Economy of Growth*. New York: Monthly Review Press.

_____1969 "Theses on Advertising," in *The Longer View*. New York: Monthly Review Press.

BARBER, B. 1996. *Jihad vs. McWorld: How Globalism and Tribalism Are Reshaping the World*. New York; Ballantine.

BARITZ, L. (ed.) 1977. *The Culture of the Twenties*. New York: Bobbs-Merrill.

BARNET, R. 1970. *The Economy of Death: A Hard Look at the Defense Budget and the Military-Industrial Complex*. New York: Atheneum.

BARNET, R., CAVANAGH, J. 1994. *Global Dreams: Imperial Corporations and the New World Order*. New York: Simon and Shuster.

BEARD, C. 1969. *The Devil Theory of War*. Westport, Conn.: Greenwood.

BECKLES, H. 1989. *White Servitude and Black Slavery in Barbados, 1627-1715*. Knoxville: Univ. of Tenn. Press.

BENERIA, L., FELDMAN, S. 1992. *Unequal Burden: Economic Crises, Persistent Poverty, and Women's Work*. Boulder, CO: Westview Press.

BERLE, A.A., MEANS, G. 1932. *The Modern Corporation and Private Property*. New York: Macmillan.

BERNAYS, E. 1952. *Public Relations*. Norman, OK: University of Oklahoma Press.

BERRY, W. 1977. *The Unsettling of America: Culture and Agriculture*. New York: Avon.

BIERCE, A. 1911/2000. *The Devil's Dictionary*. New York: Devon.

BIRD, K., LIFSCHULTZ, L. (eds.) 1998. *Hiroshima's Shadow: Writings on the Denial of History and the Smithsonian Controversy*.

BLACKBURN, R. (ed.) 1973. *Ideology in Social Science: Readings in Critical Social Theory*. New York: Vintage.

BLAIR, J.M. 1978. *The Control of Oil*. New York: Vintage.

BLIX, H. 2004. *Disarming Iraq*. New York: Pantheon Books.

BLOCK, F. 1977. *The Origins of International Economic Disorder*. Berkeley: Univ. of California Press.

BLUESTONE, B., HARRISON, B. 1982 *Deindustrialization of America*. New York: Basic Books.

_____1988. *The Great U-Turn: Corporate Restructuring and the Polarizing of America*. New York: Basic Books.

BLUM, W. 2000. *Rogue State: A Guide to the World's Only Superpower*. Monroe, ME: Common Courage Press.

_____2004. *Killing Hope: U.S. Military and CIA Interventions Since World War II*. Monroe, ME: Common Courage Press.

BOGGS, C. 1971. *Gramsci's Marxism*. London: Pluto Press.

BOIES, J.L. 1994, *Buying for Armageddon: Business, Society, and Military Spending Since the Cuban Missile Crisis*. New Brunswick, NJ: Rutgers Univ. Press.

BOK, D. 2003. *Universities in the Marketplace: The Commercialization of Higher Education*. Princeton: Princeton University Press.

BONNER, R. 1984. *Weakness and Deceit: U.S. Policy and El Salvador*. New York: New York Times Books.

BONNIFIELD, P. 1987. *The Dust Bowl, Men, Dirt and Depression*. Albuquerque: Univ. of New Mexico Press.

BORCHER, W. 1949/1971. *The Man Outside*. New York: New Directions.

BOUCHER, D. (ed.) 1999. *The Paradox of Plenty: Hunger in a Bountiful World*. Oakland, CA: Food First Books.

BOVARD, J. 1995. *Shakedown: How the Government Screws You From A to Z*. New York: Viking.

BOWDEN, W. et al. 1937. *Economic History of Europe Since 1750*. New York: H. Fertig.

BOWLES, S. 1991. What Markets Can—and Cannot—Do. *Challenge Magazine* July-August.

BOXER, C.R. 1965. *The Dutch Seaborne Empire*. New York: Knopf.

BRADY, R.A. 1933. *The Rationalization Movement in German Industry*. Berkeley: Univ. of California Press.

____1937. *The Spirit and Structure of German Fascism*. New York: Viking Press.

____1943/1999. *Business as a System of Power*. New York: Columbia Univ. Press/ Piscataway, NJ: Transaction Publishers.

BRANCH, E. D., 1929. *The Hunting of the Buffalo*. New York: Appleton Co.

BRANDS, H.W. 1993. *The Devil We Knew: America and the Cold War*. Oxford: Oxford University Press.

BRANFMAN, F. 1972. *Voices from the Plain of Jars*. New York: Harper Colophon.

BRAUDEL, F. 1979/1992. *The Structures of Everyday Life, Vol. I*. Berkeley: University of California Press.

BRAVERMAN, H. 1974. *Labor and Monopoly Capital: The Degradation of Work in the Twentieth Century*. New York: Monthly Review Press.

BREITMAN, R. 1998. *What the Nazis Planned, What the British and the Americans Knew*. New York: Hill & Wang.

BRESLOW, M. (et al.). 1999. *The Environment in Crisis*. Cambridge, MA: Dollars & Sense.

BRITTAIN, J. 1972. *The Payroll Tax for Social Security*. Washington: The Brookings Institution.

BRENAN, G. 1943. *The Spanish Labyrinth: An Account of the Social and Political Background of the Spanish Civil War*. New York: Cambridge University Press.

BRONFENBRENNER, K. 2003. "Declining Unionization, Rising Inequality," *Multinational Monitor*, May.

BROWN, Claire. *American Standards of Living, 1918-1988*. New York: Blackwell.

BROWN, Claude. 1965. *Manchild in the Promised Land*. New York: Macmillan.

BRYANT, H. 2002. *SHUT OUT: A Story of Race and Baseball in Boston*. New York: Routledge.

BUNDY, MCG. 1988. *Danger and Survival: Choices About the Bomb in the First Fifty Years*. New York: Random House.

BusinessWeek. (various issues)

CAHILL, T. 1995. *How the Irish Saved Civilization*. New York; Doubleday.

CAHN, B. (ed.). 2002. *The Affirmative Action Debate*. New York: Routledge.

CALLENBACH, E. 1996. *Bring Back the Buffalo: A sustainable future for America's Great Plains*. Berkeley: Univ. of California Press.

CAMPEN, J. (et al.). 1999. *Real World Banking*. Cambridge, MA: Dollars & Sense.

CAREY, a. 1997. *Taking the Risk Out of Democracy*. Sydney: New South Wales Press.

CARMICHAEL, V. 1993. *Framing History: The Rosenberg Story and the Cold War*. Minneapolis: Univ. of Minnesota Press.

CARSON, R. 1962. *Silent Spring*. Greenwich, Conn.: Fawcett Press.

CASH, W. 1941. *The Mind of the South*. New York: Knopf.

CATO INSTITUTE. Policy Analysis No. 24l: Archer Daniels Midland: A Study in Corporate Welfare (James Bovard), 9-26-1995

CAUTE, D. 1978. *The Great Fear: The Anti-Communist Purge Under Eisenhower and Truman*. New York: Simon & Schuster.

CHANG, I. 2003. *The Chinese in America: A Narrative History*. New York: Viking.

CHANG, L., KORNBUHL, P. (ed.) 1992. *The Cuban Missile Crisis*. New York: New Press.

CHILDE, V.G. 1951. *Man Makes Himself*. New York: Mentor Books.

CHOMSKY, N. 1969. *American Power and the New Mandarins*. New York: Pantheon.

____1970. *At War with Asia*. New York: Vintage.

____1991. *Deterring Democracy*. London: Verso.

____1993. *Year 501: The Conquest Continues*. Boston: South End Press.

CHOMSKY, N., HERMAN, E.S. 1988. *Manufacturing Consent: The Political Economy of the Mass Media*. New York: Pantheon.

CHURCHILL, W. 1997. *A Little Matter of Genocide*. San Francisco: City Lights Books.

CIRINO, R. 1971. *Don't Blame the People*. New York: Random House.

CLARK, G.N. 1947. *The Seventeenth Century*. London: Oxford University Press.

CLARKE, R.A. 2004. *Against All Enemies: Inside America's War on Terror*. New York: The Free Press.

CLOGG, R. (ed.) 2002. *Greece, 1940-1949: Occupation, Resistance, Civil War*. London: Palgrave Macmillan.

COCKROFT, J., FRANK, A.G., JOHNSON, D.L. 1972. *Dependence and Underdevelopment*, New York: Doubleday.

COLE, D. 2003. *Enemy Aliens: Double Standards and Constitutional Freedoms in the War on Terrorism*. New York: The New Press.

COLL, S. 2003. *Ghost Wars: The Secret History of the CIA, Afghanistan and Bin Laden, From the Soviet Invasion to September 10, 2001*. New York: The Penguin Press.

COLLINS, C., LEONDAR-WRIGHT, B. SKLAR, H. 1999. *Shifting Fortunes: The Perils of the Growing American Wealth Gap*. Boston: United for a Fair Economy.

CONASON, JOE. 2004. *Big Lies: The Right-Wing Propaganda Machine and How It Distorts the Truth*. New York: Thomas Dunne/ St. Martin's.

COOK, B.W. 1981. *The Declassified Eisenhower: A Divided Legacy*. New York: Doubleday.

COULTER, A. 2003. *Treason: Liberal Treachery From the Cold War to the War on Terrorism*. New York: Crown Forum.

CRILE, G. 2003. *Charlie Wilson's War: The Extraordinary History of the Largest Covert Operation in History*. New York: Atlantic Monthly Press.

CUMINGS, B. 1981. *The Origins of the Korean War*, Two vols. Princeton: Princeton University Press.

____, HALLIDAY, J. 1988. *Korea: The Unkown War*. New York: Pantheon.

CYPHER, J. 1987. "Military Spending, Technical Change, and Economic Growth," *Journal of Economic Issues* (March).

____1991. "The War Dividend," *Dollars & Sense*, May.

____1998. "Financial Domination in the US Economy," in Fayasmanesh, S. and Tool, M. (ed.) *Institutionalist Theory and Practices*. (Cheltenham, UK: Edward Elgar.

____2001. "Nafta's Lessons: From Economic Mythology to Current Realities," *Labor*

Studies Journal, Spring.

_____2002. "Return of The Iron Triangle," *Dollars & Sense*, Jan./Feb.

_____2002. "A Prop, Not a Burden: The U.S. Economy Relies on Militarism," *Dollars & Sense*, July/August.

CZECH, B. 2003. *Shoveling Fuel for a Runaway Train*. Berkeley: University of California Press.

DALY, H.E., COBB, J.B., Jr. 1989. *For the Common Good: Redirecting the Economy toward Community, the Environment, and a Sustainable Future*. Boston: Beacon Press.

DALY, H. 1996. *Beyond Growth: The Economics of Sustainable Development*. Boston: Beacon Press.

DANNER, M. 1994. *The Massacre at El Mozote: A Parable of the Cold War*. New York: Vintage.

DAVIS, D.B. 1988. *The Problem of Slavery in Western Culture*. New York: Oxford University Press.

DAVIS, M. 1998. *Ecology of Fear: Los Angeles and the Imagination of Disaster*. New York: Henry Holt

DE CASTRO, J. 1950. *The Geography of Hunger*. New York: Monthly Review Press. (republished as *The Geopolitics of Hunger*, 1990)

DENNISON, G. 1969. *The Lives of Children*. New York:; Random House.

DELANY, W. 2001. *The Green and the Red: Revolutionary Republicanism and Socialism in Irish History, 1848-1923*. New York: Writer's Showcase.

DE TOCQUEVILLE, A. 1846. *Democracy in America*. New York: Macmillan.

DE ZENGOTITA, T. "The Numbing of the American Mind," *Harper's* Magazine, April, 2002.

DOBB, M. 1937. *Political Economy and Capitalism*. London: Routledge and Kegan Paul.

_____1966. *Soviet Economic Development Since 1917*. London: Routledge and Kegan Paul,

DOBSON, A. (ed.) 1991. *The Green Reader: Essays Toward A Sustainable Society*. San Francisco: Mercury House.

DOMANICK, J. 2003. *Cruel Justice: Three Strikes and the Politics of Crime in America's Golden State*. Berkeley, CA: University of California Press.

DOMHOFF, W. 1998. *Power and Politics in the Year 2000*. New York: Oxford Univ. Press.

DONOVAN, J.A. 1970. *Militarism, U.S.A.* New York: Scribner's.

DORFMAN, J. 1934. *Thorstein Veblen and His America*. New York: Viking.

DOWD, D. 1950. "Two-Thirds of the World," *Antioch Review*, Fall.

_____1956. "A Comparative Analysis of Economic Development in the American West and South," *Journal of Economic History*, December.

_____1964/2000. *Thorstein Veblen*. New Brunswick, NJ: Transaction Publishers.

_____1965, *Step by Step*. New York: W.W. Norton.

_____1967. "An End to Alibis: America Fouls Its Dream," *The Nation*, February.

_____1978. "The CIA's Laotian Colony," in Adams, N.S. and McCoy, A.W., *Laos: War and Revolution*. New York: Harpers.

_____1982. "Militarized Economy, Brutalized Society," *Economic Forum* (Summer)

_____1989. *The Waste of Nations*. Boulder, Col.: Westview Press.

_____1993. *U.S. Capitalist Development Since 1775: Of, By, and For Which People*. Armonk, NY: M.E.Sharpe.

____1997a. *Blues for America: A Critique, A Lament, and Some Memories*. New York: Monthly Review Press.

____1997b. *Against the Conventional Wisdom: A Primer for Current Economic Controversies and Proposals*. Boulder, Col.: Westview Press.

____2000/2004. *Capitalism and Its Economics: A Critical History*. London: Pluto Press.

____2001. *And It's Each for Himself and God For All: Once More, U.S. Capitalism on a Rampage*. (Pacifica, CA: Vai Vecchio Press.

____(ed,) 2002. *Understanding Capitalism: Critical Analysis, from Karl Marx to Amartya Sen*. London: Pluto Press.

DRAKE, S. & CAYTON, H. 1992 (1945). *Black Metropolis: A Study of Negro Life in a Northern City*. Chicago: Univ. of Chicago Press.

DRAPER, T. 1991. *A Very Thin Line: The Iran-Contra Affairs*. New York: Hill & Wang.

DRAY. P. 2002. *At the Hands of Persons Unknown: The Lynching of Black America*. New York: Random House.

DREW, E. 2002. "War Games in the Senate." *New York Review of Books*, 12-5-02.

DU BOFF, R. 1989. *Accumulation and Power: An Economic History of the United States*. Armonk, NY: M.E.Sharpe.

DUBOFSKY, M. 1974. *We Shall Be All: A History of the Industrial Workers of the World*. New York: Quadrangle.

DU BOIS, W.E.B. 1989 (1903) *The Souls of Black Fools*. New York: Penguin.

DUUS, P. 1976. *The Rise of Modern Japan*. Boston: Houghton Mifflin.

DWORKIN, R. "The Threat to Patriotism," *NYRB*, 2-28-02.

EHRENREICH, B. 1990. *Fear of Falling: The Inner Life of the Middle Class*. New York: Harper Perennial.

____2001. *Nickel and Dimed: On (Not) Getting By in America*. New York: Henry Holt.

____B, & J. 1971. *The American Health Empire*. New York: Random House.

EISENBERG, C.1996. *Drawing the Line: The American Decision to Divide Germany, 1944-49*. New York: Cambridge Univ. Press

ELIOT, T.S. 1937. *Collected Poems: 1909-1935*. London: Faber & Faber Limited.

ELLIS, R. 2003. *The Empty Ocean: Plundering the World's Marine Life*. Washington: Island Press/Shearwater Books.

ELON, A. 2004. "A Very Special Relationship," *NYRB*, 1-15.

ELLSBERG, D. 1972. *Papers on the War*. New York: Simon & Schuster.

____2002. *Secrets: A Memoir on Vietnam and the Pentagon Papers*. New York: Viking Penguin.

ENGLER, R. 1961. *The Politics of Oil*. Chicago: Univ. of Chicago Press.

ENSENZBERGER, H. 1974. *The Consciousness Industry*. New York: Seabury Press.

EVEREST, L. 2004. *Oil, Power and Empire: Iraq and the U.S. Global Agenda*. Monroe, ME: Common Courage Press.

EWEN, S. 1976. *Advertising and the Social Roots of the Consumer Culture*. New York: McGraw-Hill.

____1996. *PR! A Social History of Spin*. New York: Basic Books.

FALL, B. 1967. *Last Reflections on a War*. Garden City, NY: Doubleday.

FANON, F. 1963. *The Wretched of the Earth*. New York: Grove Press.

FAULKNER, H. 1947. *The Decline of Laissez-faire: 1897-1917*. New York: Rinehart.

FEAGIN, J. & SYKES, M. 1994. *Living with Racism: The Black Middle Class Experience*. Boston: Beacon Press.

Federal Trade Commission. 1939. *Report on the Automobile Industry*. Washington, D.C.: USGPO

FEIS, H. 1930. *Europe, the World's Banker: 1870-1914*. New York: A.M. Kelley

FINNEGAN, W. 1998. *Cold New World: Growing up in a Harder Country*. New York: Random House.

FITZGERALD, F. 1972. *Fire in the Lake: The Vietnamese and the Americans in Vietnam*. New York: Random House.

_____2000. *Way Out There in the Blue*. New York: Simon & Schuster.

FOLBRE, N., et al. 1995. *The New Field Guide to the U.S. Economy: A Compact and Irreverent Guide*. New York: The New Press.

FOLBRE, N. 1996. *The War on the Poor: A Defense Manual*. New York: The New Press.

Fortune Magazine (various issues)

FOSTER, J.B. 1999. *The Vulnerable Planet*. New York: Monthly Review Press.

_____2000. *Marx's Ecology*. New York: Monthly Review Press.

_____2002. *Ecology vs. Capitalism*. New York: Monthly Review Press.

FRANK, A.G. 1979. *Dependent Accumulation and Underdevelopment*. New York: Monthly Review Press.

FRANKLIN, M. 1988. *Rich Man's Farming: The Crisis in Agriculture*. London: Routledge.

FREELAND, R. 1972. *The Truman Doctrine and the Origins of McCarthyism: Foreign Policy, Domestic Politics, and Internal Security, 1946-1948*. New York: Knopf.

FRIED, A. 1997. *McCarthyism: The Great American Red Scare*. New York: Oxford University Press.

FREUD, S. 1930. *Civilization and Its Discontents*. New York: Knopf.

FROMM, E. 1941. *Escape from Freedom*. New York: Holt & Company.

FRUMKIN, G. 1951. *Population Changes in Europe Since 1939*. New York: United Nations.

GALBRAITH, J.K. 1955. *The Great Crash, 1929*. Boston: Houghton Mifflin.

GALLETTI, M. 2001. "Le relazione tra Italia e Kurdistan," (Collected Essays), in Quaderni di ORIENTE MODERNO.

GANS, H. 1995. *The War Against the Poor: The Underclass and Antipoverty Policy*. New York: Basic Books.

GARDNER. L. 1995. *Pay Any Price: Lyndon Johnson and the Wars for Vietnam*. Chicago: J.R. Dee.

GATTO, J.T. 1992. *Dumbing Us Down: The Hidden Curriculum of Compulsory Schooling*. Philadelphia: New Society Publishers.

GENOVESE, E. 1967. *The Political Economy of Slavery*. New York: Vintage Books.

GEORGE, S. 1976. *How the Other Half Dies*. London: Penguin.

_____1979. *Feeding the Few: Corporate Control of Food*. Washington, D.C.: Institute for Policy Studies.

_____1994. (with Fabrizio Sabelli) *Faith and Credit: The World's Secular Empire*. Boulder, Colo.: Westview Press.

GERSCHENKRON, A. 1943, *Bread and Democracy in Germany*. Berkeley: Univ. of California Press.

GERVASI, T. 1986. *The Myth of Soviet Military Superiority*. New York: Harper & Row.

GINGER, R. 1969. *The Bending Cross: A Biography of Eugene Victor Debs*. New Brunswick: Rutgers Univ. Press.

GINZBERG, E. 1964. *The House of Adam Smith*. New York: Octagon Books.

GLUCKMAN, A. (et al.) 2003. *Current Economic Issues*. Cambridge, MA: Dollars & Sense.

GOODWIN, Doris Kearns. 1973. *Lyndon Johnson and the American Dream*. New York: Harper & Row.

GORDON, C. 1994. *The Clinton Health Care Plan: Dead on Arrival*. Westfield, NJ: Open Magazine Series (P.O. Box 2726, 07091)

GORDON, D.M. 1996. *Fat and Mean: The Corporate Squeeze of Working Americans and the Myth of Managerial Downsizing*. New York: Free Press.

GOULD, S. 2003. *The Hedgehog and the Fox, and the Magister's Pox: Mending the Gap Between Science and Humanities*. New York: Three Rivers Press.

GRAMSCI, A. 1967. *The Modern Prince and Other Writings*. New York: New World Paperbacks.

GREGORY, J. 1989. *American Exodus: The Dust Bowl Migration and Okie Culture in California*. New York: Oxford Univ. Press.

GREIDER, K. 2003. *The Big Fix: How the Pharmaceutical Industry Rips Off American Consumers*. New York: Public Affairs Reports.

GREIDER, W. 1994. *Who Will Tell the People?* New York: Simon & Schuster.

____1997. *One World, Ready or Not: The Manic Logic of Global Capitalism*. New York: Simon and Schuster.

____1998. *Fortress America: The American Military and the Consequences of Peace*. New York: Public Affairs.

____2003. *The Soul of Capitalism: Opening Paths to a Moral Economy*. New York: Simon & Schuster.

GRIFFITH, R.W. 1971. *The Politics of Fear: Joseph McCarthy and the Senate*. Rochelle Park, NJ: Hayden.

GROSS, B. 1980. *Friendly Fascism: The New Face of Power in America*. New York: M. Evans.

GURLEY, J. 1979, *Challengers to Capitalism: Marx, Lenin, Stalin, and Mao*. New York: W.W. Norton, Inc.

HACK, R. 2004. *Puppetmaster: The Secret Life of J. Edgar Hoover*. New York: New Millenium Press & Audio.

HAHNEL, R. 1999. *Panic Rules: Everything you Need to Know About the Global Economy*. Cambridge, MA: South End Press.

HALBERSTAM, D. 1965. *The Making of a Quagmire*. New York: Random House.

HALDEMAN, H.R. 1994. *The Haldeman Diaries: Inside the Nixon White House*. New York: Putnam.

HALLINAN, A. 2001. *Going Up the River: Travels in a Prison Nation*. New York: Random House.

HALPERIN, M., et al. 1976. *The Lawless State: The Crimes of the U.S. Intelligence Agencies*. New York: Penguin Books.

HAMMOND, J., B. 1911. *The Village Labourer*. London: Guild Books.

____1924. *The Rise of Modern Industry*. New York: Harcourt, Brace.

HANDLIN, O. 1981, *The Uprooted*. Boston: Atlantic Monthly Press.

HARRINGTON, M. 1962. *The Other America*. Baltimore: Penguin.

HARTMAN, C. 1983. *America's Housing Crisis: What is to be Done?* London: Methuen.

HAYEK, F. 1952/1999. *The Road to Serfdom*. London: Routledge.

HAYNES, H,P. 1989. *The Recurring Silent Spring*. New York: Pergamon Press.

HECKSCHER, E. 1935. *Mercantilism.* (2 vols.) New York: Macmillan.

HEINTZ, J, FOLBRE, N. 2000. *Field Guide to the U.S. Economy.* New York: The New Press.

HENWOOD, D. 1997. *Wall Street: How it Works and for Whom.* New York: Verso.

HERIVEL, T. WRIGHT, P (eds.) 2003. *Prison Nation: The Warehousing of America's Poor.* New York: Routledge.

HERMAN, E.S. 1981. *Corporate Control, Corporate Power.* New York: Cambridge Univ. Press.

_____1999. *The Myth of the Liberal Media.* New York: Peter Lang.

_____2003. "From Guatemala to Iraq." *Z Magazine,* January.

_____WUERKER, M. 1992. *Beyond Hypocrisy: Decoding the News in an Age of Propaganda* (including The Doublespeak Dictionary). Boston: South End Press.

_____MCCHESNEY, R. 1999. *The Global Media: The New Missionaries of Global Capitalism.* London: Cassell.

HERSEY, J. 1946/1989. *Hiroshima.* New York: Vintage Books.

HERSH, B. 1992. *The Old Boys: The American Elite and the Origins of the CIA.* New York: Scribner's.

HERSH, S. 1970. *My Lai 4: A Report on the Massacre and Its Aftermath.* New York: Random House.

_____1983. *The Price of Power: Kissinger in the Nixon White House.* New York: Summit Books.

HERTSGAARD, M. 1988. *On Bended Knee: The Press and the Reagan Presidency.* New York: Farrar, Straus and Giroux.

HIGBEE, E. 1963. *Farms and Farmers in an Urban Age.* New York: Twentieth Century Fund

HIMMELSTEIN, D., WOOLHANDLER, S., "We Pay for National Insurance But Don't Get It," *Journal of Health Affairs* (7-10-02)

HISS, T. 1999. *The View from Alger's Window: A Son's Memoir.* New York: Knopf.

HOARE, Q., SMITH, G.N. (eds.) 1971. *Selections from the Prison Notebooks of Antonio Gramsci.* London: Lawrence & Wishart.

HOBSBAWM, E.J. 1964. *Labouring Men: Studies in the History of Labour.* London: Weidenfeld and Nicolson.

_____1968. *Industry and Empire.* New York: Pantheon.

_____1984. *Further Studies in the History of Labour.* London: Weidenfeld and Nicolson.

_____1990. *Nations and Nationalism Since 1780.* New York: Cambridge University Press.

HOBSON, J.A. 1902. *Imperialism.* London: Allen & Unwin.

HOCHSCHILD, A. 1999. *King Leopold's Ghost: A Story of Greed, Terror and Heroism in Colonial Africa.* London: Macmillan.

HOCHSCHILD, A.R. 2004. *The Commercialization of Intimate Life: Notes from Home and Work.* Berkeley: University of California Press.

HOFFMAN, R.J.S. 1933. *Great Britain and the German Trade Rivalry.* Philadelphia: Univ. of Pennsylvania Press.

HUBERMAN, L. 1937. *The Labor Spy Racket.* New York: Modern Age.

_____1937/1955. *We, the People.* New York: Monthly Review Press.

_____1940. *America, Incorporated.* New York: Viking.

HUNT, E.K. 1979. *History of Economic Thought: A Critical Perspective.* Belmont, CA: Wadsworth.

HUXLEY, A. 1931. *Brave New World.* New York: Harper & Bros.

IGNATIEFF, M. 1984. *The Needs of Strangers*. London: Chatto & Windus, Hogarth Press.

ISHERWOOD, C. 1931. *The Berlin Stories*. New York: New Directions.

IVINS, M., DUBOSE, L. 2000. *Shrub: The Short but Happy Political Life of George W. Bush*. New York: Random House.

____2004. *Bushwacker: Life in George W. Bush's America*. New York: Random House.

JACKSON, K., ed. 1989. *Cambodia: 1975-1978. Rendezvous with Death*. Princeton: Princeton University Press.

JEFFERS, R. 1925. "Shine Perishing Republic," from *Selected Poems*. New York: Random House.

JOHNSON, C. 2000. *Blowback: The Costs and Consequences of American Empire*. New York: Henry Holt & Co.

JOHNSTON, D.C. 2003. *Perfectly Legal: The Covert Campaign to Rig Our Tax System to Benefit the Super Rich—and Cheat Everybody Else*. New York: Viking.

JONAS, S. 1991. *The Battle for Guatemala: Rebels, Death Squads, and U.S. Power*. Boulder, CO: Westview Press.

JOSEPHSON, M. 1934. *The Robber Barons*. New York: Harcourt Brace Jovanovich

JUNGK, R. 1958. *Brighter Than a Thousand Suns: A Personal History of the Atomic Scientists*. New York: Harcourt Brace

KAHIN, G. 1968. *The United States in Vietnam*. New York: Harper & Row.

____1986. *Intervention: How America Became Involved in Vietnam*. New York: Knopf.

KAPP, K.W. 1950. *The Social Costs of Private Enterprise*. Cambridge, MA: Harvard University Press.

KEANEY, M. 2002. "Unhealthy Accumulation: the Globalization of Health Care Privatization," *Review of Social Economy*, September.

KEMP, T. 1967. *Theories of Imperialism*. London: Dobson.

KESSLER, R. 2002. *The Secret History of the FBI*. New York: St. Martin's Press.

KEYNES, J.M. 1919. *The Economic Consequences of the Peace*. London: Macmillan.

____1931. *Essays in Persuasion*. London: Macmillan.

____1936, *The General Theory of Employment, Interest and Money*. New York: Harcourt and Brace.

KINDLEBERGER, C. 1978. *Manias, Panics, and Crashes: A History of Financial Crises*. New York: Wiley.

KINZER, S. 2003. *All the Shahs's Men: An American Coup and the Roots of Middle East Terror*. Hoboken, NJ: Wiley.

KLARE, M. 2001. *Resource Wars: The New Landscape of Global Conflict*. New York: Henry Holt.

KLEIN, C. 2001. "Coverage for Low Earners Dwindles," <editors@plansponsor.com>

KLEIN, N. 1999. *No Logo*. New York: Picador.

____2002 *Fences and Windows: Dispatches from the Front Lines of the Globalization Debate*. New York: HarperCollins

KOFSKY, F. 1987. *Harry S. Truman and the War Scare of 1948*. New York: St. Martin's Press.

KOHN, A. 1986. *No Contest: The Case Against Competition; Why we lose in our race to win*. Boston: Houghton Mifflin.

KOLKO, G. 1969. *The Roots of American Foreign Policy*. Boston: Beacon.

____1970. "The Decline of American Radicalism in the Twentieth Cemetery," in WEINSTEIN/EAKINS.

KOLKO, J. 1988. *Restructuring the World Economy*. New York: Pantheon.

KORNBUHL, P., BYRNE, m. (eds.) 1993. *The Iran-Contra Scandal: The Declassified History*. New York: New Press.

KORNBLUH, J. (ed.) 1964. *Rebel Voices: An I.W.W. Anthology*. Ann Arbor: University of Michigan Press.

KOZOL, J. 1967. *Death at an Early Age*. New York: Bantam Books.

____1991. Savage Inequalities: Children in America's Schools. New York: Crown Publishers.

KRUGMAN, P. 2002. "For Richer." *New York Times Magazine*, October 20.

____2003. *The Great Unraveling: Losing Our Way in the New Century*. New York: Norton.

KUTTNER, R. 1996. *Everything for Sale: The Virtues and Limitations of Markets*. New York: Knopf.

LA FEBER, W. 1976. *America, Russia and the Cold War*. New York: Wiley.

LANE, F. 1973. *Venice, A Maritime Republic*. Baltimore: Johns Hopkins Univ. Press.

LAPHAM, L. 1989. *Money and Class in America*. New York: Harper & Row.

LAPPE', F. et. al. 1998. *World Hunger: 12 Myths*. New York: Grove Press.

____F. & A. 2003. *Hope's Edge: The Next Diet for a Small Planet*. New York: Tarcher/Putnam.

LASKI, H. 1936. *The Rise of European Liberalism*. London: Allen & Unwin.

LEBOW, N., STEIN, J.G. 1994. *We All Lost the Cold War*. (Princeton: Princeton Univ. Pres..

LE CARRE', J. 1995. *Our Game*. New York: Knopf.

LEFFLER, M. 1992. *A Preponderance of Power: National Security, the Truman Administration, and the Cold War*. Stanford, CA: Stanford Univ. Press.

Left Business Observer (various issues)

LEIGH, J.P. 1995. *Causes of Death in the Workplace*. Westport, Ct. Greenwood Publishing Group.

____et. al. 2000. *Causes of Occupational Injuries and Illnesses*. Ann Arbor: Univ. of Michigan Press.

LEKACHMAN, R. 1982. *Greed is not Enough*. 1982. New York: Pantheon.

LEWIS, D.L. 2002. "An American Pastime," *New York Review of Books*, November 21.

LEWIS, M. 1989. *Liar's Poker*. New York: W.W. Norton.

LEWIS, S. 1920. *Main Street*. New York: Dover Publications.

LEWIS, W.A. 1949. *Economic Survey, 1919-1939*. London: Allen and Unwin.

LICHTMAN, R. 1982. *The Production of Desire. The Integration of Psychoanalysis into Marxist Theory*. New York: Free Press.

LIEBLING, A.J. 1961. *The Press*. New York: Ballantine.

LINDERT, P. 2004. *Growing Public*. Cambridge: Cambridge University Press.

LITWACK, L. 1980. *Been in the Storm So Long: The Aftermath of Slavery*. New York: Random House.

LIVELY, P. 1987. *The Moon Tiger*. London: Andre Deutsch.

LOCKWOOD, W. 1964. *The Economic Development of Modern Japan*. Princeton: Princeton Univ. Press.

LYND, R. and H. 1937. *Middletown: A Study in Cultural Conflicts*. New York: Harcourt, Brace & Co.

MCCAFFERTY, K. 2002. *Testimony of an Irish Slave Girl*. New York: Viking.

MCCHESNEY, R. 1999. *Rich Media, Poor Democracy: Communication Politics in*

Dubious Times. Champaign, Ill.: Univ. of Illinois Press.

_____FOSTER, J.B. 2003. "The Left-Wing Media?" *Monthly Review*, June.

_____2004. *The Problem of the Media: U.S. Communication Politics in the Twenty-First Century*. New York: Monthly Review Press.

MCCOY, A.W. 1972. *The Politics of Heroin in Southeast Asia*. New York: Harper.

MCLOUGHLIN, W.G. 1984. *The Cherokee Ghost Dance*. Macon, Ga: Mercer Univ. Press.

MCGINNIS, J. 1969. The Selling of the President. New York: The Trident Press.

MCNAMARA, R. 1995. *In Retrospect: The Tragedy and Lessons of Vietnam*. New York: Times Books..

MADRICK, J. 1995. *The End of Affluence: The Causes and Consequences of America's Economic Dilemma*. New York: Random House.

MAGDOFF, F., FOSTER, J., BETTEL, F. 2000. *Hungry for Profit: The Agribusiness Threat to Farmers, Food and the Environment*. New York: Monthly Review Press.

MAGDOFF, H. 1968. *The Age of Imperialism: The Economics of U.S. Foreign Policy*. New York: Monthly Review Press.

_____2003. *Imperialism Without Colonies*. New York: Monthly Review Press.

MALKIN, M. 2002. "Ethanol is a big fraud on consumers," (SFC, 8-28-02)

MALTHUS, T. 1798/1970. *An Essay on the Principle of Population*. Baltimore: Penguin.

MALRAUX, A. 1927. *Man's Fate*. New York: Vintage.

MANDER, J. 1978. *Four Arguments for the Elimination of Television*. New York: Morrow.

_____1992. *In the Absence of the Sacred: The Failure of Technology and the Survival of the Indian Nations*. San Francisco: Sierra Club.

MANGOLD, T. 1991. *Cold Warrior: James Jesus Angleton, The CIA's Master Spy Hunter*. New York: Simon & Schuster.

MANNING, R. 2004. *Against the Grain: How Agriculture Has Hijacked Civilization*. San Francisco: North Point Press.

MANTOUX, P. 1906. *The Industrial Revolution in the Eighteenth Century*. London: Cape.

MARABLE, M. 2002. *The Great Wells of Democracy: The Meaning of Race in American Life*. New York: Basic Civitas Books.

MARCUSE, H. 1964. *One-Dimensional Man*. Boston: Beacon Press.

MARKUSEN, A., YUDKEN, J. 1992. *Dismantling the Cold War Economy*. New York: Basic Books.

MARSHALL, A. 1890. *Principles of Economics*. London: Macmillan.

MARTINEZ, E. 2003. "Don't Call This Country America," *Z Magazine*, July/August.

MARX, K. 1844/1963. *Early Writings*. (translated and edited by T.B. Bottomore. New York: McGraw-Hill.

_____1867/1967. *Capital, Vol. I*. New York: International Publishers.

_____and ENGELS, F. 1845-46/1970. *The German Ideology*. New York: International Publishers.

_____1967. *Selected Works*. New York: International Publishers.

MATRAY, J.I. (ed.) 1991. *Historical Dictionary of the Korean War*. New York: Greenwood Press.

MAZZOCCO, S. 2003. "The Americanization of Youth Through MTV." Research Paper, University of Modena, Italy.

MAYER, M. 2002. ""Banking's Future Lies in the Past," *NYT*, 8-25-02

MEEROPOL, M. 2003. *An Execution in the Family: One Son's Journey*. New York: St. Martin's Press.

MELMAN, S. 1965. *Our Depleted Society*. New York: Holt, Rinehart & Winston.

____1970. *Pentagon Capitalism*. New York: McGraw-Hill.

____1974, *The Permanent War Economy*. New York: McGraw-Hill.

MERWIN, W.S. 1997. *The Vixen*. New York: Alfred A. Knopf.

MESZAROS, I. 1998. "The Uncontrollability of Globalizing Capital," *Monthly Review*, February.

MEYER, C. 1980. *Facing Reality*. New York: Harper & Row.

MILLER, D. NOWAK, M. 1977. *The Fifties: The Way We Really Were*. New York: Doubleday.

MILLER, H. 1971. *Rich Man, Poor Man*. New York: Crowell.

MILLER, J. (et al.). 2003. *Real World Macro*. Cambridge, MA: Dollars & Sense.

MILLER, M.C. 2001. *The Bush Dyslexicon*. New York: Norton.

MILLS, C.W. 1951. *White Collar*. New York: Oxford University Press.

____1956. *The Power Elite*. New York: Oxford University Press.

____1967. *The Sociological Imagination*. New York: Oxford Univ. Press.

MINSKY, H. 1996. *Stabilizing an Unstable Economy*. New Haven: Yale University Press.

MINTZ, S. 1986. *Sweetness and Power: The Place of Sugar in Modern History*. New York: Penguin.

MISHEL, L., BERNSTEIN, J., BOUSHEY, H. 2003. *The State of Working America, 2002/2003. An Economic Policy Institute Book*. Ithaca, NY: ILR Press. an imprint of Cornell University Press.

MITCHELL, B. 1947. *Depression Decade: From New Era through New Deal, 1920-1941*. New York: Rinehart.

MOISE, E. 1986. *Tonkin Gulf and the Escalation of the War in Vietnam*. Chapel Hill: University of North Carolina Press.

MOORE, M. 2002. *Stupid White Men*. New York: HarperCollins.

MORISON, S.E. 1965. *Oxford History of the American People, Vol 3*. New York: New American Library.

MORRISON, T. 1982. *Tar Baby*. New York: Penguin Plume.

NATIONAL RESOURCES COMMITTEE. 1939. *The Structure of the American Economy*. Washington, D.C.: U.S. Government Printing Office.

NAVARRO, V. 2002. *The Political Economy of Social Inequalities: Consequences for Health and Quality of Life*. Amityville, NY: Baywood Press.

NAVASKY, V. 1980. *Naming Names*. New York: Viking.

NAYLOR, R.T. 1987. *Hot Money and the Politics of Debt*. New York: Simon and Schuster.

NELSON, C. 1999. *Manifesto of a Tenured Radical: Higher Education Under Fire*. Evanston: U. of Ill. Press.

NEUMANN, F. 1942/1963. *Behemoth: The Structure and Practice of National Socialism*. New York: Harper.

NEWMAN, K. 1993. *Declining Fortunes: The Withering of the American Dream*. New York: Basic Books.

NEWMAN, N. 2002. "'Homeland Security as Union Busting," *Progressive Populist* (6-15-02) <www.populist.com>

NEW YORK TIMES. 1971. *The Pentagon Papers*. Chicago: Quadrangle Books.

NORDHAUS, W.D. 2004. "The Story of a Bubble," *NYRB*, 1-15.

NORDHOLDT, W.S. 1970. *The People That Walk in Darkness*. New York: Ballantine.

OFFNER, A. (et al.). 2003. *Real World Micro*. Cambridge, MA: Dollars & Sense.

O'FLAHERTY, L. 1984. *Famine*. Dublin: Wolfhound Press.

OGLESBY, C., SHAULL, R. 1967. *Containment and Change*. London: Macmillan.

OLLMAN, B. 1976. *Alienation: Marx's Conception of Man in Capitalist Society*. Cambridge: Cambridge Univ. Press.

OMI, M., WINANT, H. 1994. *Racial Formation in the United States: From the 1960s to the 1990s*. New York: Routledge.

O'NEILL, J.R. 2000. *Something New Under the Sun: An Environmental History of the Twentieth-Century World*. New York: W.W. Norton.

ORWELL, G. 1938/1962 *Homage to Catalonia*. New York: Harcourt Brace.

_____1846. *Animal Farm*. New York: Harcourt & Brace.

_____1949/2003. *Nineteen Eighty-Four (1984)*. New York: Plume/Harcourt Brace.

OSBERG, L. (ed.) 1991. *Inequality and Poverty: International Perspectives*. Armonk, NY: M.E.Sharpe.

PALERMO, J. 2001. *In His Own Right: The Political Odyssey of Senator Robert F. Kennedy*. New York: Columbia University Press.

PALMER, A. 1979. *The Penguin Dictionary of Twentieth Century History*. New York: Penguin.

PARRY, J.H. 1965. *The Spanish Seaborne Empire*. New York: Knopf.

PECHMAN, J. 1989. *Tax Reform, The Rich and the Poor*. Washington: The Brookings Institution.

PHILLIPS, K. 1991. *The Politics of Rich and Poor: Wealth and the American Electorate in the Reagan Aftermath*. New York: Harper Perennial.

_____1994. *Arrogant Capital: Washington, Wall Street, and the Frustration of American Politics*. New York: Harper Perennial.

_____2002. *Wealth and Democracy: A Political History of the American Rich*. New York: Broadway.

_____2004. "Bush Family Values: War, Wealth, Oil." *Los Angeles Times*, Feb. 8.

_____2004. *American Dynasty*. New York: Viking.

PILGER, J. 2003. *The New Rulers of the World*. London: Verso.

PITT, W.R./RITTER, S. 2002. *War on Iraq: What Team Bush Doesn't Want You To Know*. New York: Context Books.

PIVEN, F., CLOWARD, R. 1971. *Regulating the Poor*. New York: Pantheon.

PIZZO, S., et al. 1989. *Inside Job: The Looting of America's Savings and Loans*. New York: McGraw-Hill.

POSTMAN, N. 1985. *Amusing Ourselves to Death: Public Discourse in the Age of Show Business.*. New York: Viking Penguin.

POTTER, D. 1958. *People of Plenty*. Chicago: Univ. of Chicago Press.

POWELL, C. 1995. *My American Journey*. New York: Random House.

POWERS, T. 1979. *The Man Who Kept the Secrets; Richard Helms and the CIA*. New York: Knopf.

_____2002. *Intelligence Wars: American Secret History from Hitler to Al-Qaeda*. New York: New York Review of Books.

RAMPTON, S., STAUBER, J. 2003. *Weapons of Mass Deception: The Uses of Propaganda in Bush's War on Iraq*. New York: Taucher/Penguin.

_____2004. *Banana Republicans: How the Right Wing is Turning America Into a One-Party*

State. New York: Tarcher/ Penguin.

RASSELL, E. "A Bad Bargain: Why U.S. Health Care Costs So Much and Covers So Few," *D&S*, May 1993.

RAVENSCRAFT, D., SCHERER, F.M. 1987. *Mergers, Sell-Offs, and Economic Efficiency.* Washington: The Brookings Institution.

REED, J. 1917/1877. *Ten Days That Shook the World.* New York: Penguin.

REUSS, A. (et al.). 2002. *Real World Globalization.* Cambridge, MA: Dollars & Sense.

RIDGEWAY, J. 1973. *The Last Play: The Struggle to Monopolize the World's Energy Resources.* New York: Dutton.

ROBERTS, S. 2001. *The Untold Story of Atomic Spy David Greenglass, and How He Sent His Sister Ethel Rosenberg to the Electric Chair.* New York: Random House.

ROBINS, N. 1992. *The FBI's War on Freedom of Expression.* New York: Morrow.

ROBINSON, J. 1962. *Economic Philosophy.* Chicago: Aldine.

RODMAN, S. 1939. *A New Anthology of Modern Poetry.* New York: Modern Library.

ROEDIGER, D. 1991. *The Wages of Whiteness: Race and the Making of the American Working Class.* New York: Verso.

ROGIN, L. 1956. *The Meaning and Validity of Economic Theory.* New York: Harper.

ROVERE, R. 1959. *Senator Joe McCarthy.* New York: Harper.

RYAN, W. 1976. *Blaming the Victim.* New York: Random House.

SACKREY, C. 1973. *The Political Economy of Urban Poverty.* New York: W.W. Norton.

____(et al.). 2002. *Introduction to Political Economy.* Cambridge, MA: Dollars & Sense.

SALVEMINI, G. 1936. *Under the Axe of Fascism.* New York: H. Fertig.

SAMPSON, A. 1975. *The Seven Sisters.* New York: Viking.

SANDBURG, C. 1936. *The People, Yes.* New York: Harcourt Brace Jovanovich.

SAUNDERS, F.S. 1999. *The Cultural Cold War: The CIA and the World of Arts and Letters.* New York: New Press

SCHEIBER, H.N. 1964. *United States Economic History: Selected Readings.* New York: Knopf.

SCHILLER, H. 1971. *Mass Communications and American Empire.* Boston: Beacon Press.

____1973. *The Mind Managers.* Boston: Beacon Press.

____1976. *Communications and Cultural Domination.* Boston: Beacon Press.

____1989. *Culture, Inc.: The Corporate Takeover of Public Expression.* New York: Oxford University Press.

SCHLESINGER, S., KINZER, S. 1982. *Bitter Fruit: The Untold Story of the U.S. Coup in Guatemala.* New York: Doubleday.

SCHMIDT, C. 1939. *The Corporate State in Action.* New York: Columbia University Press.

SCHOR, J. 1991. *The Overworked American.* New York: Basic Books.

____1998. *The Overspent American.* New York: Basic Books.

SCHULTZ, B. & R. 1989. *It Did Happen Here: Recollections of Political Repression in America.* Berkeley: Univ. of Calif. Press.

SCOTT, P. 1972. *The War Conspiracy: The Secret Road to the Second Indochina War.* Indianapolis: Bobbs-Merrill.

SCITOVSKY, T. 1976. *The Joyless Economy,* New York: Oxford Univ. Press.

SEN, A. 1981. *Poverty and Famine: An Essay on Entitlement and Deprivation.* Oxford: Clarenden Press.

____*Development as Freedom.* New York: Knopf.

SENDER, R. 1936. *Seven Red Sundays*. New York: Liverright.

SENNETT, W. & COBB, J. 1973. *The Hidden Injuries of Class*. New York: Vintage.

SHAWCROSS, W. 1979. *Sideshow: Kissinger, Nixon and the Destruction of Cambodia*. New York: Pocket Books.

SHERMAN, H. 1977. *Stagflation*. New York: Harper.

SHERRILL, R. 1968. *The Accidental President*. New York: Pyramid Books.

_____1995. "The Madness of the Market: Dangerous to Your Health," *The Nation* 1-9/16.

SHERWIN, M.J. 1987. *A World Destroyed: Hiroshima and the Origins of the Arms Race*. New York: Vintage.

SILONE, I. 1934. *Fontamara*. New York: Macmillan.

SIMPSON, C. 1993. *Blowback: America's Recruitment of Nazis and Its Effects on the Cold War*. New York: Weidenfeld & Nicolson.

SINCLAIR, U. 1906/2001. *The Jungle*. New York/Mineola, NY: Doubleday/Dover.

_____1920. *The Brass Check* Pasadena, CA: Self-published.

_____1926. *Oil!* London: Werner Laurie.

SINGER, D. 1999. *Whose Millennium? Theirs or Ours?* New York: Monthly Review Press.

SINGER, P.W. 2003. *Corporate Warriors: The Rise of the Privatized Military Industry*. Ithaca: Cornell University Press.

SLATER, P. 1971/1990, *The Pursuit of Loneliness*. Boston: Beacon Press.

SMITH, A. 1776/1937. *An Inquiry into the Nature and Causes of the Wealth of Nations*. New York: Modern Library.

SMITH, R., EMSHWILLER, J.R. 2003. *24 Days*. New York: Harper Business.

SNOW, E. 1972. *The Long Revolution*. New York: Random House.

SOULE, G. 1947. *Prosperity Decade: From War to Depression*. New York: Rinehart.

STAMPP, K. 1956. *The Peculiar Institution: Slavery in the Ante-Bellum South*. New York: Vintage.

STARR, P. 1982. *The Social Transformation of American Medicine: The Rise of a Sovereign Profession and the Making of a Vast Industry*. New York: Basic Books.

STAVRIANOS, L.S. 1989. *Lifelines From Our Past: A New World History*. Armonk, NY: M.E. Sharpe.

STEFFENS, L. 1904-1957. *The Shame of the Cities*. New York: Sagamore Press.

STEINBECK, J. 1939. *The Grapes of Wrath*. New York: Viking.

STEINBERG, S. 1981. *The Ethnic Myth: Race, Ethnicity, and Class in America*. Boston: Beacon Press.

STIGLITZ, J. 2002. *Globalization and Its Discontents*. New York: W.W. Norton.

_____2003. *The Roaring Nineties: A New History of the World's Most Prosperous Decade*. New York: Norton.

STOCKDALE, J. and S, 1984. *Love and War*. New York: Harper & Row.

STOCKMAN, D. 1987. *The Triumph of Politics*. New York: Harper.

STONE, I.F. 1952/1958. *The Hidden History of the Korean War, 1950-51*. Boston: Little, Brown.

_____1967. *In a Time of Torment*. New York: Random House.

STREETEN, P. 1984. "Basic Needs: Some Unsettled Questions," *World Development*, Vol. 12, No. 9.

STRETTON, H. 1999. *Economics: A New Introduction*. London: Pluto Press.

SUMMERS, A. 1993. *The Secret Life of J. Edgar Hoover*. New York: Putnam.

SWARD, K. 1948. *The Legend of Henry Ford*. New York: Rinehart.

SWEDBERG, R. (ed.) 1991. *Joseph A. Schumpeter: The Economics and Sociology of Capitalism*. Princeton: Princeton Univ. Press.

SWEEZY, P. 1938. *Monopoly and Competition in the English Coal Trade: 1550-1850*. Cambridge: Harvard Univ. Press.

_____1939. "Interest Groupings in the American Economy." (see NATIONAL RESOURCES COMMITTEE)

_____1941. *The Theory of Capitalist Development*. New York: Oxford.

_____1949. *Socialism*. New York: Macmillan.

_____1972. *Modern Capitalism and Other Essays*. New York: Monthly Review Press.

SWOPE, G. 1931. *The Swope Plan for Stabilizing Business*. New York: The Business Bourse.

TACITUS. 98 A.D. *Agricola*. Cambridge: Loeb Classical Library, No.5; Harvard University Press.

TAKAKI, R. 1995. *Hiroshima: Why America Dropped the Bomb*. Boston: Little, Brown & Company.

TAIARA, C. 2002. "All Quiet in the Classroom," *San Francisco Bay Guardian*

TANZER, M. 1969. *The Political Economy of Oil and the Underdeveloped Countries*. Boston: Beacon Press.

_____1974. *The Energy Crisis: World Struggle for Power and Wealth*. New York: Monthly Review Press.

TAWNEY, R.H. 1920. *The Acquisitive Society*. New York: Harcourt Brace.

_____1926. *Religion and the Rise of Capitalism*. New York: Harcourt Brace.

TERKEL, S. 1974. *Working: People Talk About What They Do All Day and How They Feel About What They Do*. New York: Pantheon.

_____1982. *Hard Times: An Oral History of the Great Depression*. New York: Pantheon.

_____1984. *The Good War: An Oral History of World War Two*. New York: The New Press.

TUCKER, R.C. 1978, *The Marx-Engels Reader*. New York: Norton.

TURGEON, L. 1996. *Bastard Keynesianism: The Evolution of Economic Thinking and Policymaking since World War II*. Westport, Conn: Greenwood Press.

TYE, L. 1998. *The Father of Spin: Edward L. Bernays and the Birth of Public Relations*. New York: Crown.

UNICEF. 1986. *Report on the State of the World's Children*. New York: UNICEF.

UNITED NATIONS. 1990. *Human Development Report*. New York: United Nations.

UPDIKE, J. "Glad Rags," *New Yorker* (3-1-1993)

ULLMAN, J. (ed.) 1983. *Social Costs in Modern Society*. Westport, Conn.: Quorum Books.

URIBE, A. 1975. *The Black Book of American Intervention in Chile*. Boston: Beacon Press.

U.S. DEPARTMENT OF AGRICULTURE. 1999. *Advanced Report on Household Security in the United States, 1993-1999*. Washington, D.C: USGPO.

U.S. DEPARTMENT OF EDUCATION. 1999. *National Center for Educational Statistics*. Washington, D.C.

U.S. FEDERAL TRADE COMMISSION. 1940. *Report on the Automotive Industry*. Washington: USGPO.

USGPO. 2002. *Economic Report of the President*.

U.S. Senate Intelligence Committee. 1975. Alleged Assassination Plots Involving

Foreign Leaders (November); *Covert Action in Chile,1963-73.* U.S.G.P.O.

VEBLEN, T. 1898. "The Beginnings of Ownership," and "The Barbarian Status of Women," in *American Journal of Sociology*, September and November, 1898. (Reprinted in Ardzrooni, L. /Ed./. 1934. (Veblen's) *Essays in Our Changing Order*. New York: Viking.

_____1899. *The Theory of the Leisure Class*. New York: Macmillan.

_____1904. *The Theory of Business Enterprise*. New York: Scribner's.

_____1914/1946. *The Instinct of Workmanship*. New York: Huebsch.

_____1915/1946. *Imperial Germany and the Industrial Revolution*. New York: Macmillan.

_____1917/1945 *An Inquiry Into the Nature of Peace*. New York: Macmillan/Viking.

_____1918. *The Higher Learning in America: A Memorandum on the Conduct of Universities by Businessmen*. New York: Huebsch.

_____1919. *The Place of Science in Modern Civilization*. New York: Huebsch.

_____1923. *Absentee Ownership and Business Enterprise in Recent Times*. Huebsch.

_____1925/1994 *The Laxdaela Saga* New York: Routledge.

_____1934, *Essays in Our Changing Order*. New York: Viking. (Edited by Ardzrooni, L.)

WEALE, A. (ed.) 1995. *Eye-Witness Hiroshima*. New York: Carroll & Graf.

WEINSTEIN, J., EAKINS, D. 1970. *Toward a New America*. New York: Vintage.

WILCOX, C. 1969. *Toward Social Welfare*. Homewood, Ill: Irwin.

WILLIAMS, E. 1944. *Capitalism and Slavery*. Chapel Hill, NC: Univ. of North Carolina Press.

_____1984 (1970). *From Columbus to Castro: The History of the Caribbean 1492-1969*. New York: Vintage Books.

WILLIAMS, W.A. 1959. *The Tragedy of American Diplomacy*. New York: Dell.

_____1966. *The Contours of American History*. Chicago: Quadrangle.

_____1969 *The Roots of the Modern American Empire*. New York: Random House.

_____1980. *Empire as a Way of Life*. New York: Oxford Univ. Press.

WILLIAMSON, T. (et al.). 2002. *Making a Place for Community*. Cambridge, MA: Dollars & Sense.

WILLS, G. 1969. *Nixon Agonistes: The Crisis of the Self-Made Man*. New York: Houghton Mifflin.

_____1988. *Reagan's America*. New York: Penguin.

WINANT, H. 2001. *The World Is A Ghetto: Race and Democracy Since World War II*. New York: Basic Books.

WITTNER, L. 1978. *Cold War America: From Hiroshima to Watergate*. New York: Holt, Rinehart and Winston.

WOLFF, E. 1987. *Growth, Accumulation and Unproductive Activity*. New York: Cambridge Univ. Press.

_____1995. *Top Heavy: A Study of Increasing Inequality of Wealth in America*. New York: Twentieth Century.

WOLMAN, W., COLAMOSCA, A. 2002. *The Great 401(k) Hoax: Why Your Family's Financial Security Is at Risk and What You Can Do About It*. New York: Perseus Publishing.

WOODHAM-SMITH, C. 1962. *The Great Hunger*. New York: Harper

WOODHOUSE, C.M. 1990. *The Rise and Fall of the Greek Colonels*. London: Granada.

WOODWARD, C. V. 1956. *Reunion and Reaction*. New York: Doubleday; Anchor.

_____1963. *Tom Watson: Agrarian Rebel*. New York: Oxford University Press.

_____1966. *The Strange Career of Jim Crow*. New York: Oxford University Press.

WRIGHT, J. 1995. *Competing Solutions: American Health Care Proposals and International Experience.* Washington, D.C.: The Brookings Institution.

WRIGHT, M.I. 2003. *YOU: Back the Attack! WE"LL Bomb Whoever We Want!.* New York: Seven Stories Press.

WRIGHT, R. 1992. *Stolen Continents: The Americas Through Indian Eyes Since 1492.* Boston: Houghton Mifflin.

YATES, M. 1994. *Longer House, Fewer Jobs: Employment and Unemployment in the United States.* New York: Monthly Review Press.

____1998. *Why Unions Matter.* New York: Monthly Review Press.

____2003. *Naming the System: Inequality and Work in the Global Economy.* New York: Monthly Review Press.

YOUNG, M.B. 1991. *The Vietnam Wars: 1945-1990.* New York: HarperCollins.

ZAROULIS, N. & SULLIVAN, G. 1984. *Who Spoke Up? American Protests Against the War in Vietnam.* New York: Harper & Row.

ZEPEZAUER, M., NAIMAN, A. 1996. *Take the Rich Off Welfare.* Tucson, AZ: Odonian Press.

ZINN, H. 1973. *Postwar America: 1945-1971.* Indianapolis: Bobbs-Merrill.

1986/2002. *Emma: A Play.* Boston: South End Press.

____1999. *You Can't Be Neutral on a Moving Train.* Boston: Houghton Mifflin.

____2000. *A People's History of the United States.* New York: The New Press.

Z Nagazine. (various issues) + Web site: <www.zmag.org>

ZWEIG, M. 2000. *The Working Class Majority: America's Best Kept Secret.* Ithaca, NY: Cornell University Press.

About the Author

Douglas F. Dowd has been teaching and writing socioeconomic history for more than 50 years, beginning at U.C. Berkeley (where he had done his studies), and then leaving to teach at Cornell University for almost 20 years. He returned to the San Francisco Bay Area to teach again at Berkeley, U.C. Santa Cruz, and at the California State Universities at San Jose and San Francisco.

In the 1950s his research in medieval and early modern Italian economic history gained him a Guggenheim Research Fellowship, followed by a Fulbright fellowship for teaching in Italy in 1966-67. He returned in 1986 to teach there in alternate semesters for ten more years, and resumed doing so a few years ago. In addition to his university teaching, for over 30 years he has offered weekly free community classes in the San Francisco Bay Area (for which there is a web site: www.dougdowd.org)

A professor of economic history at Johns Hopkins University in Italy and also at the University of California, Douglas F. Dowd has written over 10 books critical of capitalism, including *Capitalism and Its Economics: A Critical History*, *The Twisted Dream: Capitalist Development in the United States Since 1776*, and *Understanding Capitalism: Critical Analysis From Karl Marx to Amartya Sen*.